On The Road To FREEDOM

Footprints On Indian History **1877 -1936**

Part I

Sudip Kar Purkayastha

Vitasta

Let Knowledge Spread

Published by
Renu Kaul Verma
Vitasta Publishing Pvt Ltd
2/15 Ansari Road, Daryaganj
New Delhi - 110 002
info@vitastapublishing.com

Set ISBN 978-93-82711-82-7
ISBN 978-93-82711-42-1

Reprint 2018

Cover and Layout Design by Vitasta Publishing Pvt Ltd
Printed by Vikas Computer and Printers, New Delhi

To

Young Indians in whose
hands lie the Destiny of India

CONTENTS

Acknowledgements

Foremost, my sincere thanks to Prof Manjula Bose, who first inspired me to write books.

Many thanks to the staff and officials of the National Library, Kolkata and its 'old newspaper' section; National Archive of India, New Delhi; State Central Libraries at Kankurganchi, Kolkata & Cubbon Park, Bangalore; and Raja Rammohun Roy Library Foundation (RRRLF), Kolkata. In particular I thank Samir K Banik, my friend and former official of the National Library, Kolkata and Shri Mrityunjoy Ghosh, AL&IO of RRRLF for his their help and cooperation.

I am grateful to Vitasta and my publisher Renu Kaul Verma for taking up the manuscript and Papri Sri Raman, my editor, in particular.

I have sincere appreciation for my nephews Indraneil and Tonmoy for their useful feedback on the manuscript.

I have been the beneficiary of an intellectually stimulating and emotionally supportive familyambience. Thanks to my brothers and sisters for their encouragement and valuable feedback. I can never thank my wife Jaya and sons Rituraj and Siddhartha enough for their silent, self-effacing support and also their never-ebbing encouragement throughout thislong journey that has lasted six years. I must make a special mentionof Siddhartha, who has been an inseparable part of this project in everypossible manner—arranging numerous books from India and abroad,going through manuscripts and offering valuable suggestions, besideshandling the entire computer operations. This book embodies his contribution all through

PROLOGUE

The story of India's struggle for independence from the powerful British Raj is a fascinating one. After the East India Company set up their hegemony across the subcontinent, the Indians waged their first major battle in 1857, in a bid to throw off the company's chains. It was carried out by large number of disaffected Indian sepoys of the Company, led by several valiant commanders and a number of native rulers distinguished for their valour, strong antipathy for the British and love for the motherland. The vehemence of that struggle, the gallantry and the spirit that were on display, supreme sacrifices offered by numerous named and unnamed heroes and the interminable nature of the armed challenges that kept cropping up over and again across the vast swath of the subcontinent, especially in its central and northern parts, kept the British rulers in a state of panic and dread.

That the British could come back from the precipice of certain disaster and re-establish their grip over the vast territories they had lost to the 'rebels' in a matter of months, owed primarily to the help they received from the Maharaja of Nepal (a Hindu kingdom in the Himalayas), and various native princes ruling states including inter alia Patiala, Nabha, Kashmir, Indore, Gwalior, and Hyderabad. They also got their lifeline from Indian sepoys who continued to be loyal to the Raj, in particular those belonging to the Madras regiment as well as the Sikh soldiers. Before 1859 came to an end, the Company, albeit with considerable difficulties, managed to crush the armed uprising completely. Significantly, however, they paid a heavy price for their misgovernance. They lost their possession of the colony of India to the British empire. Her Majesty's Government assumed the governance and Queen Victoria held out to Indians assurances of justice and fair play.

The Indian armed challenge against the colonial rulers had, thus, burst forth intensely in a small window of time and thereafter fizzled out rather quickly. The assurances and the promises that were held out by Her Majesty's Government had a pacifying effect and Indians, generally, looked forward with some measure of optimism to the future. Interestingly, the next round of Indian challenge against the British Raj sprouted forth rather soon. But unlike 1857, the standard bearers of the new challenge were the educated middle class intelligentsia who propagated the mantra of *swaraj* across the country and the masses. Carried by the agency of these new-look soldiers, the yearning for freedom gradually got etched on to the consciousness of the vast masses, and the series of movements eventually consumed the British Raj in 1947.

The early symptoms of the disenchantment of Indians with HMG began to manifest as early as in the 1870s, due to the condemnable attitude and actions of the government in handling the ruinous bouts of famines and famine victims. That a psyche of disdainful racial discrimination alone could be the engine of such apathy and indifference was confirmed by more racially-biased legislations that followed in close succession. In hindsight, the mega celebration of the coronation of Queen Victoria in India in the year 1877 could be seen as a politically significant event. It was apparently benign but, in fact, began to trouble, vaguely or otherwise, thinking Indians. Unseemly in the context of the widespread epidemic and extreme human miseries, this event went on with great fanfare for days while the poor famine victims were dying in hundreds and thousands. The heartless festivity stood in stark contrast to the British claim that HMG was the most civilised of all governments in the contemporary world.

This book begins its story from that signal event and meanders its way through the corridors of seventy long years to end in 1947.

The intervening period of seven decades witnessed various strands of struggles by the Indians against the Raj in quest of *swaraj*. The impatient revolutionaries wanted to expel the colonial rulers 'then and there' and resorted to violent means. The constitutionalists explored the parliamentary route to secure the right of self-government from the Raj consensually. Then there were two huge non-violent mass movements led by Gandhi, the like of which the world had never experienced, before or after. But the British Raj frustrated every such challenge, sometimes with an iron hand, some other times with feigned magnanimity and diplomatic finesse but above all by driving deep wedges amongst their Indian adversaries on the basis of religion and castes. They cultivated the Muslim fears about losing their due share of political rights to Hindus in a democratic polity with commendable success. Thus, barring very few occasions, the struggle of the mainstream Indians, led by the Congress Party, failed to enlist the support of the majority of the Muslim community. On several important junctures the Raj was able to fight some of its toughest political battles in India by gathering strength from the Muslim League. The two, in fact, shared a cosy relationship based on a 'quid pro quo', with the common objective of stalling the mainstream challengers' aspiration for *swaraj* and a united independent democratic India.

In 1941, Churchill, the new British prime minister, had made it crystal clear that the British government had no intention to abandon HMG's vast Indian empire. Till mid 1940s, the Raj showed no desire to cast away the brightest jewel from the British crown. But the ordeal undergone in course of the Great War during 1939-45 compelled them to rethink after the war was conclusively over, and the Raj had chance to reflect. Though the Allies eventually managed to win the war, Britain suffered heavy losses of human lives and it was nearly devastated in terms of physical assets and financially ruined. With regard to their Indian empire, they were subjected to another torment. The impact of the Indian National Army on the armed forces, their mainstay in the colony, had shaken their confidence badly. By 1946, for the first time, the Raj seemed to be in a mood to abandon its Indian empire, albeit reluctantly. This presented the Indians with an unprecedented opportunity to enter the post-war world as a united independent country.

Unfortunately that did not happen. The gulf between the Congress, representatives of the mainstream Indians and the Muslim League, the chief spokesperson of Muslims in the country proved to be unbridgeable. Significantly, the distrust that Jinnah harboured about Gandhi in 1947 seemed to be far greater than what Sir Syed Ahmed had displayed towards the Congress in 1885. The failure of two premier political bodies to come together, even after the lapse of a period as long as sixty-two years or more, constituted a telling commentary on the success of British diplomacy and the mindset of Indian politicians. Before they left, the Raj took their last revenge on their disloyal Indian challengers by granting them dominion status on the condition that they agreed to divide the country. The two parts of India walked into freedom amidst rivers of blood.

The above narrative is only the broad contour of the story of India's freedom struggle. The readers may find the details, spread out over eleven chapters in two parts, engrossing. The saga of the Indian struggle is a wide-spectrum account of human instincts, emotions and actions. It embodies stories of many opposites on the part of political actors—raw courage and cowardice, temperance and greed, supreme sacrifice and abject selfishness, straight-forward dealings and chicanery, clear-headed and muddled thinking. It recounts the momentous 'movements', the likes of which the world has never seen and the abrupt manner in which they were withdrawn. It describes the clashes of great ideas and also of the titans. It tells the stories of blind faith of the followers in their leaders as well as endemic mistrust between great leaders themselves. It is glorified by the spirit of peace and nonviolence and yet it has been stained by the blood of fratricide. It chronicles the subtle political art of 'divide and rule' practised by successive Viceroys and the British government in London to perpetuate the British rule in India. On the whole, the wide spectrum of Indian challenges to the British, apart from having been a freedom movement for four hundred million people, it also constitutes a captivating political story that has universal educative value. Most certainly, it has many lessons for the people of independent India and they can ignore it only to their great disadvantage.

The book has shortlisted the milestone events during the period 1877 to 1947, presented them to the reader in the newspapers style of those times, together with insightful analysis. The 'political analysts' and 'political observers' referred to in the book represent the author's analysis and interpretations based on his extensive study of history. The items presented in the style of 'editorials' are to be taken as the author's view.

The book has two part. The first parts, divided into four chapters, tracks the events that occurred till the end of 1936, together with their analysis. The second parts spreads into seven chapters, deals with rest of the period till 15 August 1947.

The author has done extensive research of available materials in multiple domains including inter alia documents, books, newspapers, magazines, websites and attempted to piece them together in a time sequence by furnishing the relevant dates, wherever available. At the same time, the readers are cordially welcome to suggest improvements in any form for incorporation in future editions.

The author may be reached at sudipkarp@hotmail.com

ONE

STRUGGLE FOR EXPRESSION

1877 - 1905

STRUGGLE FOR EXPRESSION

BRITISH CROWN ASSUMES KAISER-I-HIND TITLE

Government Spends Millions; Millions Die In Famines

January 1, 1877, Delhi: The British Indian government celebrates Queen Victoria assuming the title of *Kaiser-i-Hind*, meaning Queen Empress of India. The Queen herself has not come over to India. However, that does not matter. Viceroy Lord Lytton has been taking every step to make it a memorable event, one that people will remember through generations. He has been holding a grand 'durbar' in Delhi to commemorate the occasion. Thousands of troops, hundreds of civil servants and scores of Indian princes with their elaborate retinues have been converging on the venue of the celebrations. This ostentatious event spans over a fortnight. India is a subjugated country and it has hardly any choice in such matters. However, the grandeur and gloss of the celebrations are pricking sensibilities of many thinking, educated Indians, especially because the country has been under the grip of a terrible famine and poor Indians, in tens of thousands, are succumbing to starvation and attendant diseases. The government has been remarkably insensitive to the miseries of common Indians—their lives matter little.

It is true that majority of the wealthy, privileged and advantaged native Indians are keeping their eyes closed to such blatant injustice, indifference and failure of governmental duties to its subjects. However, some educated and enlightened Indians across the country are feeling disturbed and upset at the colonial ruler's apathy to their fellow countrymen. Scattered sparks of nationalistic sentiments are finding expression, subdued though.

Sir Syed Ahmed Khan Sees His Sapling Grow

1877, Aligarh: The school that Sir Syed Ahmed Khan had founded at Aligarh a couple of years ago to impart Western education to the Muslim community has now blossomed into a college called the Mohammedan Anglo Oriental College. Syed Ahmed Khan, a jurist, author and educator, has been concerned at the comparative backwardness of the Muslim community vis-à-vis the Hindus under British rule. He attributes this inter-communal disparity to the Muslim indifference to Western education. He also reckons that awareness of political rights and eagerness to acquire the same are dependent on modern education. He has, thus, been trying to address this important issue in earnest. But to make good for the lost time and opportunity, Syed Ahmed wants to secure the active support of the British rulers. In India, a Hindu majority country, the support of the colonial rulers would help the minority Muslims in the matter of securing due political rights. As such, he has not only been spearheading modern education amongst Muslims but also declaring loyalty to the British Empire. The students here learn English language as well as branches of Western sciences. The college is expected to play a key role in developing Muslim intelligentsia in India.

Government Tries To Throttle Vernacular Press

March 1878, Calcutta: The cruel indifference of the British government in handling the famine and reaching out to its victims have been compounded by its manner of dealing with the after-effects of the calamity. As agrarian riots erupt at several places and exploited farmers rebel against unscrupulous moneylenders in the aftermath of severe famine, the government machineries has come down hard on the hapless peasantry.

The government has also been trying to muzzle the vernacular press from reporting ground realities. The latter has been critical of the government policies driving people to despair, desperation and death. Instead of initiating policy correctives, the government has taken the criticisms of the press as affront and come down heavily on it. Newspapers have been asked to sign agreements with the government and many restrictions have been imposed on them. For example, they cannot publish anything that can arouse antipathy between persons of various races, castes or religions amongst Her Majesty's subjects. If convicted, the punishments awarded by district magistrates cannot be appealed against in any court of law. With such curbs, not only the poor and the downtrodden, even the educated and middle class Indians are feeling alienated and aggrieved.

After The Media, Now It Is A Matter of Arms

June 1878, Calcutta: Lytton's government has issued another legislation that smacks of racial discrimination. It has passed the Arms Act XI, stricter in form than the one passed in 1860. The revised and stricter Act imposes severe control on explosives and munitions. It renders keeping, bearing and trafficking in arms without licences criminal offences. Any concealment or attempt to conceal would attract higher punishments. What, however, has upset Indians is the exemption granted to Europeans, Anglo Indians and some categories of government officials.

Ilbert Bill Raises Protests In England, India

February 1883, London/Calcutta: There has been an intrinsically prejudiced position in the criminal justice system in British India, debarring Indian judges from trying criminal cases involving European accused. Viceroy Lord Lytton sought to remove such an unjust disqualification through the Ilbert Bill. This proposed bill has been introduced by Sir Courtenay P Ilbert, Law member of the Viceroy's executive council. Even before a dispassionate, objective debate could take place on the proposed bill by law makers, there have been loud protests in England as well as in India amongst the European community. In India, European and Anglo-Indian communities have been most vocal in Calcutta. Fiery speeches are being delivered in meetings convened to oppose the bill. The Anglo-Indian press has been in the vanguard of a powerful campaign seeking to vilify the bill. All shades of apprehensions are being voiced and all kinds of fears are being hyped. To whip up raw emotions, rumours have been floated that in criminal cases involving European women, Indian judges would indiscriminately misuse their newfound position to exploit them. The purpose of such campaigns, being pursued relentlessly, is to bring pressure on British law makers not to entertain such a dangerous initiative.

On the other side, the elite and educated Indians as a class find these protests not only unwarranted, disgraceful and racially prejudiced, but also demeaning to their esteem and self-respect. In fact, all these years, such a malaise existed and no one seemed to have cared much, as it was treated as a part and parcel of an archaic system. But now, the loud protests against a change proposal have exposed a deep wound. The elite, educated and sensible Indians are realising that all talk of liberal values, rationality, justice and fair play by their colonial rulers are cosmetic and can quickly vanish into thin air, if they offend the hypothesis of racial superiority. The ongoing protests are serving as stark reminders that despite all their intelligence and education, they are, after all, the subjects of a colonial ruler.

Anglo-Oriental College Churns Out British Loyalists

1883, Aligarh: Theodore Beck, a scholar at Trinity and the former president of Cambridge Union, has taken over as principal of the MAO College this year and he has already begun to lend concrete help to Syed Ahmed Khan to carry forward his political objectives. Khan has two broad aims—to bring Western education to increasing number of Muslim Indians and promote loyalty to the British Empire in them. He has been of the opinion that these will be crucial to protect and advance political interests of the Muslims in India, a Hindu majority country.

Under Beck, Muslim students are not only being imparted Western education but also indoctrinated to be loyal to the British Empire. In Theodore Beck, Syed Ahmed Khan has found a principal who is capable of translating his vision into reality.

MUSLIMS DEMAND REPRESENTATION, HINDUS UPSET

1883: Syed Ahmed Khan has been carrying forward his long-term vision of imparting Western education to Muslims. At the same time, he is also keen to ensure that Muslims as a community get their due share in the political rights that are made available to native Indians by the colonial rulers.

One of the basic steps towards the goal of self-government to Indians is to give them representations and responsibilities in municipal bodies. Fearing that they may lose out if a democratic process is adhered to in such matters, the Muslim community, led by Syed Ahmed Khan, has sought separate representation for Muslims in municipal bodies. This has generated a controversy and Hindus are upset.

Ilbert Bill Compromised
Viceroy's Legislative Council Passes Diluted Version

January 25, 1884: In the face of intense protests by Britons in general, and British settlers in India in particular, the Imperial Legislative Council has eventually passed a diluted version of the Ilbert Bill. In the new and compromised form, the Indian district magistrates and session judges, like their European counterpart, will be conferred the jurisdiction to try European offenders in criminal cases. However, a European facing charge will have the right to demand a jury of which at least half of the members are Europeans.

INDIAN NATIONAL CONGRESS IS BORN

December 28, 1885, Bombay: Allan Octavian Hume lays the foundation of the first political organisation in India. In colonial India, political aspirations of Indians were not encouraged. The sepoy mutiny against the East India Company was ruthlessly crushed following which the reins of the country were taken over by the British government directly in 1858.

At long last, some well-meaning people of the Empire have chosen to implant the seeds of democratic political institutions from Britain to India. Allan Octavian Hume is the pioneer amongst them. A retired civil servant, having served India for long years and with wide familiarity and attachment with India's people, tradition and culture, Hume has laid the foundation of the first political organisation in India. Through this maiden political organisation, named the Indian National Congress, he envisages a win-win situation for both the Empire and the Indian people. He believes that the happiness of the vast multitude of Indians is intertwined with the progress and prosperity of the British Empire. It may be recalled here that some of the British colonies in other parts of the world have already been granted dominion status and the people of these countries, though under the British Empire, have self-governance as their administrative model.

Hume wants Indians to prepare for and be given increasingly more chances to govern themselves, albeit within the British Empire. This, he feels, would be facilitated by democratisation of politics and also Indianisation of the bureaucracy. He wants more and more educated and elite Indians to come forward, identify the political problems so that the government can address these effectively. As a part of this programme he has been touring provinces, and delivering inspiring talks to his target audience to come forward and work for achieving the goals. The underlying thrust is to work in a cooperative spirit with the government and strengthen the Empire. The Indian National Congress (INC) would thus be a broad platform, which will give political workers from across provinces the scope to meet each other, exchange views, identify problems and grievances of the natives for redressal and formulate political agenda for the years to come.

As many as seventy-two delegates have converged in Bombay from different parts of the country. The congregation is clearly dominated by professionals and other elite of the society, with lawyers accounting for a chunk. Womesh Chandra Bonnerjee is presiding over the conference.

Syed Ahmed Worried, Sees Congress As A Threat

1885: Whereas the birth of the Indian National Congress has aroused enthusiasm in a large number of nationalist Indians, it is causing disquiet in certain quarters. Sir Syed Ahmed Khan views it as disturbing because he perceives this new entity has the potential to tilt the balance of political power against Muslims in India. His inference is based on the fact that the Congress is hugely dominated by Hindu elites and its objectives include achieving progressive self-governance by Indians. He apprehends, under such a scheme of things which is likely to evolve in the Western democratic tradition, Congress and its predominantly Hindu leaders are likely to grab political power by virtue of being the majority community. He does not rule out the possibility that Muslim participation in the Indian National Congress would only vest the latter with more legitimacy, without sufficiently endowing the Muslims with political powers. As such, he is calling Muslims of the country to not join the Congress. Already, he has the steadfast support of a growing band of Muslim intellectuals, thanks to the influence of the Aligarh College. Syed Ahmed's non-coperative attitude is acting like a thorn for the nascent Congress.

Congress Tries To Work Out Road Map

December 27-30, 1886, Calcutta: The Congress (INC) annual session is held in the city of Calcutta, the capital of the British Indian empire, generating considerable enthusiasm. Dadabhai Naoroji presides over the session. In the delegates, there is a pronounced domination of English-educated lawyers and journalists. Most belong to high, upper middle and middle-income groups and hardly encompass the vast multitude of poor Indians. As such, the representative character of these few hundred delegates in relation to 280 million Indians, most of whom are economically, socially and educationally very backward, is suspect. Octavian Hume, who conceived the idea of the Indian National Congress, is keen that it effectively acts as a mediator between these underprivileged sections and the government.

Further, during the long course of interactions with the Indian population in his civil services career, Hume had particularly noticed that the lower middle class Indians are both literate and intelligent, and for that very reason he has been keen that their discontents and grievances are not exploited by vested interests against the government and that the Congress act as a safety valve in between.

According to his vision, the Congress can catalyse self-governance, play an effective role in resolving the problems of the vast number of disadvantaged Indians, and simultaneously promote loyalty to the Empire.

But it is clear that the Congress, as it completes the first year of existence, is far removed from becoming a genuine representative of the average Indian, who is backward socially and economically. But these are early times as yet.

It is also too early for the government to formulate a view on the Congress. An air of civility prevails between the two. Lord Dufferin, the Viceroy, invited the delegates to his garden party.

Does Congress Have The Feel Of Real India?

December 27-30, 1887 Madras: Third annual session of the Indian National Congress is being held here and the famed barrister Badruddin Tyabji presides. The Congress still wears an exclusivist look and exudes an elitist flavour. It does not appear to have either the reach or feel of the problems and grievances of the Indian masses. Like its earlier presidents, WC Bonnerjee and Dadabhai Naoroji, Tyabji very much belongs to the top strata of the society—highly affluent and Western educated. However, the religious affiliations of these three presidents suggest that the party is trying to project a secular image—the first two were Hindu and Parsee respectively and Tyabji is a Muslim. It will not be surprising if the next president is a Christian or Sikh.

In his speech, Tyabji has stressed upon the representative character of the organisation and desired that the Muslims work shoulder to shoulder with other Indians for the common benefit. Deliberations in the annual session reflect the party's loyalty to the British government and betray its ignorance of the problems of Indian masses.

United India Patriotic Association Formed

August 1888, Aligarh: Far from emerging as a mass-oriented organisation, the Indian National Congress is still taking toddler steps in that direction, using the reach and proximity of other social and socio-religious organisations for such purposes. Notwithstanding such inadequacy, it has been trying to project itself as the sole indigenous political organisation competent to engage the British government on matters of self-government—involving gradual transfer of governmental responsibilities and powers to Indian hands.

But there are native groups who are sensing dangers and resent any such scheme or schemes that aim at transferring powers from British to Indian political parties or units. Syed Ahmed has been in the forefront of these groups and Raja Shiv Prasad of Benares has joined him. Both are united by their loyalties to the British, and they consider Congress' demands for self-government not only unjustified but also bordering on sedition. They have launched a new organisation, viz. United India Patriotic Association. Membership of this new organisation is open to all communities. The association vows to expose the seditious character of the Indian National Congress. For this purpose, it has been bringing out pamphlets and conducting a propaganda war.

Congress Aims To Be A Large Ship

December 26-29, 1888, Allahabad: Fourth annual session of the Indian National Congress is held here, with George Yule presiding. Yule is Scottish and owns some of prime industrial establishments in India. More importantly, he loves India and Indians and considers India almost as his home. His abiding concerns for the country and its people make him eminently qualified to be the president of the session.

However, the Congress itself is yet to build bridges with the Indian masses. The tag of being 'elitist and Westernised' continues to firmly stick to it. The deliberations seldom touch the issues that affect average Indians.

One way Congress is trying to overcome the blemish is by acting as a platform of other mass-based social and socio-religious organisations like the Arya Samaj, and a few others. These organisations, with intimate connections to large sections of Indian populations, are carrying the political messages of the Indian National Congress to their members.

However, the sustained anti-Congress propaganda by Syed Ahmed Khan and his followers, including the Aligarh camp, acts as a formidable roadblock for the party to attract Muslim Indians to its fold.

Another worry has begun to crop up. Although the initial government attitude towards this new organisation was benign, there are signs of change for the worse. Possibly, the British regime in India is beginning to see the Congress as a potential threat to its political hegemony. It is learnt from reliable sources that the Lt Governor of United Province, Sir Auckland Colvin, has issued a secret circular prohibiting government servants from joining the Congress. Hume, the founder of the Congress, has been shocked at such news. He finds it hard to reconcile that an organisation that has been conceived to strengthen the bond between the educated Indians and the British government has begun to be viewed with hostility. He is convinced that the Congress will promote loyalty to the British Empire while facilitating more of self-government to the Indians. As such, unfriendly government approach to this budding indigenous political institution could be harmful to both the British and Indian interests, he reckons.

Indian National Congress Establishes Presence In England

July 25, 1889, London: The Indian National Congress establishes its British Committee here. It is expected to take care of Indian interest in the British capital effectively by influencing opinions of the local public and law makers.

Rest Of My Life To The Service Of India: Wedderburn

December 26-28, 1889, Bombay: The Indian National Congress holds its fifth annual session here. William Wedderburn is presiding. Wedderburn retired from the ICS a couple of years ago. He has been known for his love of India and Indians. He also happens to be the president of the British Committee of the Indian National Congress and is known for putting across Indian causes forcefully before the British government in England. In his presidential speech, he committed himself to the service of Indians for the remaining part of his life. The delegates are mostly elite, wealthy and Western-educated. The activities in the session have been mostly in the form of deliberation of important issues identified by the Congress and adoption of resolutions commending governmental attention. The organisation has been attracting criticism from some quarters, especially Syed Ahmed, his followers and Indians who swear steadfast allegiance to the British rulers.

Tilak Joins Congress

1890, Bombay: Bal Gangadhar Tilak, a militant nationalist leader, has joined the Congress. He is thirty-four years old. He has already been in public life, rendering service to society and the masses for long. Exceptionally meritorious as a student, a graduate and holder of a degree of law, Tilak has been critical of Western education. He has been one of the founders of the Deccan Education Society (1884) and has been responsible for founding several schools. He has been editing two popular papers, viz. the Mahratta (in English) and the Kesari (in Maratha).

Revolutionary Activities Proliferate In Maharashtra

1890, Bombay: History of revolutionary activities in Maharashtra is old. The Marathas fought three fierce battles with the British before being subdued in 1818 but the fire kept raging in their hearts. In the post-sepoy mutiny period, Wasudeo Balwant Phadke had organised a revolutionary society for overthrowing British rule. Following Phadke's footsteps, more societies came up later. Foremost amongst these was the 'Rashtrabhakta Samuha' founded by Ganesh Damodar Savarkar and his brother Vinayak. It has been serving as a centre for mobilising patriots who favoured extreme means to expel the British from India. Now, this society has been renamed as 'Mitra Mela'. The government is keeping close watch on its activities.

A FLAME IS EXTINGUISHED – JYOTIRAO PASSES AWAY

November 28, 1890, Poona: Jyotirao Govindrao Phule has passed away. His death is certain to dislocate the movement for the upliftment of the depressed classes till another leader of his stature arrives on the national scene. Throughout his life, Jyotirao had been leading movements to eradicate the caste system and raise the social status of the shudras and untouchables. In 1873, he had founded the Satya Shodhak Samaj. He had made membership of the Samaj open to all to secure wide involvement in the promotion of the causes for which he stood. Such has been his dedication and spirit that Jyotirao became a legend in his lifetime. He not only gave a clarion call to the downtrodden to wake up but simultaneously sensitised many in the upper strata of Indian society, including their leaders, to the problems of the untouchables. Centuries of subjugation and persecution by the upper castes and the powerful made these vulnerable people live a life of self-effacement. If today there are some sparks, however scattered, and some signs, however feeble, seen amongst them expressing a desire to participate in political power, the credit must be attributed to this outstanding leader.

PRINCE OF MANIPUR HANGED PUBLICLY

British Set Foot In The North East

April 27, 1891, Imphal: The British government had been looking for an opportunity to bring the politically sensitive easternmost kingdom of India under its conrol for past several years. The opportunity presented itself to the Viceroy in Calcutta this year, when a serious succession trouble broke out in Manipur. The successors to late Maharaja Chandrakirti Singh had a bitter feud amongst themselves. The first occupant of the throne, prince Surchandra, was removed by prince Kullichandra who took over the reins and appointed another prince, Tikendrajit, as *Jubraj* (heir apparent) and *Senapati* (commander). The dethroned Surchandra met Viceroy Lansdowne in Calcutta and sought his intervention.

Lansdowne conferred with Lord Quinton, the Lt Governor of Assam, and deputed him to Manipur with a brief that Quinton should recognise the incumbent Kullichandra as the Maharaja but demand the 'handing over' of prince Tikendrajit, supposed to be the chief obstacle in reining in Manipur. Quinton arrived in Manipur on 22 March and was extended lavish hospitality by the royalty. But when Quinton demanded that prince Tikendrajit be handed over, Kullichandra refused to oblige. By transgressing the diginity of a good host, betraying the trust of the Maharaja and playing out a devious political plot, Quinton conducted a raid in the early morning at the residence of prince Tikendrajit two days later. However, the ill-conceived campaign was defeated by the Manipuri forces. Later on the same day, a scuffle broke out between Quinton and the Manipuri royalty when Tikendrajit insisted that the British forces disarm themselves. This led to a confrontation at the end of which Quinton, along with three other senior British officers and a burgler, were beheaded. The local fury did not end and the forces put to death two other British officers engaged in the Post & Telegraph operations in the kingdom.

Following these debacles, three columns of British forces headed to Imphal from Silchar, Kohima and Tamu. Led by prince Tikendrajit, the Manipuri forces fought valiantly against the advancing British forces but were overpowered. On this day, the foreign army entered Imphal and after an impromptu, farcical trial put Jubraj Tikendrajit Singh and General Thangal to death at Pheida Pung. They were hanged in full public view and it led to great anger and hatred against the British.[1]

Want More Indianisation, Less Discrimination

December 28-30, 1891, Nagpur: The Indian National Congress holds its seventh annual session here. P Ananda Charlu presides. In his presidential speech, Charlu demands increased Indian presence in the legislatures. He also expresses his dissatisfaction on the efficacy of the Indian council to present India's case. In this session, demands were raised to establish a military college in the country and relax the Arms Act. Incidentally, provisions in the Arms Act about entitlement to hold firearms are discriminatory against Indians and are nothing but a stigma to them. BG Tilak has brought this issue to the centre stage. He has proposed changes in the gun prohibition regulations. He has also proposed absorption of more Indians in the British India army, especially in higher ranks.

SIKH REFORMERS BEGIN TO PREPARE SIKH COMMUNITY

1892, Amritsar: Over the last few decades, the Hindus have been the beneficiaries of renaissance begun by various spiritual leaders and thinkers, many of them belonging to the *Brahmo Samaj* and the *Arya Samaj*. The latter two have been laying emphasis on the spread of education, eradication of prejudices, abolition of idolatry, liberty of thinking and more such measures to prepare the Hindus to face the challenges of modern times. Thanks to such cumulative efforts, to the mainstream Hindus, Western education is gradually becoming acceptable and even popular. As a result, Hindus, benefiting from Western education and liberal thinking, have been flourishing ahead of other religious communities in British India. Taking cue from these developments, Muslim leaders like Syed Ahmed Khan have also been trying to bring the benefits of Western education to Indian Muslims over last two decades.

A band of Sikh reformers has been seized of these developments. They are keen that the Sikhs must also march with the times. Before the British wrested Punjab, the Sikhs ruled this land of 'five rivers'. Past achievement and glory are no doubt morale boosters, but the community cannot rest on such laurels. To compete with the rest, the Sikhs must equip themselves with modern, Western education.

Towards this goal, the Sikh reformers, called Singh reformers, have laid the foundation stone of the Khalsa College at Amritsar where Sikh students would be exposed to an Anglo-Sikh system of education—they would be taught Sikh history, Sikh tenets along with Western sciences and literature.

Simultaneously, Takht Singh, a reformer of repute, is crusading for the cause of female education so that Sikh girls too, do not lag behind. Towards this noble goal, he has founded the *Kanya Mahavidyalaya* in Ferozepur. This college, meant to promote education amongst girls, would be run without government grant—and it would not charge any fees from the students.

As regards the medium of education, the Sikh reformers are keen to use Punjabi in Gurumukhi script, unlike the Hindus who prefer Hindi in Devnagri and Muslims keen on Urdu.

Congress Protests Against Inequitable Policies

December 28-30, 1892, Allahabad: The eighth annual session of the Congress is held here. Veteran leader WC Bonnerjee presides. A strong sturdy voice of protest was raised in the session by Lala Murli Dhar. He lamented the destruction of Indian handicrafts and cottage industries and narrated how this was occurring under clever government policies that aimed to benefit the industries in Britain. He criticised the inequitable trade pattern between the two countries, leading to an unacceptable rise in imports and inflation in India. He has also condemned the government policy in raising salt tax and making impoverished Indians pay that.

Muslims To Strengthen British Rule In India

December, 1893 Aligarh: Although not yet a mass-based organisation, the Congress' policies, programmes and activities have begun to reach and influence educated Indians, creating in them some kind of political aspirations, which were unknown to them even a decade ago.

The British government is somewhat uncomfortable about the manner in which the Indian National Congress is creating new aspirations amongst important sections of Indians whose opinions are likely to influence the masses in course of time. Syed Ahmed is keen to come closer to the British government, capitalising on such fears. He is prepared to keep Muslims insulated from any kind of political agitation, provided the Muslims as a community are assured of political rights, which he feels is due to them. The seed sown by him at Aligarh has already grown into a nice sapling, spreading ripples of Muslim loyalty to the Empire far and wide. Syed Ahmed wants to intensify his efforts in these lines and carry forward initiatives to other areas and forums.

In accordance, he has now founded the Mohammedan Anglo-Oriental Defence Association. Its main purposes include: (a) to place the opinions of Muslims before the government and to protect their political rights; (b) to prevent political agitation from spreading among the Muslims; and (c) to strengthen British rule in India. This new outfit is blatantly communal and especially against the Hindus. Unlike the United India Patriotic Association launched by him earlier, the membership of this new Association is open only to Muslims, and to Englishmen, with whom Syed Ahmed identifies grounds of common interest but not the Hindus. In short, it is a closed circuit political coalition between Muslims and Englishmen to protect their mutual interests to the exclusion of Hindus, the majority community. Theodre Beck, the European principal of the Aligarh College, has given Ahmed able support in starting the association and has become its secretary. Beck wants to use the new platform to drive Muslims away from Hindus and deepen their loyalty to the British.

Congress is not amused. A fight seems to be on hand with Syed Ahmed and his followers, if it hopes to attract large number of Muslims as its members.

Lahore Overwhelms Dadabhai
Swami Shraddhanand Recalls Emotional Scenes

December 27-30, 1893, Lahore: This is not the first time that Dadabhai Naoroji is presiding over an annual session of the Indian National Congress. In fact, he did so in 1886 in Calcutta, which happened to be its second session. However, the people in this smaller city are dying to have a glimpse of this legendary Indian, who has entered the British House of Commons from the liberal constituency of Central Finsbury last year. His immense stature is in sharp contrast to his diminutive physique. Dadabhai has made history, being the first Indian to enter the august house of British democracy. People are simply excited that an Indian is participating in formulating policies in the British Parliament that would influence governance in India. To the simple-minded vast Indian masses, Dadabhai has become one of their rulers and now they expect their pressing problems to get resolved. They refuse to recognise that Dadabhai is only one amongst the numerous law makers in Britain and, therefore, his abilities are very restricted.

Swami Shraddhanand, a prominent leader of the Arya Samaj attending the session, witnessed the unprecedented enthusiasm and emotions of the people in welcoming and felicitating Dadabhai. According to the Swamiji's first hand account of the events, in an unprecedented gesture of love, respect and admiration for their leader, the graduates and the elites of the city unhorsed Dadabhai's vehicle on the way to the venue of the session and pulled it themselves. During the course of the session, as the Parsi patriot assumed the presidential chair, the audience went mad with enthusiasm. When Dadabhai asked his audience to allow him to forget his identity for a moment and to rejoice with them that an Indian had got into the British Parliament, tears of joy were seen coursing down hundreds of cheeks.[2]

Dadabhai Naoroji Backs Indian States

December 1893, Lahore: Indian states ruled by princes have a kind of special relationship with the Indian National Congress. They are viewed and called as the 'Indian India' compared to the provinces under direct British rule, which are referred to as the British India. These princely states not only provide employment opportunities to the educated Indians, but also act as patrons of various Indian art forms including painting, music, dance, literature etc. Above all, these states are testimonies of the Indian capacity to govern. Intriguingly, however, these six hundred plus states of various sizes widely vary in regard to their competence in matters of governance. On the one hand, there are large and highly efficient states like Baroda, Mysore, Travancore and a few others. On the other hand there are many which are characterised by autocratic and oppressive governance, much worse than the British rule.

Though the Congress has been concerned with issues of governance and political aspirations of the people of British India, it pursues a conscious, condescending 'hands off' approach in relation to the same set of issues in the Indian states. It is significant that a number of rulers and princes of these states help the Congress financially, some of them substantially. Critics attribute the Congress' aloofness to the above reason. Incidentally, Dadabhai himself has been the beneficiary of the financial largesse of Gaekwad Sayaji Rao of Baroda.

It has been Congress' policy not to intervene in the internal affairs of the Indian states in favour of the subjects and against the rulers. However, in matters of conflicts between a state and the British government, Congress has generally been supportive of the native princes. In his presidential address, Dadabhai, while dwelling upon the relationship between Indian states and the British government, has deplored the unnecessary irritation and dissatisfaction therein. The indication as to who should mend the relationship is obvious.

INDIA AN AGRICULTURAL COUNTRY: MALAVIYA

December 1893, Lahore: In the annual session of the Congress held last year, Lala Murli Dhar had raised a voice of protest against the government's trade policies. Madan Mohan Malaviya now takes the issue forward. In the annual Congress session held here, he criticises the way British goods have flooded India and Indian exports have virtually disappeared. He also alleges that government policies have turned India into 'a primitive agricultural country'.

Per Capita Income Of Indian Ten Times Less Than A Briton's

December 26-29, 1894, Madras: Congress holds its tenth annual session here. Alfred Webb, an Irish member of British Parliament, presides. The selection of the president and his acceptance of the invite are being seen as goodwill gestures from both sides and expected to promote better understanding between two countries.

In his speech, Webb expresses discomfort at the strikingly low level of per capita income in India, which is nearly ten times lower than that in Britain. He has also voiced anxiety at the expenditure pattern of the British Indian government—very high on 'military' and low on 'education'. Such criticisms from a British MP are food for thought for the Indians in general, and Congress delegates, in particular. The session criticises the government policies, curbing the growth of Indian enterprise. It slams imposition of excise duties on cotton manufactured in India, which is paving the way for import of cotton from Britain.

Controversy Surrounds Congress Social Conferences

December 27-30, 1895, Poona: Holding a social conference in the venue of the Congress' annual session, following its conclusion, has become customary wherein various social ills and maladies that warrant attention are discussed, including those where the government ought to take initiatives. However, this tradition has now suffered a jolt as BG Tilak and few other leaders supporting him have registered strong protests against this practice. They are of the opinion that social and religious issues are closely connected, and any space granted to the government based on such deliberation would be to invite the colonial government to intrude into the religious lives of Indians and, as such, not warranted. So vehement has been their protest that the organisers are seriously thinking of discontinuing this practice of appending the social conference to Congress' annual session.

However, another section of leaders is worried about some of the longstanding, pervasive maladies of the wider Hindu society. They feel the social conference has been acting as a platform to create awareness about these issues, by bringing them into the open for a discourse at the national level. Now these will remain hidden beneath the carpet. The caste-related social evils and the millennium-old social injustice perpetrated upon the depressed classes in Hindu society constitute an example. It is true that leaders like Tilak are distinguished social reformers in their own rights, but certain issues warrant tackling from all fronts including initiatives from the government of the day. They recall the laudable efforts of Raja Rammohun Roy in the previous century in putting an end to the evil practice of 'Sati' by roping in the government of the East India Company.

The Congress is, thus, caught in the cross currents of two opposing schools of thoughts. However, according to inside information, chances for decoupling of the two are more.

Ranade Quits PSS, Forms Deccan Sabha – Tilak Offended

1896, Poona: Simmering conflict between Justice MG Ranade and BG Tilak over the past few years has come to a head with Ranade moving away from the Poona Sarvajanik Sabha (PSS) and founding the Deccan Sabha. Though Ranade had been playing a crucial role in conducting the affairs of the PSS for over two decades, he has been losing ground to Tilak in recent times. The two leaders have radical differences in approaches on several issues. Those aggravated significantly since Tilak made Ganapati puja a mass festival in 1893, and intercommunal differences began to crop up on issues such as music played by the processions of worshippers in front of the mosques. Not satisfied with the stance of the Sabha on such disputes taken under the influence of the Tilak group, most of its Muslim members resigned. Whereas Tilak wanted settlement of the dispute between the two communities based on reasoning, Ranade preferred to adopt the legal and secular approach. This led to a drift between the two.

In 1895, the two camps again came on a course of confrontation on the issue of holding the social conference in the venue of the Indian National Congress. Tilak and his followers opposed the practice, following which the Ranade group retreated.

It may be recalled that by that time, Tilak had come to command the support of the majority members and his followers consolidated their hold over the managing committee of the PSS.

Gokhale, who treats Ranade as his mentor, has been working tirelessly for the Sarvajanik Sabha for the last few years. The fact that Tilak had virtually forced Ranade out of the PSS, an organisation that the latter had built assiduously over long years, hurt Gokhale more than Ranade himself. Upset by these developments, Gokhale was keen to resign from the PSS. Ranade, however, took these adverse developments in his stride. Continuing with his long tradition of public service, he founded a new organisation, viz. the Deccan Sabha with like-minded persons. The inaugural meeting was attended by one hundred and one eminent citizens of Poona. On the occasion, Ranade said that the new society would represent 'Liberalism and the Moderates'.

Tilak, affronted by the floatation of the parallel sabha and Ranade's claim of what it would stand for, posed a counter—whether Ranade felt Tilak and his followers in the PSS were 'illiberal and immoderate'. Tilak apprehends that Ranade's action in starting a new sabha would reduce the importance of the PSS to the government.

Evidence At Royal Commission – Naoroji Writes To Ranade

June 18, 1896, London: Dadabhai Naoroji, a member of British Parliament, writes to MG Ranade in Poona, inviting him to England to give evidence before the Royal Commission on Indian Expenditure, headed by Lord Welby. Dadabhai and Wedderburn are amongst its members.

The formation of the Royal Commission has been the fruit of sustained work by Allan Octavian Hume and his colleagues. Way back around 1888-89, they realised that in order to achieve the Congress goals and objectives, much help could be accrued if pressure of public opinion and press could be generated in England. Accordingly, they founded the British Committee of the Indian National Congress. Wedderburn was appointed its chairman. The next important step to build up an India lobby was taken by constituting the India Parliamentary Committee after Dadabhai and Wedderburn were elected to the British Parliament in 1892 and 1893 respectively.

The rising government expenditure and the falling level of public welfare has been a burning issue in India for past several years. The India Parliamentary Committee pressed the British government to conduct a thorough enquiry into the issue. In response, the latter has constituted a thirteen-member committee under the chairmanship of Lord Welby. The body of members include Dadabhai and Wedderburn.

Dadabhai, in his letter, has written that this would be a golden opportunity for Ranade to highlight the critical issues that ail the functioning of the British Indian government, imposing hardships on Indian people.

CRUSADER MOHANDAS GANDHI VISITS INDIA

Looks To Enlist Indian Support

1896, Bombay: Young barrister Mohandas Karamchand Gandhi is in India, criss-crossing the country to bring to the attention of Indian people and leaders the miserable plight of the Indian community living in South Africa. He had gone to South Africa in connection with a legal brief and has been continuing to reside there.

Like India, South Africa is another British colony and it is governed by local British settlers there. They have been practising an aggressive form of racism against the black and the brown people.

Since landing in that country, Gandhi has been subjected to a series of racist insults and humiliations by the white people and the government machinery. As a result, his attention was attracted to the distressed and degraded life enforced on the Indian immigrants there and the black natives.

Political observers say the condition of Indians in South Africa is no isolated case. The plight of general Indian immigrants in various countries forming part of the British Empire across the world is also pathetic. This even applies to Indian immigrants to developed commonwealth countries. The irony is that the Indians in mainland India are generally unaware of these hard facts. The sordid tale of the oppressed Indians in South Africa would also have remained buried, like the others, had Gandhi not brought it before India and also the world at large.

Gandhi has been organising the Indian community in South Africa and conducting resistance movement using non-violent methods. Simultaneously, he has been trying to secure intervention of the British government in England to end the injustice against the immigrant Indians. He is hopeful of strengthening his movement in that land by securing the support of the Indian National Congress, Indian media and Indian people in general.

He arrived at Calcutta from Durban on 4 July this year. Since then he has been touring places and meeting important people in pursuit of his South African mission.

During his sojourn in India he wrote a pamphlet, called the 'green pamphlet', on the actual condition of Indians in South Africa, printed 10,000 copies and sent it to all the newspapers and leaders of every party in India. In this connection, he met Pheroze Shah Mehta in Bombay, Gokhale, Tilak and Bhandarkar in Pune, Surendra Nath Banerjea in Calcutta. In Madras, the *Madras Standard*, *The Hindu* and in Calcutta, *The Statesman* gave good coverage of his case. It seems Gandhi has been able to generate some degree of awareness on this issue in India.

'The Himalaya, The Ocean And The Ganges'

Gandhi On Pheroze Mehta, Tilak And Gokhale

1896: As a part of his South African Mission, Gandhi has been trying to meet important Congress leaders to make them aware and enlist their support for the cause of the immigrant Indian. During his visits to Bombay and Poona, Gandhi has come in personal contact with some of the top Congress leaders. The persons who have impressed him much are Sir Pheroze Shah Mehta known as the Lion of Bombay, whom he felt, was as grand and lofty as the Himalayas. He has been equally impressed by BG Tilak whose depth appeared to him like that of an ocean. He, however, has become most friendly with Gopal Krishna Gokhale. Gandhi has perceived him as the sacred Ganges who, unlike Mehta and Tilak, was not beyond reach—interacting with him was refreshing, rewarding and illumining. On his part, Gokhale too has been impressed by Gandhi, his experienced eyes identifying the future leader in the latter. Gokhale extends his unqualified support to the cause Gandhi is propagating.

TILAK FIGHTS FOR FAMINE VICTIMS, RELIEF CODE

December 1896, Poona: India's misfortune as a colonised nation has been aggravated in recent years by famine attacks. Famines have been striking various parts of India at disturbingly close intervals. The British government had framed a 'famine relief code' based on the experience of the famines of the 1870s, to tackle future famine situations and provide relief to the victims. However, there is little implementation at the ground and people continue to suffer as before.

This year there were ominous portends of famine in large parts of western India, especially in the Deccan and Konkan. By December, different parts of Bombay presidency came under severe spell of grains scarcity. People began to die out of starvation and diseases. But the Bombay government made little, if any, efforts to recognise the situation and take action. It does not seem to have learnt any lessons from the past.

Way back in 1877-78, between five to six million people had succumbed to famine in the country which prompted Lord Lytton, then Viceroy, to appoint a Famine Commission to determine the principles and practices to be adopted in future to tackle famine. The commission, led by Sir Richard Strachey, had submitted its report in 1880 and since then the provincial governments had devised 'famine codes' in the light of the government's famine policy.

Unfortunately, now, when Bombay and surrounding areas have been reeling under the spell of a vicious famine, an overall Famine Relief Code remains on the shelf. The government neither allowed the affected farmers remission of land revenues nor provided any other relief to the starving victims. Tilak has been fighting against such colossal cruelty and injustice. He has sent members of the Poona 'Sarvajanik Sabha' to various districts of the Deccan and Konkan to enlighten people of their legal entitlements to the relief measures as per the 'Famine Relief Code'. The Sabha members have been extensively touring these places and helping the affected farmers file applications for relief. Such has been the intensity of the campaign that the land revenues from these parts of the presidency have dwindled significantly. The district administration, especially the police, have been keeping watch over the members of the Sabha canvassing in the districts. In a few cases, they have also arrested the Sabha members who made even technical errors in informing the peasants about the provision of the famine relief code.

YOUNG MONK RETURNS AFTER SPIRITUAL CONQUEST

January 26, 1897: India has been a colony of the British for more than a century. The long period of subjugation has robbed Indians of all self-respect and they look down upon their own culture and heritage. The small coterie of West-educated Indians who occupy positions of importance and are capable of exercising influence over public life, tend to imitate the West in every walk of life. In such a setup, while the small numbers of privileged Indians tend to ruthlessly exploit their own vast vulnerable brethren, there is an all-round attitude of servility to the white colonial rulers and Western civilisation.

Vivekananda, a young spiritual leader from India, has just returned from the USA and Europe after accomplishing a spiritual conquest of those lands. He had first gone to Chicago in 1893 to attend the Parliament of World's Religions. There he presented the eternal messages that he claimed were useful to the entire humanity to realise their spiritual aspirations. Thanks to his elevated persona, masterly discourse, eloquence and strength of conviction, he left an indelible impression on the parliament delegates. Thereafter, he toured various parts of America and Europe delivering discourses. At least some important sections of people in the West have begun realising that India's rich, ancient wisdom, which can guide the world towards its spiritual destiny.

In his own country, the news of his spiritual conquest has shaken Indians out of their stupor, making them conscious of their own glorious past. This is possibly for the first time that an Indian has spoken about his country with pride and respect. He represented himself as native of India, the spiritual capital of the world and not, of course, as a shrunken citizen of a slave nation. He could, thus, initiate a process of change in perceptions about India in both the West and more importantly in India. He returned from Europe to Colombo on 15th January in 1897. From there he has crossed the sea by a steamer and reached India today at Rameshwaram. Large number of people gathered to welcome this young monk.

'Awake, Arise And March Ahead'

Vivekananda's Call To Slumbering Indians

April 1897: Since his return from the West in January this year, Vivekananda has been visiting places and people are turning up in large numbers to hear him speak. In Calcutta, Raja Benoy Krishna Deb and Congress leaders extend a warm welcome to this spiritual warrior at a thickly attended meeting.

Vivekananda is urging Indians to awake, arise and march ahead. He is asking them especially to render service to the depressed, downtrodden and vulnerable Indians whom they should embrace as their own brethren. Although he is away from politics, he is describing bondage as a curse and urging Indians to shed their 'shackles' to realise the glory of total emancipation. He is advocating equality amongst people as all souls are potentially divine.

Although essentially a spiritual leader, Vivekananda is not undermining the need for the Indians to advance in all spheres of life, spiritual and material. He is attacking lethargy, and indolence that are crippling Indians. He wants them to dust away the cobwebs of prejudices, mindless rituals and emerge as a self-respecting, vibrant nation. His messages have been electrifying and motivating Indians, especially the youth.

His lectures and utterances are bringing some of the core issues relating to Indian masses to the centre stage, which the Indian National Congress has failed to achieve over the last twelve years or so. There is urgency in whatever Vivekananda is doing.

Critics say, hitherto Congress has been dominated by drawing-room politicians who could hardly be trusted with the task of tearing asunder the shackles of slavery. After Vivekananda's arrival in national life, it looks plausible that the future leaders, or at least quite a few of them, may attempt a different brand of politics. He has, in fact, generated a new force that will exert its own influence over leaders and events.

Govt Derecognises Poona Sarvajanik Sabha

April 1897, Bombay: Bombay government has been much perturbed by the activities of the Poona Sarvajanik Sabha under the leadership of Tilak, especially in regard to the assistance by them to famine victims. As per the famine relief code, a farmer whose crop production has fallen to four annas in a rupee is exempted from paying land revenue. The government contends that due to misleading campaign by the Sabha members, even those ineligible for the relief have also stopped paying land revenue. To add fuel to the fire, Tilak has been writing strong editorials in his paper *Kesari*, denouncing the government apathy and unwillingness to apply the provisions of the famine relief code.

After some of the Sabha members campaigning in the countryside were arrested and charged for inciting the peasantry by wrong interpretation of the famine relief code, the government asked the Sabha if they were its accredited agents. When the Sabha gave a vague reply, the government took the opportunity and declared that the Sabha in its present form would cease to be recognised as a body, which had any claim to address the administration on public policy.

This government move has come as a setback to Tilak as he has been using the Sabha as an effective and government-recognised platform to reach a wide population and try to get the people justice and help from the government.

My Work Here Is My Gurudakshina: Gokhale

April 1897, London: MG Ranade, unable to present himself due to compulsions of judicial services, deputed Gokhale to London to give evidence to the Royal Commission on Indian Expenditure. Gokhale made a splendid presentation—based on sound reasoning and plethora of facts collected from official sources. He conclusively established the facts of rising government expenditure and the falling levels of public welfare and in the process highlighted the lacunae of the government policies and administration. His evidence was followed by cross-examinations by members of the Commission, in the course of which he made a great impression upon them. Thereafter, he has been on a lecture tour in Britain and forcefully presents India's point of view to the citizens there.

Although accolades are being showered upon him from several quarters in India and England, Gokhale is a modest person. He has dedicated all his work here to Ranade as his *gurudakshina*.

VIVEKANANDA FOUNDS RAMAKRISHNA MISSION

May 1, 1897, Calcutta: Vivekananda has founded the Ramakrishna Mission at Belur, a suburb of Calcutta, to spread the message of his master Ramakrishna Paramhamsa. There are at least two important aspects of this mission. One, it stresses on service to the distressed humanity with humility and reverence. Two, it does not undermine any religion and says all religions lead to the same God. Vivekananda is not a political leader, nor has he begun a political movement for independence. He, nevertheless, condemns bondage of every kind as a handicap for the human soul to realise its spiritual goal. By thoughts, speeches and actions, he has been a great source of inspiration to all patriots and freedom fighters. Some of the finest minds of educated Indians are joining the Mission. Although political freedom does not constitute the basic tenets of the Swami or the Ramakrishna Mission, most of the people attached to the Mission are deeply patriotic and have soft corners for the cause of freedom of Indian nation.

PLAGUE, THE LESSER EVIL?

Poona Burns In Helpless Anger, Rand Indifferent

May 1897, Poona: Last year Bubonic plague broke out in the western part of India, engulfing Bombay, Poona, Surat, and Karachi. Bombay city remained under its vicious grip during October 1896 to February this year. According to some reports, about half of the city dwellers deserted the city. For past sometime, Poona has been reeling under the scourge and people are succumbing to it in large numbers. Ironically, the miseries of people here have aggravated manifold after the Bombay government appointed a plague committee with WC Rand as its chairman to tackle the epidemic and placed the army at his command to carry out his task. The committee has been granted wide powers to stamp out plague. Towards this end, it can inter alia supersede the local authorities, search for infected buildings, segregate people suspected to be suffering from plague, demolish tents and temporary structures.

Rand's men, who include both army and civic officials, began to comb Poona right from March this year. Teams supported by cavalry and infantry have been raiding suspected plague-affected areas to segregate the diseased from the healthy people. While doing this, the British soldiers have been destroying properties, desecrating places of worship, and handling the aged and women in very uncivilised manner, encroaching upon their dignity. While segregating, people are being herded like animals in open spaces. It is heard that two women have committed suicides after they were violated upon by the soldiers. Those exposed to the excesses feel even 'plague' is kinder than these notorious, cruel men.Rand has been completely impervious to complaints against his men and simply brushes these aside. Poona is fuming in helpless anger, especially against Rand. Tilak has been protesting against such mindless atrocities through the editorials in his papers.

TILAK CELEBRATES 'CHATRAPATI' ANNIVERSARY

June 1897, Poona: This year, Tilak is holding a 'coronation anniversary' to commemorate Shivaji's assumption of the tile 'Chatrapati'. Tilak had organised celebration of the Shivaji festival last year on the great hero's birth anniversary. There was excellent response and Tilak could raise a good sum of money to reconstruct Shivaji's samadhi that was lying neglected for long years. There were discourses and Tilak addressed the gathering on Shivaji's strategies against enemies in the course of winning 'swaraj' and building up his empire. Clearly he wants to remind the people of their glorious past and history of *'swaraj'*. There was a discussion on Shivaji's planned murder of Afzal Khan. Tilak, in his presidential address, justified Shivaji's actions in the context of the latter's noble objectives by drawing references from religious scriptures.

Thereafter, on the eve of the jubilee celebrations of Queen Victoria, Tilak has, in his *Kesari* editorial, questioned its propriety when the country was reeling under famine, plague and earthquake. He has lamented the plight of the natives who, he said, have become so miserable and lifeless that anyone could lord over and tyrannise them.

Tilak's lecture on the occasion of the Shivaji festival and his editorials have stirred up people. At the same time, the government is sensing sedition.

PLAGUE COMMISSIONER RAND KILLED

June 22, 1897, Poona: Walter C Rand, the plague commissioner, has fallen to the bullets of Damodar Hari Chapekar, a revolutionary patriot hailing from nearby Chinchwad. Damodar has been, since long, organising patriotic young men by imparting them with both physical and military training with a view to overthrowing the British regime.

He has been deeply moved by the mute sufferings of the people of Poona at the hands of Rand and the army acting at his command. Today midnight, while Rand was returning from the Government House after attending the 'Queen's jubilee celebration' ceremony, Damodar and his brothers, Balakrishna and Vasudev, chased Rand's carriage. In another carriage an army officer, Lt Charles Egerton Ayerst, was following.

In a desolate spot, Damodar opened fire at Rand causing the latter grievous injury. By that time Balakrishna was close behind Ayerst's carriage, following it. Suspecting that the army officer had watched Damodar's action and could act, Balakrishna shot him dead.

Thereafter, the Chapekar brothers disappeared. Rand has been severely injured and admitted to the hospital. Chances of his survival are bleak.

The police have not been able to identify the assassins. Many stories are doing the rounds. They have begun a manhunt for the assassins.

Gokhale Links Assassination And Operation Plague

July 1897, London: News of the assassination of WC Rand has spread across India. It has reached England too and it is upsetting the British people. Gokhale is here. While speaking on this issue to a local newspaper, he opined that there is a link between the assassination and the manner in which 'Operation Plague' was being conducted under Rand. He also contended that the two women who committed suicide were violated by British soldiers. Gokhale's view on the matter has annoyed the British government, the British Indian government in Delhi and also the provincial government in Bombay.

Tilak Sentenced To 18 Months Of Jail

Divided Jury Convicts Him For Seditious Editorials

September 1897, Bombay: British Indian government has strong suspicion that Tilak has had a hand in the assassination of Rand. However, it did not have clinching evidence. As such, it has implicated him for his public address during the Shivaji celebration and for writing seditious editorials in his newspaper *Kesari.* He was arrested on 27 July this year and charged under Section 124 of the Penal Code for sedition. The jury comprised six Europeans, two Hindus and one Parsee judge. There was clear dichotomy in the jury—the six European judges pronounced him guilty while all three Indian judges found him innocent. Based on the majority verdict, the court awarded him eighteen months of rigorous imprisonment.

There is gloom in Bombay and Poona after the sentence. One thing is certain. The forcible indictment of Tilak has given a huge boost to his popularity.

Congress President SN Banerjea Applauds Tilak

December 27-29, 1897, Amravati: The thirteenth annual session of the Congress is held here. C Sankaran Nair, ex-member of the Viceroy's executive council, presides. The issue of plague in Poona and its handling by Rand and the armed forces come under sharp criticism.

Sankaran Nair and Surendra Nath Banerjea, two stalwarts, lavish praises on BG Tilak in relation to the famine and the epidemic, paying him rich tributes. Nair regrets that Tilak is not being treated as a political prisoner. SN Banerjea, a veteran leader from Bengal, strikes an emotional chord when he says the whole nation is in tears due to Tilak's conviction.

Gokhale Heckled, Booed

December 1897, Amravati: Upon his return from England to India, Gokhale felt intense pressure all around him. Notwithstanding the accolades he won for his immaculate presentations to the Royal Commission on Indian Expenditure, things went sour after he spoke on the 'Rand assassination'. In India, the Bombay government was much annoyed—taking Gokhale's view as aspersion cast on its functioning.

In Poona, right since Rand's assassination, the government let loose oppression. Tilak was implicated and sentenced to imprisonment. The administration has been out to throttle any voice of dissent. Gokhale was confronted by the police and pressurised to disclose the sources of the news upon which he gave his press interview in England. Under such suffocating circumstances, Gokhale fully retracted his statement and tendered an apology to Sandhurst, the Bombay Governor.

Gokhale is suffering inner turmoil over his action. He is upset. Tilak has criticised Gokhale for showing lamentable lack of courage. Gokhale's cup of woes spills over when he is heckled and booed in the annual session of the Congress held here.

TO THE GALLOWS WITH BHAGAVAD GITA IN HAND

April 18, 1898, Yeravada prison, Poona: Damodar Hari Chapekar, the revolutionary, who assassinated Rand was later arrested, charged and awarded death sentence. He is being adored and revered by people for his peerless patriotism and revolutionary spirit. According to reports received, Damodar today went to the gallows with a c opy of the 'Bhagavad Gita' in his hand.

People close to him say that this copy of the divine literature was given to him by BG Tilak and Chapekar held it as precious possession till his dying hour.

Damodar's sacrifice is being seen as an important step forward in the country's struggle against colonial rulers and towards swaraj.

Annie Besant Founds The Central Hindu College

July 1898, Benares: Annie Besant has founded the Central Hindu College in this holy city. She, the daughter of Irish parents, had come to Madras in 1893 at the age of forty-six years and since then has made India her home. While in Europe, she was active in public life and was known for her commitment to causes like women's rights, secularism, birth control, rights of the working class and freedom of thoughts of individuals.

What particularly distinguishes Anne Besant is her uncompromising attitude in her quest for the truth. It is due to the latter that her interests in religion extended beyond conventional Christianity and she became attracted to the Theosophical Society. She has also been deeply interested in the theory of 'karma' and 'reincarnation'.

In India, she has been trying to rediscover and re-establish the hidden glories and heritage of the Orient that could be useful to the world at large. No surprise, she has chosen to start the Central Hindu College here—the oldest surviving city of the world and an abode of ancient Hindu heritage. It may be added that Besant shares Indian aspirations for self-government and has been engaging herself actively towards that end.

Congress Bats For Indian Princes

December 29-31, 1898, Madras: This is the third consecutive year that the Congress has passed a resolution urging the Government of India not to depose Indian princes for mal-administration or misconduct until an enquiry establishes the facts of the charge. With more than six hundred native states in India—some of which are quite small, the British government has generally been high-handed in its dealing with the rulers of many states. But, Congress has been sympathetic to their causes—due to self-interest and a generally soft approach towards the Indian India.

The princes and their ministers have been invited to annual sessions of the party from time to time. Some rulers have also been contributing to the Congress fund. Prominent among them are the rulers of Mysore, Travancore, Cochin, Baroda, Kolhapur, Junagadh and Bhavnagar. On its part, the Congress has refrained from meddling in the internal affairs of the states, notwithstanding the autocratic and repressive policies concerning the subjects in many Indian states.

Youth Driven To Extremism By Government Policies

1898, Bombay: Thanks to increasing awareness of the gradually growing tribe of educated Indians, a number of whom are educated under the British system, more and more native schools and colleges have been coming up in India. The British government is concerned at the large turnout of young men from these Indian institutions. Its worries are two-fold: first, the young people passing out under the extant curriculum are not adequately prepared to take up practical careers; second and more important, the students are politically indoctrinated to turn against the Empire. To pre-empt the possibility of the country and the government getting inundated by crowds of such disloyal and indisciplined youth, the government has now prescribed that no educational institution for the instruction of youth should, under any circumstances, have any connection with political writings, political speeches, political assemblies and political parties. All educational societies have been instructed to incorporate these principles in their constitutions if they wished to receive government assistance.

This fresh directive, shutting out students from political activities, has been achieving an objective that the government surely did not have in mind—it has been driving more and more youth to the secret revolutionary societies. Many of these societies have independence of the country as their goal and believe that armed revolution is the means to attain it. In the Bombay presidency, organisations like Mitra Mela are witnessing steady influx of young revolutionaries. Reports from the IB are causing concerns to the British government in Bombay and Calcutta.

THE VIVEKANANDA IMPACT

December 29-31, 1898, Madras: The Congress holds its fourteenth annual session here. Ananda Mohan Bose presides. The president has given a call to educate people to deal with problems that affect the vast masses, who have practically no voice in deciding how they would like to be governed. This appears to be a welcome change in approach—puts the archlight on the mute millions. According to some political observers, the spirited lectures and speeches of Vivekananda in recent times, exhorting people to serve the distressed and downtrodden Indians in the sense of worship of God, may have begun to touch the thoughts of the politicians.

The Best Way To Help Indians Is Self-government

December 27-30, 1899, Lucknow: The Congress holds its fifteenth annual session here. Romesh Chandra Dutt, retired divisional commissioner of Burdwan, a celebrated writer and intellectual, presides. His presidential speech was deeply analytical, constituting a slight departure from the past trend. He compared India with other self-governing colonies of the British Empire, in the process bringing her miseries including the recurrent famines under sharp focus. Based on facts and arguments, he made a strong case for self-governance for Indians. That is the best way to help India's people, he contended.

If this is harbinger of a trend, it may be concluded that the Congress has begun to shift from its initial position of blind loyalty to the British and is showing willingness to examine issues more objectively.

Congress Attempts To Lure Muslim Delegates Critics Ask Congress To Shed Off Cosmetics

December 27-30, 1899, Lucknow: The annual session of the Indian National Congress is held here and its organisers make every possible attempt to make it appear representative of all sections of Indian people. Enlisting more Muslim delegates has been posing particular difficulty all these years and the Congress makes specific efforts to overcome the challenge this year. But, Lucknow is not far from Aligarh and its Muslim inhabitants are very much subject to the charisma of Sir Syed Ahmed Khan. On the eve of this annual session, the Aligarh camp has become hyperactive to thwart the Congress aspiration by resorting to active propaganda amongst the Muslim community, dissuading them from attending the Congress show.

According to Swami Shraddhanand attending the session, the situation has been like a tug of war, the Congress given a helping hand by moneyed Hindu men of means who are reportedly spending liberally to fund large number of Muslim delegates from Lucknow by arranging for their ostentatious attires, delegate fees, expenses for boarding and lodging. They are, in fact, trying hard to allure the minorities to the session—they have a single objective—to demonstrate that the Congress represents minorities as much as the majority. Critics, however, say that such manipulations merely demonstrate the hollowness in the show. According to reliable sources, out of a total of about 433 Muslim delegates, merely 30 have arrived here from the outside, the rest have been mobilised from Lucknow. They say Congress had better shed such a cosmetic approach, if it really wants to get a foothold amongst Muslims.

Tilak Is The Real Champion Of Swarajya Amongst All Carpet Knights: Shraddhanand

December 1899, Lucknow: There were many illustrious Congress leaders attending the annual session. However, special accolades were reserved for Bal Gangadhar Tilak—not only a fiery speaker but a leader brimming with patriotism and a man of the 'masses' and 'action'. He is back after serving his prison term. The audience listen to him in rapt attention. Swami Shraddhanand, greatly impressed by him, felt that Tilak is 'the one real champion of Indian swarajya among all the carpet knights assembled there'.

HINDI ACCEPTED IN GOVERNMENT OFFICES

Communal Temperature Soars

April 8, 1900, Allahabad: The language permitted to be used in the law courts and government offices concerns common people and, therefore, is of importance. In the United Province, Urdu has been enjoying that status. This means, to file a petition at a court or government office, a common man has to get the appeal written in Urdu. The vast majority of Hindu population has been representing for long that Hindi in Devnagri script be allowed for this purpose. At long last the government has acceded to this request. However, this has led to a bitter communal acrimony. Many Muslims resent this new government directive and some Muslim organisations are holding protest meetings across the province. Joining the issue, Hindus are also holding counter meetings in support of the government directives. The disharmony that has erupted only shows the sensitive nature of inter-community relationship and the readiness of the communal elements to exploit every opportunity that comes their way.

Congress Leaders Attack Punjab Land Alienation Act

October 1900: According to the government, the Punjab Land Alienation Act 1900, by imposing restrictions on sale and mortgage of agricultural land and their conversion for non-agricultural uses, protects the interests of the common peasantry against the unscrupulous zamindars, land sharks and money landers. Predictably, the zamindars, land sharks and the moneylenders are upset. However, the peasantry are dismayed as a number of Congress leaders too have been attacking the legislation.

Critics say, criticising a public welfare-oriented legislation like this is unfortunate and betrays the fact that the Congress has not yet been able to shed its elitist mindset and it still continues to protect the interest of the rich and the affluent. Even if a process of fermentation in favour of the common people has begun in the party, as some insiders insist, nothing is visible as yet on the ground. To be able to emerge as a mass organisation, the Congress Party has to go a long way, they contend.

Victoria Memorial To Epitomise Might Of British Raj

February 6, 1901, Calcutta: Viceroy Lord Curzon has unveiled a plan to construct a magnificent memorial in this British Indian capital in honour of late queen Victoria. He wants it to symbolise the might of the great British Empire. No doubt, this would continuously remind the Indians about their status as a colonised nation.

British Arrogance Hurts Educated Indians

1901, Calcutta : As the new century dawns, a new and confident India is gradually emerging. A number of British leaders claim that the credit for it must be given to the introduction of Western education system in this country, which has been bearing fruit. Be that as it may, the fact remains that intellectually many of the educated Indians have been posing serious challenges to a sizeable section of middle and lower levels of British bureaucracy, who are in their position of authority because of their lineage and colour of skin, despite being of mediocre calibre. Unable to assert their superiority morally and intellectually, and on the contrary feeling threatened by the educated Indians, these officials have been resorting to oppression and repression, misusing their position and power. Such behaviour are further alienating the educated Indians, especially the middle classes, which have many aspirations but no avenues to fulfil them. The recent spiritual conquest of the West by Swami Vivekananda has invested Indians in general with a new sense of self-respect and patriotic spirit.

Against this backdrop, the Indian National Congress, supposed to be the political representative of the Indians, has still been pursuing a pliant approach towards India's colonial ruler—one that is based on prayer and appeal, with little assertiveness. This is leaving many educated Indians dissatisfied and disquiet. What must cause worry to the government is that some of them are being attracted to revolutionary ideas and secret societies to realise their political aspirations. The pinpricks by the highhanded British officials are catalysing this process. Calcutta and greater Bengal are emerging as the fertile soil, encouraging revolutionary activities.

New Kid On The Bloc

NORTH WEST FRONTIER PROVINCE

November 9, 1901, Peshawar: British Indian government has carved out a new province from the Punjab. The new province, called the North West Frontier Province, bordering Afghanistan comprises some settled districts like Bannu, Dera Is mail Khan, Hazara, Kohat and Peshawar and agencies of the Khyber, Kurram, Malakand, Tochi and Wana. The aim clearly seems to be to protect the sensitive north Western border of the country from Afghan invasion. It has been placed under the charge of a chief commissioner.

British Indian Government Is The Most Expensive

December 26-28, 1901, Calcutta: The seventeenth annual session of the Congress is held here. Dinshaw Eduji Wacha presides. Wacha has been involved with the Congress for quite some time and has served the organisation as its secretary for a few years. In his presidential speech, he has carried the trend of antagonism against the government a little further. He criticises the British government for running perhaps the most expensive administrative machinery in a poor country like India.

The session has demanded Indians be admitted to police competitive examinations in London, and also more employment in senior positions in the army.

Congress Passes Gandhi Resolution On Immigrants

December 1901, Calcutta: Gandhi is in India. One of the important objectives of his India visit is to bring the plight of the suffering Indian immigrants in South Africa to the attention of the Congress leaders in the annual session in Calcutta. His indefatigable spirit, sincerity and devotion to the cause has earned him the admiration and support of Gopal Krishna Gokhale, a Congress stalwart, whose friendship he had secured during his visit to India way back in 1896. Gandhi wants to introduce a resolution on the issue of the Indian immigrants in the Subjects Committee, and get the matter discussed in detail by the delegates so that they develop right appreciation of the underlying problem. Gokhale has assured him all help.Gandhi, however, gets a feel of the formidable bureaucracy operating within the Congress as he is kept waiting till midnight while one after another resolution is introduced. As regards adoption by the committee, more than the intrinsic worth of a resolution what mattered was the weight of its sponsor. In the ordinary course, there is little scope for a newcomer to get his resolution introduced. Thanks to Gokhale's efforts, Gandhi gets a chance but his turn comes almost in the midnight, at the fag end of the session. At that inconvenient hour, when the thin body of delegates present are fatigued and not in a receptive frame of mind, Gandhi is given only five minutes to speak as he introduces the resolution. While the resolution is passed without any deliberations, Gandhi becomes upset as his hard work fails to serve the core purpose—create appropriate awareness amongst Congress delegates.[3] But he has to reconcile to the state of affairs in the Congress.

'Lord Curzon's Khansamas' – Gandhi is shocked

February 1902, Calcutta: Gandhi comes here to attend the annual session of the Congress. After the Congress session, he visits Burma and then returns to Calcutta in the first week of this month. He decides to stay here for some time, along with his mentor cum friend Gopal Krishna Gokhale. On one occasion, Gandhi is shocked to see that in a durbar held by Lord Curzon in the city, the rajas and maharajas put on trousers and shining boots befitting khansamas. On enquiry, he comes to know that the native royalties are treated as 'khansamas' of Lord Curzon, and it would be an offence if they are to attend the function in their usual royal dress. Gandhi is appalled to witness this kind of racial discrimination right in India, and that too at the highest social strata.

Gandhi Is Greatly Impressed By Gokhale

February 1902, Calcutta: Gandhi is having an extended stay in the city, his purpose being to meet important people to advance the cause of Indian immigrants in South Africa and also study the religious and public institutions here. Gokhale, more familiar with the city and connected to the leaders and renowned people here, is also staying back in connection with his own work and has invited Gandhi to stay with him while in Calcutta. During nearly a month-long stay together, Gandhi feels it is as much a joy as education to see Gokhale at work. Out of a wide range of qualities that Gandhi observes in Gokhale, one striking factor is that his personal life is dedicated for public good and he never wastes a minute. India's freedom is the one and the only thing that engages his attention. They have turned good friends and Gokhale has requested Gandhi to return from South Africa, settle in Bombay, practise in the Bombay Bar and help him in public work in India.

ANUSHILAN SAMITY IS FOUNDED

An Ominous Signal For The Raj?

March 24, 1902, Calcutta: Today, some of the prominent nationalist individuals inspired by revolutionary ideals have come together to found the 'Anushilan Samity'. According to reports, it will act as an umbrella organisation for three societies founded already by Satish Chandra Bose, Sarala Devi and P Mitter. Its goals and agendas may be coterminus with its constituents, though of course, it can as well act as the leader, showing them the path and also coordinate their activities.

Its professed objectives are health, culture and training in martial arts for the youth and prepare them for socially constructive activities like flood and famine relief. Needless to say, a current of patriotism and intolerance of the colonial rulers runs in the veins of all its members and leaders. Clearly, the Samity has not only social but political goals as well, even if hidden and may not hesitate to pursue unconventional path to realise these goals. The Samity has, reportedly, the blessings of many nationalist leaders of Bengal.

SWAMI VIVEKANANDA AWAKENS INDIA
Then Leaves Mortal World

July 4, 1902, Belur: Swami Vivekananda passed away today at the young age of thirty-nine. This great monk not only showed the spiritual path to India and the world, but also taught the world how spiritual salvation could be achieved through service to humanity. Although he did not involve himself in politics, he did say that slavery was a curse and encouraged Indians to be independent.

Vivekananda might be addressed as the father of modern Indian nationalism. BC Pal has called him a 'prophet of nationalism'. His message 'arise, awake and stop not till the goal is reached' has a profound appeal for teeming millions of Indians. According to Aurobindo Ghosh, Indians were so stimulated by Vivekananda's message and actions that they would have brought about an upsurge like the French revolution in this country if only they had been politically trained. Vivekananda's was the voice of the soul. Effortlessly, he reached the heart of the nation and exhorted it to stand firmly on its feet. Even though he is no more, his thoughts and speeches have begun to motivate many leaders of the Congress and revolutionaries, besides the vast masses across this subcontinent.

More Revolutionary Societies May Grow In Bengal
Aurobindo Plans To Send Emissaries From Baroda

1902, Calcutta: Sarala Devi Ghoshal has founded a School of Physical Culture at Ballygunj Circular Road in the city. Sarala Devi is a highly courageous lady with independent spirit. She is the niece of poet Rabindranath Tagore. It is being said that renowned barrister P Mitter and Okakura, a Japanese gentleman known for his love of India, are involved in this enterprise. In the School's first meeting, Barindranath Ghosh, a brother and emissary of Aurobindo Ghosh, a fierce patriot serving the princely state of Baroda as a senior official, participated. Barindranath is a revolutionary in his own right.

Apparently, a well-intentioned move to improve the health of the youth and engage them in social activities, this new school of physical culture is making the government suspicious. According to the intelligence branch reports, the school is a guise to train young people to carry out terrorist activities against the government. Even citizens are whispering that young persons will be trained here to assassinate officials and supporters of the British government. In certain closed circles it is being discussed that Aurobindo Ghosh is keen to see more revolutionary societies grow on the soil of Bengal to work for Indian's emancipation. As a part of this exercise, Barindranath Ghosh, already here, is likely to visit other parts of Bengal to encourage setting up of more secret societies. It is significant that BG Tilak has already started a Shivaji cult in Maharashtra, his chief aim being to carry out aggressive patriotic activities. Political observers say that in the foreseeable future, the revolutionaries in Bengal, Maharashtra and Gujarat might attempt to build a network and work in coordination.

BHIKAJI CAMA ENLISTS SUPPORT FOR REVOLUTION

1902: Growing dissatisfaction with the colonial British government and the yearning for freedom has begun to be seen and heard even outside India. Madam Bhikaji Cama, a Parsee nationalist, epitomises their spirit. Bhikaji, wife of a rich Parsi businessman, attracted countrywide attention six years ago when she had rendered exemplary service to the plague victims in Bombay by nursing the patients and inoculating the people. In the process, she herself became affected. Though she survived, she grew very weak and came to Europe for recovery. In this continent, she, as an associate of Shyamji K Verma, another famous ex-patriate nationalist leader, has been touring various parts of Europe and America and making revolutionary propaganda against the British rule in India. She is getting encouraging responses, especially from expatriate Indians. This patriotic woman leader is setting an example. She is certain that if there is greater awareness and appreciation about the problems and aspirations of the Indians in other parts of the world, this would help the cause of Indian emancipation.

Congress Resents Hefty Increase In Capitation Charges

December 28-30, 19 02, Ahmedabad: The Congress has held its eighteenth annual session here with Surendra Nath Bannerjea presiding. In recent years, educated Indians are becoming aware of the huge burden being imposed by the British government to maintain large armed forces in their country. Considering India's poor economic condition and pervasive poverty, such lopsided expenditure appears to be obscene. In striking contrast are the meagre expenditures on education and public health. The session has deliberated on these issues and criticised, in particular, a fat increase effected recently in the capitation charges thrust upon India for keeping the British armed forces on this land.

RC DUTT STEERS PARADIGM SHIFT IN INDIAN THINKING

1902, Calcutta: Long years of British rule have been instrumental in exposing a section of Indian society to Western education. The British regime has been consciously attempting to promote servility and blind loyalty. Unfortunately, most of the Western educated intellectuals are compromising their integrity to curry favour with the government of the day. Even many top leaders of the Indian National Congress swear loyalty to the British Empire. In such a climate of intellectual depravity, Romesh Chandra Dutt's book titled, *Economic History of India,* has shaken the government and taken complacent Indians by storm.

This book provides a masterly exposition and a scholastic analysis of the economic history of India, together with the causes of its illness. Dutt has sharply criticised the imperialist policies and programmes that have been contributing to economic maladies of the country. Through hard facts and strong arguments, Dutt has torn asunder not only the grandstanding by the British government but also the servile mindset of many Indian intellectuals.

Lord Curzon is much antagonised, but he finds it hard to counter the objectivity of Dutt's scholarly work. The book is compelling Indian leaders and thinkers to take a re-look at the merits and demerits of colonial rule. This one masterly work has taken at least some lustre off the proverbial British Empire. Both, the rulers and the subjects, will certainly look at each other from somewhat changed perspectives from now on—that is for sure.

CURZON WANTS TO DIVIDE BENGAL

December 1903, Calcutta: Lord Curzon has begun to work on a plan that could turn Bengal into a volcano—to divide Bengal and carve out a Muslim majority province. His plan involves segregating districts of Dacca, Chittagong, Mymensingh and Tippera Hills and conjoin these with Assam to create a combined Muslim majority province of Eastern Bengal and Assam. While critics see a deliberate attempt to create a religious divide in the plan, the government justifies the move as an administrative compulsion. It says Bengal is too unwieldy to be governed by one Lt Governor.

It's Time We Relate To The Masses: Congress President

December 28-30, 1903, Madras: The nineteenth annual session of the Congress is held here and Lal Mohan Ghosh presides. In his speech, Ghosh has sharply criticised the pomp and show of the coronation durbar in a poor country. He urges the Congress to be sensitive to the needs and problems of the masses. He says, the Congress' policies must be formulated keeping them in view. He also exhorts the delegates to educate the masses.

Challenges Against The Old Order

The Indian National Congress is almost twenty years old. A change in its orientations has been much awaited—from being elitist to pro-people. At last this seems to be happening.

A contest is emerging for the leadership of the Indian National Congress—it is between the wealthy, Westernised, elite leaders professing unswerving loyalty to the British Empire and those who are closer to Indian heritage, culture and people and look at British presence as undesirable and want to expel them. Both groups are educated and enlightened, but their objectives and approaches are different. The first group, includes leaders like Sir Pheroze Shah Mehta, Sir Surendra Nath Banerjea, Dadabhai Naoroji, Gopal Krishna Gokhale, and such others.

Not only have they been significant beneficiaries of the British rule, they have firm faith and trust on the goodness and sense of justice of the Empire. They are firm believers in the constitutional means and trust that the British will grant the Indians self-government in due course of time and they see their role as facilitators of that process. On the other hand, the second group, comprise leaders like Bal Gangadhar Tilak, Aurobindo Ghosh, Lala Lajpat Rai, Bipin Chandra Pal and many others. Though highly educated and erudite, they hold deep respect for Indian culture and heritage. Between the two groups, the latter are closer to the Indian soil and understand the Indian aspirations better. But they are impatient to achieve freedom for the country, if possible here and now, and not hesitant to adopt revolutionary means for this purpose. In any event, they find the policies of 'prayers and petitions' adopted by the Congress all these years as simply inadequate and unsatisfactory. They have so far tolerated the hegemony of the other group in the organisation. But now they are sensing the change in the air and that the time has arrived to assert their views. Political analysts predict a serious confrontation between the two groups for the leadership of the Congress, sooner than later.

Life Beyond The British

Centuries of colonial rule have destroyed the belief of Indians on their ability to govern themselves—a kind of dependency syndrome has established a vice-like grip over their psyche. However, in recent times, with the occurrence of certain events in India and in the rest of the world, sections of Indians have begun to think afresh about their political future. This is reflecting not only in a simmering conflict between the two groups for control of the Indian National Congress, but also in a budding predilection amongst a section of Indians in favour of armed opposition to the British government. The latter want outright independence as soon as possible and are ready to examine the possibility of armed revolution to expel the British. All these years, Western superiority over the oriental nations was considered axiomatic truth. However, the Japanese victory over the Russians, constituting the triumph of an Asian power over a European rival in recent times has changed notions. Calcutta is excited. Some overtly patriotic Bengalis are drawing inspiration from the episode and taking to the path of armed resistance. The government suspects, new secret societies are coming up in the city that aim to carry out violent activities against it and its supporters.

Abhinav Bharat – Mitra Mela In New Avatar

Revolutionary Society Changes Name Yet Again

1904: If the spurring of revolutionary societies and activities are matters of last three or four years in Bengal, their history is older in Maharashtra. The Rashtrabhakta Samuha was the foremost revolutionary organisation in Maharashtra and it changed its name to Mitra Mela in 1890. Now it has emerged in a new avatar and re-christened itself as Abhinav Bharat. The society remains a prominent face of revolutionary activities in Maharashtra. It may also be recalled that the Chapekar brothers had chalked out before the country's revolutionaries the path of political assassination way back in 1897. It is also being said that revolutionaries in these two far ends of the empire—east and west of India—are trying to establish linkages to coordinate their programmes and enhance their impact.

Secret Societies Spread Wings Northwards

1904, Saharanpur: Secret Societies spread beyond the provinces of Bombay and Bengal to other parts of the country as well. After west and east, the amber of revolutionary spirit has begun to glow now in the northern part of India. A secret society has been formed here, led by SM Chatterjee. A host of leading revolutionaries from Punjab including Lala Hardayal, Sufi Amba Prasad and Ajit Singh are also helping in organising its activities. The society is both collecting and manufacturing arms to carry out its programmes and activities.

Henry Cotton Moots United States Of India

December 26-28, 1904, Bombay: The Congress holds its twentieth annual session here with Sir Henry Cotton presiding. Cotton was the chief commissioner of Assam. He has abundant concern for India and Indians and has been working for the benefit of India in Britain. He, however, sees India only as an integral part of the British Empire. In his presidential speech, he has made an interesting suggestion—to form a federation of free and separate states to be called as United States of India. He foresees that this USI, vested with local autonomy, will gel together with other self-governing British colonies.

BENGAL DIVIDED: GOVT PLAYS COMMUNAL CARD

Swadeshi Movement Launched

October 16, 1905: Viceroy Lord Curzon had in February this year, proposed the partition of Bengal, ostensibly to secure better governance of the large presidency encompassing Bengal, Bihar, Orissa, Assam, princely state of Sikkim and tributary states of Orissa and Chotanagpur. According to this proposal, a new province comprising East Bengal and Assam will be created while the rest would remain as the western part of Bengal and the two would be placed under separate Governors.

The partition is supposed to change the demographic profile in the two provinces with obvious political implications. Pre-partition, the Bengal presidency had a large Hindu majority. Post-partition, the west of Bengal has even higher concentrations of Hindu people—42 million Hindus and 9 million Muslims. However, the new province of East Bengal has a clear majority of the Muslims—18 million Muslims and 12 million Hindus. In the densely populated East Bengal, there are huge concentration of Muslims—mostly peasants and artisans—lagging behind socially, educationally, economically and politically. The government says that the partition would help these backward people to receive preferred administrative attention.

On 19 July 1905, the Government of India formally passed the resolution for partition. Right since the time the proposal was known in public, numerous requests had flooded the government to stall the move. But Curzon remained unconvinced. Secretary of State Brodrich sanctioned the proposal in June and a proclamation of formation of the new provinces was made in September. Finally, the new provinces have come into existence today. The Bengali Hindus have been deeply resenting this move right since the time the idea was made public and staging unprecedented agitation. It may be mentioned that caste Hindus had dominated undivided Bengal all these years. Their hegemony has been undisputed even in the eastern part (now organised as a separate province). In fact, the educated middle class Bengali Hindu intelligentsia have been leveraging their hold over such a large presidency to dominate even at the national level. The partition is sure to upset the extant power equation between the two communities. Bengali Hindus are not convinced of government justification and see in this government action a despicable design to create division amongst the two communities. Today, they have launched a mass movement declaring it a Black Day. They are calling it the 'Swadeshi Movement' and drawing from the Chinese precedent of boycotting American goods to use as one of the strategies to conduct the movement, ie. boycotting British goods.

Aurobindo Combines Spirituality With Nationalism

November, 1905, Calcutta: Aurobindo Ghosh was the vice-principal of the State College in Baroda and held in good respect by the Maharaja. However, he left the well-paid job and moved to Calcutta. This is in accordance with his plans to accelerate the freedom struggle of India, his motherland. Calcutta, the capital city of the British Empire as well as the abode of intense political activities—both of Congress and the revolutionary societies—obviously suits his scheme.

Aurobindo has been deeply influenced by the philosophies of Ramakrishna Paramhamsa and Vivekananda. A splendid intellect, which even his British adversaries grudgingly admit, he is impatient to see India independent and restored to her pristine glory.

The government is apprehensive of his presence in Calcutta as he has been intimately involved with secret societies, pursuing violent means to destabilise the government. The threat has grown much bigger as Aurobindo is participating also in mainstream politics through the Indian National Congress. His presence is giving the Congress a new sheen as he excels as a leader, speaker and editor. Recently he organised a huge rally in Calcutta. His natural leaning is towards the faction in the Congress that advocates extreme stance against the British government rather than the constitutionalists who recommend petitions, prayers and at the best, processions. His rapport with Congress leaders like Bal Gangadhar Tilak, in particular, is said to be excellent and together they constitute a huge threat to the present leadership of pro-British Pheroze Shah Mehta, his friends and followers.

Gokhale Founds Servants Of India Society

1905, Poona: Gopal Krishna Gokhale sets up the 'Servants of India Society' here on 12 June this year. The society's aim is to serve the country with a religious spirit and to select and train men for this purpose. The society also wants to promote national interests by all constitutional means. Gokhale is a man of impeccable integrity and public spirit. His life is a living testimony of the ideas and values he professes. No wonder, the society is attracting many worthy persons. However, enrolment as member in this society is not easy. There is a rigorous selection process and one requires recommendations of at least three ordinary members and the first member (president) to be granted membership.The society has been doing commendable social and educational work. In the political sphere it associates with the Congress.

Political analysts cannot help but observe Gokhale's differences in approaches in regard to political issues from BG Tilak, though both come from the same part of the country. Tilak is a militant nationalist, looks at the colonial rule as an unmitigated curse responsible for various ills of the country and he would like to achieve swaraj at any cost. Gokhale recognises both evil and good consequences of the British rule while being keenly aware of the former. He also wants India to get rid of the British, but would like to use only constitutional means to achieve this objective. Both are, however, great activists and pursue their goals with single-minded devotion. Yet another common factor in the two is their peerless love for India and Indians.

Another Secret Society In Manicktala

1905, Calcutta: Yet another revolutionary society has come up in Calcutta. Some of the important members of the Anushilan Samity have taken the initiative to bring it to existence—Barindra Kumar Ghosh, Aurobindo Ghosh's brother, is prominent among them. This new society has been holding its meetings and programmes in the Manicktala garden house of the Ghosh brothers. It is being called as Manicktala Secret Society.

After Calcutta, Anushilan Now in Dacca

November 1905: The Anushilan Samity, by now the most organised revolutionary society in the country, headquartered in Calcutta, has spread its wings in East Bengal. It has opened a prime office in Dacca with Pulin Behari Das as its leader. This is disturbing news to the government.

Swadeshi Is One Of The Noblest Concepts: Gokhale

December 27-30, 1905, Benaras: Congress holds its twenty-first annual session, with Gopal Krishna Gokhale presiding. The partition of Bengal has created ripples in the session. Gokhale has lauded 'swadeshi' as one of the noblest concepts. However, there is no consensus on how far the Congress should go to bring pressure on the government to annul the partition. On the issue of welcoming the Prince and Princess of Wales, due to visit India, there are sharp differences of opinions between two groups. The radical nationalists have opposed the resolution that welcomed the royal couple. Clearly, the bitterness caused by Bengal's partition has influenced the issue.

TWO

BOILING CAULDRON

1906 - 1918

BOILING CAULDRON

PARTITION: UNREST GRIPS TWO BENGALS

On the issue of partition of Bengal, the British government feels the ongoing agitation is completely unjustified. It says this step had become necessary and in fact, overdue, to tone up the administration. Bengal was too large to be managed by a single Governor. But evidently, there are other important political considerations behind this decision.

This government move has been silently welcomed by large sections of Muslims of the eastern province. There is an undercurrent of assent in this community though they are not able to express it publicly, so fierce, vocal and emotional has been the protest against the partition. Reports from the countryside suggest that vast numbers of Muslims, especially the peasantry in the east, are welcoming this government initiative. They feel post-partition, they will receive preferred attention by the government, a necessity for progress, educationally and economically. The fact that their co-religionists have a significant numerical majority in the new province is also comforting them. Now they have a geographic area, where the elite Hindus will have lesser role and they hope to wield real political power.

The educated, enlightened, economically progressive Hindus,

especially the middle class intelligentsia are seeing the partition as a 'nefarious design' of the crooked British Empire to sow divisions amongst Bengalis by inciting their religious sentiments. Bengali political leaders and intellectuals are urging the general public to unite as Bengalis and protest.

On the whole, it is the protesters that dominate the empire's landscape. It is their voice that is being heard everywhere. whether Dhaka, Calcutta or London.

Bidhir Badhan Bhangbe Tumi Ki Emoni Shaktimaan

Unrest Grips Calcutta And Bengal

1906, Calcutta: As protests against Bengal's partition get strident and violent, the British government is getting visibly perturbed. They feel it ironical that the movement is being steered by the present crop of educated Bengalis who owe their prosperity and all-India prominence to none other than their British rulers, a sapling that has been watered by the British all these long years. They are finding these protests hard to endure—possibly too much of a reaction to a prima-facie administrative decision!

However, British perceptions hardly matter. The agitation has been snowballing into a huge movement. The slogan 'Vande Mataram' reverberates in the cities, towns and villages. Angry protesters are projecting Shivaji as the National Hero. The Bengali Hindus, because of their pre-eminent position in every walk of life held for long, have been able to spread the agitation against the British government far and wide, so much so that even Muslims are not actively opposing them, despite being obvious beneficiaries of the government initiative. Powerful litterateurs including Rabindranath Tagore are also supporting the movement on the ideological ground that the government is trying to create a rift between the two communities. Highly motivating songs and poems written by Tagore and other patriotic poets fuel the movement. Tagore's song 'Bidhir Badhan Bhangbe Tumi Ki Emoni Shaktimaan', (are you powerful enough to snap the chord between people that the Almighty has ordained?) throws an open challenge to the British government, which is seen as a villain bent upon dividing the people of Bengal. Feelings against the government run high. People make bonfires of clothes made in England. So intense and yet extensive has been the 'swadeshi movement' that even the Congress Party in Bengal has begun backing it.

Bengal Boils: Government Clamps Down On Agitations

1906, Calcutta: Bengali leaders have a remarkable presence in the top brass of the Indian National Congress, and they have, at least at the provincial level, extended support to the ongoing movement against the partition of Bengal. To add to the concern of the British government, the Congress has given a call for boycott of foreign goods too. In different parts, agitated people are burning vast quantities of Manchester Cotton Cloth on pyres. There is new craze in people to buy and wear swadeshi cloth, which the British business lobby has kept out of the market for the last few decades by intrigue and manipulation. This 'swadeshi' economic bullet is certain to hurt Britain more than anything else. For British industry and economy, Indians as consumers of their manufactured goods are critically important. They cannot simply accept the loss of such a huge market overnight. The involvement of the INC in the movement has the dangerous potential to spread the cult of 'swadeshi' to other parts of India as well. To the consternation of the government, Bengali Congress leaders are completely embroiled in this movement. With highly spirited leaders like Aurobindo and Bipin Chandra Pal taking interest in the movement, softliners like Sir Surendra Nath Banerjea have been compelled to follow suit.

To add to this, revolutionary societies are channelling public anger in violent activities directed at government officials and their supporters. Unless the issue is tackled properly and promptly, the agitation runs the risk of creating anarchy in Bengal.

The Viceroy is in a piquant situation. He cannot accept this impudence—this growing turbulence and chaos. Before his eyes, this movement has begun to breach the ancient loyalty of the natives to the Crown and build up a new national consciousness, making them see virtues not only in 'swadeshi' cloth but other institutions such as education. At the same time, the Viceroy is also not willing to recommend annulment of the division of Bengal—which would be construed as a political surrender. In the circumstances, he has gone for the easy and tempting option—let loose government repression —and this is being done sans limit. Worse for the natives would, however, be any covert measure aimed at fanning the communal feelings between Hindus and Muslims—this too looks a distinct possibility.

SN Banerjea Taken Into Custody

April 16, 1906, Barisal: Congress holds its provincial conference in this town in Eastern Bengal. Bampfyide Fuller, Lt Governor of this new province, has been much peeved by the sustained anti-partition agitation, supported by the Congress and want police to act tough. Under his instructions, the police dispersed the gathering and also went to the extent of arresting Congress stalwart Surendra Nath Banerjea. Such high-handed government actions add fuel to the fire. The anti-partition movement is likely to become stronger. The Viceroy himself is said to be unhappy about the manner in which Fuller has tackled the situation.

We Will Listen No More To Old Lullabies: Aurobindo

1906, Calcutta: Although, the Congress, as an organisation, has been traditionally under the firm grip of leaders loyal to the British Empire, alternative visions and voices are being raised with force and determination. Tilak has been a militant nationalist for nearly two decades. In addition to Lajpat Rai in Punjab, and Bipin Chandra Pal in Bengal, he has a formidable ally in Aurobindo Ghosh whom he has known since the latter's Baroda days. Together, they are thrusting a new agenda on to the centrestage of Congress politics. When these leaders speak, and they often do so through the print medium, Indians sit up and listen in rapt attention. They are for swaraj and prepared to wage a hard war to attain that. They are proud of the Indian philosophy, culture and heritage and feel that the real development of Indians shall proceed on the basis of an Indian model. Their fierce patriotism, love for freedom and disdain for the imperial rule have made others refer to them as 'extremists'. Events like the partition of Bengal and the ensuing protests are coming handy for these leaders to look within, to evolve institutions and programmes of actions to take the nation ahead, shedding dependence on the colonial government.

Aurobindo Ghosh has been speaking forcefully to Indians, condemning the servility that holds the country down. He is critical that the people of India, unaware of their own culture and heritage, are complacent at some sprinkling of charities by the British and the meagre political rights allowed to Indians. Through his paper, he has communicated:

> For the last century, since our confrontation with Western civilisation began, we have been constantly discussing national progress and the attainment of political rights. In practice however, we have not progressed but declined....
>
> Far from getting political rights, our political and economic life, our arts and science, intellectual faculties and religious spirit have all become fettered. We look to others for our good, for the clothes we wear, for our education, political rights, intellectual developments and thought systems. There is no end to our gratitude to the English for the few toys they have given us. When a people is dependent on others in both mind and body, railways, telegraphs, electricity, municipality, universities, National Congress etc, all the discoveries of Science and all the paraphernalia of Western political life, all are merely toys.... Only what is won by one's own efforts is a right, not what others give as charity. Therefore, these are not real rights, we have no permanent claim on them. Childishness is a principal feature of our political life. The habit of servility is another. We are slaves even if we get high posts: the civilian judge,..., member of legislative council, all are wearing chains and acting on a stage. But we have become so petty that we are not ashamed to boast of these chains being made of gold or silver! Servility has permeated our entire life like a thick fog.
>
> What is heartening is... we have now opened our eyes and begun to realise our abject condition. This subservience to others is no longer tolerable. Throughout the country the idea is generally spreading that, we must, by whatever means, win independence of our education, economy and political life. This is the hope of the future. This is the sign that

we have awakened and will listen no more to the old lullabies. We will heed no obstacle and stop at no one's comment. We will surely arise.[4]

Minto's Initiative Is A Wakeup Call?

August 15, 1906, Calcutta: Viceroy Minto has appointed a five-members committee from his executive council under Sir T Arundale as chairman, to advise the government on some profound issues of reforms that the colonial government are likely to be confronted with soon enough, given the rising political aspirations of the Indians. These include placing an Indian in the Viceroy's executive council, developing a council of native princes, increasing Indian presence in both Indian and provincial legislative councils and providing a mechanism for debate on budgets in the legislative councils. These proposals, particularly, increasing Indian presence in legislative councils, have instantly put political India on alert.

A Schism Is Growing Within Congress

A schism is growing within the Congress as regards political strategies to be adopted for securing self-governance. The faction headed by Pheroze Shah Mehta, Dadabhai Naoroji, Surendra Nath Banerjea, Gopal Krishna Gokhale and their supporters are for moderate means—they believe in the sense of justice and reasonableness of the British. They want self-government under British but they also want the Indian people to prepare and become worthy of the same. For this purpose, they want to utilise the existing institutions, administrative machineries and the government. They want to work with the government in a cooperative frame. They want to take gradual steps towards the goal of self-governance. To them, the objective is important—but so also are the means. The rival faction, led by Tilak, Lajpat Rai, Bipin Chandra Pal, Aurobindo and their supporters are adopting a strident posture—they are advocating self-dependence, self-rule and open opposition to British rule. They see the primacy of political freedom and believe once that is obtained, other problems will get sorted easily. To them, good governance is not a substitute for self-governance. They consider swaraj as an inalienable right of the Indians and want aggressive action programmes against the government that include boycotts of various kinds—starting from foreign goods to foreign institutions like Westernised education, law courts, and even payment of taxes. They contend that political rights are to be claimed, not begged. If moderates are reformist, these leaders believe in revolutionary changes. They want swaraj, here and now, if possible. Leaders like Aurobindo would even support insurrection and uprisings.

In Bengal, the issue of partition of the province and the relentless protests have been strengthening the case of the extremist faction. It is true that the pressure of public opinion has compelled even the moderate faction in Bengal to oppose the government decision. But, in keeping with their overall strategy, the moderate leaders here have been exploring constitutional remedies to the issue. They held a meeting at the town hall in the city on this issue and sent a memorandum to the Secretary of State in accordance with a typical constitutional methodology. As if to give them a strong rebuff, the extremists in Calcutta held the Shivaji celebrations on a grand scale. In a significant gesture of solidarity with their Bengal counterparts, extremist stalwarts from Maharashtra like BG Tilak, GS Khaparde and BS Moonje made it a point to attend the programme. This created lots of pressure on the Bengal moderate faction to adopt a more aggressive posture—especially keeping in view the colossal insensitivity of the government to the partition issue.

We Deserve Special Treatment, Muslims Tell Government

October 1, 1906, Simla: A deputation of Muslim leaders from all over India, led by Aga Khan II, has visited Lord Minto, the Governor General, here with their demand for separate electorate for the Muslims. Mohsin-al-Mulk, secretary of MAO played a key role in organising the event. A striking thing about the delegation is that it represents a wide range of Muslim opinions in the country. The deputation contended that the Western model of democracy, where the idea of a nation is territory-centric and all people comprising the nation constitute a general electorate, is not suitable for a country like India. It further contended that the political right of the Indian Muslims should not be determined on the basis of numerical strength but in terms of their political importance and services rendered to the Empire. As such, it argued that extreme care was called for in introducing or extending electoral systems in whatever sphere—municipal, provincial or federal and that the government must ensure that Muslims are represented in every political power structure as a community.

The deputation made it clear that they had no confidence in the Hindu majority and they were unwilling to accept a general electorate on the basis of a homogenous nation. According to sources, the Governor General's reaction was intriguing. In his reply to the deputation, he is reported to have assured the Muslims that their political rights and interests as a community would be safeguarded by any administrative reorganisation under him. The acceptance of the deputation and the response of the Viceroy have, for the first time, raised the Hindu-Muslim conflict in India to the constitutional plane. If actions and attitude of Minto are any indication, it seems sure that separate electorate for Muslims shall be accorded statutory recognition in future—it is only a matter of time. Some critics say that this deputation under the leadership of Aga Khan was engineered by the Governor General and, therefore, it should be construed as a command performance by the British government itself.

It seems that the Indian National Congress, the premier political face of the Indians that claims to represent Indians of all caste and creed, has not been able to comprehend the long-term implication of this deputation and the condescending attitude of the Governor General to its demands. It would like to believe that this was a stray and transient demand put up by some fundamentalist Muslim leaders at the instigation of the British government, a demand that would fade away with time. However, political analysts are of the opinion that the Congress is grossly neglecting an extremely sensitive political issue and that the institution of separate electorate could create eternal enmity between Hindus and Muslims. Some analysts say that the simmering tension between the moderates and the extremists and issues like the partition of Bengal may have contributed to its lack of due seriousness in responding to this critical development.

Simla Deputation – The Handiwork Of Governor General?

1906, Simla: The British government has been contemplating small measures of self-governance for Indians at the provincial level. Viceroy Lord Minto had appointed the Arundel Committee to look into the prospect of extending the representative elements in the legislative council. As soon as the matter became known, indigenous political activities began. Congress grew enthusiastic for understandable reasons—being the sole political party, it was bound to claim the lion's share of the rights, so achieved. And, for that very reason, Muslim interest groups became worried. Congress, in their eyes, has been a protector of Hindu interests. With Sir Syed Ahmed Khan no longer alive, the Aligarh intelligentsia came forward to protect the political interests of the Muslims. They reckoned under general franchise, Muslim candidates had slender chances of getting elected in an overwhelmingly Hindu majority country.

As a result, as soon as the government's plan was announced, the Aligarh intelligentsia formed a new interest group called the Mohammedan Educational Conference, in conjunction with the aristocratic elite of East Bengal to protect Muslim interests. Mohsin-al-Mulk, secretary of MAO College, a prominent politician and a mentor of the Aligarh movement, has reportedly taken keen initiatives to organise a deputation to Lord Minto to advocate setting up of separate electorate for Muslims. It has been learnt that AJ Archbold, the British principal of Aligarh College, is also assisting in this exercise.

Political observers say that the Muslim demand for separate electorate is likely to be considered favourably by the government. According to reliable sources, the Governor General himself has been taking active interest in this matter and is, in fact, encouraging the delegation. The growing disenchantment of the government with the progressively rising political aspirations of the Congress and especially its strident opposition on certain issues, including the partition of Bengal recently, may have something to do with the ongoing developments, they insist. The government possibly thinks that by conferring extra political weight upon the Muslims through separate electorate, it would be able to use them as counterweight against the increasingly assertive Congress.

COLONISATION BILL CREATES SUSPICION IN PUNJAB

1906, Lahore: The provincial government has introduced a new Bill, viz. Colonisation of General Lands (Punjab) Bill, 1906 which seeks to introduce a new method of recording the right of government tenants and provides for imposition of fresh conditions upon the government tenants in Punjab colonies. The Bill also bestows certain special powers to executive officers, which are not granted by ordinary law. What causes concern to many is the stipulation that these new provisions shall apply to existing tenants too. Numerous tenants, already settled in government colonies, feel uncomfortable and suspect the intentions of the government. In particular, there is clear restlessness in Jhelum and Chenub colonies, where many Sikh soldiers were allotted land by the British government in consideration of their service during the Sepoy Mutiny. The settlers in these colonies, by their hard labour, had turned their habitation into very prosperous areas. The Bill introduces various new restrictions and limitations on the rights of the tenants, eg. erection of building, prohibition against alienation. These settlers view the new Bill as attempts to infringe on their rights and liberties. The dissatisfaction has gradually spread across the state, particularly amongst ex-soldiers who are most affected.

ALL-INDIA MUSLIM LEAGUE IS BORN

Muslim Interests Lie In Preservation Of British Empire

December 30, 1906, Dacca: There is a flurry of political activities in India and much of these are occurring in Bengal. In Dacca, a new communal political party, the Muslim League has been formed, with the professed objectives of protecting the interests of the country's Muslims.

Muhammedan Educational Conference of the Aligarh intelligentsia and the Muslim aristocracy of Bengal, led by Nawab Salimullah Khan, a close friend of Curzon, the former Viceroy, have played key roles in promoting this new political outfit.

The League has been set up on this day, following the end of the twentieth session of the All-India Mohammedan Education Conference held in this city. After the closure of the education conference, the delegates re-assembled in the pandal to take a momentous initiative—form a political organisation of Indian Muslims. Nawab Salimullah, one of the key initiators of the project, proposed Maulvi Mushtaq Hussain as the chairman and accordingly the latter was elected. As many as 58 Muslim leaders attended the founding session.

Mushtaq Hussain, in his presidential speech, explained the rationale, objectives and programmes of this new organisation. He tried to take a sneak peek into the distant future when the British might withdraw from India, handing over political power to Indians. In such a scenario, the future of the Muslims—their lives, properties, honour and faith might be placed at the mercy of the Hindus who are four times more in number. In order to guard against any such catastrophe, he stresses upon the need for an exclusive party to protect the political rights of the Muslims. Even though the Congress is an all-India organisation representative of all caste and creed, the conference viewed it only as a Hindu-dominated organisation and not one that Muslims can trust. In recent years, the loud and insistent demands for constitutional and administrative reforms placed by the Hindu-dominated Congress, upon the government has had unsettling effects on the Muslims. Lest these make the government bring in changes that adversely affect the Muslims as a community, they must organise themselves for political action, the president contended. According to him, though Muslims have a past to be proud of in the country, their weak numerical strength leaves them no alternative than to protect themselves through an exclusive political party.

As strategy, the newly-formed Muslim League has professed its loyalty to the British Empire. Its leaders have identified their community's interests and aspirations closely with the consolidation and perseverance of British rule in India. As a quid pro quo for their loyalty to the British crown, they foresee distinct advantages accruing to their community from the British government. Especially in the context of the Congress' growing assertiveness and stridency, its offer of loyalty and support to the British Crown is certain to fetch the Muslim League better bargains in all political negotiations.

Lord Minto is reportedly happy as the new party rents the air with its birth cry—he has got an ally and a hammer to beat the Congress with. Moreover, according to the British government, the very fact of its birth has put a question mark on the demand of the Indian National Congress that it, indeed, is the real representative of all communities.

Grand Old Man Naoroji To Preside Over Congress Session

December 1906, Calcutta: The annual session of the Congress is to be held in this city. Bengal has been like a live volcano these days. Protests against partition of the province are erupting at several places in various forms, relentlessly. Extremist leaders like Aurobindo Ghosh have established firm grip over large chunk of Congress workers and the public in general. They are keen to use the impending annual session not only to strengthen the protests against the partition but also compel Congress to adopt a much more militant and nationalist position vis-à-vis the British government.

It is learnt that moderate leaders from outside Bengal are neither that enthusiastic about the partition issue nor are they keen to effect any radical changes in strategy against the government. Given that both the camps have strong convictions about respective ideologies, the session is likely to be stormy. Both the sides fought bitterly over the election of a party president. After much acrimony, both sides agreed to the candidature of Dadabhai Naoroji, the Grand Old Man of Indian politics, to preside over the forthcoming session. He is seen as holding a somewhat neutral position.

Bengal Congress Supports Anti-partition Movement

If the deliberations in the annual sessions here are any indication, the movement against the Bengal partition is forcing changes in Congress policies and programmes. An important offshoot of the protest movements is the emergence of a strong demand, even if somewhat vague, for swaraj—a development that the British Government views as ominous. The boycott of foreign goods, and adoption of swadeshi goods—two major planks of the ongoing movement against partition—have been connected to the demand for swaraj. Emanating from the platform of the Congress, the prime political organisation of the country, the demands have acquired some legitimacy and a life force. Although the exact meaning of the term 'swaraj' has not yet been offered, and leaders are attaching varying interpretations to it, and the government is quite disturbed. To leaders like Naoroji and Mehta, the term means self-government as under 'dominion status'. However, leaders like Tilak see in it much more. To them 'boycott' presents an opportunity to be used as a weapon to achieve a broader political goal for India. They argue that boycott need not be confined to merely foreign goods but can encompass much more—they would like Indians to boycott every facet of British rule and things that exert harmful Western influence over the natives like law courts, schools, legislative councils, taxes etc. Though the moderate leaders do not subscribe to such radical views, a debate has begun to rage within the Congress organisation on these issues. It is becoming clearer that the Bengal partition will begin to influence the political agenda of the Congress Party in the days ahead.

Extremists Bulldoze Moderates

December 26-29, 1906, Calcutta: As the annual session of the Congress Party progresses, the simmering tension between the moderate and the extremist groups becomes more palpable. The issue of Bengal's partition is subjecting their relationship to severe strain. Noticeably, under the leadership of Aurobindo Ghosh, the demands of the extremist group have become much wider, extending beyond partition to include swaraj, boycott of foreign goods and a set of initiatives for national education. Obviously, if the Congress decides to adopt the resolutions on all these and pursue their implementation, the impact will be observed in other parts of India as well. On their part, moderate leaders, other than that of Bengal, are of the opinion that the partition issue is essentially a provincial grievance and the band of four resolutions proposed by the extremists are disproportionate to the gravity of the matter.

As the two groups locked horns on the issue of these four resolutions, Bengal extremists received huge encouragement when Bal Gangadhar Tilak and his vociferous followers rise to support their position. Buoyed by such strong endorsement, they simply swamp the moderates. Moderate leaders from Bengal have been rendered passive spectators in confrontation—they are under tremendous local pressure as the venue is Calcutta and emotions run high, the underlying issue being the partition of the province. Moderate leaders from outside Bengal are dismayed that their Bengal counterparts do not lend them any help.

Mehta Heckled And Humiliated

December 1906, Calcutta: The annual session of the Congress here witnesses bitter acrimony amongst moderates and extremist leaders. The Bengal partition issue has been one of the key drivers. To the moderate leaders other than those from Bengal, and which includes veterans such as Mehta and Naoroji, the partition issue has no doubt been important but nonetheless a provincial grievance—they are not in favour of accoding it disproportionate weightage. However, for all extremist leaders and all leaders of Bengal including the moderates, this has been a crucial issue. The differences between the two groups surfaced very early—right from the stage of selecting the office-bearers of the Reception Committee and then escalated as the session progressed. Mehta tried to stonewall the 'partition' issue by proposing an enquiry committee to send the matter to the deep freeze. However, the resolution against the 'partition' was still carried out—so vociferous was the demand. The moderate leaders of Bengal joined hands with the extremist factions on this issue, much to the discomfiture of Mehta and Naoroji. Three more important resolutions were passed on swaraj, boycott, and national education. None of these were to the liking of the moderate leaders. But they were helpless against a militant and vocal opposition. Things went to such a pass that senior leaders like Mehta and Naoroji were heckled and insulted by some extremist young members. Under such disagreeable circumstances, Mehta quietly left the city without formally taking leave of the Bengal leaders. He was, however, very bitter while parting—particularly shocked at the behaviour of the Moderate leaders of Bengal who did little to contain the extremist agenda and conduct.

Pagri Sambhal O Jatta, Pagri Sambhal Oye

Punjab Burns – Lala Banke Dayal Warns People

March 5, 1907, Lahore: Punjab is reeling under nature's fury and incompetent governance. Lack of monsoon drives the prices of cotton and grains sky-high. The poor struggle to sustain themselves. To make matters worse, plague has spread and it is taking a huge toll of Punjab's population. According to government data, the death rate is about 62.1 per thousand people. The government has proved itself both unwilling and incompetent to tackle the epidemic. To add to the woes of the people, the government has introduced the new Colonisation Bill in the provincial legislative council today. Numerous settlers in government colonies are a worried lot. As if all these are not enough, the government has also announced hike in canal rates, another burden on the distressed farmers and eventually on the price of food grains. There are intense feelings against the government amongst the masses. Popular leaders like Lala Lajpat Rai, Sardar Ajit Singh and others have been travelling through the province and addressing them. Lala Lajpat Rai has published several articles on the economic crisis affecting the people. The newspapers have been highlighting the misery of the people and are vocal against apathy and incompetence of the imperial government to handle the crisis. Lala Banke Dayal, editor of *Jhangsial*, has been exhorting the people with the poem: 'Pagri Sambhal O Jatta, Pagri Sambhal Oye'. This poem, of great relevance these days, has become folklore in the land of the five rivers.

Loyalty In Smithereens – Ibbetson Warns Viceroy

April 30, 1907, Lahore: Today Denzil Ibbetson, Lt Governor of Punjab, has written to Lord Minto, the Governor General, describing the situation in Punjab as exceedingly dangerous and called for immediate action. In his missive he has mentioned that the air of sedition is blowing across the province and people in various cities and towns like Rawalpindi, Sialkot and Lyallpur in particular, are openly carrying out ant-British campaign. Villagers are being told to withhold payment of government revenues, water rates and other dues. They are even being persuaded not to extend any kind of cooperation to government officials. Pamphlets exhort villagers to even refuse supplies and carriages to these officials. Ibbetson has expressed concerns that even the Sikh military pensioners are being inducted in the anti-government agitation. The Governor holds the Arya Samaj responsible for masterminding the ongoing agitation. He has been particularly critical of Lajpat Rai and has cited a story doing the rounds—that the Lala is in correspondence with the Emir of Afghanistan against the British Empire. On the basis of such diagnosis, Ibbetson has recommended that Lajpat Rai, along with another revolutionary leader, Sardar Ajit Singh, be arrested and deported from India.

However, critics say Ibbetson looks at things with jaundiced eyes. If this prosperous and once highly loyal province is in a crippling bind today, it has been solely due to mis-governance and successive wrong policies. Instead of applying policy correctives and initiating sensible public-welfare measures, Ibbetson, possibly out of personal bias, attacks the very people and organisations that try to render service to the distressed people. They also feel, Lala Lajpat Rai is a very venerable, popular public figure and any insensible steps against him might arouse severe public unrest.

Lajpat Rai Arrested Under Draconian Law

May 9, 1907, Lahore: After securing order from Lord Minto, the Punjab government has arrested Lala Lajpat Rai under Regulation III of the 1818 Act. He is being deported to Mandalay. The government has resorted to this infamous regulation because it does not have concrete evidence against these leaders, particularly Lala Lajpat Rai whose public image is impeccable. This draconian regulation provides for preventive detention and for attachment of property without court order. It is in the nature of a suspension of the writ of habeas corpus. The legality of the arrest cannot be challenged in a court of law.

PUBLIC MEETING ORDINANCE TO STIFLE PROTESTS

May 10, 1907, Calcutta, Lahore: Both Punjab and Bengal are burning with rage. Draught, famine, plague have been stalking Punjab for some time. Government initiative in the form of the Colonization Bill and raising of canal rates have inflamed public anger further. Arrests of the two popular leaders have made people go wild—they have erupted in violent protests all across the province. In Bengal, the situation is no better. The anti-partition movement has assumed serious form and revolutionary activities are growing by the day. Under these circumstances, the Government of India has on this day issued an 'Emergency Ordinance' in Punjab, Eastern Bengal and Assam. Public meetings have been banned and Indian press has also been placed under tight leash. The government is determined to muzzle voices of protests.

Bureaucracy Has Thrown Gauntlet, We Take It Up: Aurobindo

May 1907, Calcutta: News of arrest and deportation of Lala Lajpat Rai has caused great anger and indignation not only in Punjab but across the country. If *Jhangsial*, a patriotic paper in Punjab condemned the deportation of the Lala as an act of oppression, barbarism and cowardice, the *Bande Mataram* from Calcutta issued a bold challenge:

'… hours of speeches and fine writing is over. The bureaucracy has thrown the gauntlet. We take it up. Men of the Punjab. Race of the Lion. Show these men who would stamp you into the dust that for one Lajpat they have taken away, a hundred Lajpats will rise in his place. Let them hear a hundred times louder your war cry—*Jai* Hindustan.'[5]

Government Retreats – Punjab Celebrates

November 18, 1907, Lahore: The popular confidence in constitutional methods has also suffered a serious setback with the government decision to arrest and deport Lala Lajpat Rai. This single act of indiscretion on the part of the British government has begun to give a boost to revolutionary activities in the province. The subsequent oppressive measures unleashed by the provincial government further strengthened such activities. Things went from bad to worse causing all-round degeneration in law and order. On reconsideration and introspection, Governor General Minto felt the arrest and deportation of the two leaders were based on slender evidence, hasty and unjustified and wrote accordingly to Morley, Secretary of State. Morley agreed and a decision was taken for their acquittal.

Today, both Lala Lajpat Rai and Sardar Ajit Singh were released. There was festivity in Lahore, holidays declared in schools and colleges, sweetmeats distributed, fireworks displayed. Across Punjab, numerous public meetings were held in celebration.

Bengal Lt Governor Has A Narrow Escape

December 6, 1907, Narayangarh: Today a team of revolutionaries belonging to the Anushilan Samity derailed a train here using bombs, and made an unsuccessful attempt to kill Andrew Fraser, the Lt Governor of Bengal, who was aboard. The police are on manhunt.

Extremists and Moderates Lock Horns In Bengal

December 7, 1907, Medinipur: Dress rehearsal of the impending moderate-extremist encounter at the all-India level has been enacted in Bengal in Medinipur, the venue for the district conference of the Congress. Although during the Calcutta session of the Congress, the Bengali moderate leaders did not actively support their counterparts from rest of the country, like Mehta, on the partition and associated issues, the extremist group were not happy with them either. The extremists expected them to have been much more vociferous, as the issue of partition was dear to the heart of the Bengalis. Since then, the two groups have been sharing a kind of estrangement in relationship.

On the occasion of the district conference, Aurobindo Ghosh had arrived here with a strong force of extremist leaders and workers, but avoided meeting the moderate stalwart Surendra Nath Banerjea, camping in town. Such deliberate action, where a courtesy meeting was keenly expected, created lots of tension in both camps. There was a tug of war as the conference began, with both the groups attempting to wrest control of the proceedings. As the moderates somehow managed to hold the reins, Aurobindo held a separate meeting. Whereas the extremists passed a resolution on swaraj, the moderates passed a resolution on colonial self-government. As if he could foresee the shape of things to come at Surat, Aurobindo also proposed that a separate extremist Congress session be held at Nagpur on the lines of the one he had done in Calcutta.

Ajit Singh Attempts To Form Secret Societies In Punjab

December, 1907: According to reports of the intelligence branch, Sardar Ajit Singh is trying to form secret societies in all principal towns in Punjab. Other prominent members of his group are Sufi Amba Prasad, Lal Chand Falak, Krishn Singh, Swarn Singh, Zia-ul-Haq and others.

Surat Substitutes Nagpur
Venue For Congress Session Changed Abruptly

November 10, 1907, Bombay: Pheroze Shah Mehta has not forgotten the insult hurled at him in the Calcutta Congress. He has been planning to drive out the extremist elements from the Congress Party and even sideline the moderate leaders of Bengal. Earlier in the Calcutta session, Nagpur was selected as the venue for the next year's session. Nagpur happens to be a stronghold of extremist leaders like Tilak and Moonje. After the bitter experience in Calcutta, Mehta does not want to give another chance to the extremists to influence the proceedings. In a meeting convened in his bungalow, Mehta has taken a decision to shift the venue to Surat in Gujarat— a place far from the reach of the extremists. Mehta is sure Surat would be a strong wicket for the moderates and he can undo many of the wrongs committed under extremist pressure in Calcutta last year.

On the other hand, reports from the extremist camp suggest they have been able to read through Mehta's move. Tilak would have been happy with Nagpur. But in the changed circumstances, he has plans to be present in Surat with a large band of his followers to counter the intrigues of the moderates.

Aurobindo To Pursue Tilak Line

December 1907, Poona: Aurobindo, the leader of the extremist group in the Congress, has been sceptical of Mehta's move in changing the venue from Nagpur to Surat and has proposed that the extremist group hold their session in Nagpur. According to sources, Tilak did not view this proposal favourably. He is determined to take over the reins of the entire party from the moderates led by Pheroze Shah Mehta. He is also confident that the extremists will succeed in this endeavour. He is organising a large body of followers to accompany him in Surat, where he expects to get valuable support from Aurobindo and his followers of Bengal, and also other extremist leaders, especially from Punjab. He has made his views known to Aurobindo and the latter has reportedly agreed to pursue the Tilak line.

As Congress Session Begins, Swords Are Unsheathed

December 26, 1907, Surat: On the eve of the Congress session, the air here is thick with intrigues. Both camps have arrived with adequate preparations. Mehta, the general, commanding the moderate group, is moving his pieces on the board very thoughtfully. In a bid to bring about a division in the extremist group, the moderate camp has proposed the name of Rashbehari Ghosh, a Bengali moderate leader as the president of the session–their calculation being this move will wean away the extremist delegates from Bengal from Tilak because of regional affinity. On their part, the extremists are determined to have the president from their camp. They want either Tilak himself or Lala Lajpat Rai to preside and they want no compromise on this issue.

To add to the tension, a strong rumour is doing rounds that the moderate camp is preparing to drop all the four resolutions on swadeshi, boycott, national education and swaraj passed in the last annual session in Calcutta. To facilitate this agenda, Mehta has manoeuvred to appoint only his own men in the reception committee. But the extremists are determined to not allow any mischief on this count. They are determined not to allow any reversal or retracement. The swords are out even before the session has begun and these are not likely to go back in their sheaths without spilling blood—that is for sure.

Chaos Spells Doom Over Congress' Annual Session

December 27, 1907, Surat: As the morning dawned on the banks of the river Tapti, the battle formations by two camps in Surat came under clear view. Tilak was commanding a well-knit, energetic, aggressive band of few hundred delegates drawn from Maharashtra, Central Provinces and Madras. He also had the support of the extremists led by Aurobindo Ghosh from Bengal. In a total attendance of about thirteen hundred, about six hundred committed delegates backed him.

On behalf of the moderates, Mehta has been busy trying to formally ensconce Rashbehari Ghosh as the president and drop the 'four resolutions' adopted against his wishes in the Calcutta session. The extremists had proposed Lala Lajpat Rai as the president. Tilak was furious when the moderate camp reportedly rejected Lala's candidature on the ruse that this would invite the wrath of the government upon the Congress. He decided to make an issue of the presidential election.

Tilak was keen on defending the 'four resolutions' passed in the Calcutta Congress last year. He was prepared for an all out war, when he was informally assured by Surendra Nath Banerjea, a moderate stalwart, that these Calcutta resolutions would not be tampered with. A temporary truce occurred. But after the proceedings began, the moderates went ahead with their game plan. Realising that they have been deceived, Tilak, greatly infuriated, climbed on the dais and wanted to address the delegates about the nomination for presidency, but he was not allowed to speak by the chairman. Tilak stood his ground and demanded the right to speak before Rashbehari Ghosh could speak to the audience. He refused to leave the stage despite repeated insistence by Ghosh, Mehta and other moderate leaders. There was total chaos and someone from the audience hurled a shoe at Tilak. It missed the target and hit Banerjea and Mehta seated on the stage. Thereafter, mayhem broke loose and the two factions charged at each other with chairs and sticks, which flew in all directions. Finding it impossible to continue with the proceedings, the president dissolved the session. The police took over. The Surat session of the Congress has, thus, ended with a bitter taste.

Manicktala Secret Society Now Kown As Jugantar

1907, Calcutta: Manicktala Secret Society, though born only a year ago, is emerging as a major headache for the government due to its anti-establishment activities. It may be mentioned that Barin Kumar Ghosh, who is one of its main promoters of the Manicktala Society, also happens to be the editor of *Jugantar*, a political weekly. Barin's revolutionary spirit echoes through strongly-worded editorials of the *Jugantar*, attracting large number of young natives. Barin later on transferred editorial responsibility to Bhupendranath Dutta, who too matched Barin in terms of militant tone and content. As the members of the Society are also involved with the *Jugantar* weekly, it is being referred to as 'Jugantar' by both the public and the police.

REVOLUTIONARY BRINGS BOMB TECHNOLOGY TO INDIA

January 1908, Calcutta: Hem Chandra Kanungo, a revolutionary and an associate of Barin Kumar Ghosh, had gone to Paris last year primarily to study revolutionary politics. There he had interactions with French and Russian anarchists from some of whom he learnt the technology of making bombs. Hem always had an interest in this branch of chemistry and he acquired the knowledge with ease and well. Now he has come back and rejoined the team of revolutionaries in the Manicktala garden house. Hem's knowledge and skill in handling of explosives are being seen as a huge boost to the strength of the team. With this, Jugantar is certain to pose much more difficulties to the government.

Moderates And Extremists Are Gulfs Apart

> Although, some serious political observers had prophesied after 1906 that the more vocal and energetic extremist group would take over the reins of the Indian National Congress, things have turned differently. The moderates have been able to retain Congress' name and hold on to the organisational structure. After a brief display of fireworks at Surat, the extremists, notwithstanding their revolutionary passion, verve and anti-imperialist fervour, seem to have turned into a scattered force. Some of them, at this point, are realising the merit of Aurobindo's suggestion earlier that they hold a parallel session in Nagpur instead of attending the Surat session. This could have possibly given birth to a strong unified lobby to take the moderates head on for the control of the whole Congress by now.
>
> After the din and dust of Surat have settled, the moderates, in command of the organisation, are in a mood to rediscover the Congress' basic tenets, which in their opinion, is one of loyalty to the British Empire and the use of strictly 'constitutional means' to achieve their goal of self-governance similar to that available to other self-governing members of the British Empire. As a part of this exercise, they want to completely exorcise the recent aberrations—when they yielded to the demands of the extremist groups in Calcutta and had to be a party, albeit unwilling, to the passing of the four unpalatable resolutions.

Mehta Vows To Purge The Congress Of Extremists

April 19, 1908, Allahabad: Pheroze Shah Mehta is taking every initiative to drive the extremists out of the Congress. He had learnt bitter lessons in Calcutta and Surat. Mehta has begun the purge, starting with the Bengali moderates whom he suspects of having been hand-in- glove with the extremists. First, he set them aside, leaving them in no position to influence his next course of action, which has been to drive out the extremists from the Congress in droves. Thereafter to nip in the bud any future infiltration of the extremists in the organisation, he has now arranged a convention in Allahabad, where the Bombay group is declaring its 'loyalty to the British government' loud and clear. As if to teach the Bengali leaders a lesson and send a strong message to all the extremist leaders across the country, the convention has drawn up a Congress creed expressing firm loyalty to British rule. The goal of the Congress has been stated—to become self-governing under the British Empire. Every delegate has been asked to accept the goal in writing. Banerjea and other moderate leaders are attending the session but they have been rendered just meek observers.

Calcutta Reacts Violently To Allahabad Convention

April 1908, Calcutta: Deliberations in Allahabad are being sharply criticised by both the extremist Congress leaders of Bengal and also the local press. They feel moderate leaders like Banerjea have just jettisoned the interests of Bengal by remaining meek, passive spectators. Leaders like Aurobindo seem to have lost confidence in moderate leaders from Bengal. Aurobindo has written in *Bande Mataram* that between conventionalism and nationalism there can be no truce henceforth.

To be fair to them, the discredited moderate leaders of Bengal had made some efforts and requested Mehta to examine the case of re-entry of the extremists to Congress. But Mehta brushed their pleading aside, treating these as 'mawkish sentimentality'. On account of this seemingly unreasonably hardened approach, the Bengali press has been enraged and they are levying harsh criticism on Mehta.

KINGSFORD ESCAPES BID ON LIFE

Prafulla Chaki Commits Suicide

April 30, 1908, Muzaffarpur: Revolutionary societies in Bengal seem to have acquired confidence to strike at the mighty British Empire. By now they have been able to indegenise the bomb technology. This has emboldened them. Anushilan Samity has already grown in stature in public eyes as the most disciplined and well-organised revolutionary society in the country. Jugantar is the second important revolutionary outfit that is acting as a loose confederation of a number of secret societies, and thus has the power to strike at targets across wide areas. It had sent two of its young, committed members, Khudiram Bose and Prafulla Chaki to kill Kingsford, the oppressive district magistrate of Muzaffarpur, a place far away from Calcutta. Khudiram, a young man of barely nineteen years, has been impatient with the colonial rule and the humiliations faced by Indians, like members of a slave nation. The high-handed British act to partition Bengal, in complete disregard of persuasions and protests by millions of natives, had also aroused deep aversion in these two young souls and they grabbed this opportunity to eliminate one of their oppressors.

As part of their plan, the two young men were to launch a bomb attack on Kingsford's carriage. Unfortunately, they hurled bombs on a wrong carriage, killing two British ladies—the wife and daughter of Barrister Pringle Kennedy—together with one of their Indian servants. Cornered by the police, Prafulla committed suicide. The police have launched a massive manhunt for Khudiram.

While the incident has stirred up the government, the use of bombs in the attack is causing it further worries.

AUROBINDO GHOSH ARRESTED

Police Raid Family Garden House At Manicktala

May 2, 1908, Calcutta: Following the Muzaffarpur attack, the government has let loose unprecedented repression. The police have launched extensive search and to start with, have arrested thirty-three persons. The use of bomb in the attack has alarmed the government. Based on the intelligence collected, the police have gone all out to trace bomb-making activities in Calcutta city. Today, the police raided the Manicktala Garden house of Aurobindo Ghosh and it is reported to have found a small bomb-making factory. The police have arrested a number of activists including Aurobindo Ghosh and his brother Barindranath. Aurobindo has been put in solitary confinement in

Alipore Presidency jail. The police are accusing him of planning and overseeing revolutionary attacks.

BOMB-SCARED GOVERNMENT ENACTS NEW LAWS

June 8, 1908, Calcutta: Government of India has today passed the 'Explosive Substance Act' and the 'Newspaper Act' to put a lid on revolutionary activities and prevent spreading of anti-government feelings amongst people. According to some political observers, the use of bombs by the revolutionaries and the power of editorials such as that of Tilak, and Aurobindo on the public psyche have been the proximate cause of these new legislative initiatives.

Muzaffarpur Bomb Case Fallout: Tilak Arrested

June 24, 1908, Bombay: The Muzaffarpur bomb attack and the government repression following the incident have sent ripples across the country. In distant Poona, Tilak in his paper, *Kesari*, has been advocating the case of the revolutionaries and urging the government to allow swaraj to Indians. Highlighting that both the rulers and the subjects have mutual duties and responsibilities to each other, Tilak contended that even if there is no punishment for treason by the king against his subjects or 'prajadroha' in the modern penal code, such a thing very much exists in the penal code of God, the King of kings. When such crimes are committed by kings, the mental state of people become inflammable and kings are destroyed like moths in fire. He opined that in a way, the government repression is uniting Indians, infusing in them a feeling of a common nationality.

On 12 May, he wrote an editorial titled, the 'Country's misfortune' on the Muzaffarpur incident, supporting the case of the accused. On 9 June, he followed up the issue by writing that the government may take away muskets and guns from its subjects or even stop the manufacturing of these, but would it be possible to stop or do away with the bombs by means of laws or the suppression of people by the official or the busy swarming of the detective police?

The 'bomb' is more like knowledge rather than a bullet, it is magic, it is a sacred formula, an amulet, Tilak contended. The government finds his outbursts too dangerous. Today, Tilak was arrested in Bombay for sedition.

TILAK SENTENCED FOR SEDITION

Bombay Comes To A Halt

July 1908, Bombay: As the eyes of patriotic India remain riveted on Tilak's trial in the court room, the judge announces his verdict. Commenting that Tilak's journalism is a curse for the country, the judge sentences him for six years of imprisonment and a fine of Rs 1000. A jury of seven Europeans and two Parsis heard his case—there was no Hindu. The verdict is 7-2. Initially Tilak had thought of engaging young barrister, MA Jinnah, but the two could not agree on a common approach to fight the case. As such, Tilak defended himself. While pleading for freedom he said, as the newspaper editor he had his special duty or religion to perform. The judges were not impressed. Tilak took it in his stride. He said: '...There are higher powers that rule the destinies of men and nations and I think it may be the will of Providence that the cause I represent may be benefited more by my suffering than by my pen and tongue'.[6]

The news of his sentence spreads like wild fire in the city. Dozens of mills go on strike and even cotton exchange, cloth, grain, freight and the stock market closes down. Apprehending that Tilak's continued stay in Bombay or nearby places could pose a threat to the law and order situation, the government quickly shifts him to the Sabarmati jail. From there he will be sent to Mandalay. Nationalistc Indians throughout the country are aggrieved and agitated.

Bagha Jatin Takes Over Reins Of Jugantar

1908, Calcutta: Now that both Aurobindo and Barin have been arrested and charged in the Manicktala bomb case, another top-ranked revolutionary, Jatindranath Mukherjee, has taken over the leadership of Jugantar, the revolutionary outfit, responsible for ordering the murder of Kingsford. He was earlier associated with the Anushilan Samity, the older sibling of Jugantar. Jatindranath earned the prefix 'Bagha' for having killed a tiger in a one-to-one fight without a fire arm. Besides possessing immense physical strength, Jatindranath has also been a leader par excellence—charismatic, courageous, meticulous planner and a visionary. Bagha Jatin's taking over of the control of Jugantar has infused great enthusiasm amongst the revolutionaries. Deeply influenced by Swami Vivekananda in his early youth, he became a disciple of Bholanand Giri later. From Vivekananda's speeches and teachings, Jatin became convinced that the political independence of India can lead to the spiritual progress of both, Indians as well as humanity at large. He believes in it and has been working hard at it. Aurobindo Ghosh is also playing a role in shaping his political philosophy.

KHUDIRAM GOES TO THE GALLOWS WITH A SMILE

August 11, 1908, Muzaffarpur: Khudiram Bose, arrested and tried in connection with the Muzaffarpur Bomb case, was awarded death penalty. Guided by the teachings of Bhagavat Gita, the young man sang the glory of the free spirit, not caring the least about death or physical sufferings. He went to the gallows, smiling. Death could not scare this young man but he has infused fear in the hearts of India's British rulers. His courage, patriotism and poise are being talked about everywhere.

Long After He Is Dead And Gone, His Words Will Be Echoed And Re-echoed – CR Das Defends Aurobindo

1908, Calcutta: Aurobindo Ghosh was arrested by the police in course of a search operation in his Manicktala Garden house in the city in May this year and has been put to trial. CR Das, the celebrated Congress leader and also a famous barrister, has been defending Aurobindo so well that an acquittal seems likely. Besides building up an impeccable defence of his clients technically, Das also made an emotional appeal to the jury on Aurobindo's exalted personality that rests on universal values. His deep admiration and regards for Aurobindo permeated his submission to the court as he made it strong and compelling.

'...long after this controversy will be hushed in silence, long after this turmoil, this agitation will have ceased, long after he (Aurobindo) is dead and gone, he will be looked upon as the poet of patriotism, as the prophet of nationalism and the lover of humanity. Long after he is dead and gone, his words will be echoed and re-echoed, not only in India, but across distant seas and lands.'[7]

The court seems to be getting convinced about the unsustainability of the charges brought against Aurobindo by the prosecution.

Fraser Survives Another Assassination Bid

November 7, 1908, Calcutta: Lt Governor of Bengal Andrew Fraser had another lucky escape today when a student shot at him at a meeting of the YMCA in the city but missed. The government is clearly perturbed at the daring of the revolutionaries, despite a plethora of oppressive legislations and police clampdown.

Punjab's Fire-brand Leader Visits Revolutionaries' Citadel

November 1908: According to IB reports, Sardar Ajit Singh, the revolutionary leader from Punjab, has visited Calcutta in a bid to establish linkages with revolutionaries in Bengal. Both have a common goal—securing freedom of the country by driving out the British.

Government Wants To Pin Down Revolutionaries

December 14, 1908, Calcutta: Deeply perturbed at the growing revolutionary activities, which the government views as nothing but abominable terrorist actions, the Government of India has passed the Criminal Law Amendment Act today to facilitate expeditious trials of the accused under terms of Regulations III of 1818 Act and to suppress societies or associations formed to carry out illegal acts. It is being said that the Bengal government may go the whole hog in using the Amendment Act to suppress the anti-partition agitation. The government in Punjab may not lag behind.

Extremists Are Cornered, Moderates Reign Supreme

December 28-30, 1908, Madras: The annual session of the Congress is in progress here and the moderates, led by Pheroze Shah Mehta, are in complete control of the proceedings. Only moderate faces are seen all around. Bengali moderate leaders are, of course, attending the session, but they have been kept under tight leash. Mehta has not forgotten their hobnobbing with the extremist leaders during the Calcutta session a couple of years ago. Neither has he forgotten the insults and humiliations that he had to suffer personally. Mehta has not been satisfied with the Allahabad clampdown on and subsequent purging of the extremists. His juggernaut is still rolling. Such has been the pressure on Bengali moderate leaders that they are no longer talking about 'boycott' here, although the partition remains a live issue and a festering wound in the Bengali psyche.

Rashbehari Or Rashab Bihari – Taunts Bengali Media

December, 1908, Calcutta: The manner in which the Congress annual session has been conducted in Madras has come in for criticism by the press here. However, more than Mehta, the Bengali moderate leaders are being attacked for their meek surrender to the Mehta camp. Rashbehari Ghosh, who was elected to preside over the Surat session, is being ridiculed with the appellate 'Rashabh Bihari', meaning one seated on an ass.

Political observers are disturbed by the kind of high-handed and autocratic attitude exhibited by the Mehta camp in stifling the democratic spirit in the Congress organisation. They feel, the wholesale expulsion of the extremist members does not augur well for the future of either the Congress or the country.

Congress Extremists Face Systematic Persecution Driven To Revolutionary Politics

December 1908: The extremist faction, not finding accommodation in the main body of the Congress, had been trying to hold a parallel Congress in Nagpur. However, the British government has suitably deterred their efforts. Leaders like Aurobindo feel there is no longer any possibility of a rapprochement between the 'conventionalists' and the 'nationalists'. He foresees the dissolution of the old Congress and coming of a revolution. Political observers fear that denying any constitutional channel to the extremist faction for political activities may push them to strengthen the hands of the revolutionaries, whom the government describes as 'terrorists'.

Revolutionary Outfit Undergoes Radical Changes

1909, Calcutta: Since Jatin took over the reins of Jugantar, the outfit has undertaken radical changes in terms of strategy and growth. The links between the headquarters at Calcutta and several branches spread across Bengal, Bihar, Orissa and Uttar Pradesh have been greatly revitalised. As a result, revolutionary activities are significantly spurred not only in Bengal but across the country. One of his outstanding skills lies in his ability to keep his own role secret from the government. He accomplishes this by developing a decentralised federated body of loose autonomous regional cells of secret societies. As if the INC itself was not enough of a trouble, the emergence of such revolutionary outfits is adding a new dimension to the government's problems. What makes matters still worse is the moral influence that Jatindranath exerts over not only the members of these secret societies, but also on a significant section of the civil society.

PUBLIC PROSECUTOR FALLS TO BULLET IN COURT

Revolutionaries Warn Native Collaborators

February 10, 1909, Calcutta: Like other cases against the revolutionaries during the course of hearings of the Manicktala bomb factory case, Asutosh Biswas, the public prosecutor, had been taking extraordinary interest and going out of the way to get the accused revolutionaries convicted. It may be recalled that Aurobindo Ghosh himself was one of them, although he had to be released later. The revolutionaries in the city have been watching Asutosh's role closely and found his enthusiasm unwarranted, bordering on treason against the motherland. In a daring act to punish Asutosh and also send a strong message to native collaborators of the British government, Charu Chandra Bose, a 19-year-old revolutionary, belonging to Jugantar, shot him down in broad day light in the court precincts. There are rumours that Bagha Jatin had ordered this action. After the event, the young Charu calmly courted arrest. According to insiders, the police are torturing him in the lock up, but Charu has not given them any clue about his fellow revolutionaries, leaders and Jugantar.

Aurobindo Ghosh Acquitted

May 6, 1909, Calcutta: As anticipated, barrister CR Das has finally been able to secure the acquittal of his distinguished client, Aurobindo Ghosh, by tearing asunder the prosecution allegations and suggesting that the court look at the sterling character of his client in terms of universal human values. Today Aurobindo Ghosh was acquitted of the charges of complicity in the recent bomb conspiracy case by the Alipore sessions court.

Minto-Morley Reforms: Sprinkles Of Charity Or Poison?

May 25, 1909, London, Calcutta: The Indian National Congress has been striving to achieve self-governance for Indians all these years. There has also been bitter acrimony in recent years among the moderates and extremists over the quantum and form of the self-government and the mode to obtain it. As fallout of the long conflicts between the two factions, the moderates have managed to drive out nearly the whole extremist group from the organisation. They have been relying on British sense of justice and fairplay to grant the Indians, in phases, political rights. Way back in 1906, Lord Morley, Secretary of State for Indian Affairs, had announced in the British Parliament that his government wanted to give more powers to Indians in legislative affairs. Moderates were all praise for such holy intention, while extremists found nothing great to rejoice over. Since then, the British government has taken nearly three years to announce the reforms it promised. In the meanwhile, of course, it has planted the seed of communal politics on

Indian soil by lending ear to the demands for a separate electorate by the Muslims.

The present set of reforms incorporated in the Indian Council Act, 1909, duly passed by the British Parliament, has become an Act today. Viewed carefully, it seems nothing more than sprinklings of British charity, which could, ironically, be potential poison for India's struggle for self-government. The Act allows Indian presence in the legislature, but bulk of it would be selected or nominated by the Raj. Not only would the elected Indians constitute minority in the legislature, even the franchise electing them would be severely restricted in a manner that caters to the interests of the Empire. These reforms are, therefore, just peanuts and unable to satisfy the large section of the politically aware nationalist Indians. The worst part is the institution of separate electorate for the Muslims. Moreover, they would also be able to take part in elections by mixed electorates. Critics say, this would divide Hindus and Muslims of the country forever, and that the British would continue to reap dividends from the resultant communal conflict.

As the extremist group has already been expelled, there is no robust intellectual debate occurring in the Congress, pointing out the loopholes of the reforms. On the contrary, the moderates are singing the glory of British magnanimity. They are rejoicing over the provision for Indian presence in the legislature, but in that euphoria, are unable to foresee how the institution of communal electorate could establish a vice-like grip over Indian politics in the years ahead.

INDIAN COUNCIL ACT, 1909 – THE FINE PRINT

It was way back in 1906 when Lord Morley, Secretary of State for Indian Affairs, had announced in the British Parliament that his government wanted to give more powers to local people in legislative affairs. Lord Minto, the Governor General of India in 1906, also joined Morley in bringing to fruition the promised reforms. A committee was appointed to propose a scheme of reforms. The Act of 1909 has been passed in accordance with its report and after its approval by both Morley and Minto.

The Act has increased the number of members in the Imperial

Legislative council from 16 to 60. The number of members has also been increased for provincial legislatures—to 50 each for Bengal, Madras and Bombay and 30 each for the others. Besides the elected representatives, the members of Legislative Councils both at the Centre and in the provinces would belong to three categories, viz. (a) ex-officio members (Governor General and the members of his executive council), (b) official members—who must be government officials nominated by the Governor General, and (c) nominated non-official members—who too would be nominated by the Governor General but not being government officials. At the Centre, nominated official members would form majority whereas in provinces it would be nominated non-official members. The right of separate electorate has been given to the Muslims. The Governor General has been empowered to nominate one Indian member to his executive council. The reforms also allow two Indians to be nominated to the Council of the Secretary of State for Indian Affairs in London. The Act of 1909 has not only given the Muslims the right to elect their representatives by separate electorate, but also the right to vote in general constituencies. In addition, they are also given weightage in representation. This is not based on plain demography or presumption of a homogenous nation, but considering the political importance of the community and its contribution to the Empire, as the Muslim leaders had represented to the Raj. It is clear the British government is bent upon playing the communal card in the years to come and this Act has begun that game. The Muslims are happy. Even the Congress moderates, seemingly in an expansive mood with British charity in the form of some reforms at least, are happy. They have possibly not fully realised the significance of the separate electorate system. They are glad that this new Act, 1909 has added 135 elected representatives to legislative councils spread across British India. The moderates are also excited as the Secretary of State for India in England may also induct Indians to his own council of India to reflect Indian aspirations.

A Splendid Intellect Has Become Mentally Deranged?

May 30, 1909, Uttarpara, Calcutta: Aurobindo Ghosh has been one of the most popular political leaders in Bengal and naturally his prosecution in the Alipore bomb case had aroused intense public interest. Today, he came to Uttarpara, a suburb of Calcutta, to address a large gathering. The news soon spread and over ten thousand people assembled to listen to what he had to say.

They were eager to see him take up the reins of the Congress in Bengal, especially when the extremist group was in complete disarray in the province and the partition of Bengal continued to hurt people. The audience also included intelligence branch officials in disguise. The government was keen to get an idea about Aurobindo's next intended political move.

However, what he said could break many hearts. His utterances surprised people so much that many did not know how to react. Aurobindo shared his unique experience of divine realisation inside the prison. He said, during his prison term, he used to have vision of Vasudev (Lord Krishna) all around him—in four walls, trees, and also in judges hearing his case. He gave hints of a withdrawal from politics and henceforth devoting his life to carry out the divine command.

Intelligence branch officials, keeping a track, are reported to have briefed the government that a splendid intellect has become mentally deranged. However, the government is heaving a sigh of relief—a formidable political adversary is going out of the fray.

I Attempted To Shed British Blood: Madanlal Dhingra

July 1,1909, London: Indian discontent and protest against the high-handed and heartless British rule were registered today at the very heart of the British capital, when Madan Lal Dhingra, an Indian revolutionary carried out the assassination of Sir William Hutt Curzon Wyllie at the Imperial Institute here. Wyllie happened to be the ADC of Secretary of State for India. Dhingra justified his action, saying that he did this intentionally and that he 'wanted to shed British blood on purpose as a humble protest against the inhuman transportations and hanging of Indian youths'[8] by the colonial regime in India. It may be mentioned that since the passing of the Criminal Amendment Act last December, the government persecution of the revolutionaries in India has gone up significantly. Using the Act as a weapon, the government has begun to dish out disproportionately harsh punishment to not only revolutionaries but even ordinary political workers.

It may be mentioned that Dhingra belongs to India House—an exclusive group led by Shyamji Krishna. The group has as members such distinguished persons as Madam Bhikaji Cama, Lala Hardayal, Sardar Singh Rana and many others. Shyamji himself is a prominent name in Britain, especially amongst the Indian community, being the founder of the famous 'India House' in London and also the journal Indian Sociologist. For past some time, the British government had been suspecting that Indian revolutionaries were using Indian House to conspire against the Empire. This daring attack in the heart of London not only confirmed their apprehensions but also made the British government wary. It is likely to come down heavily on Shyamji and his associates.

SHYAMJI KRISHNA VARMA AND INDIA HOUSE

Shyamji Krishna Verma has been one of the distinguished Indian revolutionaries working abroad indefatigably to advance the cause of India's independence. Like Gandhi and Jinnah, a Kathiawari by birth, he was influenced by the Arya Samaj beliefs in early years. Over the years, he has come to be influenced by thoughts of Herbert Spencer and developed a revolutionary ideology. Spencer's maxim, 'Resistance to aggression is not only justifiable but also imperative' has been deeply influencing him in carrying out strident nationalist programmes and activities against the oppressive colonial rulers of India. As an expatriate Indian in England, Shyamji has not joined the British Committee of the Indian National Congress. On the contrary, he has been following his revolutionary beliefs. He founded India House in 1905 for the benefit of overseas Indian students who have been victims of racial bias in securing residences in London. Indian stalwarts like Dadabhai Naoroji, Lajpat Rai and Bhikaji Cama were present at the opening ceremony.

Located in 65, Cromwell Avenue, High Gate in north London, Indian House has evolved over the years as the rendezvous of Indian revolutionaries in Britain. Shyamji believes that Indians cannot expect Britain to give them anything on their own and that they must themselves be firm, determined and obsessed about freedom, to be able to secure independence from their colonial rulers.

Over the years, patriotic Indians like Bhikaji Cama, VD Savarkar, Virendranath Chattopadhyay, Hardayal, Sardar Singh Rana, VVS Iyer, MPT Acharya and many others became members of India House and have been putting their might in advancing the Indian cause in Britain and Europe.

In 1905, Shyamji started a publication, the 'Indian Sociologist', 'to propagate the nationalist cause' and anti-colonial views in powerful language. It has been stressing on the need for armed revolution to secure Indian independence. The publication has been banned in India. The British government has been distinctly uneasy about Shyamji and India House's activities. Though it has kept this group under surveillance, it has so far not taken any drastic step. Now the assassination of Wyllie by one of its members may change its attitude altogether. Madanlal Dhingra was tried expeditiously and hanged on 17 August, 1909. Indications are afoot that the government may come down hard on the group and initiate series of vindictive actions.

'Karmayogin' A Symbol Of National Awakening

1909, Calcutta: After his release from jail, Aurobindo has not been directly participating in political activities. However he started his paper, *Karmayogin* (English) on 19 June and *Dharma* (Bengali) on 23rd August this year. Indians, especially the youth, are reading these with avid interest.

In a short time the *Karmayogin* has become a symbol for national awakening and given him wide reach. Today, his charismatic appeal goes out to people across the country. Abul Kalam Azad, a young man fuelled by nationalist fervour and eager to see India free from the colonial rule, went to meet Aurobindo two or three times. He has been deeply influenced by Aurobindo's thoughts.

AJIT SINGH ESCAPES TO PERSIA

September 1909, Hoshiarpur: Since he came back to the Punjab from the Mandalay prison, Ajit Singh had resumed revolutionary activities with missionary zeal – his goal is to throw British out of India. In 1907, he attempted to motivate soldiers of some units of the First Division of the Indian Army and also some other units at Bannu to wage a strike for higher pay. He also arranged to distribute leaflets amongst students of DAV College and Islamic College in Lahore.

For past some time, Ajit Singh has been trying to form secret societies in all principal towns in Punjab in association with other revolutionaries like Sufi Amba Prasad, Lal Chand Falak, Krishan Singh, Swarn Singh, Zia-ul-Huq and a few more. He visited Calcutta in November last year and established liaison with revolutionaries in Bengal. He paid a repeat visit to that capital city in May this year. The government has been suspecting him and tracking his movements.

The police, in the course of searching the Tilak Press in the town, have stumbled upon a revolutionary document, which contains a plan to overthrow the British rule in India and bears reference to Ajit Singh and a few others. Before the government could get hold of him, he has reportedly escaped to Persia. Some of his close associates, including Lal Chand Falak, have been arrested. They are likely to be awarded harsh punishment for sedition.

Tilak, The Real Life Karmayogi, In Mandalay Prison

1909, Mandalay: Following the editorials he wrote supporting the case of the accused in the Muzaffarpur bomb case, Tilak was arrested, tried and sent to prison to distant Mandalay. He had appealed to the Privy Council against the order, which he felt was unjust. But his hope was extinguished on 3 March 1909, when the Privy Council in England passed order rejecting the appeal. Tilak accepted the outcome with equanimity. He said there are higher powers that rule the destiny of things and it may be the will of Providence that the cause which 'I represent may prosper more by my suffering than by my remaining free.'

In Mandalay, Tilak has begun to work on his book *Gita Rahasya* or the *Secret Meaning of Gita*. In his life, Tilak has always been stressing on disinterested action in the service of his motherland rather than on quietism or ascetic renunciation. Given his extraordinary merit and deep knowledge of scriptures, this new project may be a valuable addition to the treasure of philosophical literature.

INDIAN NATIONAL CONGRESS

Gokhale Sees A Bleak Future

September 1909, Poona: With hardly three months to go before its annual session in Lahore, the Congress Party is in a state of despair. Since the Surat incident in 1907, the moderates led by Pheroze Shah Mehta have been systematically decimating the extremists. His job became much easier as the British government too targeted their leaders like Lajpat Rai, Aurobindo Ghosh and Bal Gangadhar Tilak, implicating them in court cases. Separated from the leaders, the extremists were given a kind of burial in the Madras session.

Against this backdrop, some moderate leaders are introspecting. Level-headed leaders like Gokhale are also realising that squeezed between the repressive government and the revolutionaries, the moderates do not have the necessary public spirit and energy to hold together effectively for long.

The paltry offerings of the Indian Council Act 1909 are also loaded with mischievous potential aimed at inciting communal politics in the country. The sober, easygoing, peace loving moderate leaders loyal to the British Empire are not up to the task of challenging the government on this count. The daring, the spirit, the vitality, the resilience and the courage to take the imperial government head on, which characterised the extremist group and its leaders, are sadly being missed at this juncture. The deep-rooted antagonism against the British has begun to be expressed in revolutionary activities.

In a letter written recently to his friend Wedderburn, Gokhale has lamented that under the extant circumstances, political terrorism has been throwing the political equilibrium in disarray. In an obvious reference to Bengal, he has written that provincialism is on the rise and that is throwing the national movement out of gear and also that there was no influence available in the country to stem that process. Critical of the Bengal moderates, he observed that, they are so preoccupied with the partition of their province that they were hastening the process of disintegration of the national movement. Gokhale is obviously realising the value of the maxim 'united we stand, divided we fall'.

DISTRICT MAGISTRATE SHOT DEAD

December 21, 1909, Nasik: Following harsh sentences imposed on a large number of revolutionaries in the Kolhapur bomb case, Anant Laxman Kanhere, a young revolutionary from Aurangabad has shot dead AMT Jackson, the district magistrate of Nasik in a theatre hall. The incident has sent a shock wave across the bureaucracy.

Improve Plight Of South African Indians, Gokhale Makes Passionate Appeal In Congress Session

December 27-29, 1909, Lahore: Congress' Lahore session has begun amidst poor turnout of delegates. Bengal seems to be conspicuous by near absence and even the host province of Punjab is not displaying any enthusiasm. Though Pheroze Shah Mehta was the president-elect, he refused to preside and asked Gokhale to take over. But even Gokhale was not inclined. Eventually, the public-spirited leader, Madan Mohan Malaviya, took up that onerous responsibility.

In an otherwise lacklustre show, Gokhale made a soul-stirring appeal to Indian patriotism to support the crusade led by Gandhi in South Africa, against the discriminatory policies of the racist white government persecuting the Indian immigrants in that country. Gokhale has been in close touch with Gandhi and keeping track of the struggle pursued by the latter on non-violent lines in that distant land. Gokhale has been helping this cause for long and if there is significant awareness of this issue amongst Congress members, much of the credit goes to him.

Congress Session Ends In A Whimper

December 1909, Lahore: The Congress session here has come to an end. Coming in the wake of the Minto-Morley reforms, this should have been a very important event deliberating the pros and cons of the reforms, but precious little has been achieved. Though Madan Mohan Malaviya, in his presidential address, dealt with the issue, this was not followed by any vigorous, fruitful debate and action. Malaviya criticised the separate electorate system, saying that the actual purpose of the government is not to favour the Muslims but to lure them away from their Hindu brethrens, so that they do not agitate for real reforms. He said by granting the Muslims separate electorate as well as the right to take part in elections in the mixed electorates, the British regime has granted one community undue and excessive importance, to the exclusion of others.

The session was marked by exceptionally poor attendance. As Gokhale had rightly apprehended earlier, many Congress leaders remained so obsessed with regional issues, that issues of national concern like the 'separate electorate' were not rigorously debated to offer a substantial response to the government or chalk out the road map for future political action. The absence of the extremist group due to expulsion, made the session even more sterile.

CID Report: This Congress Not A National Organisation

December 1909, Lahore: Just concluded Congress session here has witnessed the poorest attendance. The apathy of the 'all-India Congress leadership' about the partition of the province has antagonised Bengal so much that it clearly reflected on the exceptionally poor strength of the delegates from that province. Not only the extremist group, even the moderate leaders from Bengal had to face humiliating treatment in Allahabad and Madras sessions on the issues of partition and boycott. All of these engineered a 'disconnect'. The bulk of Punjab was not only indifferent but even hostile. The government was insensitive in handling public grievances and their popular leaders while the Congress, despite being the premier political organisation, did little to help matters. With the extremist groups virtually out, Congress as an organisation has also been robbed of its vitality and resilience to a great extent. The current leadership has not been able to inspire much confidence that they can squarely address the political issues and engage the British government successfully. As such, the prospect of a good turnout was low and it turned out to be exactly so. A CID report says that the attendance was so pathetic that it posed a threat to the status of the Indian National Congress as a pan-India organisation.

Secret Societies Proliferate In Bombay Presidency

December 1909: Bal Gangadhar Tilak's imprisonment and deportation to Mandalay has been alienating people from the government across the country. However, the reaction has been severe in Bombay province. Some feel so intensely about the issue that they are denouncing even constitutionalist leaders like Gokhale, whom they charge with having had a role in Tilak's arrest. Although such cynicism seems to be unfounded, it is indicative of the amount of distress caused to the people by Tilak's arrest by the British regime.

It is bad news for the government that following Tilak's deportation, a renewed interest is being witnessed in revolutionary activities in the province. In addition to Abhinav Bharat, many new secret societies have sprung up. In areas like Bombay, Pune, Nasik, Bassein, and Kolhapur factories have been set up by revolutionaries and their sympathisers for manufacturing bombs. The government is worried and has been taking repressive measures to curb such activities.

POLICE OFFICER FALLS TO BULLET

Revolutionaries Target Native Collaborators

January 24, 1910, Calcutta: Many revolutionaries arrested in connection with the Manicktala bomb case were handed down harsh punishments including life imprisonment and transportations. Jugantar, the premier revolutionary outfit, has been seeking revenge and keeping a watch over the government officials who played key role in the arrests and trial in this case. Today, its member, Biren Dutta, has shot to death Samsul Alam, the Dy Superintendent of Police on the stairs of the Calcutta High Court. Earlier, Charu Chandra Bose, a Jugantar member, had assassinated Asutosh Biswas, the public prosecutor, who was taking unduly high interest in securing conviction of the accused revolutionaries. This is the second important retaliatory action.

Imperial Legislative Council Meets Under 1909 Act

January 25, 1910, Calcutta: Following the passing of Indian Council Act 1909, the Imperial Legislative Council has assembled for the first time. Whereas the government is viewing it as a significant reform for India and the Congress moderates also consider this as a positive step, the revolutionaries are bent upon removing the colonial ruler.

Government Beware!
Members May Be More Than Rubber Stamps

1910, Delhi: Indian Council Act 1909 has paved the way for extending the size of the council. The Governor General feels, notwithstanding the increase, the council will not hamper his unrestricted power and authority in any manner and that the extended council will essentially serve as a mere rubber stamp. However, political observers feel that his complacency may come in for a rude shock with stalwarts like Gopal Krishna Gokhale, Motilal Nehru, Mohammad Ali Jinnah and Surendra Nath Banerjea, amongst others, entering the council.

Plan To Overthrow British – Bagha Jatin Is Charged

1910, Calcutta: Jatindranath Mukherjee, alias Bagha Jatin, was arrested on charges of waging war against the Crown. Based on further investigations, he has been charged with inciting Indian soldiers belonging to the Jat regiment posted in Fort William and also soldiers posted in Upper Indian Cantonments. It is being alleged that Jatin was expecting Germany to declare war against England and he was planning to exploit such an occasion to organise an armed uprising amongst Indian soldiers in various regiments. About forty-seven people are on trial.

Along with Jatin, many prominent revolutionaries operating in various parts of Bengal have also been arrested and charged for sedition. This case is being referred to as the 'Howrah-Sibpur' Conspiracy case.

Are Revolutionary Societies Thinking Big?

Arrest of Bagha Jatin, and the police thereafter claiming to have unearthed a revolutionary plot to incite the British Indian Army against the King Emperor in order to end colonial rule in the country, suggests that revolutionary societies are thinking well beyond killing of individuals, and in terms of organised armed rebellion against the government. Although their might as yet is paltry vis-à-vis the formidable Empire, their new strategies are much broader in scope and involve key institutions of the government and, therefore, are causing the latter considerable disquiet. Especially when a leader of Jatindranath's stature is at the helm, the possibility of a countrywide revolutionary uprising cannot be discarded as outright utopian.

In recent times, Ajit Singh had made similar attempts in Punjab. According to intelligence branch reports, before escaping to Persia to avert arrest, he had visited Calcutta and that revolutionary societies in these two provinces have been trying to develop some coordination.

In faraway USA, Lala Hardayal, an ex-patriate Indian revolutionary, has founded Jugantar Ashram. He has been organising Indian immigrants in the distant Pacific coast against discriminatory treatment meted to them by local governments, and also for the cause of India's freedom. Hardyal has been attempting to organise revolutionary activities in Punjab too.

In the United Province, Rashbehari Bose has been trying to build strong bulwark of local revolutionaries. Jatindranath Banerjee, an ex-Anushilan Samity leader, has settled in Vrindavan, in the guise of Swami Niralamba, to escape government attention. He is working to strengthen the revolutionary network in coordination with Rashbehari Bose.

The expulsion of the extremists has also dealt a serious blow to the Congress. By sowing seeds of communal divide, the government is trying to decimate the Indian aspiration for self-government. As such, the revolutionary struggle, which even a couple of years ago seemed to be impractical romanticism, has begun to acquire semblance of an alternative strategy for India's freedom struggle.

Watchword Should Be Hope, Conciliation: Wedderburn

December 26-29, 1910, Allahabad: Promised reforms on self-government were offered to Indians in 1909 with a barb. Although the Congress in the Lahore session did not adequately attempt to extract the thorn, ie. the issue of separate electorates, the experience over the last one year has been frustrating. This new institution has been driving a wedge between Hindus and Muslims, exactly the way the British government wanted—they are thus happy. But the communal temperature is rising. Though a few nationalist Muslims, Jinnah included, have not welcomed this system, none of them have spoken out against it. After all, this looks like a special privilege to the community, a huge lever of political power and difficult to give up. Although as a political organisation, the Congress does not seem to be ready to fight tooth and nail against it, a number of its Hindu members find it difficult to digest. They have been organising themselves under pro-Hindu leaders in the Congress. It may be recalled that Madan Mohan Malaviya has been a strong critic of the new system which he feels would be bad for both the communities and, of course, the national unity.

The rising tension between the two communities became a cause of concern on the eve of the Allahabad session of the Congress. Reckoning that a statesman ought to be called to preside over to reconcile and resolve the raging conflict between the two communities, Congress has invited Sir William Wedderburn. He has been known for his abounding love for India and Indians and, has earlier presided over a Congress session in 1889. Gokhale finds in him not only a friend but a person with vision and wisdom—he in fact considers Wedderburn as a 'Rishi' of modern times. In his address, Wedderburn assures the assembly of his enormous goodwill towards them and the cause they represent. Urging them to march ahead, he says, 'our watchword must be hope, conciliation and united efforts'.

In this session, Congress has adopted a resolution against extension of the separate electorate system to the local level. Resolutions were also adopted opposing the Press Act and the Seditious Meetings Act, which the government has been using to suppress political aspirations and movement of the Indian people.

Bagha Jatin Acquitted

February 1911, Calcutta: Bagha Jatin was being tried along with forty-six others on the charge of conspiring against the Emperor in the Howrah-Sibpur conspiracy case. Their trials were being watched with avid interest by the media and local people, given the popularity of Jatindranath. Eventually, Jatindranath had to be released for want of adequate evidence. He has been leading Jugantar using a decentralised organisational model, where many regional outfits with allegiance to the central body function more or less independently. As such, it was difficult for the police to gather sufficient evidence to prove his role or complicity. The person most upset with his acquittal is Lord Hardinge, the Viceroy. The rising revolutionary activities have been upsetting him and he had hoped Jatin's indictment in this case would give the government much respite. He is personally convinced about the key role played by Bagha Jatin in the whole episode.

PARTITION ANNULLED BUT BENGAL DISMEMBERED

December 12, 1911, Delhi: The Coronation ceremony of King George V is being celebrated with great fanfare in Delhi. On this occasion, the King has made announcements of two major decisions—one, annulling the Bengal partition and two, shifting the capital from Calcutta to New Delhi.

The annulment of partition, though it has been a long-standing demand of the Bengali Hindus, has not brought them much cheer.

Reasons are not far to seek. Though the partition has been rescinded, the Bengal presidency is slated to undergo a massive surgery. Unified Bengal will no longer include districts of Bihar, Orissa and Assam. These have been prised away. Districts of Sylhet and Cachar are also to be severed. Unified Bengal, therefore, will be much truncated and have essentially Bengali-speaking areas minus Manbhum. Outside of Bengali-speaking areas, if at all, only the Darjeeling hill sub-division will become its part. Thus, at one stroke, the hegemony of the Bengalis over a wide swathe of territories have been threatened. To compound their woes, the capital of the vast empire is also scheduled to shift. The elaborate government establishment moving away from the province is bound to hit the Bengalis hard.

Through this territorial re-engineering, the government has created a Muslim majority province in the re-unified Bengal. This is likely to help them in political manoeuvring.

Some sections of Hindus are upset about the demographic upheaval in Bengal. They feel the government has created a synthetic Muslim majority in the unified province by tempering with the largely Hindu majority Bengal presidency, to suit its political purpose.

Many Muslims too are not exactly rejoicing. First, they view the annulment as a capitulation of the government to Hindu revolutionaries, whom, they, like the British, call terrorists. Second, in eastern Bengal, they had unquestionable political domination for the last five years. In the united Bengal, notwithstanding their numerical majority, they would find the political space fiercely competitive, due to the traditional hegemony of caste Hindus in Bengal politics and their overall majority being only slender. The discontentment against the government decision is not confined to Muslims in Bengal but seems to have spread amongst politically aware Muslims across the country. Together, they consider this a betrayal as they have been pledging their loyalty to the British crown and have so far kept themselves distant from demands like swaraj and self-governance. Should their loyalty have been reciprocated this way- they wonder!

What, however, is hurting Bengali Hindus and Muslims alike is the British decision to shift the capital of British India from Calcutta to Delhi.

King Lays Foundation Stone For India's New Capital

December 15, 2011, Delhi: King George V has today laid the foundation stone for the new capital city for his Indian empire here.

ASSASSINATION BID ON CEREMONIAL PROCESSION

Viceroy Escapes With Injury, Mahout Killed

December 23, 1912, Delhi: An unidentified revolutionary has thrown a home-made bomb at the 'howdah' of the elephant on which Lord Hardinge was passing through the Chandni Chowk suburb, in course of his state entry into the city. The Viceroy was seriously injured, but survived. Vicereine Lady Hardinge escaped unhurt but she went into a state of deep shock. The Mahout of the elephant was killed in the attack. The Viceroy is undergoing treatment in hospital.

It is being heard that the conspiracy to kill him was hatched by a network of revolutionaries in Bengal and Punjab, headed by Rashbehari Bose. The Viceroy was on the elephant on the occasion of shifting of the capital from Calcutta to Delhi.

The police are hunting for the assassin. Visibly upset at this audacious attempt, the government has become determined to crush the network of revolutionaries in Punjab and Bengal.

Congress Leader Jinnah Attends Muslim League Meeting

December 31, 1912, Bankipur, Bihar: Muslim League was launched about six years ago. However, unlike the Congress, its progress as a political party has been rather tardy. Its leadership has identified Jinnah as a person who can help the party to grow rapidly. Jinnah's exceptional legal acumen, oratory, experience as a legislator and stature as a leader may have generated their interest in him and made them keen to get him into the League's fold. At this juncture, they are, however, not demanding that Jinnah sever his relationship with the Indian National Congress. They are prepared to wait and would be happy to augur a relationship. At their insistence, Jinnah has agreed to attend the meeting of the council of the League. However, he continues to be a member of the Congress and professes his loyalty to it.

SPARK OF REVOLUTION REACHES NORTH AMERICA

April, 1913, San Francisco: Indian freedom struggle has found a new base in the distant land of United States. The immigrant Indians in the west Pacific coasts have taken it upon themselves to carry out this war. A big push towards this was given when the erstwhile Hindi Association of America, founded in a lumber mill at Oregon by Baba Sohan Singh of Bhakna and Lala Hardayal, re-christened itself as the Hindustan Ghadar Party, the word 'Ghadar' meaning 'revolution'.

With its headquarters in San Francisco, the party has been fighting to improve the miserable plight of Indian immigrants in countries like Canada, Philippines, Hong Kong, China and the USA, all of which are connected in some way or the other with the British Empire. It holds the British Empire responsible for their miseries, has deep seated grievances against it and wants to expel it from India. Its top leader, Hardayal, is a deeply patriotic person and has also been visiting India at intervals and organising revolutionary outfits in Punjab and the United Provinces. With intimate connections to the revolutionary societies in India, he has also set up Jugantar ashram in this distant land.

For past some time, Hardayal has been in contact with Bagha Jatin in Bengal and Rashbehari Bose in the United Province and they are planning to stage a big armed revolt against the British Empire in India, taking advantage of the wars in Europe, which appears a distinct possibility in the near future. They are also trying to secure international help for this purpose.

The Ghadar party is recruiting cadres in this part of the world to fight the upcoming Indian war of independence. The party is planning to send large number of its members at the opportune time to India to take up arms and carry out the revolt.

LEAGUE PERSUADES JINNAH TO BECOME MEMBER

October 10, 1913, Bombay: Following his attendance in the Muslim League session last year, Jinnah has also attended the plenary session of the League held at Lucknow in April this year. After that, he was approached by League leaders, Maulana Mohammad Ali and Syed Wazir Hassan, to become a member of the All-India Muslim League. Jinnah has agreed but made it clear to the League leadership that this would not dilute his commitment and loyalty to the larger national cause—the freedom of the country—to which he said his life was dedicated. Jinnah has today enrolled himself as a member of the All-India Muslim League. Maulana Ali proposed and Wazir Hassan seconded his membership.

Ghadar Party Sounds Bugle

'There Begins In Foreign Lands War Against The Raj'

November 1913: Ghadar party is deeply imbued with revolutionary spirit and wants the British to leave India. It has begun publishing its official mouthpiece *Ghadar* which contains writings with strong patriotic appeal. In its very first issue this month, it says:

'Today there begins in foreign lands a war against the British raj. What is our name? Mutiny. What is our work? Mutiny. Where will mutiny break out? In India. The time will come when rifles and blood will take the place of pen and ink.'[9]

In the 'wanted' column, appears:

Wanted: Enthusiastic and heroic soldiers for organising Ghadar in Hindustan.

Remuneration: Death

Reward: Martyrdom

Pension: Freedom

Field of work: Hindustan

Revolutionaries Plan 1857 Type Revolution

With the cloud of a great war gathering in the Western world, Indian revolutionaries have begun preparations to use that occasion to stage a 1857 type revolution. They are strengthening coordination amongst themselves and also looking for help from outside India. Towards this objective, revolutionary networks of Bagha Jatin in Bengal, Rashbehari Bose in the United Province and Hardayal in Punjab have come together. Hardayal-led Ghadar party in the USA is also joining hands and planning to send its cadres to India at an appropriate time. As part of their strategy, the revolutionaries aim at securing the cooperation of sections of British Indian Army as well. Rashbehari Bose is reported to have initiated talks with native officers posted in Fort William in Calcutta, before returning to Benares where he proposes to organise scattered forces towards this goal. Army units in Punjab are also being contacted.

German And Austrian Ships Seized In Indian Ports

August 4, 1914, New Delhi: A big war has already broken out in Europe and pitted Great Britain against Germany. As a fallout of the above, today the Government of India has ordered the seizure of all German and Austrian ships in Indian ports.

British India Pledges Support In War Against Germany

September 8, 1914, New Delhi: British India has formally entangled itself in the ongoing war in Europe. The Imperial Legislative Council has passed a resolution of support to Britain in the war against Germany and other members of central power. As a colonised nation with practically no voice in governance, Indians could hardly raise a contrary opinion. The Congress Party in particular, as the prime political organisation, has lent positive support to the British war efforts.

Harsh Treatment Meted Out To Returning Indians

September 1914, Lahore: Many Indians, a bulk of them from the Punjab, emigrated to countries like USA, Canada, Hong Kong, Philippines, and China in search of livelihood. However, their being citizens of British India often earned them discriminatory treatment in those countries rather than privileges. This year, due to the war-induced recession and contracting job opportunities overseas, many of them have decided to come back to the Punjab, with stories of their woes and miseries in foreign lands. In ordinary circumstances, such mass ingress would not have caused any extraordinary worries to the government in Punjab or Delhi. However, upon briefing by the intelligence branches about Ghadar party's plans of staging an armed revolt in India, the government of India has been trying to check the entry of returning Indians by proclaiming the Ingress Ordinance. In terms of the Ordinance, every returning immigrant is being watched from the port of landing. Any one suspected to be a Ghadar activist is being interned. The government is permitting those it considers harmless to live in their native villages, with restrictions on their movements outside.

SIKH IMMIGRANTS MASSACRED IN BUDGE BUDGE

September 29, 1914, Calcutta: Today the police opened fire at unarmed passengers, mostly Sikhs, who had disembarked at this port city from the Japanese ship Komagata Maru, after a long and arduous sea voyage and were refusing to board the Punjab bound train arranged for taking them to their native province. It is being learnt that at least 18 people have died and 25 wounded due to the police firing.

According to reports, Komagata Maru started its voyage on 4th April this year from Hong Kong, bound for Vancouver. Its passengers included 351 Sikhs and 21 Punjabi Muslims. Upon arrival at the destination, these passengers were not allowed to disembark by Canadian Immigration Authorities. As the ship began its return voyage with these passengers on board, the current war broke out and they were not allowed to disembark even at Hong Kong—the port of embarking, either. Under the circumstances, the ship sailed towards India—the motherland of the immigrants.

After Komagata Maru reached Hooghly, the government carried out extensive search on the ship, suspecting the passengers to be Ghadarites. Not finding any arms, they were permitted to disembark and then they were herded to a special train arranged for them by the Punjab government. However, many Sikh passengers refused to board the train and headed out towards Calcutta city in a procession, with the holy Granth Sahib in hand. The disobedience led to a scuffle and skirmish, when police opened fire at the unarmed and fatigued immigrants, killing and injuring many.

This news spread like wild fire in the city and generated a lot of popular anger against the British government. It is being predicted that people in Punjab will rise in protest as soon as they come to know of the brutal massacre of these innocent Sikhs.

Indian Revolutionaries Sense Opportunity

September 1914: A great war was triggered in Europe with the assassination of Archduke Ferdinand, heir to the throne of Austria-Hungary, by a Yugoslav national on 28 June this year. The Habsburg Empire then served an ultimatum on the Kingdom of Serbia. Within two weeks, the nations in the continent have begun to take sides and started a bloody war. An assessment of the alignment of the nations indicates a likely confrontation between Germany and Britain, heading two camps as the war gathers momentum. Expatriate Indian revolutionaries are sensing an opportunity in this European war, which might keep Great Britain engaged. An international pro-India Committee that was formed in Zurich earlier has merged into a bigger body to form the Berlin Committee. It is also being called the Indian Independence Party. It has many prominent Indian revolutionaries among its members and has also managed to secure the support of the German government, which has an interest in destabilising the British government in India, to gain an upper hand over them in Europe.

The Indian revolutionaries have chalked out a plan to stage an armed revolt in India, taking advantage of the war situation. The revolutionaries could persuade the German government to help their cause by supplying arms and ammunitions. Jugantar, led by Bagha Jatin, in Calcutta, is expected to play a key role in the scheme. Rashbehari Bose is to carry out the plan in the United Province and Punjab which includes enlisting the support of a section of British Indian Army at the right time. The Ghadar party of Hardayal has already sent many of their members into Punjab and they are waiting for the call to strike the government.

This extensive plan is being called the Zimmerman plan, after Arthur Zimmerman, the State Secretary for Foreign Affairs of the German Empire. As part of the plan, the German ambassador in

Washington would be sending large consignments of arms and ammunitions to the eastern coast of Bay of Bengal in India for use by the revolutionaries across the country.

Ottoman Caliph Joins Global War

Indian Muslims Keep Fingers Crossed

December 1914, Istanbul: The Ottoman Empire has joined the Great War that is raging in Europe and has engaged in fierce fights against Britain in southern Arabia. These two are trying to expel each other from Aden and Yemen respectively. Since the Ottoman Emperor is acknowledged as the Caliph by many Muslim countries, Germany being enemy of Britain, is trying to turn the Muslim sentiments against Britain. William , a German agent in Istanbul, has made contacts with pan Islamic revolutionaries to promote 'jihad' against the British Empire. Many politically-conscious Muslims in India are supporting the Ottoman Emperor in this war as they accept him as the Caliph of the Islamic world. They resent Britain's role and designs in fighting Turkey.

Tilak Enormously Popular, Still Unwelcome In Congress

December 1914, Madras: Since 17 June this year, when Tilak was released, there has been considerable debate about his re-induction in the party. Pheroze Shah Mehta had amended the Congress constitution in Allahabad, way back in 1907, to pre-empt such a possibility. As expected he and his supporters have been opposing Tilak's rehabilitation. Gokhale has also been in agreement. The intra-party politics has increased manifold over this issue as the annual session of the Congress is held in the city.

Right since the time Tilak returned to India from Mandalay, Annie Besant has been working tirelessly to bring about reconciliation between Tilak and Gokhale, and thereby between moderates and extremists. But she failed to convince Gokhale. The memories of hijacking the control of the Poona Sarvajanik Sabha and the Surat split are still vivid in his memory. It is being heard that he does not want the Congress constitution to be amended in any manner that can facilitate Tilak's re-entry. The bottom-line is that the Congress session here has not invited Tilak. As a mark of protest, the extremist groups of Bengal have boycotted the session. According to some sources, other provinces too have joined the protest and the numbers of delegates in Madras have dipped.

GANDHI RETURNS TO INDIA

To Embark Upon Bharat Parikrama

January, 1915: Notwithstanding the facts that there have been many important political developments nationally and now even internationally as the great war has begun to pick up momentum, the Congress, as the prime political party, has not been able to forge together appropriate responses. The moderate leaders, at the helm, are all soft-paddlers, excessively loyal even to understand the long-term implications of the current government actions. Their capacity to achieve self-government at any foreseeable future seems suspect.

Gokhale, the level-headed leader and one who is closer to the people than most other moderates, has been sensing a big void in the political space—a big disconnect between the Congress and the popular aspirations. For past some time he has been asking Gandhi to return to India and take up public service here. Gokhale has been impressed by Gandhi's work and his non-violent struggle in South Africa. Gokhale's persuasion has a role in Gandhi's decision to return to his motherland at the conclusion of his Satyagraha struggle in Africa.

Gandhi began his return journey from England on 19th December and landed in Bombay in January. On return, he was put under the protective custody of Pheroze Shah Mehta briefly. Then Gandhi went to Pune to meet Gokhale, where he was flooded with affection by Gokhale and the members of the Servants of India Society. Gandhi wanted to set up an ashram where he could settle with his family and co-workers from South Africa. Gokhale consented to the proposal and agreed to bear all the expenses of the ashram. Gokhale, however, extracted a promise from Gandhi that Gandhi whould travel in India for gaining experience and express no opinion on any public issue until he has finished the period of probation for a year. During this period he has only to see and learn, not do anything. Gandhi has agreed. He is preparing for the *parikrama*, which he intends to take up with due seriousness.

Gandhi Highlights Jinnah's Religious Identity

January 14, 1915, Bombay: It was supposed to be a happy occasion when two famous leaders hailing from Kathiawar met in a welcome party in the city. Following Gandhi's return to India from South Africa, a Gujarati Society (Gurjar Sabha), led by the well-known Congress leader MA Jinnah, arranged a garden party at Mangaldas House, Girgaum in the city to welcome him. Kasturba accompanied her husband. While welcoming Gandhi, Jinnah made laudatory references to Gandhi's arduous struggle for not only indentured Indians in South Africa but also of the motherland. He also praised Kasturba for her support to Gandhi undaunted by the trials, sufferings and sacrifice in a hostile environment including courting of prison term. While responding to Jinnah's urban and secular welcome, Gandhi said he was 'glad to find a Mohammedan not only belonging to his own region's Sabha but chairing it.'[10] These remarks came as a shock to Jinnah. He is reportedly upset at a communal identity being thrust upon him.

PLAN FOR ARMED UPRISING

Revolutionaries Give Final Touches To Plans

February 1915, Lahore: The European war has grown into a much bigger World War already, and major powers like Britain and Germany are at each other's throat. To give final touches to their plan, Rashbehari Bose has arrived in Punjab from Benares and set up his local head quarters. Another famous revolutionary, Vishnu Ganesh Pingley, arrived in Punjab December last year to participate in the upcoming revolt and he is camping here. The revolutionaries have fixed 21 February as the date for the general uprising. Villages have been organised, pistols made, flags made ready, instruments collected for destruction of railways and telegraph, and even the declaration of war against the British has been drawn up.

Ghadarites Wait For The D Day

February 1915, Lahore: Over the last one year or so, many Ghadarites returned to Punjab. Whereas they have been subjected to the strict provisions of the Ingress Ordinance, Bhai Paramanand, a trusted aide of Lala Hardayal, lent them a helping hand in the matter of rehabilitation. Unfortunately, they could not manage to remain a disciplined force till the 'D' day arrived. On the contrary, many of them engaged in activities like attacking rail stations, robberies and looting of treasuries in a bid to raise resources to fund revolutionary plans and activities. Thus, despite attracting sympathy in early days following their return, the Ghadarites have, by now, begun to arouse fears in their neighbourhood. Clearly, they have failed to get themselves assimilated into the society to which they returned after a long gap.

Simultaneous with attempts to enlist mass participation, albeit unsuccessfully, the Ghadarites have been contacting units of the British Indian armies at different camps and cantonments to participate in the coming armed revolution. Reports say they have established contacts with the 23rd cavalry at Lahore, 28th Punjabis at Ferozepur, 28th Pioneers and 12th cavalry at Meerut, trying to enlist the latters' participation in the upcoming rebellion.

GHADAR CONSPIRACY BUSTED

February, 1915, Lahore: Rashbehari and his Ghadarite comrades were rudely shaken after they realised that some of the insiders had betrayed and informed the government of their plans. Apprehending complete dislocation of their carefully designed plan, they advanced the date of the general uprising by two days, ie. to begin on 19th February. However, the government had come to know much more than what the revolutionaries imagined. A police informer, Kirpal Singh, had enrolled as a member of Rashbehari's party. He divulged the plan to the government. Before the revolutionaries could act, the government force raided Rashbehari's head quarters. Once the full plot was revealed, the government immediately disaffected the suspected regiments, disarmed them, court-martialled the suspected soldiers and executed them. The police have begun to make large-scale arrests of suspected Ghadarites in the province.

ZIMMERMANN PLAN EXPOSED

1915, Washington: As part of the Zimmerman plan, the German ambassador in Washington was to arrange despatch of huge quantities of arms and ammunitions by ship to the Indian revolutionaries in the east coast of India along the Bay of Bengal. The Germans kept it a closely guarded secret. The successful execution of the plan for revolt in India could seriously undermine the British war resources in Europe.

However, a Czech espionage network operating in the USA and devoted to a relentless mission to find out German secret plans and designs, had stumbled upon the Zimmerman plan. The Czech overseas spy networks, upset because of German conquest of their motherland, have shared this information with the USA and Britain, their enemy's enemy. The discovery of this dangerous plan has sent the British Indian government in a tizzy. It has immediately alerted its navy to seal off all the sea approaches on the eastern coast along the Bay of Bengal.

India Loses A Worthy Son

February 19, 1915, Poona: Today Gopal Krishna Gokhale breathed his last. He was only 49 years old. His premature death is being seen as a big loss to the Indian struggle for self-governance. Political India is mourning. Gandhi, who considered Gokhale as his mentor, is in Shanti Niketan. He is shocked to get the news. Gokhale was a role model for many and his popularity cut across all barriers. Jinnah had also said he wanted to be a Muslim Gokhale.

Government Arms Itself With Special Power

March 1915, New Delhi: Government of India has passed the Defence of India Act which confers draconian powers to it. The Act allows detention of political suspects without charge or trial. It also empowers provincial Governors to appoint commission of three judges to try political cases without a jury. In the face of the Indian support for the British war efforts, the assumption of the new power seems to be unusual. However, experts say the government is wary of the revolutionaries and also the pan-Islamists who have been against Britain attacking Turkey and trying to foment troubles in the name of jihads, particularly through Afghanistan.

ALL-INDIA HINDU SABHA IS BORN

To Build A Hindu State By Legal Means

April 1915, Hardwar: Although the Minto-Morley reforms introduced an apparently well-meaning but potentially dangerous system of separate electorate that could drive a permanent wedge between Hindus and Muslims, the Indian National Congress has not dealt with the issue with due seriousness—at least such has been the feeling amongst a large section of people in India.

In the Lahore session last year, many Hindu Congress workers had a feeling that while the Congress has been bearing the brunt of national struggle, the Muslims would be walking away with the cake, through the institution of separate electorates. Although all through its existence, the Congress has remained an organisation representing Indians of all castes and creeds, this partisan move compelled a section of its workers and leaders to think that Hindus needed an exclusive organisation to protect their political interests, too. The concern has also begun to be shared in the wider Hindu community outside the Congress.

Neraly a decade ago, a Punjab Hindu Sabha was started in December 1906, and it had established its branches in districts in the province in a couple of years. However, its focus was essentially confined to issues affecting middle class Hindus within the confines of the province.

Now, leading Hindus of Allahabad have joined hands to found the All-India Hindu Sabha with its head quarters at Haridwar. Its formation has come in Hardwar at a time when the Kumbh Mela, a holy festival of the Hindus, is in progress. Maharaja Manindra Chandra Nandi has presided over the session. Madan Mohan Malaviya, the veteran Congress leader, is one of its founders. Other Congress stalwarts lending strength to the Sabha include inter alia Lajpat Rai from Punjab, B S Moonje from Bombay. This new outfit is expected to link up the activists and leaders of Hindu Sabhas across the country.

The Sabha also seeks to establish by legal means, 'a Hindu state built on Hindu culture and tradition so that Hindu ideology and way of life have a home land of its own.'

YOUNG BASANTA SENT TO THE GALLOWS

May 11, 1915, Ambala: Today the young revolutionary Basanta Kumar Biswas has been hanged in the central jail here. He was tried for throwing a bomb at the Viceroy, Lord Hardinge, in December 1912. Basanta is said to be only twenty years of age, and has become one of the young revolutionaries to sacrifice his life in the service of the motherland.

After the bomb attack on Hardinge, Basanta escaped arrest for more than a year. Last year on 26th February, he had gone to his home village at Nadia in Bengal to perform the last rites of his deceased father. He was arrested there and later on tried. He was convicted for the bomb episode. Besides Basanta, Amir Chand and Avad Behari were convicted in the same case and all of them awarded capital punishment. It is being heard that Basanta was too young to be awarded life sentence and as such, the government had fudged his age in jail records.

Rashbehari Bose Escapes To Japan

May 12, 1915: Rashbehari Bose has been a nemesis for the British government. Apart from his leadership role in respect of a wide network of revolutionaries especially in upper India, he had planned for the assassination attempt of Lord Hardinge. Rashbehari also played a key role in architecting the Zimmerman plan. With the government now literally in a hot chase for him, Rashbehari has escaped to Japan. Obviously, the network of the Indian revolutionaries outside the country will be benefited by his experienced presence. In Japan, he can pursue his plans with greater freedom.

Gandhi Sets Up His Ashram

May 25, 1915, Ahmedabad: Gandhi has set up his ashram at Ahmedabad. It has been named 'Sevashram'. There are twenty-five inmates. Under Gandhi's leadership they share common spiritual goals. They are tied by a common thread. They have a common kitchen and they live as one family.

BERLIN NEW ABODE OF INDIAN REVOLUTIONARIES

1915, Berlin: After two young, patriotic Indian students, Virendranath Chattopadhyay and Abinash Bhattacharya, set up a committee here, many overseas Indian nationalists—students and others, have been joining them. Bright young Indian students pursuing higher education in Europe have been exposed to the modern, liberal, democratic world. Such new experiences have only made them keenly realise the pain and ignominy of living under colonial rule and kindled a keen desire to unshackle their motherland.

After the assassination of Wyllie in London, Shyamji and his associates, many members of the India House including Shyamji himself, and Bhikaji Cama have left England in the face of government persecution and moved over to Paris and Germany. Quite a few of the India House members joined the new group in Berlin and added to its strength. In fact, the top rung of ex-patriate Indian revolutionaries like Hardayal, Barkatullah, Dr Dhiren Sarkar, NS Marathe, Dr JN Dasgupta, Chanji Kerasasp, Champak Raman Pillai and others have swelled its rank. The organisation has come to be known as the 'Berlin Committee' and its young, dedicated members are doing exceptional work with the aim of liberating India from British rule through revolutionary programmes. They have sighted a clear opportunity in the ongoing war in Europe, to bring Britain under considerable pressure.

The Committee shares a common ground with the German government—fighting the British. In Europe, Britain and Germany are posited against each other, leading the Allied and the Central powers respectively. Berlin Committee leaders have been able to secure promise of help from the German government in the form of money, men and ammunitions. Two of its members have been sent to Washington to meet Von Berstoff, the German ambassador there, to finalise despatch of ammunitions to coastal India.

The leaders of the Berlin Committee were in touch with Bagha Jatin in Bengal, Rashbehari Bose in northern India and Ghadar Party in the USA in a bid to enact an armed rebellion against British Raj in mainland India.

FIERCE GUN BATTLE AT BALASORE

Injured Jatindranath Dies In Hospital

September 10, 1915: In the wake of unearthing of the Zimmermann plan, the police had intensified its watch over revolutionary societies, in particular Jugantar and and its leader Bagha Jatin. Time was running out and the promised German arms and ammunitions were yet to reach the Indian shore. In such circumstances, Jatin's followers felt their leader's stay in Calcutta had become untenable and he could be arrested any time. Accordingly Jatin, along with some of his trusted followers, moved to Balasore, a coastal town in Orissa along the Bay of Bengal. They reckoned, by this strategy he could keep the police at bay and simultaneously be near the place where the ship carrying German arms was planned to arrive.

However, the police in Calcutta came to know of his movements from an insider of Jatin's party. A strong contingent of police, reinforced by the armed forces of the native ruler, arrived at Balasore and approached Jatin's den in a pincer movement. The revolutionary with indomitable courage was not upset. He fought against a numerically much larger and better-equipped force with few followers and old-fashioned mauser pistols. The uneven fight continued for at least seventy-five minutes in the form of a fierce battle. It came to an end only after Jatin and his followers ran out of ammunitions. Jatin was seriously injured, brought to Balasore hospital where he breathed his last.

Ghadarites Are Crushed But Their Spirit Lives On

No doubt, their violent activities like sabotage, looting and robbery of the treasury for about a year had alienated the Ghadarites from the wider society in Punjab. But as their goals and plans became public knowledge, and the government began savage retaliation, a wave of sympathy for these revolutionaries flooded the province. In hindsight, people are discussing their devotion and commitment. On the whole, the movement of the Ghadarites, even though collapsed, has created a deep impact on the Sikh psyche. Yet another consequence has been that it has drawn Sikhs nearer to the mainstream national struggle for independence. This has happened as during the course of their movement, Sikh activists and leaders came in close touch with leaders from other parts of India. Appeals with wider connotations were issued by Ghadar party through poems and articles in the Ghadar magazine. The fight against tyranny was presented as a duty of a true Sikh. In this struggle, memories of Sikh heroes and martyrs were invoked. To take up the sword to fight injustice as the last resort was presented as an injunction of Guru Govind Singh. The heritage of Sikh struggle was presented in terms of struggle for 'national liberation', and the 'Khalsa Pant' by the 'country'.

Though the government has come down very hard on the Ghadarites and it is trying to uproot the movement, they have been able to make a lasting impact upon the psyche of the local people and their influence may refuse to disappear in a hurry.

CONGRESS EXTENDS SUPPORT TO BRITISH WAR

1915: Opinions amongst 'politically aware' Indians on how India should respond to the War-induced situation vary. On the one hand, the revolutionaries, within India and overseas, have been trying to leverage the war situation as an opportunity to wrest freedom from the British. On the other hand, the Indian National Congress has been of the opinion that Indians should rise in support of the British Empire at their hours of crisis. Some of the Congress leaders are lauding the role of British men and women who, they feel, are sacrificing their lives so that scores of others can live freely.

Congress Expects Reward For Cooperation

1915: The political situation of Britain has dramatically changed in recent times. It has been engaged in a fierce encounter with Germany, ostensibly to save freedom of other nations under attack from Germany and its accomplices. Englishmen are fighting in many countries, apparently for the causes of democracy and freedom. In its crusade for the freedom of nations across the world, Britain has been generously supported by India with lives, money, supplies and equipment of every sort to conduct and wage war at different theatres—whether Mesopotamia, Egypt or Gallipoli. All the while, the Congress has stood like a rock by the government's side. In fact, the Congress responded with warm support for the overall Allied cause too. Gandhi, a returnee from South Africa, himself campaigned for recruitment of Indians in the British army. In the above backdrop, Indians are fervently hoping that the English will be the first people to realise and appreciate the great insistent desire in the hearts of Indians for self-government. Indians are sure of British reciprocity after the Allied victory—that the crown will grant them self-government as a quid pro quo.

Government Unhappy With Nationalist Urdu Press

1915: Maulana Abul Kalam Azad has established a press and has been publishing his journal *Al Hilal* since 1912. Being the first Urdu journal carrying nationalist contents, it has earned rapid popularity. In the process, Azad and his paper antagonized the Muslim leadership of the Aligarh camp, who have been the trustees of Sir Syed Ahmed's policies. The basic tenets of their policies have been 'loyalty' to the British Crown and aloofness from the freedom movement. Azad's paper has been questioning these doctrines and appealing for Hindu-Muslim unity in their common struggle against the colonial exploitations. The government is unhappy with Azad's philosophy, policies and publication. It has confiscated his press. This can be seen as a conscious attempt to keep the Muslims, as a community, at bay from the mainstream struggle for freedom.

Moderates Manage To Stonewall Tilak's Entry

December 27-29, 1915, Bombay: The annual Congress session is in progress here. It has lost two moderate stalwarts, viz. Gopal Krishna Gokhale and Pheroze Shah Mehta. Gokhale died on 19 February and Mehta in November. Their absence is being felt acutely. On the other hand, these losses have raised the possibility of Tilak's re-induction in the Congress. But still, there were some lingering objections from other moderates. This has made Tilak abstain from the annual session. During the course of the session, however, a consensus has emerged that the conflict need not be dragged on any longer and that the Congress constitution be amended suitably to allow Tilak to attend the next session, if he so desires.

PROVISIONAL GOVERNMENT OF INDIA IN EXILE SOLICITS INTERNATIONAL SUPPORT

1916, Kabul: Afghanistan has been a hotbed of political activities by pan-Islamists and Indian revolutionaries for past some time. For the former, the immediate cause of anti-Britishism is Britain's war against the Sultan of Turkey, who happens to be the Caliph of the Islamic world. In October last year, a group led by Maulana Ubaid Allah Sindhi and Mahmud al-Hasan arrived at Kabul to engineer rebellion against the British Indian government and to throw them out. Whereas Ubaid Allah has been trying to persuade the Amir against the British, Mahmud went to Hejaj (kingdom of Saudi Arabia) and managed to get a declaration of war against the British, signed by Galib Pasha, the Turkese military Governor of Hejaj. Mahmud has been planning a rebellion against British Indian government. These pan-Islamist groups here have been getting significant support from the Berlin Committee. As a result of their combined endeavour, plans have been set afoot to involve not only Germany but also the Caliph of Turkey and the Khadeve of Egypt who was dislodged by the British in 1914. Towards this end, efforts have been made to prod the tribes in the Indo-Iranian border, NWFP and Kashmir to attack British interests.

Last year, Indian groups operating here established a Provisional Government of India in Kabul with Raja Mahendra Pratap as its president, Maulana Barkatullah as the Prime Minister, Maulana Ubaid Allah Sindhi as the Minister for India and Champak Raman Pillai as the Foreign Minister. Mahendra Pratap, a prince of a native state in Aligarh district and educated in Anglo Mohammedan College Aligarh, had left India at young age with the mission of liberating India with outside help. Consumed by a burning desire to unshackle India, he traversed through several countries before reaching Afghanistan and has taken over the reins of the provisional government as its president. Provisional government has been trying to procure support from Russia, China and Japan in its fight against the British government.

There has been decisive influence of the Indian revolutionary activities on the local politics in Afghanistan. Siraj al Akhbar, the prime newspaper of the country, has been publishing a series of anti-British articles. Raja Mahendra Pratap himself has written many of these. Indian groups have been trying every means to make the Amir of Afghanistan to declare war against the British. But so far, they have not succeeded, the Amir is acting cautiously.

Abolition Of Indentured Indian Labour

Malaviya Supports Gandhi's Initiatives

March 1916, Delhi: Out of a number of struggles Gandhi undertook in South Africa, an important one was the abolition of indentured Indian labour. Under the system, Indian labourers who were lured to emigrate to South Africa were bound to work under the indenture for five long years, often under inhuman conditions.

The terms of the indenture pinned them down–they could not disengage themselves. Now in India, Gandhi wants to carry on with the movement and bring it to its conclusion—he wants Indian legislatures to try for its abolition. At his instance, Madan Mohan Malaviya moved a resolution in the Imperial Legislative Council for the abolition of the indenture system. Lord Hardinge, the Viceroy, has accepted the resolution and announced that he has obtained His Majesty's Government's promise for abolition of the system in due course of time.

Since no time frame was specified Gandhi has been meeting some leaders, writing in the media and trying to create public opinion to hasten abolition of the cruel, inhuman system.

Tilak Founds Home Rule League, People Enthusiastic

April 28, 1916, Poona: Not a man to be dissuaded by adversities and challenges, as the moderates in the Congress have been posing to him right since June 1914, Tilak has established Home Rule League here with a view to accelerate the achievement of 'swaraj'. The objectives of the League are to secure a representative government and management of own affairs by Indians themselves. Thus it wants the councils to be represented by the Indians.

Large numbers of Congressmen have been unhappy at the moderates' attitude towards Tilak since he returned from Mandalay. They have begun to look at the new organisation Tilak has founded, with keen expectations. Large numbers of people, including Congressmen are eagerly registering themselves as volunteers.

SPHERES OF INFLUENCE – HOME RULE LEAGUE

September 3, 1916, Madras: Annie Besant has set up Home Rule League here. The objective of the League is to secure self-governance for India through constitutional methods. The League, however, foresees continued relations with Great Britain—it envisages that as a free nation, India would remain within the Empire. The League acknowledges the role of the Congress, pledges support to and undertakes to work to strengthen it.

Whereas Tilak's Home Rule League has become active in the Central province, Karnataka, Bengal and parts of United Province, Besant's League may direct its activities to other parts of India. Together, they are hoping to gather and marshal the scattered nationalist forces in the struggle for self-government. Large numbers of Congressmen, disillusioned with their moribund organisation, are joining this new movement.

Home Rule Movement Takes People Away From Congress

1916, Bombay and Madras: Role of the moderate leaders controlling the Congress has not been inspiring public confidence—if they are to be relied upon, the issue of self-governance seems to be contingent on British charity. The Home Rule League Movement, on the contrary, has raised new hopes. Tilak's Home Rule League has attracted large number of people—volunteers are enrolling in tens of hundreds. In Madras, Annie Besant, is reaching her large audience through two journals, viz. *The New India* and *The Commonwealth*—both edited by her. It appears the Home Rule Movement is placing before India a concrete scheme of self-government and trying to pursue the goal actively.

ANTI-BRAHMIN PARTY TAKES BIRTH IN TAMIL LAND

November 26, 1916, Madras: Domination by Brahmin leaders of the Madras provincial chapter of the Indian National Congress has for long been resented by the non-Brahmin castes and things came to a head between the two groups on past several occasions. But the former, with the support of the central leaders, have managed to retain their grip upon the provincial Congress. To realise their political aspirations, the non-Brahmin leaders of Madras presidency formed the South Indian Liberal Federation (SILF) and they issued a manifesto on 20th of this month. Today, a conference was held and the SILF was reshaped into the Justice Party. The Justice Party will work to protect and advance the interests of non-Brahmin communities and has demanded reservations for non-Brahmin castes in the legislatures, local boards, education, and government services. To the protagonists of reservations, the institution of separate electorate granted to the Muslims has served as a precedent. To the list of warring groups in the country like Hindus and Muslims, Moderates and Extremists, now this Brahmin and non-Brahmin divide has become another uncomfortable addition. Political analysts say the newly-formed party is likely to pose grave challenge to the political hegemony of the Congress over the Tamil land in future.

Congress Session Vibrates With Life After Long Years

December 26-30, 1916, Lucknow: Congress session is held here. In pursuance to the decision adopted in the Bombay session last year, steps were taken to facilitate Tilak's re-entry. Both Tilak and Annie

Besant have landed at the session with large contingents of Home Rule League volunteers, converting the assembly to a huge gathering. After long years, the annual session of the Congress reminds people of its past glory.

Tilak is being given a hero's welcome. His presence has raised the prospects of a reunion between the moderates and extremists, whatever is left of it.

Mohandas Karamchand Gandhi, a leader who has become famous for his crusade in South Africa, is also attending. So far he has kept himself essentially confined to the South African Indian question. Significantly, the people of the country want a younger leader of vision and dynamism to emerge, one who can connect with them, deliver the Congress from its moribund state. Mehta is no more and Tilak is physically exhausted after six years of exile. They want Gandhi to come ahead and participate more actively in the Indian struggle for self-government.

Jawaharlal Nehru, son of Motilal Nehru, is attending the Congress session. His political indoctrination has been by his father but this is the first time he is attending a big event. He is much impressed by stalwarts like Tilak, Malaviya and others. Simultaneously, Gandhi has made deep appeal to his mind.

HOME RULE IS MY BIRTHRIGHT AND I'LL HAVE IT: TILAK

December, 1916, Lucknow: BG Tilak has been a star attraction in the ongoing Congress session. His patriotism, spirit, and long prison term in Mandalay for loving his countrymen have already made him legendary.

Since he began his 'Home Rule' movement in Bombay following his return from Mandalay, the movement has attracted large number of people—the delegates here are eager to hear him. Clad in simple dhoti and Marathi chappal, as Tilak rose to speak, the whole audience at the Lucknow session was hushed into pin-drop silence. And as he roared, 'Home Rule is my birthright and I will have it', the assembly greeted his utterances with thunderous applause.

Muslim League Tries To Come Closer To Congress

December 29-31, 1916, Lucknow: Although Jinnah continues to be an important leader of the Congress, he has also been a member of the Muslim League in recent years and the latter has obviously benefited from his perspectives and advice. The fact that last year the League had held its annual session in the same place as the Congress, and that the League continues to project some kind of closeness to the Congress are attributed by some analysts to Jinnah. They say the League, as a strategy, is trying to build up pressure on the British government at a time when the Governor General Chelmsford and Secretary of State Montagu have begun working on the next phase of self-government for Indians. Congress has already been the prime political party. Now the proximity of the two parties and presentation of some common, radical demands is likely to add to the importance of the League, at least as the second most important political party. The Muslims have been given the benefit of a separate electorate. Now, the Muslim League would like to protect that right and improve upon it, if possible. The visibility of the party in the centre stage of national politics as an equal of the Congress, or at least along side it, will add to its weight in negotiations with the government.

In keeping with such strategy, this is the second year in succession that the League is holding its annual session in the same place as the Congress. The Congress has conceded to separate electorate for the Muslims and also weightage in the minority provinces. In return, it has persuaded the League to raise a set of demands jointly on governance. The two have decided to tell the government that they expect these to form part of the forthcoming constitutional reforms. These include: unacceptability of any resolution, Bill or clause affecting a community if opposed by three-fourth of that community; enlargement of both central and provincial legislatures and increasing the proportion between the elected and nominated members to 4:1; ensuring incorporation of Indian members in both the central and provincial 'councils' elected by respectives legilslatures; providing that a vetoed resolution still becomes a law, if it is passed by the respective council following the veto. While the above conditions are some of the nitty gritties, the core demand of the Congress is self-government to India and lifting the country from its present state of despondency, to be an equal partner in the British Empire with the other self-governing nations. The League has conceded to this core concern of its partner and agreed to lend it its voice. The speeches made at both the venues are reported to be identical in tenor and theme and these have bearings on the forthcoming reform measures that are being worked upon presently. Jinnah has urged the Muslims to galvanise themselves for political action, the need for which, Jinnah reckons, has already arisen.

The government is, predictably, not quite comfortable at this unexpected bonhomie between the Congress and the Muslim League.

Congress-Muslim League Bonhomie
Euphoria Engulfs Indian Politicians

December 26-30, 1916, Lucknow: Congress has been holding its annual session here. It is marked by exuberance and optimism. The prospect of an Allies' victory in the ongoing global war has kindled hope among Congress leaders of British generosity in the matter of granting Indians self-governance in the next round of reforms, which could even occur earlier, coinciding with the end of the war. After all, the British, with the willing cooperation of the Congress, has drawn large resources from India, in men and material, to fight the central powers led by Germany at different parts of the globe. No doubt Jinnah had called India's service and sacrifice as 'willing service of the people of India' and he had also clarified that India's loyalty to the Empire had set no price on itself. But the fact is that the Indian people have enormous expectations of a commensurate reciprocation. Taking into account the turn of the War in favour of the Allies, they hope soon the British government will get the opportunity to return the favour.

Yet another factor for keeping the Congress leaders in an expansive mood is that some kind of rapport was struck with the Muslim League last year, while both the parties held their annual session in Bombay, a unique precedent that is being repeated this year. Despite many efforts, Congress has not so far been able to enlist Muslim members on a large-scale, owing to consistent opposition first by the Aligarh camp, a trend accentuated by the Muslim League later on. The newly-found rapport with the League is giving it an artificial satisfaction of winning the Muslim confidence.

In the apparent bonhomie in which the Congress seems to be exuberant and the Muslim League discreet, the two parties have agreed to a formula that guarantees certain percentage of representation for the Muslims on both councils—central and provincial. Jinnah, now a common leader in both Congress and Muslim League, has proposed this formula and the Congress has accepted it with enthusiasm. Except for a few like Pandit Madan Mohan Malaviya and CY Chintamani who are against communal representation and communal voting, most other Congress leaders, oblivious of the long-term implications of the separatist politics, are seemingly euphoric about such quick-fix solutions. Sarojini Naidu has called Jinnah the ambassador of Hindu-Muslim unity. And AC Mazumdar, the Congress president, has gone to the extent of declaring that the Hindu-Muslim question has been settled. With self-government round the corner and the communal issue tackled so easily, the time is apt for celebrations! Political analysts have reservations about the overflowing enthusiasm displayed by some top-ranked Congress leaders.

CONGRESS ENDORSES GUARANTEED REPRESENTATIONS

All-India Hindu Sabha Deeply Upset

1916, Lucknow: In its annual session this year, the Congress has accepted Jinnah's formula, which prescribes certain guaranteed percentage of Muslim legislators in every council—whether provincial or central. Hindu Sabha is feeling upset at this Congress gesture. It feels that a guaranteed percentage of legislative posts for any community is against basic principles of democracy, whether it is by way of agreeing on a certain quota or through separate electorate. The Sabha feels this is an undesirable attempt and against the overall interest of the country. But the Congress is dismissive of any such criticism and on the contrary, feels Hindu Sabha has a communal perspective on the issue.

Some political observers see merit in the Hindu Sabha's stand. They contend that the British had introduced the system of separate electorate to drive a wedge between two communities, and so far carried a sense of guilt. It is so because, the British themselves claimed the credit for creating a new Indian nation comprising of many different communities and, therefore, there was no need to create a division in that nation by this move. However, now the Indian National Congress itself has accepted the British principle by passing a resolution according certain guaranteed quota in the councils to the Muslims. These observers argue that by this initiative the Congress has committed a grave error. From now on, the Muslim League would be emboldened to ask for special political rights for Muslims in future negotiations without any qualm.

Congress-League Proximity Irritates Government

December, 1916, Delhi: British Indian Government has been keen to divide Hindus and Muslims to keep native political movements under check. Since 1906, it has been following a studied policy to insulate the Muslim community by granting it a separate electorate. It has been working well till sometime ago. It is not amused at the growing closeness of the Congress and Muslim League in recent times—especially with the outcome of the annual session of the Congress in Lucknow. The government is concerned that the tool of separate electorates could lose efficacy as Congress is seeking to guarantee certain percentage of Muslim representation in the councils. Political observers say, such apprehensions on the part of the government may not augur well for the reforms measures that have been promised to the Indians—its fresh offerings may be much restricted than what Indians expect. The last thing the government would like to face is a combined demand for accelerated self-government by both Hindus and Muslims.

ANNIE BESANT IS INTERNED

June 1917, Ootcamond: In the eyes of the government, Anne Besant played a significant role in bringing together the moderates and the extremists in Lucknow session last year. It has been displeased about such initiatives and is mulling appropriate actions. The government also suspects her linkages with revolutionaries in Bengal. She has now been interned in this hill station to prevent her from engaging in further activities of similar nature. The government action is being decried all around as high-handed and unwarranted. It has also been bringing the moderates and the extremists closer than ever before. There is growing clamour for her release.

INDENTURED LABOUR IN SOUTH AFRICA ABOLISHED

Gandhi's Struggle Bears Fruit

July 1917, Delhi: Although Malaviya had moved a resolution on this subject as early as March 1916 and the then Viceroy Hardinge accepted it, the government kept dillydallying. In February this year, Malaviya asked for leave to introduce a Bill for the immediate abolition of the system but Lord Chelmsford, the present Viceroy, refused permission. This made Gandhi tour various places like Karachi, Calcutta etc. and conduct meetings as a preparation to begin an all-India agitation on the issue. His campaign attracted enthusiasm everywhere. Eventually, the government has now announced the abolition of the 'indenture'. Gandhi had been working to stop this system of semi-slavery right from 1894. This development has given him a lot of satisfaction and has also enhanced his stature as a leader.

British Government Not To Defraud India With Reforms

November 10, 1917, New Delhi: Edwin Montagu, Secretary of State for India, is in India. He would be in the country for six months—tour places, interact with people and organisations and collect inputs for listing the next round of reforms facilitating increased measures of self-governance. His visit is in accordance with the decision of the British war cabinet taken in August this year, which wanted him to undertake such an exercise. Predictably, his present visit is raising lots of public expectations.

Montagu is expected to work out with Chelmsford, the Viceroy, to achieve the British government's professed objectives. He feels concrete steps are required to be taken to save the credibility of the British government in India. He has observed:

'If the results of our deliberations are either something which India will not accept, or a niggling, miserly, grudging safeguard, fiddling with the existing order of things, we shall have defrauded and defrauded irreparably—for they will never believe us again—a vast continent whose history is our glory, and whose hopes and aspirations, fears and tribulations it is pathetic to see.'[11]

All Is Not Well In Hindu Society

November 11, 1917, Bombay: It seems that the subterranean discontent of the depressed classes in the Hindu society over centuries has now begun to surface. Today, about 2,500 people belonging to the depressed classes, have held a conference here under the chairmanship of Justice NG Chandavarkar. The conference has brought to light discriminations against the people of the depressed classes by the caste Hindus in the matter of admission to public school, access to hospital, court of justice and public offices and even such fundamental things like access to public wells. The conference has urged Hindu society to take steps to remove various disabilities imposed by religion and custom on the depressed classes for centuries. It has passed six resolutions. The fourth one is politically significant. It prays that the British government protect the interests of the depressed classes by guaranteeing them the 'right to elect their own representatives to the councils in proportion to their numbers'.

The holding of a conference of this nature and the nature of the deliberations clearly show that the slumber of the people in the outermost fringes of the caste-ridden Hindu society is at last breaking and it is only appropriate that the Congress takes note and initiates action. In recent times, the Congress has begun to forge alliance with the Muslim League, but the question remains if the Hindu society itself is united? This conference has pointed out the deep fissures within the Hindus.

Interestingly, even though Congress has not so far done anything concrete on this issue, Montagu and Chelmsford had earlier, in course of their countrywide tour, listened to the voices of the depressed classes while collecting feedback from various cross-sections of people for incorporation in the forthcoming political reforms for India. At that time, they received at least ten applications from the people of the depressed classes, demanding representations in the legislative bodies. Critics say Congress must aggressively address this issue, unless it wants to be overtaken by the British government.

RED FLAG FLUTTERS IN RUSSIA

Kindles Hopes Of Emancipation In India

November 1917, Moscow: Russia has been under great turmoil over the last several years. In March this year, the Tsar had declared dissolution of the Duma but its members refused to oblige. The Tsar himself abdicated. Thereafter, a semblance of stability was perceived after Kerensky, a leader of the Socialist Revolutionary Party, formed a provisional government. However, his government, which wanted to pursue with Russia's participation in the ongoing war, proved unpopular and had to go. Recently, an all-Russia Soviet Congress met in which a clear majority of 390 out of a total strength of 676 were Bolshevik delegates, led by Vladimir Lenin. Following that meet, the Bolsheviks have formed a temporary government of 'workers' and peasants' in the country. They have also passed a resolution for 'peace', and 'dispossession of landowners'. They declared that their temporary government would continue to function till the decision arrived at by a democratic constituent assembly.

Russia has been an essentially backward and agriculture-based country, where peasants have been dipped in poverty and brutally exploited by the landowners. The condition of the workers of factories and the soldiers, recruited mostly from the poor peasantry, are equally pathetic. The installation of the Bolshevik government is giving a new hope to the peasants and workers against the landed gentry and other vested interests. This is the first time that a government has assumed office on the basis of Marxist ideology. The development in Russia is being keenly watched by Britain and other imperial countries with concern. The royalties in various European countries are interconnected, many of them through blood relations. They have been bitter about the expulsion of the Tsar by the communists.

To the vast millions of subjugated Indians, the red flag in

Moscow has kindled feeble hopes of removing their own shackles. Geographically, Russia is nearer to India than Britain and a government of the proletariats is being perceived to be friendly to the people of a colonised country and expected to help in their struggle for freedom.

Throw Out Plunderers Of Your Land
Bolsheviks Urge Indians

November 24, 1917, Moscow: Russia's Bolshevik government has begun to evince interest in the colonised countries sooner than anticipated. The council of the peoples' commissars have exhorted the people of India and the Middle East to throw away the yoke of the powers that have been plundering their lands for a hundred years. Imperial Britain obviously had cosy relationship with the Tsarist Russia. In the post-revolution era, she is finding a potential enemy in the Bolshevik government, which can create serious problems in her Indian Empire by propagating communist ideology.

Victory Of Moral Force Over Brute Power
Gandhi Emerges As A Towering Leader

November 29, 1917, Champaran: Till a year ago, Gandhi was much talked about and admired on account of his success in South Africa but his capability remained to be tested in Indian conditions. Now he has emerged before the country at the head of a successful and popular socio-politico-economic movement at Champaran. This is the first of its kind to be achieved by any political leader in India. He locked horns with the powerful British regime, using popular struggle and non-violent means and emerged victorious. This victory may be over a small battle but it is symbolic and, therefore, being viewed as of much significance.

Gandhi was invited to Champaran, a small quiet locale in Bihar inhabited by docile, illiterate, peace-loving, simple farmers steeped in abject poverty, ignorance and diseases, to deliver them from the savage exploitation by local landlords and the European indigo planters. Victims of several kinds of persecution by the rich and the powerful men, the helpless tenant farmers, in this land full of mango grove, were bound by a mindless '*tinkathia law*' compelling a farmer to plant indigo in three out of every twenty parts of his land for his landlord, without or with very measly compensation. Their miseries were much more exacerbated since 1914, when a famine visited the land and in that aggravated condition, the government raised taxes on the impoverished farmers.

Invited by Raj Kumar Shukla, a public-service minded local peasant leader, Gandhi had arrived at Champaran in April this year, en route Patna, Muzaffarpur and Motihari. Starting at Patna and till he reached this village, he had talked to a number of influential people and leaders on this issue. He was surprised that barring one or two like Rajendra Prasad, a Congress leader of repute, most others betrayed colossal apathy and indifference to the miseries of their fellow countrymen.

Gandhi put to experiment, his ashram experience and method of peoples' movement in this case. He set up an ashram at Champaran and began an extensive programme of welfare work. He undertook extensive cleaning campaign, established schools and hospitals. As the activities unfolded, he called some of his ashramites from Sabarmati to Champaran to carry ahead the struggle. Securing the confidence of the villagers through a series of such missionary activities, he also campaigned for removal of purdah amongst women.

As public awareness grew, Gandhi involved the simple villagers in launching a Satyagraha against the tyranny by the landlords, indigo planters and government. His movement began to be spoken about nationally. Young nationalist leaders like Jawaharlal, Rajendra Prasad, Sri Krishna Sinha and a few others were attracted to him and received excellent grooming on Satyagraha.

At the peak of the movement, the British government arrested Gandhi on the charge of creating unrest amongst people. However, hundreds of villagers, who felt themselves more empowered now, vociferously protested—they thronged the jails, police stations and courts wherever Gandhi was taken. So overwhelming was the public reaction that the court had to release him, albeit unwillingly. In the face of the Satyagraha, the government also had to cancel the hike in taxes till the famine ended and agreed to give more compensation and control to the farmers. In August this year, the Champaran Committee appointed by the government agreed for abolition of 'tinkathia'. The detailed negotiations continued even thereafter. Today, the Champaran Bill has been introduced in the Council.

Gandhi has emerged a much more confident man. He has used his novel method of mass struggle, developed in South Africa, for the first time in India and achieved sterling success. Indians, on their part, are seeing the unmistakable inklings of a true mass leader in him.

Is Besant Expecting Too Much From Britain?

December 26-29, 1917, Calcutta: The annual session of the Congress is held here. Annie Besant presides. After interning her for about three months, the government had to yield to popular demands and release her in September. Besides her hard work for self-government for Indians and untiring efforts to establish unity between Congress' factions, her recent internment has made her popularity soar and she has almost become a cult figure.

According to some extremist delegates, Besant has rather too high expectations from the forthcoming reforms, almost like the moderates. This is possibly due to the positive statements and utterances of Montagu.

Rowlatt To Inquire Into Political Disorders

December 1917: If Montagu's visit has been raising expectations about radical reforms, the news of the appointment of Sir Sydney A T Rowlatt, to lead a committee of enquiry regarding political disorders in India, has been generating some doubts about British intention in the informed circles. According to political experts, the British government, despite its war success thus far, has been wary about the 'Zimmerman Plan', Berlin committee activities, pan-Islamists' movement in Afghanistan, presence of a provisional Indian government in that country and so on. They suspect linkages between such overseas networks and Indian revolutionaries. Rowlatt has been asked to make a thorough inquiry and suggest if any legislative initiatives are necessary to address the extant situation.

Britain Won't Be Vindictive Towards Turkey: Lloyd George

January 5, 1918, London: British Prime Minister Lloyd George has issued a statement that appears to be aimed at assuaging the fear amongst some sections of the Indian Muslims about the future ofTurkey and its Sultan who holds the position of the Caliph. Turkey had joined the great war against the allies but has not only been soundly defeated but also been exposed to the risk of dismemberment, in the process losing large part of its territories, especially in Asia Minor and Thrace. Lloyd George has said that Britain would not adopt a vindictive policy towards Turkey.

Owners And Workers Settle Disputes
Gandhi's Fast Bears Fruit, Mill Strike Ends

March 18, 1918, Ahmedabad: Gandhi came back from Champaran to guide the mill-workers in Ahmedabad who had resorted to strike in support of some longstanding demands. Trusted by both the mill owners and workers, he had a delicate task on hand. While guiding workers, he laid down the conditions for a successful strike thus: (a) never resort to violence (b) never to molest blacklegs; (c) never to depend on alms; (d) remain firm, no matter how long the strike continues and to earn bread during this period by any other honest labour.

Here he met Vallabhbhai Patel, a gutsy Congress leader. Gandhi found in the latter a trusted supporter cum follower. Every day, the workers paraded the streets of the city peacefully, and at the end of the day they reviewed the day's developments under the guidance of their leaders. After two weeks, there were signs of fatigue and wavering. The Strike began to weaken and the attitude to the blacklegs became increasingly hostile. Gandhi then resorted to a hunger strike, to discipline the striking workers and vowed not to touch food unless the workers rallied and continued the strike till a settlement was reached or till they left the mills altogether. The fast lasted for three days and yielded result. The mill owners and workers have come to agreement. Mill owners have distributed sweets to workers as both reconciled.

World Will Be Watching What Happens Tomorrow Viceroy Chelmsford To Gandhi

April 27, 1918, New Delhi: The British government has been facing the heat of stepped up German aggression in Europe. This has made Chelmsford, the Viceroy, explore the possibility of obtaining increased support from Indians. Towards that end he convened a war conference on the morrow. Amongst Indian leaders attending, Gandhi is distinguished both by his stature and commitment. He has agreed to make a personal appeal to Indians for increased recruitment in the army. The Viceroy sent him a message today that betrays his tension. The whole world- especially all in England—will be watching with anxiousness what happens tomorrow...'[12]

India Keenly Awaits A Liberal Dose Of Self-governance

Peace is gradually returning to countries worldwide following the cessation of war hostilities. However, the war has transformed the mindset of a large number of Indians in certain ways. The capitalists, who had made obscene profit during the war time, have turned greedier. The large Indian middle class has developed more intense yearnings for self-government. Indian soldiers who had fought for the British Empire at various war theatres across the world, grew conscious of the racial discriminations within the British Indian army. They have carried back home, loads of discontent. It is particularly manifest in soldiers coming from the peasantry, who were forcibly recruited. They suffered ordeals and discovered how they were ill-treated vis-à-vis British soldiers. These few years of exposure have added considerably to their mental maturity. On the whole, Indians, are expecting more from the British government today, than what they did before the war began.

States' People's Group Emerge In Indian India

1918, Baroda: Even though in existence since 1885, the Indian National Congress has been consciously keeping itself away from grievances and problems of the people of the princely states. It has a cosy relationship with the Indian princes. As a result, even though rulers in many states are more autocratic and oppressive than the British government and the rights of people to resort to political activities have remained severely restricted, the Congress has mostly chosen to remain aloof.

As a matter of fact, there have been undercurrents of grievances and unhappiness in many of these princely states. As the Congress has not shown willingness to mentor the political activities in them, people themselves began working in that direction. Such efforts have now culminated in the formation of the first states' people's group in the princely state here. The people have organised themselves under the banner of the Baroda People's Conference.

SOCIALIST REVOLUTION MUST THROUGHOUT THE WORLD: LENIN

1918, Moscow: The Bolshevik government, led by Lenin, has consolidated its position. It has completely suppressed the other two wings, viz., the Mensheviks and the Socialist Revolutionaries in the Russian Socialist Democratic Labour Party. The leaders of these two adversary parties have been imprisoned and their delegates expelled from the Soviets. As such, the Communist Party stands as the only legal party in Russia.

Lenin, however, is not complacent. He recognises the threats to his nebulous communist government from the imperialist countries and their allies all around. He has expressed his conviction that socialist revolution would be successful if it occurs throughout the world. It is clear that communist Russia under Lenin will play a proactive role towards such a possibility in its own interest. These are disturbing news for the imperialist countries. Britain is clearly not amused.

DEPRESSED CLASSES DEMAND SEPARATE ELECTORATE

1918, Bombay: Since November 11 last year, when a large conference of the depressed classes was organised by the Depressed Classes Mission in Bombay, a few more conferences were held in quick succession, displaying increased awareness and aspirations of these sections of socially and politically disadvantaged people. After a week of that event, Bapu Namdeo Bagade chaired a meeting of 2,000 delegates and the conference raised the demand for representations of the depressed classes according to their numbers in the total population. Earlier this year, the Depressed Classes Mission held its second conference which was chaired by Gaekwad of Baroda. Tilak also attended, lending it additional political importance. Yet another conference of the depressed classes was held here under the leadership of Subhedar Ganpatrao Govind Rokde, a leader belonging to the Mahar community. This conference raised a new demand—it wanted not only representations but also separate electorate for the depressed classes in the legislative bodies in the line of the Muslims.

Considering the chain of events over the last one year, it is clear that the political demands of the depressed classes have begun to erupt like a long-sleeping volcano waking up suddenly. It is also evident that the Congress has not kept itself in alignment with the political aspirations of this segment of the Indian people. Its top leadership has possibly been taking the depressed classes of Hindus for granted while vying to enlist the support of the Muslims.

Congress' efforts on this issue has rather been tokenist and superficial. It appointed a sub-committee to attend to this issue and from time to time it issued appeals to the Hindu religious heads to help reform Hinduism. Predictably, precious little has been accomplished so far. The present development reminds the Congress that the issue is complex and the depressed class Hindus are bound to explore more and more avenues to assert their social and political rights.

Gandhi – Messiah For The Oppressed Farmers Of Kheda

June 29, 1918, Kheda: Kheda is Gandhi's next destination after Ahmedabad. He came to this famine-struck district of Gujarat, to the rescue of its distressed peasantry. While a severe famine has ravaged its agrarian economy, the insensitive government of the Bombay presidency hiked the taxes on the farmers by a whopping twenty-three per cent. The disconsolate natives tried to persuade the government by numerous prayers and petitions sent through various civil bodies to give them relief. But when all their cravings fell on deaf ears, the people approached Vallabhbhai Patel and Gandhi to deliver them from the impending ruin.

Under Gandhi's overall leadership, Vallabhbhai Patel organised a well-knit civil disobedience movement on non-violent lines. Gandhi stressed that the people must be freed of fear of the government officials and at the same time they should be civil in their heart and actions. As a part of this Satyagraha campaign that began on March 22 this year, the villagers refrained from paying taxes altogether in spite of threat, arrests and confiscation of properties. The government for some time issued threats, adopted coercive measures and in some cases resorted to such extreme steps like confiscating property and putting these to auctions. But the movement was so total that practically no one came forward to bid for these properties. All through the movement, Patel ensured exemplary discipline and unity.

In this confrontation between the government and the *Satyagrahis*, the government blinked first. It relented and suspended tax for the year in question and also the next year, besides declaring a cut in the increased rate. It also promised to restore the confiscated properties.

After Champaran and Ahmedabad, Gandhi's novel methods of movements against oppressive forces have once again proved a remarkable success. The rest of India is watching the efficacy of Satyagraha as a political weapon with keenness and expectations.

Ottomans Are Driven Out Of Damascus

Muslim Sympathies For The Vanquished Caliphate

October 1, 1918, Damascus, Syria: The Ottoman Empire of Turkey has been a prime sufferer of the World War. The ever-growing might of the Ottoman Empire, seeking deep penetration into Russian land, met with strong resistance from the Russians in 1444. Since then, its forces were gradually pushed back from the Russian land. The recent World War proved the last straw on the camel's back. The war with the British forces precipitated their discomfiture and disintegration. Ottoman military might has been comprehensively decimated and even its Asian possessions have begun to wither. Today, British major TE Lawrence, accompanied by the charismatic Emir Faisal, made a victorious entry into Damascus, a very important city of the Arab world, by driving out the Ottoman force. The liberation of the city from Ottoman rule is being celebrated enthusiastically and the Emir is likely to be crowned as the king of Syria. This development has come as a great setback for the Ottoman Empire—the seat of the Caliph of the Islamic world. In a departure from an earlier statement by the British Prime Minister against plans for dismemberment of Turkey, now it seems the British government is preparing plans for division of the Ottoman Empire once complete victory is achieved.

Although, Syria, part of the Islamic world, is rejoicing the emancipation, many Indian Muslims are deeply concerned over these developments involving Turkey, which houses the institution of the Caliphate. They are viewing the development as a direct affront to their religious head.

Berlin Committee Undergoes A Metamorphosis

November 1918, Berlin: World War has come to an end. With the victory of the Allies over the Central powers, the fate of the Berlin Committee, which later on came to be called as Indian Independence Committee, has also been sealed. Evidently, Germany, the vanquished side, is no longer in a position to lend support to Britain's rebellious subjects in her land.

In the meanwhile, there has been a metamorphosis of the Committee. Since the occurrence of the Russian revolution, the interactions between its members with the Bolshevik leaders have been on the increase. On number of occasions, the members of the Berlin Committee were invited to Russia and Bolshevik leaders from Moscow visited them in Berlin. Through such exchange visits and sustained interactions, Russian leaders have been encouraging the Berlin Committee members to form a communist committee. This has borne fruit. The cream of the committee including VN Chattopadhyay, Bhupendranath Datta, K Panduranga and a few others responded to the communist persuasion and became involved in this exercise. A silent revolution has indeed occurred and the committee has undergone a near-complete communist transformation. It is likely that many of them will move over to Moscow, the Mecca of international communist movement. If at all, now on, they may try to engineer revolution in India based on communist ideology from Russia. So it seems.

PROVISIONAL GOVERNMENT OF INDIA WOUND UP

1918, Kabul: The Provisional Government of India in Afghanistan tried hard to secure the support of other countries against British government, but without much success. Immediately after the revolution in Russia in February last year, it began to correspond with the new Russian government. This year, Mahendra Pratap met key Russian leader Trotsky in Petrograd, followed by another meeting with Kaiser in Berlin. But he could achieve precious little. On the other hand, the Amir of Afghanistan came under pressure from Britain to act tough against anti-British activities in his land. The Amir, in awe of the victorious Britain, has fallen in line and withdrawn all cooperation to the provisional government. This has sounded the death knell for the provisional government headed by Mahendra Pratap. It is closing down.

THREE

Raj Under Siege

1919 - 1931

RAJ UNDER SIEGE

COMMUNIST INTERNATIONAL IS FOUNDED

March 4, 1919, Moscow: First communist government in the world under Lenin has taken an important step to propagate socialism, facilitate revolutions in other countries and emancipate the proletariat masses across the world from the oppression of the capitalists. It has invited delegates from communist parties and left-wing socialist groups of various countries to constitute an appropriate forum for this purpose. Fifty-two delegates have turned up from various parts of the world and established the Communist International. Each delegate has presented a report on the state of affairs in his country in terms of preparedness for revolution. This was followed by discussion on the prospective role of the Communist International.

Though there was no paper on the Indian situation in this inaugural session of the Comintern, it may be recalled that in the spring of 1918, the Bolshevik government had released a 'blue book' that examined in depth the relations between Tsarist Russia and India, drawing inputs from secret documents from the archives of the erstwhile Russian Foreign Affairs ministry. In that book, its editor KM Troyanovsky, had scathingly indicted the British regime for the successive famines in India.

It looks probable that the Indian situation will sooner than later, attract the attention of the international communist movement. Its abundant natural resources and huge population, much-exploited by a ruthless colonial regime cannot escape the eyes of the Comintern for long.

LEGISLATIVE COUNCIL PASSES ROWLATT ACT

Britain's Gift To India For Wartime Cooperation?

March 18, 1919, New Delhi: With British victory in the World War, in which the Indians had lent extraordinary help and support, they had been expecting far greater civil rights, liberties and self-governance, in lieu. But like a bolt from the blue, the first legislation passed by British India's Imperial Legislative Council, titled the Rowlatt Act, has extended the martial law in India into the peacetime. People are stunned, infuriated and calling this a 'Black Act'.

This legislative initiative has shown that the British government is back to its old mindset. After the Allied victory, Britain appears to have reverted to its pre-war cold imperial disdain for Indian civil and political demands. According to some political observers, these seemingly inexplicable harsh measures could be due to the series of revolutionary activities in recent years undertaken by the pan-Islamist groups, the Berlin Committee, and local revolutionaries culminating into the Zimmerman plan. Even though the British government has been able to largely suppress all of these, the possibilities of more such activities cannot be ruled out altogether in times to come. It is aware that Indian communists have built up a base in Russia and the pan-Islamist groups are continuing their endeavour to involve Afghanistan against the British Indian government. They are possibly looking at the need for a strong legislation to tackle such activities against the Empire and hence the Rowlatt Act.

The mainstream politicians and bulk of Indians who gave British Raj full-throated cooperation during the War feel that, taking revenge on the whole nation, for the acts of a section is disproportionate and unwarranted. To young Congress leaders like Jawaharlal Nehru, these first fruits of the post-war British policy have come as a rude shock. They are certain that these proposals for special laws will let loose much more repression.

India and Indians helped the British government in the just-concluded World War. Ironically, the beneficiary of their goodwill and sacrifice, in return, is now seeking to severely curtail their civil liberty and freedom. Towards this end, it has vested atrocious powers on the police to arrest and keep people they suspect in prison without trial. People are referring to this Draconian Act as *'na vakil, na appeal, na dalil'*.

Congress Gropes For Response, Looks Up To Gandhi

March, 1919, Bombay: People of India are shocked at British ingratitude and harshness. A perception is dawning that the government treats prayers and petitions as signs of weaknesses. The time has arrived to confront and demand. There is all-round search for a leader who can effectively channelise the discontent against the Rowlatt Act and challenge the colonial rulers. At this juncture, the Congress is veering round to Gandhi, a leader who has not only achieved success in fighting for the rights of Indians in South Africa but also led popular movements in Champaran and Kheda against the British Indian government successfully. He seems to be the man of the hour. Within the Congress, a silent shift is occurring in favour of mass-based leaders, away from the Anglophile ones who had so far been calling the shots.

So intense is the Indian dissatisfaction that even many moderates are joining the agitation against the government. Gandhi is being irreversibly inducted into the mainstream by the turn of events. Congress and the public at large feel he has the capacity to lead the injured nation in this hour of distress and crisis. Gandhi is mulling his first countrywide agitation. As strategy, he has set up Satyagraha Sabhas, which have pledged to disobey the Rowlatt Act. The members of the Sabha are to court jail openly and deliberately. The country is looking expectantly at Gandhi, for his next plan of action.

Gandhi Meets Rajagopalachari An Instant Rapport Is Struck

March 18-31, 1919, Madras: Gandhi has been organising protest movement against the Rowlatt Act. He is known for his meticulous planning and organising skills. He has already conferred with leaders like Vallabhbhai Patel, and addressed meetings attended by Sarojini Naidu, Horniman, Shankerlal Banker, Anushuyabai and others. Based on his experience in South Africa, Gandhi has recently founded Satyagraha Sabhas with headquarters in Bombay. With a view to mobilise public opinion against the Act, Gandhi is also touring the country. In Madras he has met CR Rajagopalachari for the first time. Impressed by the shy, gentle, hospitable and enlightened personality of Rajagopalachari, a rapport has quickly developed between the two leaders. They have reportedly discussed ways and means to oppose the Rowlatt Act, including the option to resort to civil disobedience. Gandhi had earlier written a courteous appeal to the Viceroy, together with a warning in connection with the Rowlatt Act, but the Viceroy did not care to respond. In clear disregard of his entreaties, the Bill was passed in the Imperial Legislative Council and converted to a statute on 18th of this month.

Based on his interactions with several leaders including Rajagopalachari, Gandhi decided to observe a countrywide general *'hartal'* on 30th March, in the form of Satyagraha when people across India would fast and suspend all their business to mourn the passing of the Rowlatt Act. Later on, the date of the 'hartal' was deferred by a week, now to be held on 6th April in order to ensure that appropriate communications can reach the organisers across the country well in time.

SHRADDHANAND FACES BAYONETS BARE-CHESTED

The Story Spreads Like Wild Fire

March 30, 1919, Delhi: In Delhi, Swami Shraddhanand and Hakim Ajmal Khan were to take the lead role in making a success of the 'hartal' called to protest against the Rowlatt Act. Delhi observed the hartal on 30th March itself as the telegram deferring the date reached the organisers late. Since morning the streets were desolate and transports did not ply—people were observing the hartal peacefully. But in the noon, the police opened fire at unarmed people who had asked some shop owners near the railway station not to open shutters. At least fourteen innocent people were reportedly killed in the shootout and the situation thereafter turned grave. Shraddhanand reached the spot, pacified the mob and diverted them to a venue where he addressed them, highlighting the need to remain peaceful despite provocations—one of the fundamental conditions of Satyagraha. After the meeting, as he was leading the homebound Satyagrahis through the clock tower, Gurkha soldiers stationed there opened unprovoked fire at the people. As the Swami protested against this atrocity, they threatened to pierce him down with bullets. At this, the *Sannyasi*, with his stout physique, stood bare chested, challenging the soldiers. The situation was saved when a British officer reached the spot and ordered the Gurkhas to retreat. This story spread like wild fire across the whole country. The Swami's courage and defiance of brute force have begun to do rounds like folklore, they are being told and retold.

Civil Disobedience Spreads Far And Wide

April 1919: People of India are responding to the call for civil disobedience by Gandhi. Huge protests have been reported from Bombay, Ahmedabad and Punjab resulting in large-scale disturbances and consequent police atrocities on people. In Bombay, on the morning of the 6th of April, thousands of people had flocked to Chowpatti for a bath in the sea after which they moved in a procession to Thakurdvar. Volunteers sold two books written by Gandhi—*Hind Swaraj* and *Sarvodaya*, both proscribed by the government—and people bought these with great enthusiasm, many paying much more than the printed price. The proceeds are to be used for furthering the civil disobedience movement. Gandhi has now been invited to Delhi and Punjab by local leaders and people. In both these places, people have been responding to the call for civil disobedience with remarkable enthusiasm. Expectedly, the government is vexed and it is bent upon not allowing Gandhi a free entry into these places in the northern part of the country.

Gandhi Emerges A Towering Political Leader

Till last year, Gandhi was seen essentially as an apolitical person, a social reformer and a humanitarian. Even the government publication, India 1919 wrote that Gandhi is generally considered a Tolstoyan of high ideals and complete selflessness. On account of his crusade on behalf of Indians in South Africa, he has been commanding among his countrymen all the traditional reverences that are bestowed upon a religious leader of acknowledged asceticism in the East. However, after he took over the leadership of the mass movement against Rowlatt, his image has gone through a complete makeover. Following the launch of the Rowlatt Satyagraha, he has leapt into fame and prominence all over India as a political leader.

Amritsar In The Throes Of Intense Violence, Dyer Conducts Flag Marches

April 12, 1919, Amritsar: Troubles have been brewing in the city since the day before when people, angered at the detention of two Congress leaders, Dr Saifuddin Kitchlew and Dr Satyapal, staged angry protests at the European cantonment. British troops, incensed by this audacity, retaliated by opening fire that resulted in the death reportedly of thirty agitators. Thereafter, the mob went berserk, destroying property. Reportedly, a few civilians and an off-duty British soldier also fell victim to mob fury.

Yesterday, Brigadier General Reginald EH Dyer arrived in the city with 1,100 troops. Today, he conducted flag marches at several places in the city and thereby served a stern warning to the people against any kind of law-breaking.

GOVT SAVAGERY AT JALLIANWALABAGH

Troops Open Fire, Hundreds Massacred

April 13, 1919, Amritsar: This morning the government had imposed prohibition on unlawful assemblies in the city. The people, already victim of government 'excesses and violence', assembled in thousands in Jallianwalabagh an enclosed park in the city late afternoon, to protest against the latter's highhandedness. British atrocities reached a peak when Brigadier General Dyer, without giving any warning to the gathering, ordered his troops to open fire on these unarmed protesters, gathered in the walled space.

Dyer was standing on a raised platform and he had a clear view that the space was shut on all sides by houses several storeys high. Only on one side, for about a hundred feet or so, there was no house but a low wall of about 5 ft height. Upon his order, when the soldiers began to mow down the unarmed protesters, the hapless people rushed to that wall and tried to scale it. The fire was then directed toward the wall to prevent people from crossing over it. When all was over, the biggest heaps of dead and wounded lay on either side of the wall.

Such savage massacre by British forces in India occurred for the first time since the brutal suppression of the Sepoy Mutiny in 1858. According to reports received, about 379 people died in the shootout and 1,200 persons suffered injuries, many grievous. Betraying height of insensitivity, Dyer left the venue with his force, without rendering any aid to the wounded. Sources close to Dyer say he had no regrets whatsoever. Rather, he was satisfied, having imparted the Indian people a good moral lesson against sedition. The government has put Amritsar under a firewall. It has banned both ingress into and exit from the city. Even the press is not being allowed in.

Martial Law Clamped On Several Districts Punjab Gripped By Tension

April 15, 1919, Lahore: Tension, fear and panic have gripped Punjab. Following yesterday's genocide, martial law has been clamped on Amritsar, Lahore, Gujranwala, Gujrat and Lyallpur districts. According to reports received, under the veil of martial law, the government has been arresting large number of people on charges of participating in mob violence. It has also been using disproportionate force to crush the slightest of public unrest. There are also reports that people have been made to crawl on their bellies while passing certain streets.[13] It is difficult to ascertain the veracity, as the authorities have drawn the iron curtains on flow of information.

TAGORE RENOUNCES HIS KNIGHTHOOD
'Such Badges Of Honour Make Our Shame Glaring'

May 30, 1919, Calcutta: As the gory facts of Jallianwalabagh are coming out, millions of Indians who have been traditionally loyal to the British Empire, are turning anti-British. A new spirit of nationalism has engulfed the country. Millions of Indians converted overnight from being British loyalists to non-cooperative anti-British nationalists.

The whole country has risen as one body in condemning Dyer and the British government. In Calcutta, the Noble laureate, poet Rabindranath Tagore, has renounced his knighthood conferred by the King as a protest against the heinous act against humanity.

In his letter to Viceroy Chelmsford, Tagore wrote:

'The enormity of measures taken by the government in the Punjab for quelling some local disturbances... revealed to our minds the helplessness of our position as British subjects in India. The disproportionate severity of the punishments inflicted upon the unfortunate people… are without parallel in the history of civilised governments… the very least that I can do for my country is to take all consequences upon myself in giving voice to the protest of the millions of my countrymen… The time has come when badges of honour make our shame glaring in the incongruous context of humiliation, and I for my part, wish to stand, shorn of all special distinctions, by the side of those of my countrymen who for their so called insignificance, are liable to suffer degradation not fit for human beings. And these are the reasons which have painfully compelled me to ask Your Excellency, with due deference and regret, to relieve me of my title of Knighthood… which I had the honour to accept from His Majesty the King at the hands of your predecessor, for whose nobleness of heart I still entertain great admiration.'[14]

MN Roy – A Key Architect Of Communist Party Of Mexico

September 4, 1919, Mexico City: Narendranath Bhattacharya, a young and militant political activist, left India in 1915 to explore Indian freedom through armed revolution and travelled a few countries, including USA before landing in Mexico. His political indoctrination was by Aurobindo Ghosh and Jatindranath Mukherjee. The latter, while, organising an armed revolution in India with Germany's help, had sent him to Batavia to make a deal with German authorities. From there Narendranath travelled through a number of countries, using various names, in quest for arms. After the British unearthed Jatindranath's plot, leading to the latter's capture and death and the collapse of the scheme of the armed revolution, Narendranath arrived in San Francisco in June 1916.

Though he could not achieve his immediate objective, his life took a decisive turn during his stay in the USA. There, he made extensive study of socialism, became attracted to the idea and established contacts with like-minded people. He also changed his name to Manabendra Nath Roy for security reasons.

In Mexico, he has played an important role in setting up the Communist Party. Incidentally, it is the first Communist Party in the world, outside Russia. Roy is keeping a close watch over the development in Russia, including the formation of the Comintern. He also continues to be firmly committed to the cause of liberation of India from the colonial British regime.

HINDUS, MUSLIMS FAST FOR THE KHILAFAT CAUSE
Gandhi Begins Groundwork For A Giant Movement

October 17, 1919, Delhi: Khilafatist leaders amongst the Muslim community have been trying unsuccessfully to convince the British regime to extend honourable terms and treatment to the Sultan of Turkey who happens to be the Caliph, or religious head of the Muslim world. They have been holding parleys with Gandhi and have been able to get the latter's endorsement of their cause. Gandhi has agreed to project 'Khilafat' as a common cause of concern for both Muslims and Hindus, to the government.

It may be recalled that when he began protests against the Rowlatt Act, Gandhi had experimented with 'hartal' (a shutdown protest) as an instrument to generate awareness and mobilise public support. He has again used that innovative tool today to generate countrywide public awareness about the issue of Khilafat and unite both Hindus and Muslims for this cause. During the day, Hindus have joined Muslims in fasting, observing 'hartal' and taking out processions across the country. The response has been quite encouraging.

Government Committee To Enquire Into Punjab Violence

October 29, 1919, New Delhi: The legislative council of the Government of India has set up a committee, to be led by Lord William Hunter, to enquire into the incidents of violence in Amritsar and other places in Punjab. Hunter would be assisted by five Englishmen and four Indians. Many are questioning the inordinate delay in appointing the committee.

Congress Appoints Enquiry Panel On Jallianwalabagh

November 14, 1919: India has been seething in grief and anger in the wake of the Jallianwalabagh massacre. The government, in a bid to assuage the public anger, has appointed Hunter Committee to enquire into the incident. However, Congress has announced its own enquiry team, which will visit the site, meet people and submit its findings. Madan Mohan Malaviya, the Congress president, has appointed leaders like MK Gandhi, Motilal Nehru, CR Das, Abbas Tayabji, and MR Jayakar as members of this committee. They have distributed themselves over various places for the purpose of the enquiry. Jawaharlal Nehru has been given an opportunity to assist the veteran leader CR Das. The young promising politician is looking at his assignment as a valuable learning opportunity.

Congress Committee Startled

November 1919, Amritsar: Atrocities committed on people by the government and the despotism of its officials were monstrous, as the Congress-appointed Committee is finding out. It has held its first open session on the 3rd of the present month. It is ironic that such brutal excesses were inflicted on people of a province, which had furnished the largest number of indigenous soldiers to the British government during the just-concluded war. It is becoming clear that the government will have to pay a heavy political price for this act of indiscretion by the Punjab government and Brigadier Dyer.

Congress Liberals' Gaze Riveted On Reforms

1919: The Jallianwalabagh incident has sent shockwaves across the whole country, attracting wide-scale anger. There is no doubt that the Congress moderates or Liberals, as they call themselves presently, are also shocked. Motilal, as the Congress president, has issued a moving appeal to them to join the Congress session to forge a unified response against the British government. However, the liberals seem to have simultaneously set their eyes on the outcome of the Montagu-Chelmsford reforms. It seems, they have not yet completely lost faith in the government's promise of giving India self-government.

Jamiat-ul-Ulema-i-Hind backs Gandhi's Programme

November 1919: Muslim Wahabis and divines have been traditionally averse to the British, who built up their empire by wiping out the Moghuls from Delhi. Now Muslim divines have formed an organisation called Jamiat-ul-Ulema-I-Hind and it is backing Gandhi's programme of non-cooperation to the hilt. Also Khilafat delegates, led by Mohammed Ali, Shaukat Ali, Abul Kalam Azad, the leaders of the Deoband and the Islamic Theological Centre of Firangi Mahal of Lucknow are firmly standing behind call for boycott of schools, courts and the councils.

Genesis Of the Khilafat Movement

Right from the early days, the institution of the caliphate combined the seat of the religious and the political head in Islam. Over centuries, the institution of caliphate travelled from Medina to Damascus to Baghdad to Egypt (for a brief period) and then to Turkey, in that sequence. During its heydays, the Ottoman Empire of Turkey extended to Europe, Africa and Asia adding to the glory of the Caliphate.

Since the beginning of the twentieth century, Islamic countries, one after another, have come under the subjugation of the Christian countries of the West. If Afghanistan came under British influence, the Anglo -Russian convention of 1908 reduced Iran to a mere dependency. Egypt has also been turned into a cipher state. Worst of all, the Ottoman empire in Turkey, that happened to be the pride of the Islamic world and the seat of the caliphate – the most important politico-religious institution of the Muslims – also began to wilt at the face of a resurgent Christianity in Europe. The growing fortune of the Ottoman Empire had hit a roadblock for the first time in 1529 with the failed siege of Vienna. Since then, it has been declining, slowly. However, the downfall has been very stiff in recent years. In the just-concluded World War, Turkey sided with Germany against the Allied powers. But, the war was won by the Allied powers and Turkey suffered major reverses along with its partners. The Treaty of Versailles (1919) reduced its territory significantly. At that time, one consolation was that the victors promised to protect the Ottoman emperor's status as Caliph. But the very next year, under the Treaty of Sevres, further territories such as Palestine, Syria, Lebanon, Iraq, and Egypt were also severed from Turkey's possession, causing the Caliph great humiliation.

With the last vestige of Islamic superiority under threat of obliteration, the Muslim leaders in India are taking it upon themselves to ensure that Turkey gets a better deal from the Allied powers. For that purpose, they would like to move the government in India and even the British government in England. Muslim leaders like Ali brothers—Muhammad Ali and Shaukat Ali—Abul Kalam Azad, Dr MA Ansari and Hasrat Mohani organised a Khilafat party with the following objectives: (a) To maintain the Turkish Caliphate; (b) To protect the holy places of the Muslims; and (c) To maintain unity of the Ottoman Empire. These leaders have been known to be close to Gandhi and together, they are exploring solutions to the Khilafat issue. When persuasions with the government did not bring results, the Muslim leaders formed the All-India Khilafat Committee and agreed to launch a non-violent non-cooperation movement under the leadership of Gandhi, and eventually resolved to wage twin movements jointly with the Congress.

HINDUS, MUSLIMS ARE SONS OF THE SAME MOTHER
Gandhi Pledges Support Of 30 Crore Indians

November 24, 1919, Delhi: The Khilafat workers and leaders held a two-day conference here. Yesterday the Muslims deliberated and adopted several resolutions. Today, the attendance was much broader, there were people from Hindu, Christian and Parsi communities. While addressing the large gathering, Gandhi emphasised that the twenty crore Hindus stood by the side of the eight crore Muslims of the country. He described the two communities as sons of the same mother and that both belong to the same soil. He said it was but natural that one brother would render all possible help when the other is justifiably aggrieved. He made it clear that the 'Khilafat' cause was justified and a big one that belonged to the whole country. However, he did not approve of one of their resolutions that called for progressive 'boycott' of British goods in certain event. Gandhi advised them, they should instead resort to 'withdrawal of cooperation'.[15]

GANDHI TAKES OVER KHILAFAT LEADERSHIP
The Gathering Storm

For the Aligarh intelligentsia, whom many view as the political rival of the Congress, the important issue, in recent times, has been the treatment of the Ottoman Empire of Turkey by the British Empire—the vanquished by the victor. To them, this issue is not simply one of a war victory, but involving the dignity of the institution of the Caliphate itself. The intensity of involvement of the prime Muslim intelligentsia of India with the cause of the Caliphate, at a distant Turkey, is puzzling to many. But political analysts attribute this phenomenon to the fact that Muslims in India under British rule and without a sovereign of their own, feel more comfortable to pledge their loyalty to the politico-religious head of the Islamic world, which lies in the Caliphate in Turkey.

Maulana Muhammad Ali and Maulana Shaukat Ali, two brothers who are seen as part of the Aligarh intelligentsia, have been in the vanguard of a movement that has been started to protect the institution of the Caliphate and ensure dignified treatment of the Ottoman Emperor by the British. Both the brothers are Oxford graduates. While Muhammad is a journalist of repute, Shaukat held a high post in the excise department in the government. They have been mobilising Indian Muslims for this cause for the past some time and have represented their case to the Viceroy. When this did not yield desired result, the promoters of the movement became busy, exploring other options to bring pressure on the British. With armed revolt or protest clearly an impossibility against the mighty British, Ali Brothers have realised that a leader with a proven track record in conducting popular struggle against powerful governments can help them achieve their goal, and they have then decided to open negotiations with Gandhi.

Gandhi, who is already leading the Congress' agitations against the government on the Rowlatt Act and the Punjab issues, has agreed to lead the Khilafat movement too. He is exploring the possibility of using non-violent non-cooperation to create pressure on the government to accept the Khilafat demands. To take over the reins, Gandhi has imposed conditions—the Khilafat leaders must have complete confidence in him and follow his guidance. Gandhi has told them that the strategy of deputations would not work and that pressure must be created on the government by determined and extensive non-cooperation. The term 'non-cooperation' has occurred to him for the first time and he at once became convinced about its efficacy and appropriateness. When resort to arms is impossible or undesirable, the only effective resistance to the government would have to be cessation of cooperation with it—people should return government titles, give up services, boycott courts etc. Khilafat leaders initially grumbled because they did not agree with some cardinal assumptions. For example, on the issue of non-violence, they believed Islam indeed permitted use of force for righteous cause. But they reconciled after it was pointed out that Islam does not forbid its followers from following non-violence as a policy. They also did not have any alternative, other than to follow Gandhi to achieve their goal. Therefore, after prolonged deliberations, the Khilafat leaders have agreed to the strategies of non-cooperation and non-violence.

All these years, since 1885, large sections of Indian Muslims have refrained from joining hands with the Congress against the British government. Now, such a possibility has arisen with Gandhi being the common leader. According to sources, Gandhi may try to bring about coordination between the ongoing agitations of the Congress, with the prospective Khilafat movement by convincing the leaders of both the camps. It is also being learnt that the government has been feeling disturbed and irritated at these developments.

Congress Finds Mont-Ford Reforms Stingy

December 23, 1919, Delhi: The report on constitutional reforms for India, prepared by Lord Montagu, Secretary of State for Indian Affairs along with Governor General Lord Chelmsford and presented last year to the British Parliament, has now been approved and received the royal assent today.

The new Act restricts the Secretary of State's power in 'transferred subjects' and also in matters on which the Governor General and his legislature are in agreement. The Governor General has been given wide powers—he can nominate as many members to his executive council as he wants. The central legislature is to be composed of two houses, viz., Council of the State or upper house and Legislative Assembly or the lower house. In both houses, the proportion of elected members has been raised. However, the executive council would not be responsible to the legislature and the Governor General himself would not be obliged to act as per its advice. In other words, the natives get very little in terms of actual power of governance, notwithstanding the rise in the proportion of elected members. As regards another sensitive issue of separate electorates, the Act now extends it to other minorities like Sikhs, Christians, Europeans, and Anglo Indians, in addition to the Muslims.

The meagre reforms, and the Rowlatt Act, betray the government attitude to Indian aspirations. If the Act was one of plain disdain, the reforms reflect indifference and neglect. Many in the Congress are clearly unhappy.

Mountain Delivers A Mouse
Indians Are Dismayed, Disappointed

December 1919, Delhi: Now that the contents of the reforms of Montagu and Chelmsford are out, speculations are over and India has to face stark realities. Against mountains of expectations built on the basis of their enormous war-support to the British, paltry reforms have been offered.

In hindsight, loaded promises made by Montagu in the British Parliament earlier seem to have been deceptions practised on unsuspecting Indians. The much expected 'dominion status' is nowhere in sight. What has made the current offerings still bitter is the imposition of the Rowlatt Act preceding it. India feels hurt and disappointed.

Only a small section of Congressmen, incorrigibly optimistic, are in favour of seeing the positive side of the new reforms. Possibly they are happy with some charities like raising the proportion of elected members. Opportunist people, who want to acquire political powers by election or selection, entering legislature or executive councils, find something positive in this next phase of self-government.

In Congress, important leaders like Motilal Nehru and Jinnah have resigned from the Viceroy's Council showing their disappointment. The main body of the Congress, unhappy with the meagre British offerings, has decided to continue with its agitation programmes.

GOVT OF INDIA ACT 1919

Montagu-Chelmsford Reform

December 1919, London: The main features of the 1919 Act are:

- The council of the Secretary of State will now have 8 to 12 members, three of them Indians and at least half should have spent at least ten years in India. Their advice would be binding on the Secretary of State;
- The Secretary of State's power to interfere in the administrative matters of the provinces is curtailed. He would not intervene in the affairs of the designated 'Transferred Subjects' and also in matters on which the Governor General and his legislatures are in agreement;
- Governor General shall have the power to nominate as many members to his executive council as he wants;
- The legislature at the centre shall comprise of two houses—Upper House or Council of the States and Lower House or Legislative Assembly. The Upper House is to consist of 60 members of which 33 are to be elected and 27 nominated by the Governor General. The Legislative Assembly is to consist of 144 members, of which 103 to be elected and 41 nominated by the Governor General;
- Both the Upper and the Lower Houses would have equal legislative powers. However, the power to vote would be available to the Lower House only;
- The executive council is not responsible to the Legislature and the Governor General is not obliged to act as per its advice;
- Provincial legislature would be unicameral with 70% members being elected and remaining 30% nominated;
- System of diarchy is introduced in the provinces;
- The system of separate electorates will now be extended to Sikhs, Christians, Anglo Indians and Europeans besides Muslims;
- New reforms are to be considered after ten years.

Secret Societies Proliferate In The Country

December 1919, Calcutta: Even though the government has crushed the Ghadarites, exterminated Bagha Jatin and foiled the Zimmerman plan, secret revolutionary societies continue to flourish. The policy of oppression by the British government and its indifference to legitimate aspirations of the Indian people are encouraging more young men and women to join secret societies to give vent to their anger and frustrations. This is more pronounced in Bengal. In Dhaka, the Anushilan Samity headed by Pulin Bihari Das has reportedly built up a membership base of over five hundred. Then there are numerous other revolutionary groups, each autonomous but coalescing with other revolutionary groups for action on occasion. Many of them are constituents of Jugantar. What is, however, striking in both the groups is the orientation of their members—they are highly disciplined and committed.

Detractors Question Gandhi's Involvement In Khilafat

1919: Gandhi's consent to lead the Khilafat movement has stirred a controversy within the Congress and in wider society. Those who have welcomed the move say that if this issue can bring both the Congress and the Khilafatist leaders on one platform, the British government would be put under real pressure and made to accede to legitimate demands of the Indians. This is because, they contend, of the very nature of the issue. Khilafat is a highly emotive issue that would push large number of Muslims, who have been since 1885 anti-Congress and pro-government, to come forward and agitate against the government.

However, Gandhi's critics say he has committed a blunder by entering into a pact with a few Muslim leaders, who neither have a mass base nor a clear perception of where lie the priorities of Indian Muslims. The pact has some underlying assumptions—that the interests of the Indian Muslims are different from the interests of other Indians and that they have a distinct political identity. Critics say Gandhi, by entering into this pact, has unwittingly accorded sanctity to these assumptions, although he may not actually agree to these. Many are just amused that these few Muslim leaders have staked so much for issues relevant to faraway Turkey, while ignoring the 'bread and butter' issues at home. One thing, the critics say, is certain, Gandhi has given legitimacy to a section of Muslim leaders with distorted view of history, society and politics by entering into a pact with them. Interestingly, a section of the Muslim League leaders is also voicing their concerns at Gandhi's taking up the Khilafat leadership. They, as a political party, have been professing absolute loyalty to the British in order to get more favourable treatment from the government than the Hindus. They are of the opinion that the Muslim participation in Khilafat under Gandhi is misguided and would work to the disadvantage of the Muslims as a community by antagonising the government. Gandhi is, however, not unduly perturbed by the League's criticism. At present the Khilafat Committee seems to be far more representative of the Muslims than the Muslim League, whose leaders are mostly pro-British and happily hunting the safe sanctuary of government jobs.

Edged Out, Congress Moderates Now Wear 'Liberal' Tag

December 1919, Calcutta: Gandhi's emergence as the supreme commander of the Congress in recent years has generated considerable intra-party politics. The moderates have now been compelled to move out of the party under the intense heat generated by the Gandhi-led movements. The relations between the two groups became irreconcilable on the issue of the 'approach to the reforms' offered by the GOI 1919 Act. The moderates believed the government's offerings constituted substantial improvement over the extant conditions and ought to be welcomed. They also stuck to their customary position that India could secure the best attainable future under the aegis of the British Empire. On both counts, the Gandhi-led nationalist Congress held diametrically opposite views. The coexistence under a common roof has become impossible.

The formal separation occurred during November last year when the moderates met in Bombay under the presidency of Surendra Nath Banerjea and tried to preserve and consolidate their members. They adopted the name All-India Moderate Federation and decided to spread its branches across the country. After a gap of about a year, the moderates hold their second conference here. Sivaswamy Ayer presides. Stalwarts like Surendra Nath Banerjea, Srinivasa Sastry and Tej Bahadur Sapru attend. Ayer has announced the strategy of the moderates—cooperate with the government wherever possible and oppose them when necessary.

The conference has adopted three important resolutions. First, it has welcomed the GOI Act 1919 as a definite and substantial step towards the progressive realisation of responsible government. Second, it has criticised both the government as well as the mob for the genocide and mass reactions in Punjab. Third, it has renamed itself as the National Liberal Federation of India.

It has also become clear that the 'Liberals' would begin preparing in earnest to participate in the elections to be held next year.

Hurt, Bruised India Looks For A Messiah In The Non-violent Warrior

December 26, 1919, to January 1, 1920, Amritsar: Annual session of the Congress is held here amidst heightened anger against the British government. As the gruesome details of the mass-murder in Jallianwalabagh and subsequent repression came to light, public rage has spilled over. Its reflections are evident in the Congress session. Congress is trying to pull together appropriate responses to channelise the deep-seated anger and frustration of the Indian people. Motilal Nehru presides over the session and Shraddhanand acts as the chairman of the reception committee.

In the backdrop of the Rowlatt Act and Jallianwalabagh massacre, the Congress session has acquired unusual importance. People expect the Congress to formulate the right roadmap to achieve self-governance from the British Raj, whose motive is suspect. Motilal Nehru has sought cooperation from the moderates (presently called liberals) with a view to putting up an united front against the atrocities of the martial law. Given the grim situation, other veterans are also attending the session. BG Tilak has taken a prominent part in the deliberations. However, most gazes have been fixed on Gandhi. His leadership in the form of Satyagraha against the Rowlatt Act has already made him a household name.

In view of his track record as a people's leader, an expectation has built up that he may be able to take on the might of the British. Majority of delegates and large crowds outside look to him for the roadmap.

On Reforms, Congress Accepts Gandhi's Roadmap

December 26, 1919 to January 1, 1920, Amritsar: There are discerning differences in approaches amongst the leaders about what ought to be the 'approach' of the Congress regarding the Mont-Ford reforms, one of the prerequisites being to contest the election to be held under the new constitution. There are three distinct camps. Important leaders including inter alia CR Das, BC Pal strongly oppose the new reforms. Much revered BG Tilak does not, however, want to reject the new reforms altogether. He wants the Congress to accept that part of the new reforms which is useful and beneficial, and reject those which are useless or harmful. Gandhi, convinced of the good intention on the part of the British, wanted to give the new reforms a chance. So strong has been the support in his favour amongst the delegates that eventually, Gandhi's line has been accepted. The Congress has resolved to work out the constitution based on the Mont-Ford reforms. This is notwithstanding the strong anti-government feelings and ambience in the wake of Jallianwalabagh and its aftermath.

Gandhi To Mobilise Congress Support For Khilafat

January 19, 1920, Delhi: A meeting was held in the presence of Gandhi and other Congress leaders to support the stand of Indian Muslims on the Khilafat question. A deputation was sent to the Viceroy to acquaint him with the feelings of the Muslim on the issue of Khilafat and Turkey's future. The Viceroy promised he would help and facilitate a deputation to England to present the Muslim viewpoint to the British government but expressed his own inability to do anything. Muslim leaders are dejected and angry. In response to the Viceroy's unwillingness to consider the Muslim demand, Gandhi suggested all support to government be withdrawn, all government titles be returned, law courts and educational institutions be boycotted, and the people resign from government services and refuse to take any part in the legislatures to be newly constituted.

Truly speaking, with the Khilafat Committee agreeing to Gandhi's guidance, it will be a test of Gandhi's non-violence non-cooperation programme in India. If Gandhi's domination of Congress continues, it is very likely that the Congress too will switch over to this novel form of movement in the near future.

British Prime Minister Dismisses Khilafat Delegation

March 19, 1920, London: Today, a delegation of Indian Muslims, led by Maulana Muhammad Ali, waited on British Prime Minister Lloyd George on the question of treatment of post-war Turkey standing on the verge of dismemberment. Maulana Ali contended that the delegation represented 72 million Indian Muslim subjects of HM's government and it also had the full backing of their 200 million Hindu counterparts. The delegation appealed to the British government for preservation of the temporal powers of the Caliph adequate for the defence of the faith, the Caliph's wardenship of Holy Places of Islam and exclusive Muslim control over the 'island of Arabia' as defined by the Islamic Scholars.

Quite unlike his assurances in 1918, British Prime Minister Lloyd George sounded curt and unfriendly to these concerns. He insisted on the application of 'self-determination' to the Turkish question, which implied 'dismemberment' of Turkey. He also insisted that the views of sincere, earnest, zealous Mussalmans on the issue of temporal powers of the Caliph were widely different from that of the delegation led by Maulana Ali.[16] This is a kind of clear message that the Khilafatists and their supporters have little to expect from the British government. Political analysts say the failure of the delegation is likely to push the Khilafatists closer to Gandhi.

Tilak Wants To Make The Best Out Of The 'Reforms'

April 20, 1920, Poona: If moderates have left the Congress to form their own outfit, all those who remain do not necessarily agree on a common agenda. Veteran leaders like Tilak, Lajpat Rai, CR Das and some others do not endorse Gandhi's line of boycotting the council—a requisite under non-cooperation movement. Tilak, though unhappy with the inadequacy of the reforms brought by the 1919 Act, is still of the opinion that Indians ought to gather as much strength from these offerings as possible and then demand more. He proposes to work the reform for all it is worth and for accelerating the growth of full responsible government. He is for cooperating with the government tactically. Right since 1916, Tilak has been working assiduously for Home Rule by Indians. In 1918-1919, during his sojourn in England, he had pursued this cause there. The reforms now on offer may be a trifle but constitute some milestones towards the destination of 'self government'. He does not want to dissipate the opportunities coming in the way, but work upon it pragmatically, consolidate the gain, and ask for more. Tilak has now founded the Congress Democratic Party, which pays allegiance to the Congress. The objective of the new party is to attain dominion status for India based on the principle of self-determination. While considering the reforms as inadequate and disappointing, the new party proposes to work the reform for all it is worth and is for accelerating the grant of full responsible government. Tilak wants the party to take part in the elections by the end of this year. He cannot obviously allow the pro-British Liberals to monopolise the legislatures. At the same time, he is also preparing for a battle with the Congress. He does not want it to embark upon a policy of boycott of council and thrust it on everyone else.

Hunter Committee Report Shocks Indians

May 26, 1920, New Delhi: The Hunter Committee's report on violence in Punjab, including the Jallianwalabagh massacre, is out. The Committee, while observing that the assembly at the Jallianwalabagh was not pre-arranged, concluded that the riot in the city had turned into a rebellion. In that context, it held the declaration of martial law in Punjab as justifiable and also that Dyer was justified in firing at the mob. The Committee, however, felt that Dyer ought to have given notice to the people before opening fire and reduced the operation time. The report has attracted wide public revulsion. To them, it betrays the typical insensitivity of a colonial dispensation. Gandhi has reportedly been upset by the findings of the report and become sceptical about the intention of the government. Sources say he might even revisit his earlier 'stance' of cooperating with the government in the matter of working out the reforms.

Khilafat Committee To Start Noncooperation Movement

June 9, 1920, Allahabad: Khilafat Committee had earlier served an ultimatum on the government to accept its demands by February this year. But the government refused to budge. Today, the Khilafat committee has met here and decided to launch non-violent non-cooperation movement to protest against the government's policy. The Committee accepted Gandhi's suggestions and has asked him to lead the movement.

Gandhi Serves Ultimatum To Viceroy

June 22, 1920, Bombay: Gandhi has written today to the Viceroy, serving the latter with the notice of the impending non-cooperation movement. He has written this has become necessary to protest against the unjust peace terms offered to Turkey by the Allies. He made it clear that he has advised his Mussulman friends to withdraw their support for the government and the Hindus to join them 'should the Peace terms not be revised'. He has also stated that he succeeded in weaning away the Muslims from violence, not on moral but on utilitarian ground, and convinced them to agree to non-cooperation. At the same time, Gandhi also added that the 'non-cooperation' practised by a mass of people is also fraught with grave risk. Thereafter, he sounded a warning: 'Not to run some risks now will be to court much greater risks, if not virtual destruction of law and order.'[17]

Gandhi has also been disillusioned by the manner in which the government handled the Jallianwalabagh incident and subsequent atrocities in Punjab. Thus, despite having played a prominent role in persuading the Congress, in the Amritsar session, to cooperate with the government in working out the Mont-Ford reforms, he has undergone a radical shift in approach since the publication of the Hunter Committee report. There are dual issues before him—wrongs by the government on Khilafat and Punjab atrocities. Knowledgeable sources say Gandhi is finding a synergy in the two causes. He may try to bring in the two organisations—Congress and the Khilafat Committee—together to make the government make amends.

Comintern Accepts Theses Of Lenin And MN Roy

July 19 to August 7, 1920, Moscow: Vladimir Lenin, the redoubtable leader of the USSR, has given a call from the rostrum of the second Congress of the Communist International to forge a vast united front of all anti-imperialist forces. He meant coming together by the nationalists, communists, reformists and revolutionaries. Lenin is well aware of the leadership role of the nationalists in most colonial and backward countries, where the communist movement is still nebulous. Lenin has presented his viewpoints in a paper that has been accepted by the Congress as the main theses.

MN Roy, representing the Mexican Communist Party, is attending the event. He has presented a supplementary thesis with specific reference to countries like India. In his thesis he has argued that the revolutionary communist parties in these countries should organise separate working class movements, aiming at national liberation rather than assisting the bourgeois leaders. Amplifying his ideas, Roy mentioned about two concurrent movements underway in India—first, a bourgeoisie democratic nationalist movement that aims at political liberation while trying to conserve the extant capitalist order; second, a struggle of the propertyless peasants for their liberation from every kind of exploitation. He has contended that the first is often controlling the second. The Comintern must fight against such control, he argues. He also postulated that the creation of communist organisations of peasants and workers to lead them to revolution is an important and necessary task. He has further argued that the class consciousness in the masses in these countries can be developed under the leadership of the proletariat of the advanced countries. He, therefore, clearly foresees a role for the Comintern.

Critics say irrespective of the differences in approaches of top leaders, the fact remains that the international communist movement would impinge significantly on Indian politics, sooner or later.

Indian Communist Leaders Gather In Russia

1920, Moscow: It may be recalled here that since 1918, a number of Indian nationalists and revolutionaries including the members of the erstwhile Berlin Committee tried to cross over to Soviet Russia at great personal risk to enlist support of Bolsheviks and the world communist movement for India's liberation. Included in them are Virendranath Chattopadhyay, Maulana Barkatullah, Dr BN Dutta, Sardar Duleep Singh Gill, Abani Mukherjee and recently, MN Roy. They are forming a group of ex-patriate Indians who believe in Marxist ideology.

SWARAJ AND KHILAFAT

Gandhi To Lay Siege Around 'Raj'

September 4-9, 1920, Calcutta: A special Congress session is deliberating on the contours of both the Khilafat movement and the Congress' next agitation programmes. There is abundant enthusiasm—Congress and Khilafat specials are being run from Bombay to Calcutta and the gatherings of delegates and visitors here are mammoth. Lajpat Rai presides over this session. Gandhi has drafted a resolution proposing non-cooperation to the government to redress the wrongs of Punjab atrocities, excesses of martial law and Khilafat. At the instance of Motilal Nehru, the absence of swaraj in the country was also considered a grave wrong and added as an important reason for the proposed non-cooperation movement. So the agenda comprises Punjab atrocities, Khilafat wrong and absence of swaraj.

The special session has considered the programme of action prepared by Gandhi. It encompassed non-cooperation as well as affirmative actions like socially constructive work. The purpose of non-cooperation would be to refuse the alien government help to exploit India. Gandhi has suggested a number of things Indians should boycott to achieve their goals—of titles given by the British government; official functions; official schools and colleges; councils under Montagu Chelmsford reforms. To be applied in a calibrated manner, the boycott would later extend to civil and military services and payment of taxes. Programmes for constructive work would encompass hand-spinning, promotion of Hindu-Muslim unity and removal of untouchability amongst Hindus, while arbitration would substitute the government law courts.

Many stalwarts like MM Malaviya, Annie Besant, BC Pal, CR Das,

Motilal Nehru and others are not convinced about the wisdom of the boycott, especially the legislature. Even Lajpat Rai, the president, does not subscribe to Gandhi's agenda. Incidentally, the veteran leader Tilak was preparing to enter council. Though he died recently, his loyalists like Moonje, Khaparde and others are determined to contest the ensuing elections.

Gandhi has mooted a programme of progressive non-violent non-cooperation that would involve boycott of legislature, law courts and educational institutions, besides British goods and their replacements by indigenous substitutes.

Bengali leaders like BC Pal and CR Das have pointed out the inadequacy of strategies like boycott of British goods, hand-spinning and national education, all of which were tried out in movements against the Bengal partition in the last decade but failed to achieve much. They contended that Gandhi was now trying to replicate similar strategies across the country. But Gandhi has been unfazed at such opposition—he feels his programme of non-cooperation is necessary if Indians wish to achieve swaraj, obtain redressal for Punjab atrocities and solve the Khilafat problem. After long deliberations, the non-cooperation resolution has been passed by 1,855 out of total 2,728 votes. The decisions arrived in this special session would require to be confirmed in the annual session to be held in Nagpur, later this year.

To make a success of the programmes approved here, Gandhi has declared his plans of a nationwide tour to arouse public awareness and support for these programmes.

From 'Class' To 'Mass' – This Is A New-look Congress

September 4-9, 1920, Calcutta: An important move by Gandhi in the Congress session here has been to broad-base Congress membership. He is planning to convert the Congress into a truly mass organisation. Hitherto, a preserve of educated middle classes, lawyers, journalists, businessmen and dominated by the Western educated Anglophile leaders, the Congress Party has now begun to welcome common men in its fold. The effects have begun to show—

khadi replacing Western attires and either Hindi or local languages substituting English in the sessions. A new life, enthusiasm and earnestness have been in evidence in the audience in the Calcutta session. In the changing landscape, anglophile leaders are clearly feeling suffocated. Prominent amongst them is Jinnah, who was responsible for bringing the Muslim League closer to the Congress. However, now in the company of the khadi-clad commoner speaking in vernaculars, he has begun to feel out of place.

AMBEDKAR ON THE RISE

To England To Pursue Higher Education

September 1920: Bhimrao Ramji Ambedkar has been emerging as a promising young leader of the depressed classes. As a student he has been outstanding. He has carried his natural talents into the fields of journalism, social and political activities. Already, he has achieved significant success in an academic career and he continues to pursue it simultaneous with other activities. His sheer brilliance saw him through many layers of higher education in India and abroad. Considering his merit, the Maharaja of Baroda helped him financially to go to the USA to take up higher studies. He had returned to India in November 1917 under instructions of the Maharaja, after securing a Masters in Economics from Columbia University, USA leaving another higher study half-finished in England.

More than his own career, Bhimrao has been determined to improve the lot of the depressed classes. He is realizing that it calls for tenacity and sustained struggle. In January this year, with the help of the Shahu Maharaj of Kolhapur, he started a fortnightly newspaper *Mook Nayak* (Leader of the Silent), to propagate his views. This journal announced the arrival of a new and powerful actor in the national struggle.

Bhimrao realises the centrality of higher level of education to his role and efficacy as a political leader serving the cause of the down-trodden people. Over the last nearly three years, he has collected funds and has now left again for England where he intends to complete his higher studies.

GOLDEN TEMPLE LIBERATED

Singh Reformers Clinch Victory

October 12, 1920, Amritsar: Sikh social activists, popularly referred to as Singh reformers, have been attempting to bring about socio-political reforms in the Sikh community by putting the 'control of gurdwaras' as the nucleus of their movement. They are aware of the central role religion plays in Sikh lives and, therefore, acutely concerned about the fact that most of the gurdwaras have turned into shelters of corruption and immoral activities. Sikhs have, therefore, been agitating against the control of gurdwaras, by Mahants of doubtful character and integrity. They allege, many Mahants, mostly Udasi Sikh or Hindus, have violated the sanctity of the gurdwaras by encouraging unethical and immoral activities in these holy shrines. Since these Mahants enjoy a cosy relationship with the British regime, the Sikh fight for the control of gurdwaras is also bringing them in conflict with the latter.

Sikh agitations have been going on at the Golden Temple—the seat and symbol of Sikh religious power—where the ruling Mahants have been routinely oppressive to the ordinary practising Sikhs and resorting to discriminatory practices against low-caste Sikhs. Besides, the Sikh psyche was grievously hurt when Arun Singh, officially appointed in-charge of the Golden Temple, honoured Dyer with 'saropa'—Dyer, the very person responsible for the massacre in Jallianwalabagh last year. The injured psyche was waiting for an opportunity to burst forth.

Today, Khalsa Beradari, an organisation of the backward-caste Sikhs, congregated in a religious assembly at Jallianwalabagh where several new persons were inducted into the Khalsa Brotherhood. At the conclusion of the ceremony at that venue of the martyrs, a large procession went to the Golden temple to offer 'karah prasad' and 'ardas'. When the clergy there refused to accept 'prasad' from the untouchables, a theological debate ensued. The reformers quoted appropriately from the hymns of the Holy Book to justify their stand. The clergy, then, had to agree, albeit reluctantly, to accept the 'prasad'.

Thereafter, the 'Sangat' proceeded to the 'Akal Takht' to pay their homage. Seeing the vast humanity approaching them, the clergies there grew scared and fled, leaving the 'Holy Seat' unattended. In such circumstances, the reformers took control of the Holy Shrine. They have appointed a jathedar and a band of volunteers to protect and serve the Holy Seat.

Today's incident is being seen as one of momentous importance for the Sikh reforms movement.

ÉMIGRÉ COMMUNIST PARTY OF INDIA FOUNDED

October 17, 1920, Tashkent: Responding to an invitation from Lenin to attend the second congress of the Comintern, MN Roy came down from Mexico to Russia in May this year. He struck rapport with important Russian leaders like Trotsky, Stalin, and Bukharin. He not only presented a thesis on the role of the Communist Party in India but also highlighted the help that was needed from the Comintern to take the revolutionary movement forward. He, with his wife Evelyn, who too is committed to socialism, travelled to Tashkent from Mexico and set up an institution here to impart training in the communist ideology. It is reported that some of the Indian Mohajirs, out on jigrat, have been coming to Tashkent in trickles. They are being indoctrinated and sent back to India.

Now, Roy and few other Indian communists in Russia have founded the Communist Party of India in this distant land. This émigré party has as its founders MN Roy, Evelyn Trent (MN Roy's wife), Abani Mukherjee, Rosa Fitingot (Abani Mukherjee's wife), Mohammad Ali, Mohammad Shafiq Siddiqui and MPT Acharya.

Roy in his thesis had stressed upon the necessity of raising the peasants' and workers' organisations in India. He has taken the first significant step towards that direction. He is training Indians in communist ideology here and intends to help the communists and communism develop in India through publication, counselling and funding.

AITUC IS BORN

A Milestone Reached In Indian Trade Union Movement

October 31, 1920, Bombay: Today is a red-letter day for the trade union movement in India. In the presence of 801 delegates representing sixty unions, an apex body of trade unions, viz. the All-India Trade

Union Congress has been formed. Another forty-two unions subscribed to the foundation by sending letters of endorsements. Congress veteran Lajpat Rai has been elected as the first president of the newly-formed organisation.

Other important leaders present on the occasion are Annie Besant, CF Andrews, Motilal Nehru, Vithalbhai Patel, BG Horniman, NM Joshi, Diwan Chaman Lall and BP Wadia. The last three persons have been at the vanguard of labour movement in the country.

The ideological stance of the Indian National Congress on the labour-capitalist issue has been based on 'higher idea of partnership' and not 'class conflict'. Though the Congress has not yet given calls to workers to join the struggle for independence, it regularly appeals to the patriotism of both workers and their employers.

The formation of AITUC is being seen as the beginning of a genuine effort to incorporate the bourgeoning labour movement within the frame of the national movement. Recent attempts, especially by Gandhi, to transform the Congress as a mass-based organisation seems to have facilitated the birth of the apex body of Indian trade unions. Communist leader MN Roy has complimented Gandhi saying the latter has ended the class insularity of the Indian National Congress, which had so far remained an elitist organisation. However, he has expressed doubts that Congress leaders have scientific understanding of various social forces.

It is becoming clear that the Congress has to redefine itself to accommodate more interest groups to continue to lead the national movements.

1920 Elections Amidst Congress, Khilafatist Opposition

November-December 1920: First election under the GOI 1919 Act has been held amidst push and pull by opposing forces. The British government has been keen to showcase it, to prove to the world the success of the reforms they just introduced. On the other hand, both, the Congress and the Khilafatists have already committed to every form of non-cooperation with the government, carried out vigorous anti-election propaganda. In fact, so intense has been their campaign that people have begun to look at anyone in the electoral fray as loyalist of the Raj.

The Liberals had no problem with such a tag because they consistently welcomed the 1919 Act and committed to make a success of the reforms. They happened to be the only organised political party to contest and predictably reaped rich dividend. They told people that there were only two groups of people—one who wanted to make a success of the reform and another, who wanted to wreck it.

Elections were held for 104 seats in the Central Legislative Assembly and 657 seats in the provincial assemblies. The size of the electorates was narrow—eligibility was determined on the basis of tax, income and property ownership. For the legislative assembly in the centre, the total eligible voters numbered only about nine lakh (900,000). In the unfriendly ambience crated by sustained propaganda by the Congress and the Khilafatists, only twenty-five per cent people cast their votes.

The Liberals are ahead in most places except in the Punjab and Madras. Other winners are mostly government loyalists and independents. Overall, the quality of the elected representatives leaves much to be desired. Their capacity to advance the cause of self-governance for the Indians seems suspect.

GANDHI FASHIONS CONGRESS GOALS

Swaraj Within Or Without The Empire

December 26-31, 1920, Nagpur: The Thirty-fifth annual session of the Congress is in progress. Vijayragahavachariar presides. The session has assumed much importance, coming soon after the special session in Calcutta where some momentous decisions were taken on the nature and modalities of the movements to be launched.

Taking part in the deliberations, Gandhi presented the goal of the Congress as the attainment of swaraj within the British Empire, if possible and without it, if necessary. As regards the second part of the goal, ie. swaraj without the British Empire, he had differences with leaders like Malaviya, Annie Besant and Jinnah, who wanted to limit the goal of swaraj 'within the British Empire' only. However, Gandhi has prevailed. At the same time, in the resolution that was adopted, Gandhi clarified that the means for the attainment of swaraj should be 'peaceful and legitimate' instead of 'constitutional' as at present. He has further expressed his conviction that if the movement is carried out on the right path, India will obtain 'swaraj' within one year.

There were serious reservations in certain sections of delegates about the non-cooperation movement that provided for, inter alia, boycott of councils. Leaders like Moonje and Khaparde, who were disillusioned with the proceedings in the Calcutta session three months ago, hoped that those would be set right in Nagpur and Congressmen permitted to contest elections. They hoped to receive support from Bengal and Punjab delegates.

Unfortunately for Gandhi's opponents, the teeth of their opposition had grown somewhat blunt as the elections were already over and thanks to the Calcutta session, the Congress refrained from taking part in it. Nothing worked against Gandhi in Nagpur. He held out the dream of swaraj within a year, and presented a plan of action in the form of an extensive non-violent non-cooperation movement. He demanded blind adherence to it.

His plan carried the prospect of uniting Hindus and Muslims, for the first time against the formidable Raj and it won the day. His appeal came like an avalanche from a mountain top and swept past everything enroute. He talked about swaraj in a year and the masses of delegates felt that it was almost achieved.

They did not want to look at any other vision, hear any contrary voices so much so that the Punjab delegates prevailed upon Lajpat Rai to fall in line with Gandhi. Bengal veteran CR Das too cooperated in the passing of the non-cooperation resolution. By the end of the session, Gandhi was able to secure endorsement of most stalwarts like Lajpat Rai, CR Das and Motilal Nehru to his programmes. It is clear Nagpur has scripted the blueprint of a formidable struggle. An enormous movement for swaraj, alongside the one on the issue of 'Khilafat' are likely to lay a siege around the Raj.

Khilafat Committee To Join Hands But Not Merge With Congress

December, 1920: Now it is only a matter of time that the twin movements for swaraj and Khilafat would burst forth upon the British Indian government. Significantly, though Gandhi is being seen as the common commander-in-chief for both the movements, the All-India Khilafat Committee would not merge with the Congress. It would retain its separate entity and carry out the movement in accordance with the agreed guidelines across the country. Political analysts observe obvious synergy in the joint movement and foresee an unprecedented mass mobilisation against the government in the near future.

Jinnah Mulls Parting Ways With Congress

December 26-31, 1920, Nagpur: A Congress session is in progress here. The enthusiasm generated in the Calcutta session earlier, on account of the united participation of Hindus and Muslims is undiminished here too. But Jinnah has been upset by the mass hysteria that is sweeping the Congress session. He is not happy with Gandhi's approach to political problems of Indians. But Gandhi has already captured the imagination of the delegates, who have unequivocally chosen him as the commander of the forthcoming Khilafat and non-cooperation movements. According to some reports, the reverence and feelings for Gandhi has reached such dizzy height that Jinnah was strongly booed by the audience, when he referred to Gandhi as Mr Gandhi in his address, unlike others who in their speeches mentioned him as 'Mahatma Gandhi'. This has allegedly upset Jinnah greatly. But he refused to oblige the audience and stuck to his gun.

Congress' Loss Is Muslim League's Gain?

December 26-31, 1920, Nagpur: Jinnah is not happy with what he calls a pseudo-religious approach the Congress has adopted, nor is he comfortable with the attempted mass mobilisation by Gandhi. Jinnah feels such programmes are aimed at working up mass hysteria. To Durga Das, a young journalist, Jinnah talked of his plan to part company with the Congress.

The All-India Muslim League is looking at Jinnah's sense of alienation with the Congress and his impending separation with eagerness. Jinnah has been a member of the Muslim League right since 1913, but his major political activities have so far hovered around the Congress. As a political organisation, the Muslim League presently has only but a tenuous hold over the Muslim community. Politically, Indian Muslims have at least three other organisations available to express their views—these being the Indian National Congress, the Association of Ulemmas of India (Jamiat-ul Ulema-I-Hind), and the Khilafat Committee led by the Ali Brothers. In order to consolidate its grip over Muslims, the League wants a leader who could rival the Congress leaders. The League, therefore, could become a beneficiary of Jinnah's decision by involving him more in its organisational rejuvenation.

GANDHI OVERHAULS INDIAN NATIONAL CONGRESS

December, 1920, Nagpur: Gandhi has overhauled the organisational structure of the Indian National Congress, with a view to extend its reach to the farthest end of the country and infuse a new life and vigour into it. The Congress has divided India in twenty-one provinces on the basis of languages spoken. These are Andhra, Ajmer-Marwar-Rajputana, Assam, Bengal & Burma valley, Berar, Bihar, Bombay, Burma, Central Province, Delhi, Gujarat, Karnataka, Kerala, Madras, Maharashtra, NWFP, Orissa, Punjab, Sind, and United Province. The Congress plans to have provincial Congress committees in each of these provinces. Not only that, it also plans to establish subcommittees at the district, sub division, taluq and even village level. At the top level, the AICC would have 350 members, representing different provinces. The working committee, which would act as the supreme executive, would consist of fifteen members. Clearly, upon such re-organisation, the party structure is likely to be as elaborate as the government machineries. This would certainly help organise the people from the grass root.

Gandhi has also held out a programme of action for all Congressmen in the form of hand weaving, hand spinning, activities for removal of untouchability and raising Rs 10 million for a Tilak Memorial Fund. The common members have responded to these measures enthusiastically, as these have given them opportunities to involve themselves in Congress activities. To them, these are akin to working for the nation.

Congress Not To Intervene In The Affairs Of Indian States: Gandhi

December 1920, Nagpur: Although Congress under Gandhi has declared swaraj as the goal, this is in relation to British India. The general perception in the Congress has been that the people in the princely states are already enjoying swaraj. The delegates attending the session from the native states are, however, not convinced. They contend that if swaraj only means rule by Indians, an opinion the Congress seems to hold, the people of the native states would be keen to see that such rule becomes more democratic. Taking cognisance of such rising political aspirations of the states' people, the Congress has asked all the sovereign princes of the Indian states to establish full responsible governments in their states. However, at the same time, Gandhi has assured them they would have a place in the future governance of India and declared that the Congress would not intervene in the internal affairs of the princely states. Gandhi's declaration is acting as a sure dampener to delegates from the states—they are unsure of the Congress support to their political programmes and activities. Political analysts say the Congress decision will deal a severe blow to the political aspirations of the states' subjects.

Swaraj – An Ambiguous Term?

The word swaraj is a Sanskrit term and it lends itself to varying interpretations. Congress leaders have been using it and at present the Congress is projecting it as a goal of its non-cooperation movement. But the Congress has not spelt out the exact meaning of this term to its supporters. At the least, Congress ought to clarify whether it means complete political independence, dominion status under British Empire or any other kind of restricted form of self-governance. Gandhi, the present commander-in-chief, has, so it seems, consciously refrained from explaining its exact meaning. To pointed enquiries he has chosen to remain vague.

Not surprisingly, to leaders—old and young—the meaning of the term, therefore, is not uniform, still worse, not even clear. Young leaders like Jawaharlal feel uncomfortable about this vagueness. Critics say clarity would have helped the cause of the movement.

From Dar-ul-Harb to Dar-ul-Islam

The Migration Picks Up

1920: Many Muslim leaders are angry and upset at the way the victors of the World War I, viz. the Allied powers led by Britain are treating Turkey and its Sultan, who happens to be the Caliph of the Muslims the world over. They are alleging that Britain, in order to enlist Muslim support for her war efforts, had earlier assured that in the event the allies won, Turkey, a nation that supported the German block, would be treated in a humane way. But now that they have achieved victory, they are humiliating Turkey and its Sultan in the same way they are dealing with other vanquished nations.

Upset, but helpless against Britain's military might, some Muslim religious leaders have declared British India as Dar-ul-harb (land of war) and exhorted Muslims to migrate to Dar-ul-Islam (land of Islam). While such a call appealed to some sections of religious devouts amongst the Muslims, Ammanullah, the Amir of Afghanistan and a traditional foe of the British, gave them a real-life choice for migration—he invited the Indian Muslims to Afghanistan, projecting his country as Dar-ul-Islam.

For past some time, many Muslims have been responding to the call for migration known as 'Hijrat'. Few thousand Indian Muslims have turned 'Mohajirs'—they have already made their way to Afghanistan through the NWFP and more are following suit. Some Mohajirs are reportedly going further up, to Russia.

It appears that the Hijrat has been further strengthening the Khilafat movement, because it is being seen as the extreme form of persecution of the Muslims by the government, forcing them out of the land. Clearly, the government is not amused and is keeping close watch over the Indo-Afghanistan border.

Political analysts say the call for Hijrat is simply impractical and unsustainable, and based on ephemeral religious emotion. Judging the vindictive mood of the British Indian government, they also prophesy that the migrants will have a hard time re-entering India, should they decide to do so later on.

Non-violent, But Movement Strikes Empire Hard

January, 1921: Government is under a lot of stress due to the impact of the non-violent non-cooperation movement launched by the Congress and the Khilafat Committee. The Khilafat Committee was the first to agree to the non-violent non-cooperation movement. After the Congress adopted this novel method of protest too, the two movements are gradually converging into a powerful force, taking into their fold both Hindus and Muslims across the country.

It is true that the Muslim League leaders have kept away from it but the lack of their participation is proving inconsequential. Such has been the involvement of the common people across both the communities that the communal elements have had to keep a low profile, lest they attract public fury. The joint movement is getting intense by day.

The Congress has already boycotted the election and thus the legislature. There are increasing instances of boycott of law courts by the natives. Instead, they are approaching the arbitration boards under the Congress control and these boards are rising in numbers. Students, as a community, have been boycotting government educational institutions and swelling the ranks of the protesters. Then, taking cue from Gandhi's ashram, many more ashrams have come up across the country and these are promoting hand weaving, hand spinning besides serving as abode for political workers and sometimes local offices of the Congress. As such, these indigenous small establishments are playing a significant role in shaping people's participation in the non-cooperation movement.

Upon analysing the strength of the movement, Jawaharlal Nehru feels that there has been a strange mixture of nationalism and politics and religion and mysticism and fanaticism—all these elements have combined into a huge movement. Agrarian discontent in the countryside and a rising working class movement in cities are fuelling it.

Chamber Of Princes To Bring Indian India Closer To Raj

February 8, 1921, New Delhi: While the Indian masses in the British Indian provinces are craving to organise themselves against the British Raj under the Congress banner, the colonial regime is coming closer to the native rulers. Today, the Government of India has held the first meeting of the 'Chamber of Princes'. This would be an institutional mechanism available to the Indian princes to express their views on important issues and hold informal talks with the Viceroy. In a nutshell, it would help the Indian India to come closer to the British Raj and explore areas of mutual cooperation.

NANKANA GURDWARA LIBERATED
What Is Next?

March 3, 1921: The 'Gurdwara movement', seen as an important means for reforming the Sikh community, has been spreading far and wide. After the Sikh crusaders liberated the Golden Temple from the oppressive Mahants, they have achieved another significant victory now in Nankana. The control of the famed Nankana Gurdwara has been wrested statedly from corrupt Mahants, and this is being seen as another milestone in the ongoing movement.

The struggle at Nankana began on 20 February, when over a hundred Akalis entered the Gurdwara, to take over its control. Mahant Narain Das, in charge, grew apprehensive and used hired goons to attack the Akalis, most of whom were wounded or killed and burnt on the spot. As the news spread, Akalis began arriving at the Gurdwara in thousands. This got converted into a strong popular movement. Even though the Mahant was supported by the British regime, the tide of the people could not be checked. Being conducted on non-violent lines, it derived synergy-driven strength from the nationwide non-violent, non-cooperation movement that has been currently underway. Many are seeing the event as a victory for the Sikh Gurdwara Prabandhak Committee (SGPC) and also of Gandhi's method of non-violent protests.

If the present Sikh mood and spirit are any indication, Nankana is not the end of the journey. A great movement is in progress and may strive to liberate many more religious shrines before it ebbs. The movement by the SGPC has support from the Central Sikh League. Some enthusiastic Sikh leaders are calling it the 'Third Sikh War'.

At the same time, due to being conducted on non-violent lines, it has also been receiving support from the Indian National Congress. Today Gandhi visited the Holy shrine.

Muhammad Ali Let Off, Thanks To Gandhi's Intervention

May 1921, New Delhi: Last month Lord Reading, the former lord chief justice of England, took over as the new Viceroy of India from Lord Chelmsford. Chelmsford's tenure came under cloud owing to the Rowlatt Act, Punjab atrocities and a biased report by the Hunter Committee. Owing to the distinguished legal background of Reading, many Indians are hopeful of getting just and fair treatment by the new Viceroy.

Reading held a meeting with Gandhi, in which he had informed the latter of his plan to prosecute Maulana Muhammad Ali, for appealing to the Muslims to resort to violence. Gandhi reportedly assured the Viceroy to extract a promise from Ali to eschew violence in future. Ali later issued a statement accordingly and the Viceroy dropped the matter.

For many, the Ali brothers are perceived to be the two arms of Gandhi and they are playing crucial roles in spreading the current movement amongst the Muslim community. Out of the two, Muhammad Ali has been particularly known for delivering fiery and rousing speeches. Their arrests would have meant a real handicap for Gandhi, and this made him go all out to salvage the situation. However, knowing Muhammad Ali's penchant for anti-British rhetorics, it is difficult to say how long he can be made to stick to his promise!

MOHAJIRS ARRESTED IN PESHAWAR
Government Suspects Communist Conspiracy

June 1921, Peshawar: Police have arrested Mohammad Akbar and a few others in Peshawar. They are said to be the first batch of Mohajirs who went to Russia via Afghanistan on Hijrat, and have now returned from the Marxist land. The police suspect that they were indoctrinated in communism in Russia and have been sent back in order to spread communist ideology in India.

There are conflicting views on the charges being levelled against the Mohajirs. According to some sections of the nationalist press, these are absurd, baseless and offshoot of British phobia of communist Russia. However, there are also reports that a few hundred Mohajirs indeed went to Russia from Afghanistan. From there, some of them even ventured to reach Turkey, the land of the Caliph. However, having failed, they too returned to Russia. While in Russia, a section of the Mohajirs came under the influence of communism and MN Roy. The latter has been training communist workers and leaders of various countries in Tashkent. Therefore, they contend that the British fears about the Russian design of spreading communism in India through the Mohajirs may not, after all, be completely unfounded.

Appeal To Muslim Police And Soldiers
Khilafatists Earn British Raj's Wrath

July 8-10, 1921, Karachi: The All-India Khilafat Conference holds its session here. Maulana Muhammad Ali presides. The political temperature is already high. Muhammad Ali has made substantial contribution to it through his militant public statements over the past four months. His utterances in Madras in April and in Broach and Belgaum last month are being seen as open defiance of and challenge to the British government. He has been warning the British government against fighting Kemal Ataturk in Turkey. The Khilafatists are looking at Kemal as the 'sword of Islam' and the potential saviour of the 'Caliphate'.

In the meanwhile, a group of distinguished ulemas have drafted a 'fatwa' which reiterates the previous fatwa issued in favour of 'non cooperation', but does not stop at that. Significantly, it highlights the clause that the service in British military or police is religiously unlawful and a 'sin' as it involves firing upon Muslim co-religionists. Such actions, the fatwa points out, entitle the violators the eternal fire of 'hell'. This fatwa has been printed and distributed widely, including in the present conference.

Muhammad Ali, one of the top leaders of the Khilafat Committee, has been delivering fiery speeches encouraging Muslims to resort to violence against the government. In May this year, he was let off the hook by Viceroy Reading as he had promised to eschew violence' and Gandhi had pleaded for him. However, in this conference, he has spoken even more stridently and given a call to drive the British out of India. The conference has adopted several resolutions. One of the resolutions says that in the present circumstances, the holy Shariat forbids every Muslim to serve and enlist himself in the British army or to recruit for it. The resolution also urges Muslims in general and ulemas in particular to convey this religious commandment to Muslim soldiers in the British army.

The conference also threatened that in the event the British government acted against Kemal in Turkey, the Khilafatists would not only resort to civil disobedience along with the Congress, but declare India's independence. The intelligence branches are keeping a close eye over the conference. From sources close to the government, it is learnt that the government is considering the developments in Karachi as ominous and contemplating some hard steps.

SUBHAS MEETS GANDHI IN BOMBAY

July 16, 1921, Bombay: Subhas Bose son of Janakinath Bose—a leading lawyer of Cuttack has returned to India from England, giving up the highly 'sought after' ICS career, to participate in the country's freedom struggle. Subhas, a young man, is deeply influenced by Ramakrishna and Vivekananda, and imbued with deep patriotism.

While in England, he corresponded with CR Das, the veteran Congress leader expressing his desire and determination to serve his motherland. The ongoing non-cooperation movement for swaraj under the stewardship of Gandhi has been stirring Indians in England. In particular, Gandhi's promise of swaraj within a year has made every one keenly interested in the movement. Subhas has many queries on the issue and he wants to have these clarified by Gandhi himself.

Today Subhas has landed in Bombay and he rushed to Mani Bhavan to meet the 'commander' of the Indian struggle. He was granted an appointment and he tried to make fullest use of it. Subhas wanted to know exactly how Gandhi proposed to accelerate the movement from 'boycott' of foreign goods and government institutions to 'stop payment of taxes', thus facilitating the achievement of swaraj. The veteran of several battles tried patiently to reply to the questions raised by the young patriot. At the end, however, Subhas felt Gandhi had no clear answers on several issues. He felt this could be either due to lack of clarity in Gandhi's own thinking or the latter's unwillingness to reveal all of his strategy. Before Subhas left Mani Bhavan, Gandhi advised him to get in touch with CR Das in Calcutta.

Subhas Begins His Political Voyage

July, 1921, Calcutta: Upon reaching Calcutta, Subhas hurried to meet CR Das. Gandhi advised him to meet CR Das who happened to be a national leader of high repute. Aware of CR Das's stature and involvement in the national struggle, Subhas himself had written to him from England, expressing his eagerness to serve his motherland. Subhas has been much impressed by Das, in whom he has discovered a statesman with clear cut thinking and pragmatic approach coupled with burning patriotism. Subhas felt Das was a person who could give everything that he had for his country and countrymen, and in turn could demand everything people were capable of contributing.

Subhas has begun his political apprenticeship under Das. To start with, Das has entrusted Subhas with the task of organising the National Volunteer Corp.

TWIN MOVEMENTS ENGULF INDIA

The non-violent non-cooperation movement has been running on the twin engines of 'swaraj' and 'Khilafat'. Though Gandhi is the supreme commander, the Khilafatists are looking at their own leaders, particularly the Ali brothers, viz. Maulana Shaukat Ali and Maulana Muhammad Ali, for guidance and instructions. Notwithstanding the above, this is the first time, the two major communities have come together in a mass movement of this magnitude. A synergy has been struck and the movement is snowballing. Boycott has taken extensive form—starting from foreign clothes to school, courts and councils. Liquor shops are being picketed and open bonfires made of foreign articles. A strong wave has surged across the land, engulfing even the hitherto unpolitical pockets and people. Members of the Muslim League are, however, not joining. Traditional ally of the British, they have been unhappy by the way Gandhi is making an inroad into the Muslim constituency.

In recent times, Khilafatist leaders have begun to mount pressures on Gandhi to take the movement to the next level—to begin civil disobedience. Gandhi, however, is taking his time. He knows the difficulties and risks in asking the police and the military to join the movement, and defy government order. He also knows the difficulty in keeping the civil disobedience movement under control in a large country like India. He is mulling appropriate options. The Khilafatists are, however, strident. They have begun to appeal to the Muslim police and soldiers to resign from services and join the movement.

KHILAFATIST MOPLAHS ERUPT IN REBELLION

Non-violence Thrown To The Winds

August 1921, Malabar: As the tidal wave of the non-violent non-cooperation movement sweeps the country, one of its twin engines, viz. the Khilafat agitation has stumbled and derailed in the south Malabar district in Kerala. The Moplahs, who were spearheading the movement there, have reportedly embraced violence as means to achieve their goal and come into confrontation with the British regime repeatedly.

The Moplahs are descendants of Arab Muslims who settled in this part of the country in the eighth and ninth century. For centuries they have been living alongside the Hindus. Mostly tenants in a district where Hindu Nairs and Namboothiris-Jenmis have been the landlords, Moplahs, usually fierce by disposition, have resorted to violence at times to settle scores with their Hindu landlords.

When Gandhi and the Ali brothers had given call for Khilafat and swaraj, the Moplahs responded enthusiastically. Clearly, they have not understood the subtleties of non-violence. Violence, in any case, is not barred by Muslim religious scriptures, for righteous causes. They saw in these movements a unique opportunity to establish Khilafat Raj on their land by force, if necessary. The provocative speeches by Muhammad Ali, one of the Ali brothers, in Madras in April and later in Broach and Karachi gave great impetus to their violent spirit.

Unlike other parts of India, where the twin movements have been carried out on non-violent lines, the Moplahs bearing grudges against the British rulers and also the local landlords, chose to use violence to retaliate against British oppression of the Khilafat movement. More specifically, the problem began when the British came down heavily on the Khilafat movement and the Khilafatists in the two taluks of south Malabar. The Moplahs responded in kind—they retaliated violently by using arms. The clashes soon spread to other areas. The Moplahs cut down telegraph lines, severed railway lines, raided and burnt post offices, government offices and even police stations. Occasionally their ire has also been directed against the local Hindus.

Although Gandhi had secured a promise from the Khilafat leaders that the movement will be conducted purely on non-violent lines, the unfolding events in this idyllic land have been causing great embarrassment to the Indian National Congress and Gandhi. Although some leaders are trying to rationalise the Moplah agitation as a spontaneous outburst of patriotism, violent events are striking at the very root of the principle of non-violence. In Ernad and Valluvanad, the Moplahs have driven out the government forces and declared these as a 'Khilafat Kingdom'. They are in no mood to listen to anyone, including Gandhi. The British government is contemplating vigorous action to quell the movement, which it considers as nothing less than an open rebellion.

Ali Brothers Arrested

September 1921, Karachi: Government has been upset in the wake of the Karachi meet of the All-India Khilafat Conference, which could potentially impinge on the loyalty of the Muslim armed forces to the government. Though it decided to round up the seven main protagonists of the rebellion call in Karachi, it did not take any immediate action and waited for the right time. Now it has swung into action.

The first to be arrested was Maulana Shaukat Ali. The Bombay police arrested him at midnight and sent him to Karachi. On 14th of this month, Muhammad Ali, was picked up in Waltair station, while he was travelling with Gandhi from Calcutta to Madras. He too has been sent to Karachi.

All the seven arrested Khilafatist leaders are now in Karachi. The government has charged them with conspiracy to tamper with the loyalty of the armed forces.

Indian Legislative Assembly Set Up Under New Constitution

September 21, 1921, New Delhi: Today the Indian Legislative Assembly has been set up under the new constitution.

COMMUNAL RIOTS BREAK OUT IN MALABAR

An Ominous Signal For The Future

November 1921: The Khilafat movement in Malabar, that had transformed itself into a violent armed uprising against the British, has eventually metamorphosed into a programme of ghastly massacre of Hindus. This radical degeneration of a non-violent mass movement came about after the British government swooped on the Moplahs with full force in a bid to crush them. The Moplahs suspected some sections of Hindus of colluding with the British and providing the latter with local intelligence. The traditional animosity of the tenants against the landlords fuelled their anger. Unable to confront the government counter-attack, the Moplahs' full ire fell upon their Hindu neighbours. Infuriated, they went in for unprecedented violence against the Hindus. Reports indicate that they committed all sorts of brutality—males were deskinned and burnt alive, women raped, pregnant women brutally murdered, properties burnt and so on. The rebellion spread over 2000 square miles in South Malabar.

Despite various points of differences—economic, social and religious—the Hindus and Muslims have been amicably living in this district for many centuries. Ironically, this has happened when Gandhi had sought to bring about greater communal harmony between the two communities through the twin movements for swaraj and Khilafat. The communal elements, who were clearly unhappy about Gandhi's taking over the leadership of Indian Muslims, stoked the fire of communal hatred by joining in the massacre. As the gruesome details of the events reach other parts of the country, quite a few eminent and nationalist leaders are preparing to visit the land to find facts and provide help and assurances to the riot victims.

According to political observers, the Moplah rebellion is sending out a clear signal as to the difficulties involved in maintaining the integrity of a non-violent movement by its leadership when emotions run deep. It has also proved that mere wishful thinking that communal unity could be established by launching political agitation would not help matters, especially when the people do not have deep conviction in the underlying ideology. They feel the outbreak of the riot in Malabar has struck a 'body blow' at Hindu-Muslim unity that was being attempted by the Congress through the Khilafat movement.

Government Crushes Moplah Rebellion

November 1921, Malabar: It began as a Khilafat movement against the British government in August this year and then turned into an armed rebellion. In its final phase, it turned into horrible communal riot against the Hindus. Eventually, the government has been able to crush the movement and with equal savageness. At least 2,337 Moplah rebels are said to have been killed in the government operations. After the rebellion was contained, ninety Moplah prisoners were sent to the central prison in Podanur in a closed goods wagon. Since there was no room in that prison, they were sent back and on the way, more than sixty of them died by suffocation.[18] Khilafatists say, the government has used disproportionate force and extreme cruelty against the Moplahs, which could certainly be avoided by a civilised government. The government could punish the culprits following due process of law, they contend.

Hindu Mission Is The Need Of The Hour: Malaviya

1921: The vehemence of the communal riots against Hindus in parts of India, despite the country having an overwhelmingly Hindu majority population, has both surprised and shocked many. The Moplah episode has made Hindus in many parts of the country feel alarmed and initiate steps for self-defence. Hindu Mahasabha has taken serious note of the event, and it is viewing the matter with anxiety. According to Madan Mohan Malaviya, a veteran leader of both the Mahasabha and the Congress, it has become necessary to organise a Hindu Mission in India, where proselytisation by other faiths has been going on for centuries.

India Restless On The Eve Of Prince Of Wales' Visit

November 1921, Delhi: The British Indian government has been tense about the visit of the Prince of Wales to India by the end of this year. The tension is in view of the countrywide non-cooperation movement that is going on in full swing under Gandhi's leadership. Gandhi has been able to cast a spell on all classes of people. It appears that the bulk of India is following him, without a question. In such circumstances, arranging proper felicitations for the royal couple would indeed be difficult, if not impossible.

The Country Turns Into A Vast Prison

Non-violent non-cooperation movements of the Congress and the Khilafat committee have engulfed the country. This is the first of a mass movement in the country in which both the Hindus and Muslims are participating. Gandhi has contrived the movement in such ways that the masses can participate in it without difficulty.

Even though the movements are non-violent, these involve withdrawal of cooperation from the British government. Boycott of foreign clothes, educational institutions, courts of law etc. are not only serving as direct affront to the authority of the government, but also hurting it economically and crippling the routine government functions. And as these are spreading across the country, the government feels vulnerable. For the first time, the British government seems to be out of depth. What is particularly annoying to the government is the extensive participation by the Muslims whom they favoured by granting separate electorates. The Ali brothers, at the spearhead of the Khilafat movement, had openly tried to tamper with the loyalty of the armed forces and both were arrested. In fact, several such developments including the Moplah rebellion in Malabar, have made the government revisit its initial 'hands-off' approach to a professedly 'non-violent non-cooperation movement'. The police have been arresting not only leaders but also agitators in tens of thousands and putting them in prison. It appears the whole of the country has turned into a vast prison.

Gandhi has been at the helm of this unprecedented mass movement. Although he has led some movements in South Africa, these were quite insignificant compared to the present movement in terms of scope and complexities like the number of agitators, difference in their religious and social backgrounds, two objectives of swaraj and Khilafat running concurrently, presence of communal instigators, the might of a powerful British government etc. The wide scale and intense government reprisals are acting as great inducement to the agitators to resort to violence, but Gandhi is committed to keep it strictly non-violent—a condition which he has to uphold under all circumstances. He is finding this very tough. Although most of his confidantes have been imprisoned, Gandhi has been so far left free by the government.

Subhas Serves Prison Term Alongside His Mentor

December 1921, Calcutta: Both CR Das and his young disciple, Subhas Chandra Bose, have been arrested for leading the non-violent non-cooperation movement in Bengal and awarded six months' imprisonment. Subhas has got an opportunity to serve the prison term while being in the Alipore jail in the city with Das, his political mentor. He finds this a unique opportunity to develop his political insight.

COLD SHOULDER TO PRINCE OF WALES

Angry Government Comes Down Hard On People

December 1921: The Prince of Wales arrived in India on 17th of November and is touring the country. In this connection the worst fear of the Viceroy has come true. Since the government is not inclined to accede to its demands on swaraj and Khilafat, the Congress has decided to boycott every function and matter that is associated with the Prince's visit. Barring a confrontation between supporters of the hartal and the government, people are by and large responding to the 'boycott' call energetically but peacefully. The Congress' hold over the country seems so total that city after city has simply closed down during the Prince's visit, causing great embarrassment to the Viceroy and the government. To make matters worse for the government, the Khilafat Committee has also been adding its weight to the protests. By the time the Prince was in Allahabad, the city turned almost dead—thanks to the groundwork done by the local Congress organisation. Angry and insulted, the government has resorted to hard suppression of the non-cooperation movement. A kind of tyranny has been let loose in many parts of India. Most top-ranked Congress leaders have been placed behind bars and they include Lajpat Rai, CR Das, Maulana Azad and Motilal Nehru. Gandhi has, however, not yet been arrested. People say the government has so far not done so because they have developed a Gandhi phobia. It fears such an action might attract rebellion by police and army. But to ensure that no untoward incident occurs during the visit of the Prince, the police, on government instructions, have resorted to mass arrest of political workers and even ordinary citizens-anyone it suspects capable of creating unrest.

Triumph For The People Of Midnapore

December 17, 1921, Calcutta: In these days of repression and atrocities, the people of Midnapore in Bengal have scored an important victory under the able leadership of BN Sasmal. Two years ago, the government had passed The Bengal Self-Government Act 1919, effective from 28 May 1921, in terms of which 227 Union Boards were set up in the district. While the expenses for these boards were imposed on poor villagers by way of additional taxation, their utility was deeply suspect. The people of the district entered into a movement under the able leadership of Sasmal, a close aide of CR Das. They refused to pay taxes. The movement attracted reprisals including confiscation of property, harassment and prosecution of villagers. But under Sasmal's inspired leadership, the people faced all odds and stood firm. Eventually, the government relented. Today, 226 Union Boards have been wound up.

Viceroy Offers Congress A Swap Deal

December 19, 1921, Calcutta: When Gandhi sought Congress' approval for his non-violent non-cooperation programme in Nagpur, he had assured that these movements would fetch swaraj to India in a year's time. However, swaraj is nowhere in sight while one year is about to expire. This is so despite the intensity of the movement, and massive peoples' participation. A situation has been reached, when some sceptics have begun reminding Congress leaders about what they say was Gandhi's promise.

In such an uncomfortable situation, the Congress has, interestingly, got a face-saving offer from Viceroy Lord Reading. The ex-lord chief justice of England and the present Viceroy has been a tormented soul, as the Prince of Wales had been rebuffed in most places he visited in India. Reading, to an extent, is seeing it as his personal failure. So, in order to save at least the rest of the Prince's tour, which would be to Calcutta during the Christmas, Reading has offered a swap deal to the Congress. The deal offers release of all prisoners of the non-violent non-cooperation movement and also a promise to hold a round table conference to discuss the Congress' demands, after the Prince's visit, provided the Congress immediately recalls its movements and withdraws restrictions in attending functions arranged for the Prince.

Madan Mohan Malaviya, acting as the peacemaker on the occasion, conveyed the Viceroy's offer to top leaders like CR Das, Motilal Nehru, Maulana Azad, all of whom are in prison and they feel that it is indeed the best offer made to the Congress under the circumstances. With the one-year limit set to expire, the Congress would be able to project this offer as a capitulation by the government. And even if the government went back or dithered on its offer at a later date, it could still be counted as a moral victory by the Congress and a new movement could be launched at the appropriate time from a stronger platform. Today, CR Das and Abul Kalam Azad sent a wire from Presidency jail here to Gandhi, conveying their unanimous view that the offer of the Viceroy be accepted. Everyone is waiting for Gandhi's verdict.

Gandhi Rejects Reading's Offer – An Opportunity Missed?

December 20, 1921, Delhi: While Viceroy Reading offered a truce to the Congress, it was evident that he was treating 'time' as of essence. Understandably, the Viceroy was bent upon salvaging the tour of the Prince of Wales, which is almost in its last legs. Two days ago, Das and Azad had sent wire to Gandhi recommending to him that the Viceroy's offer be accepted. But Gandhi took a different view. On the same day, he wired back imposing a set of counter-conditions on the government. These included (a) composition and date of the proposed conference; (b) release of prisoners including prisoners convicted for fatwas, including those in Karachi. By the reference 'the Karachi ones', there was unmistakable reference to the Ali Brothers, his trusted aides, who had earned particular wrath of the government for their aggressive speeches. Gandhi's reply came as a big dampener to Das and Azad. Today Malaviya made another frantic attempt to persuade Gandhi by sending him another cable. But Gandhi, in his reply, has stuck to the stand he has already communicated.[19]

CR Das, in the prison, has reportedly been swept by strong emotions of anger and sorrow and felt Gandhi has bungled. Political analysts too feel that the Congress has indeed lost a golden opportunity.

Defy Ordinances, Flood The Jails: Congress

December 27-28, 1921, Ahmedabad: The annual session of the Congress is under way here and Hakim Ajmal Khan is presiding. CR Das, the president elect, is in prison in Calcutta. The slender opportunity that arose due to the Viceroy's offer has conclusively disappeared. Owing to the severe government repression, the Congress has allowed the non-cooperation movement to graduate into a civil disobedience programme. Already, campaigns against payment of taxes are underway in certain areas.

The session has adopted a resolution issuing a clarion call to the country to adopt a policy of individual and mass civil disobedience. Indians have been exhorted to defy the Emergency Ordinances and court imprisonment in large numbers.

States' People Vow To Fight For Political Rights 'With' Or 'Without' Congress

1921: Congress' stand in favour of non-intervention in the internal affairs of the princely states, taken in the Nagpur session last year, came as a shock to a large number of politically-conscious people of these states.

Still, some of them did not give up hope and went ahead to form people's groups to achieve their political aspirations. In May this year, the people of the Kathiawar state have formed the Kathiawar Raajakiya Parishad. This was followed by the formation of the Deccan States Subjects Conference. Thereafter, a good number of similar groups known as 'praja mandal' and 'lok parishad' have been formed across princely states. This is the early phase of life for these groups.

One of their basic demands is that the rulers include the subjects in the governance of the states. Princes are being asked to employ more state subjects and fewer foreigners in the government and bureaucracy, introduce representative legislatures based on a franchise, and guarantee certain civil liberties such as freedom of association and press. To the relief of the rulers of these states, there is no demand anywhere to end the princely rule, as yet. Not only that—on issues of conflict between the native rulers and the British government, the subjects of Indian states have generally pronounced sympathy for the former, who are often being seen as oppressed by them.

PATRIOTS TAKING UP ARMS

Are Government Policies Responsible?

Ongoing twin movements have been causing great disquiet to the British government. It has never faced an upsurge of this magnitude, which though unarmed, has been challenging the authority of the British to govern India, besides causing grave damage to commercial interests of the Europeans in India. The vengeful and irritated mindset of the government has been reflected in the arrests of the protesters on mass scale. Worse, these political prisoners are also being treated cruelly in Indian jails by the government. In one such incident at the Lucknow Central Jail, Jawaharlal was shocked to see how a young (a boy of 15 or 16 years) Indian patriot was stripped, tied to the whipping triangle and lashed mercilessly. As each lash cut into his flesh, the boy shouted 'Mahatma Gandhi ki Jai'. This further angered the authorities and the stripe kept falling on him till he fainted. This incident is by no means solitary—similar scenes are being witnessed all over India.

Roy And Stalin Set Up Communist University Of The Toilers Of The East

1921, Moscow: Young Indian communist ideologue MN Roy along with Russian leader Joseph Stalin, have played important roles in setting up a Communist University of the Toilers of the East here on 21 April this year. It has begun to impart training and education to communist workers and future leaders from different countries.

Repression Has Made Civil Disobedience Duty: Gandhi

February 1, 1922, Bardoli: India has been caught in the crossfires between government repression and the twin agitations for swaraj and Kkhilafat. The rising public participation in the agitation has put the government to distinct unease. Though most important leaders of both the Congress and the Khilafat Committee are in jail, Gandhi has not yet been touched. Some say the government is afraid that arresting him might cause rebellion in the Indian police and even the army.

At this juncture, Gandhi has today taken the next offensive and served an ultimatum upon the Viceroy. He has accused the government of launching repression of the most 'virulent type' on people across provinces, gagging their freedom of speech and association, and bludgeoning the press. In the context of such unprecedented assault, Gandhi has pointed out that it has become necessary to make attempts to regain the elementary rights of free speech, free association and free press. Descrbing the government's unparalleled atrocities as 'lawless repression', he has written that it has 'made the immediate adoption of mass civil disobedience an imperative duty'.[20]

Gandhi has clarified that under the authority conferred upon him by the Working Committee, he has chosen Bardoli to begin the mass civil disobedience, to start with, giving hints that there is scope for replicating it at the national level. Gandhi has also made a peace offer. He gave the Viceroy a notice of seven days to free all civilian non-cooperation prisoners, declare a policy of non-interference with non-violent activities of people seeking redressal of Khilafat cause, Punjab wrongs and swaraj.

NONCOOPERATION MOVEMENT TURNS VIOLENT
Policemen Burnt Alive In Chauri Chaura

February 5, 1922, Chauri Chaura: It has been reported that in the Chauri Chaura, village, situated in the quiet countryside of the United Provinces, angry villagers have burnt twenty-two policemen to death.

From details reaching the government, it appears the incident was a fallout of a confrontation between the villagers and the police force. There are more than one versions of the incident. According to one, the Satyagrahi villagers were participating in the non-cooperation movement with much enthusiasm. A couple of days ago, while picketing in front of a liquor shop in a local market, the police had fired upon them and they had to disperse. Today, a crowd of about three thousand people consisting of people from villages around, again proceeded to the same market for picketing. On the way, they had to pass through the police chowky. As they neared it, the police attacked them. A confrontation ensued and the police opened fire, killing three Satyagrahis. Numerically a much stronger force today, the mob reacted violently. Unable to control the situation, the policemen retreated into their chowky. Incensed, the protesters did not allow the matter to rest. They encircled the chowky and set it on afire. This resulted in the death of the policemen entrapped inside. The sources say, about twenty-one policemen were burnt alive.

This incident has sent shock waves across the country. There have been many sceptics doubting the feasibility of keeping a nation-wide movement involving several crore of people strictly on non-violent rails. They feel vindicated. There is widespread shock and horror.

Congress Working Committee To Suspend Movement

February 10, 1922, Bardoli: Gandhi, the supreme commander of the ongoing movements, has been insisting that civil disobedience be kept non-violent. He was shell shocked to hear the tidings from Chauri Chaura. To the Congress workers assembled here, he regretted that the country at large has not at all aeecpted the teachings of non-violence. Therefore, he said, he must immeidtalety stop the civil disobedience movement.[21]

Civil Disobedience Movement Suspended

February 12, 1922, Bardoli: The Working Committee has adopted a lengthy resolution today. Its very first clause reads that the 'Working Committee deplores the inhuman conduct of the mob at Chauri Chaura in having brutally murdered constables and wantonly burnt the Police *Thana* and tenders its sympathy to the families of the bereaved'. It also says that the mass civil disobedience at Bardoli and elsewhere be suspended.[22]

Political observers say, even after allowing for the fact that the mob indulged in an outrageous, violent act, the criticism of the Committee has come in haste without hearing the full account of the incident from the villagers' side, too.

Gandhi Begins Penance For Violence

February 12, 1922: Gandhi has begun a five- day fast as penance for violence in Chauri Chaura.

God Has Spoken Clearly Through Chauri Chaura: Gandhi

February 13, 1922, Bardoli: Violence by the protesters in Chauri Chaura has shaken Gandhi but it has also shown him the road map ahead. He feels that God has spoken to him through the incident[23] and he has not the slightest of hesitation thereafter to call the movement off. Gandhi says the withdrawal has become necessary not only to ensure future progress of Indians but also to avert any future retrogression. Simultaneous with the calling off, Gandhi has also announced a series of constructive activities that would include predominantly hand weaving, hand spinning, removing untouchability, promoting communal harmony, suppression of drug traffick, extension of national education and establishing arbitration boards for dispute resolution without offending government laws, However, many are not sure as to how his new programmes would help Indians achieve swaraj.

Gandhi's Decision Spreads Confusion

Chauri Chaura incident and Gandhi's decision to call off the national movements at the zenith have been triggering confusion across the country. Critics point out that Chauri Chaura was certainly not the first time that the tenet of non-violence was infringed. In fact, a serious breach of that principle had already occurred in Malabar last year where the Moplahs carrying on the Khilafat movement not only resorted to armed violence against the government but also indulged in violence against a fellow community. Worse still, that mindless violence spanned over few months. Though a section of people tried to justify the Moplah violence in the name of 'spontaneous nationalistic outburst by the brave Moplahs first wronged by the British', the majority view does not condone their excesses, which in any case, constituted grave violation of the principle of non-violence. Notwithstanding, Gandhi, as the supreme commander, had been continuing with both movements. However, now, a standalone incident at Chauri Chaura has given him such a shock that he has called off an unprecedented national struggle running at its peak, without attempting to finetune it. Not only are the people of the country bewildered, so also are many leaders of the Congress itself.

Gandhi Is Inscrutable, Feel Young Leaders

March 1922: Non-violent non-cooperation movement has been called off but the swaraj which Gandhi had assured Indians in a year's time, is nowhere in sight. During December last year, Gandhi got an offer of a 'round table conference' from the Viceroy to discuss swaraj, but he let it go, by imposing a set of pre-conditions. Since then, he has had no alternative other than to escalate the ongoing movements. By early this year, these movements reached a crescendo. A seemingly desperate government had put no less than 30,000 people in jail but is still clueless. The government is visibly cornered against the rising tide of nationalism. But by his decision to 'call off' the movements, Gandhi seems to have forfeited the entire advantage.

As the rationale for his action, Gandhi has said he has committed an error in launching the movement before preparing people for Satyagraha. But most of his supporters, including many Congress leaders, find this argument hard to accept. They feel it is absurd to train thirty crore Indians in the art of Satyagraha. It is also absurd to guarantee that no violence would occur anywhere, especially when there are grave provocations from the government and vested interests determined to foment trouble, as happened in Malabar. Congress leaders—old and young—lament that a golden opportunity to achieve swaraj has just been allowed to slip. Veterans like CR Das, Motilal Nehru, Malaviya, Lala Lajpat Rai or young leaders like Jawaharlal Nehru or Subhas Bose, feel the same. A national struggle of such gigantic scale takes considerable time, effort and sacrifice to build up and cannot be switched on and off at will.

Government Is Preparing To Hit Back

March 1922, New Delhi: According to reports, the government is heaving a sigh of relief at Gandhi's decision to recall non-cooperation movements. To its enormous advantage, the movements have been called off without any pre-conditions.

The government clearly has the upper hand and it is preparing to take due initiatives. It has a grudge against Gandhi and the Congress not only on account of their demand for swaraj but also for organising large number of Indian Muslims against the government, whose loyalty they had tried to secure all these years through various political and other concessions. According to a section of political observers, the government might now not only hit back at Gandhi but also bluntly encourage communal divide across the country.

Gandhi Arrested: Government Overcomes Phobia

March 10, 1922: Government, inert under its Gandhi phobia, for the whole duration of the non-cooperation movement, has gathered courage and struck back. The police have arrested him and he will be tried for inciting people against the government. In the long history of the Congress, Gandhi was the first person to launch such an intense nationwide struggle against the British regime. The government is relieved at the cessation of the movements. On their part, the Congress leaders are in a state of confusion on their future course of action.

NO MORE THE TAG OF 'PARIAHS'

March 25, 1922, Madras: Untouchables in India, have for long, nourished grievances against the caste Hindus for using such insulting terms as 'pariah' or 'panchama' to refer to them. Today, the Madras Legislative Assembly has passed a resolution, which banishes these disrespectful words. From now on, the untouchables in Tamil districts are to be called as 'Adi Dravida' and those in Telegu districts as 'Adi Andhra'. For these communities, a long struggle for recognition begins.

Is It Possible To Restart Civil Disobedience?

June 6-8, 1922, Lucknow: The AICC has met here and held extensive deliberations over the political situation in the aftermath of the suspension of the civil disobedience movement, especially with many of the top leaders including Gandhi and president elect CR Das lodged in the prison. The session here has adopted a resolution to form a multi-member 'Civil Disobedience Committee' to be led by Hakim Ajmal Khan. The Committee has been called upon to report on the extant political situation in the country, and place before the AICC all available materials so that the latter can further consider 'the question whether civil disobedience in some form or some other measures of a similar character should be adopted.'[24]

CR Das, Others Out Of Prison

July 1922, Calcutta: Gandhi has been awarded six long years of imprisonment. Although the Congress is upset by the sentence, fortunately, some of its other stalwarts have begun to come out of prison and they are preparing to take over the reins.

CR Das is out of prison and expected to play an important role at this critical juncture in carrying the Congress programmes and policies ahead. Das is bitter about the way Gandhi had handled the offer of Viceroy Reading. That opportunity was gone and Gandhi himself has been put behind bars for six long years. Das is reportedly in touch with top leaders like Motilal Nehru and few others to discuss the road map for the Congress.

END OF BOYCOTT, 'YES' TO ELECTION?

During his months' long incarceration in Alipore Central jail in Calcutta, CR Das had chance to introspect on the happenings over the last few years. He had strong differences with Gandhi on cooperating with the government in working out new reforms in the Amritsar session in 1919 when Gandhi had his way. In less than a year's time, Gandhi had changed his policy and in the special session held in Calcutta in September 1920 he had declared the policy of triple boycott of the government, including the legislature. On the last issue, Das had serious differences of opinion with Gandhi but the Congress stood by the latter. Gandhi again strongly put forth his ideas of non-cooperation movement in Nagpur in December that year and Das eventually decided to strengthen Gandhi's hands. However, Gandhi, through his policy and programmes, had failed to achieve swaraj within one year. Worse, he also brushed aside a god-sent opportunity that came through Reading's offer. Worst of all, Gandhi suspended the civil disobedience movement while it was at its peak for the fault of a handful people at the distant countryside.

Das has become convinced of the shortcomings of the programmes and policies hitherto pursued, which invited unprecedented government repression but no advancement in the matter of swaraj. He has thought of an alternative—enter the legislature and paralyse the government through non-cooperation, so as to bring into sharp focus the limitations and defects of the Constitution that is nearly a farce in the name of giving Indians greater self-government. Das has held a series of discussions on the issue with fellow political prisoners, including senior leaders inside the prison and firmed up a plan of action. After he was released from the prison, he has held discussions with like-minded leaders from other parts of the country. Motilal Nehru and Hakim Ajmal Khan in the north, Vithalbhai Patel in the west, Satyamurthy in the south are amongst senior leaders who are enthusiastic about this plan of 'council entry' and opposing the government from inside the legislature.

Babbar Khalsa Jatha

The New Face Of Sikh Revolutionaries

August, 1922, Amritsar: In May last year, a band of radical Sikhs had made abortive attempts to assassinate persons they suspected of having complicity in the massacre of Sikh devotees in the Nankana gurdwara a few months ago. The government was alarmed and set the police on a manhunt. Some of these activists who avoided being captured, joined hands with other like-minded revolutionaries and launched a new militant outfit by the name of Babbar Khalsa Jatha. It has two core objectives: vindicating Sikh faith and securing political independence. Akalis who do not believe in the indespensibility of non-violence in the political struggle are swelling its ranks.

House Throws The Bill, Viceroy Certifies It Into Act

September 24, 1922, New Delhi: A Bill titled, The Indian States (Protection against Disaffection) Bill, was introduced in the Indian Legislative Assembly. The purpose of the Bill is to suppress agitation and propaganda against the ruling dispensation of the native Indian states from British India. In its preamble, the Bill says it aims to prevent the dissemination by means of books, newspapers and other documents of matter calculated to bring hatred, contempt, or to excite disaffection against princes, or chiefs, or governments or administration of the Indian States. After the House refused leave to introduce the Bill, Viceroy Reading has used his power to certify it into an Act. Nationalist Indians, both in British India and Indian states, are considering the event as a blatant attempt to throttle the democratic aspirations of the states' people by building an iron wall amongst the two territories.

Multan In The Grip Of Communal Frenzy

September, 1922, Multan: The Hindu-Muslim unity that was in high visibility during the movement for swaraj and Khilafat was first shaken by acts of communal rioting in south Malabar. The fragile nature of the unity has shown up here in north west part of the country too. A series of riots started with an incident on the 3rd of this month, when a Tazia struck against telephone wire and fell down. The communal fire is still burning here at the end of the month and scattered acts of rioting are still taking place. Hindus have been at the receiving end. There are reports of killing and stabbing and outraging the honour of Hindu women. Their places of worships are being desecrated and burnt.

Country Is Not Ready For Resumption Of Civil Disobedience Movement

October 30, 1922: In June this year, the Congress has appointed a civil disobedience enquiry committee, led by Hakim Ajmal Khan, which toured the country, interacted with large number of people to ascertain the reasons for the collapse of the movement and suggest if it is possible to restart the movement. The members of the committee included leaders like Motilal Nehru, MA Ansari, C Rajagopalachari, Vithalbhai Patel and SK Iyenger. The Committee has submitted its report today to CR Das, the president of the Congress, to be held in Gaya a couple of months later.

While there was a consensus that 'The country is not ready at present to undertake general mass civil disobedience or a general no tax campaign in any Province or District'[25], the members were equally divided on the issue of future course of action. While Hakim Ajmal Khan, Motilal Nehru and Vithalbhai Patel favoured the 'council entry' programme, MA Ansari, Srinavasa Kasturiranga Iyenger and C Rajagopalachari were against such a course of action.

To Change Or Not To Change – Question Haunts Congress

Now that the Civil Disobedience Enquiry Committee has submitted its report, a churning has begun within the Congress. After Gandhi suspended the great movements at their peak without achieving the goal of 'swaraj in a year', the question 'what next' has been exercising the Congress leaders. Steering the organisation at this stage is posing a big challenge. Gandhi's leadership over the last two or three years have radically changed the Congress approach and the peoples' expectations. There is a gulf between the Congress today with what it was before Gandhi took over the reins. Neither is it possible to go back to the past years, nor is it feasible to have Gandhi as leader, who is likely to be out of the public arena for the next six years, ie. his prison term. There is little doubt that Gandhi alone can lead the kind of mass movements he did over last couple of years. On the basis of their own analysis, now reinforced by the findings of the Civil Disobedience Enquiry Committee, there has been a growing realisation amongst a section of senior leaders like CR Das, Motilal Nehru, Hakim Ajmal Khan, NC Kelkar, MR Jayakar, Vithalbhai Patel and a few others that the Congress ought to make a strategy shift and take the fight for 'swaraj to the legislatures'. The party had avoided the election in 1920, in deference to the policy of non-cooperation with and boycott of the government. This paved way for some undeserving people to take seats in the councils, act as the rubber stamps of the government and connive together in persecuting the nationalists. These leaders, representing a 'pro change' group within the Congress, are keen to make amends for the past lapse. They want to enter the councils and wage the fights against the government in the legislatures.

However, another group that is represented by staunch Gandhian leaders like C Rajagopalachari, Rajendra Prasad, Sarojini Naidu, Ansari and Srinivasa Iyenger are against this approach. Though Gandhi has been sentenced for long prison term, they are strongly against moving away from Gandhi's Bardoli decision of constructive activities. At any cost, they would not like to go against the spirit of non-cooperation by entering the council.

Though some leaders were trying to mediate between the two groups for the sake of unity, hardcore leaders from either side do not see much scope for reconciliation. In fact, Pattabhi Sitaramayya, a leader from the 'no changer' group, has said that 'council entry' would constitute an act of dishonesty.

Pro-changers And No-changers In Pitch Battle

1922: The issue of 'council entry' is being hotly debated and the party seems to have become evenly divided in two camps of 'no-changers' and 'pro-changers'. The division runs across the provinces. Serious disagreements erupted in the east, west, north and south of the country.

In the south, the leaders of the Madras Provincial Congress Committee are fighting tooth and nail over the issue. Satyamurti, a prominent pro-change leader is arguing that the Bardoli decision would have little or no relevance in hastening the advent of swaraj and India can hardly spend the limited amount of political energy and enthusiasm on such endeavours. He has thus proposed to MR Jayakar, the Congress stalwart of Maharashtra, to form a party within the Congress, which would adopt council entry as its main tenet. 'Council entry' would give Indians a chance to express themselves politically. On the other extreme, no-changer leader Kalyanasundaram Mudaliar is contending that the adoption of the 'council entry' programme would be to acknowledge its own defeat by the Congress, and going into the enemy's camp to surrender. This group has as its leader Rajagopalachari who wields lots of clout in the party at the national level.

As these debates go on, insiders say efforts are on within the Congress to form a party, which would contest the second council election the next year.

Das And Motilal Nehru Resign

December 26-31, 1922 Gaya: Congress is holding its annual session here. CR Das is presiding. Two rival factions representing the 'pro-changers' and the 'no-changers' have arrayed their forces with a view to influencing the Congress decision on a future course of action. Das sought to persuade the delegates in favour of contesting the forthcoming election to the councils. He said, though Congress had boycotted the election in 1920, it must prepare to capture legislature in 1923.

Das, who has the support of leaders like Motilal Nehru, Hakim Ajmal Khan and others, tried to convince the delegates that Gandhi's direct action programme has failed and Congress should, therefore, try other methods to restore public morale. He contended that the council entry is a viable alternative that would take the political fight inside the legislature. These leaders are confident of Congress' success in crossing swords with British officialdom in a tried and tested parliamentary fashion. But all the efforts of this group of the 'pro-changers', aimed at taking hold of the organisation, have been stonewalled by the 'no-changers' or the Gandhi loyalists.

Thus, when CR Das introduced a motion in favour of the 'council entry', it was fiercely resisted by the 'no-changers'. Although Gandhi himself is in prison, his loyal followers like Rajendra Prasad, C Rajagopalachari and others opposed the motion and mobilised a large chunk of delegates to resist any change from Gandhi's policies of non-cooperation. Their contention has been that the adoption of the motion would mean a formal repudiation of Gandhi's leadership. Following extensive debates and deliberations, the 'no-changers' prevailed because of their organising skills and Gandhi's unabated appeal to larger number of delegates. Das's motion was rejected by 1,748-890 votes.

In the wake of the defeat of his motion, Das has tendered his resignation as president. Motilal Nehru, the general secretary of the party, tendered his resignation too. Das, Motilal and other like-minded leaders have begun the process of forming a separate party within the Congress, to be able to go ahead with the agenda they believe in.

SWARAJ PARTY TAKES BIRTH

Bubbling Baby Delivered By Indifferent Mother

January 1,1923, Allahabad: CR Das, Motilal Nehru, Ajmal Khan and others have decided to pursue their convictions, which lie in pursuing the alternative route of achieving swaraj by participating in the legislative process, while the option of awakening the people can go on simultaneously. They contend, the two programmes of actions are not mutually exclusive. Today, while the AICC was about to take up for discussion the Congress agenda for 1923, Motilal Nehru announced a new political formation called the 'Swaraj Party' within the Congress to achieve their political goals. Other leaders supporting the line include Seshadri Srinivasa Iyengar, BN Sasmal, Vithalbhai Patel and Chaudhury Khaliquzaaman. CR Das endorsed Motilal's announcement while winding up the proceedings and tendered his resignation as president.

The 'pro-change' leaders feel that the Swaraj Party would be able to lift the sagging morale of the Congress by resorting to constitutional agitation. The leaders are confident they can effectively deal with the British in parliamentary processes and advance the interests of the Indians better, under the present circumstances.

Both Das and Motilal have given a clarion call to prepare to capture legislatures in the coming election. The leaders of the new party want to blend the rising public emotion with participation in the legislative council in a calibrated manner, to attain control over the governmental power at the shortest time frame.

Salt Tax Doubled At One Stroke!

February, 1923, New Delhi: Sir Basil Blackett, the new finance minister who was chosen by the Conservative government in England and sent to India, has given his first gift to Indians by doubling the 'salt tax' at one stroke. Though this would hurt the poor very hard, the Reading government is just not bothered! And with the Congress in total disarray, the government is not much concerned.

Swarajists Make Inroads Into No-changers' Fort

February 26, 1923, Patna: Bihar, Gujarat and Madras have been stronghold of the 'no-changers'. However, today the Swaraj Party has made an inroad in Bihar. A section of Congressmen assembled in Patna and formed the Bihar Swaraj Party.

Prevent Legal Murder Of Soldiers Of Freedom

MN Roy To Indian Working Men And Women

March 1923, Berlin: Post Chauri Chaura, the government acted with alacrity and vengeance, disregarding the fact that the incident was a spontaneous upsurge by the simple peasantry, who were provoked by the police firing on peaceful protesters. The police rounded up over a thousand people. About two hundred and twenty five people were put on trial and the court awarded death sentences to as many as 172 accused persons.

Though the court action clearly seemed to be biased and a

continuation of the government's revengeful attitude, these unfortunate people found little support. The Congress, committed to non-violence, had already condemned the peasants who resorted to violence.

These hapless peasants found a strong voice of support in faraway Berlin from MN Roy, the communist ideologue camping there. Roy, who has been keeping a close watch from Europe over the proletariat participations in national struggles, has been deeply moved by the indifference to these doomed peasants.

From Berlin, he has issued an appeal to the all working men and women of India through his journal, *The Vanguard,* to stand by the side of these accused persons who have turned victims of the court verdicts. Calling them as soldiers of the Indian freedom struggle, he has urged that a general strike be called in the country to save their soul. He has said that the atrocities of this legal murder are unparalleled even in the bloody history of British rule in India.

Swarajists Hold First Conference

March 1923, Allahabad: The Swaraj Party has held its first conference here at Motilal Nehru's house. The constitution of the new party has been drawn. The party deliberated over what ought to be its aim. While the Congress claimed its aim as 'swaraj', it fell short of defining its meaning. The Swaraj Party has sought to differentiate between immediate aim and long term goal. The party stated 'dominion status' as its immediate aim. However, it did not spell out its ultimate objective. The party has also drawn up a plan of campaign.

British Garrison Called In To Douse Communal Riot

April 1923, Amritsar: Right since the outbreak of a riot in Multan in September last year, more communal riots are occurring in different parts of Punjab with disturbing frequency. Amritsar too came under its vicious grip. Especially on the 11th and 12th of this month, violent street fights broke out. These were so severe that the government had to call in a British garrison to bring the situation under control.

No Reconciliation, Swarajists To Go Full Steam

May 1923, Allahabad: On April 24, the top leaders of both, the 'no-changers' and the Swaraj Party, met—the aim was to arrive at common programmes to be pursued by the Congress. Though some agreements seemed to have arisen there, those proved to be illusory. On behalf of the Swaraj Party, Motilal Nehru has urged the party leaders to go full steam with the party's agenda.

Ghost Of Communal Riot Surfaces In Calcutta

May, 1923, Calcutta: After Multan and Amritsar in Punjab, the ghost of communal hatred has raised its ugly head in the capital of Bengal. A serious communal riot has broken out in the city after a clash occurred over an Arya Samaji procession, playing music and passing before a mosque in the city. Arya Samajis say this has been a practice over the past several years while the Muslims say it has disturbed their worship. The warring attitude of the two communities and their worn out tolerance of each other suggest the absurdity of the high watermark of communal unity that was on display in the course of the movement for swaraj and Khilafat. The government had a hard time in restoring normalcy.

CR Das Storms Rajagopalachari's Fort

June 1923, Madras: After the division of the Congress Party in the Gaya session, the nationalist party has generally been backing the 'no changers'. This has made the Swaraj Party to send its top leaders across provinces to carry its messages amongst people. The prime responsibility for the northern part of the country rests on Motilal, of the central and west on Vithalbhai. CR Das has taken it unto himself to spread the wings of the Swaraj Party in the south. He has been touring districts extensively and getting good response. In Madras, Satyamurti and Srinavasa Iyenger have been lending Das solid help. If the response the team has been receiving is any indicator, it can be safely concluded that the Swaraj Party has a future in Madras and it is expected to throw a stiff challenge to the 'no- changers', led by C Rajagopalachari.

Khilafat Movement Is Collapsing

The Khilafat alliance has been collapsing. Critics say it was destined to die as the pact was based on artificial grounds of 'religious sentimentalism'. It had no concern with the problems of the daily lives of Indians or Indian Muslims, more specifically—with hunger, poverty, health, education etc. British treatment of the Caliph of Turkey was too abstract an issue for which neither the Muslims nor the Hindus in India could carry out a sustained political struggle for too long a period, even if it was led by a leader like Gandhi. The Moplah rebellion in 1921 had caused great suspicion among large section of Indians about the eventual outcome of the Khilafat agitation. The final blow came from Turkey itself when the charismatic leader, Kamal Pasha defeated the Greeks, and transformed Turkey into a republic. It is being said that he would also abolish the institution of the Caliphate before long.

Bonhomie Passé, Two Communities Pick Up Arms

December 1923: As long as the twin movements for Khilafat and swaraj were running full steam, the communal elements, under tremendous pressure from the Indian masses cutting across communities, kept a low profile. However, neither they nor the British government approved of the hold Gandhi, a Congress leader, had over Indian Muslims. As such, the vested interests kept raising their ugly heads whenever opportunities arose. They had made a substantial contribution in turning the Khilafat movement in the Malabar into a vicious communal massacre of the Hindus in 1921. Though the Congress had managed to keep the non-cooperation movements running at that time—critics say, by compromising on the principle of non-violence and overlooking the atrocities on a sister community, they allowed communal amity in the country to come under severe strain right since then. The situation grew grim, especially after the Khilafat movement began to wane and Gandhi recalled the movement for swaraj. The Moplah uprising was followed by a serious riot in Multan.

Over the past few months, communal riots have been spreading across the country and the British government is watching the fun rather than dealing with these with an iron hand. Indian leaders are alarmed at these developments. The secret agents of the government are, in some cases, fanning the trouble too. Distraught by silent acquiescence and even encouragement of the government to such morbid happenings, a few well-meaning leaders of both communities are taking initiatives to improve the communal environment. In Bengal, CR Das has engineered a pact between the leaders of the two communities, aimed at dousing the fire of communal hatred. But the situation seems not to be under control as yet.

Especially in north India, the relations between the Hindus and Muslims have been steadily worsening. Brutal riots are taking place in bigger cities on issues like cow sacrifice, especially on Bakri Id day. Clashes have become more when Hindu and Muslim festivals overlap. The tolerance level has dwindled so much that stray instances of playing music in processions before mosques lead to serious clashes between communities. Jawaharlal feels that want of clear ideals and objectives in the struggle for freedom have helped the spread of communalism. The masses are not able to see a clear connection between their day-to-day sufferings and the recent movements. They are, therefore, easy prey to intrigues and machinations.

HUGE TURNOUT AT HINDU MAHASABHA SESSION

August 1923, Benares: British policy of according preferential treatment to the Muslim community in the matter of political rights has been causing resentment in other communities for long. The spurts in communal violence and large-scale massacre of Hindu lives and properties in Malabar, north western provinces and other places in the country have been causing great disquiet to many Hindus. This is reflected in large turnouts in the session that has been convened by the All-India Hindu Mahasabha (earlier All-India Hindu Sabha, renamed in 1921) in this holy city. Nearly 1,500 delegates—Sikhs, Jains, Buddhists, Sanatanists, Arya Samajis and other—turned up here to attend the deliberations.

Shraddhanand Reinducts Malkana Rajputs Into Hindu Fold

August 1923: Last year, in the same month, the Kshatriya Upakarini Sabha held a meeting in Allahabad and called for a programme for reconversion of Muslim Malkana Rajputs inhabiting the western part of the United Provinces. They were Hindus converted into Islam. Now a meeting is being held, with Swami Shraddhanand in the chair, to implement the programme. The meeting has approved setting up of the Bharatiya Hindu Shuddhi Sabha to take up the task of reconversion. In fact, the process of reconversion of the Malkan Rajputs had begun early this year. Now under the leadership of Shraddhanand and with the benefit of an organised approach, better results are anticipated.

One-way Proselytisation Must Stop: Hindu Mahasabha

1923: Since its inception, the All-India Hindu Mahasabha has been deeply concerned about the British policy of driving a wedge between the Hindus and Muslims. One of the reasons for its formation was the British government's starting of the separate electorate system for the country's Muslims. The Mahasabha has been considering the move as unjust, biased, and aimed at creating a communal divide. Having been launched in 1915, the Mahasabha has been fighting for the social and political interests of the Hindus, more specifically against discriminatory treatment meted out to them as a community by the government. Under the able leadership of stalwarts like Madan Mohan Malaviya and Lajpat Rai, it has been emerging as a strong organisation.

The communal situation in India has begun to worsen since the Moplah uprising in 1921. The brutal massacre of the Hindus in the Malabar was followed by few more riots against them in the Muslim majority provinces like NWFP and Punjab, taking huge toll of Hindu lives and properties. Reckoning that the Congress has not been adequately sensitive to these unfortunate developments hurting the Hindus, the Mahasabha is coming forward to protect the interests of the victimised community. They have diagnosed that the one-way proselytisation in the country has been at the root of many of the present problems. The Hindus, the Mahasabha contends, have been a happy hunting ground for conversions by both the Muslims and the Christians for ages and this process has, by and large, been one-sided. Its leaders are feeling the need for an organised mission who could prevent this bleeding of the majority community. In this connection, they recognise the untiring Shuddhi campaign that has begun under the leadership of Swami Shraddhanand, and is currently under way to reconvert the Rajput Malkana Muslims.

Pro-changers And No-changers Pursue Their Agenda

September 15, 1923, Delhi: The Swaraj Party was formed in January this year but its differences with the 'no-changers' had not been reconciled all these months. The AICC had held successive meetings at Allahabad in February, Bombay in May and Nagpur in July to sort out the differences between the two warring camps but failed to achieve results. Ultimately, in its special session being held here, the logjam has ended.

In this session, presided by Maulana Abul Kalam Azad, it has been resolved that both pro- and no-changers would be free to pursue their own programmes. The resolution said:

'While reaffirming its adherence to the principle of non-violent non-cooperation, this Congress declares that such Congressmen as have no religious or other conscientious objections against entering Legislatures are at liberty to stand as candidates and to exercise their right of voting at the forthcoming elections; and this Congress, therefore, suspends all propaganda against entering the councils. The Congress, at the same time, calls upon all Congressmen to redouble their efforts to carry out the constructive programme of their leader, Mahatma Gandhi, by united endeavour to achieve swaraj at the earliest possible moment.'

This resolution has, thus, put to rest the controversy over boycott of councils and non-cooperation movement that began during the Calcutta Congress held in 1920 and reached a climax in January this year with the formation of the Swaraj Party.

The Power Of The Wireless Message!

September 1923, Delhi: According to inside sources, Delhi was qualitatively different from Gaya. Swarajists have gathered considerable strength across the country right since their birth. In Delhi they turned up in large numbers. CR Das brought a huge contingent along with him. Therefore, the Swarajists negotiated from a position of strength.

Interestingly, one of the distinguished delegates, Maulana Mohammed Ali, also played a role, though some say it was a coincidence. Just before this session, both, Mohammed Ali and Dr Saifuddin Kitchlew, were released from prison. Mohammed Ali informed the delegates that he had a wireless message from Gandhi, who is still in prison, to bring about a compromise between the rival groups. Some say the Maulana's words had a magic effect upon many. Even some of the so-called rationale men also succumbed to the charm of the extraterrestrial communication.

Nabha Teaches Congress 'Caution' In Meddling With State

September, 1923: In Punjab, the Akali Dal has been carrying on its agitation programmes against the government to secure control over the gurdwaras for past few years. To this has been added a new protest movement on the issue of restoration of Maharaja Ripudaman Singh to the throne of the native state of Nabha. Suspecting that the Maharaja had been helping the Akalis in the gurdwara movement, the British government managed to dislodge him from the throne. To give the episode a constitutional sanctity, the government allegedly forced the Maharaja to resign, as if he abdicated the throne on his own. In protest, the Akalis have been regularly taking 'jathas' to Jaito in the native state, facing police repression and courting arrests.

Although an advocate of a policy of non-interference in the states' politics, the Congress has been supporting the Akali movements carried out in non-violent manner in Punjab. This autumn, the Congress passed a resolution condemning the resignation forced upon the Maharaja. Congress' interest in the issue became more pronounced when on the twenty-first day of the present month, Jawaharlal, accompanied by Dr Gidwani and K Santhanam, followed an Akali Jatha and journeyed from Muktasar inside British India to Jaito, in the Nabha state. His objective was to observe first hand, the allegedly brutal treatment of successive Akali Jathas by the state police, which were being taken out to protest against the resignation forced upon the Maharaja.

Upon arrival at Jaito, Jawaharlal and his associates were ordered to leave the state of Nabha immediately. On non-compliance, they were arrested, handcuffed and sent to Nabha. It is learnt that their arrests were ordered by the British representative in that state. In Nabha, they became victims of a farcical judicial process and had to stay in the prison for a few days. During his brief sojourn in this part of the country and interaction with the government machineries, Jawaharlal has come to realise how native states like Nabha combined the vices of both feudalism and modern bureaucratic machinery. As an organisation, Congress has come to realise that there are many practical hurdles involved in state politics. On the one hand, the Congress does not have the required hold over local political parties or the peoples' groups as shown in this case by Akali Dal's refusal to heed the Congress advice. On the other hand, there are no appropriate legal safeguards available in these states unlike in British India. The reinforced lesson is that the Congress must tread with caution when it comes to dabbling in state politics.

Swaraj Party's Election Manifesto

Indian Struggle To Be In The 'Council Houses'

October 14, 1923, Allahabad: Swaraj Party has issued its election manifesto. In it, the party has demanded the right for Indians to control their own government. Expressing their unhappiness over the unsatisfactory reforms introduced by the 1919 Act, the party promised it would make these reforms unworkable and bring the administrative machinery to a standstill. They also indicated their intention of moving resolutions for the advancement of the constitution and bring a proposal for new legislations towards this end. Generally, it would strive to bring the government in alignment with the Indian way of thinking. The party also promised that 'outside the council', it would support Gandhi's constructive programme.

Revolutionaries Found Hindustan Republican Association

December 1923, Brahmanbaria, East Bengal: A large section of the patriotic Indians were heart-broken when Gandhi had abruptly called off the non-cooperation movement. They were further hurt by a series of communal violence across the country, which they suspected as the joint venture of the vile communal elements and the secret agents of the British government. Their growing anger and frustrations against the government have been fuelling the revolutionary activities across the country.

Anushilan Samity, a prominent revolutionary society based in Calcutta, has been able to establish a large network across provinces. According to reliable sources, it has over a hundred branches and nearly nine thousand members.

A new revolutionary organisation, adopting the name Hindustan Republican Association, has now taken birth in Bholachang village in Brahmanbaria district in the eastern part of Bengal. It has been founded by Sachin Sanyal, Pratul Ganguly, Narednranath Sen and a few others, all committed revolutionaries. The founders have ambition to spread its branches across the country. The object of the association shall be to establish a Federated Republic of the United States of India by an organised and armed revolution.[26]

Voices Of The Depressed Classes Travel In Wilderness

December 1923, Bombay: In August this year, the Bombay Legislative Council had passed a resolution allowing untouchables the use of public wells, dharmashalas built or maintained out of public funds or administered by government-appointed bodies and also public schools, courts, offices, dispensaries, and other facilities. The Bombay government had issued a directive to its departments in September this year. However, the resolution is proving to be toothless. Down the line, district collectors are advising local bodies to consider accepting the recommendations. Implementation is far from satisfactory and the depressed classes in the province continue to be discriminated against.

Rival Communities Organise Themselves In Self-defence

1923: By latter half of 1922, and right from the early part of this year, the north and north west of the country have been rocked by communal violence. Several communal riots occurred in Multan, Amritsar in Punjab and Kohat in NWFP. Some ambitious communal Muslim elements planned to use pan-Islamic connections to re-establish Islamic rule in India. Thus, a virile community has been set up under Tanzeem and Tabligh, who threatened to make common cause with Afghanistan and other Muslim countries to establish Islamic rule over India. An eminent leader like Dr Saifuddin Kitchlew has reportedly taken keen initiative in promoting this new movement.

On the other hand, upset at the growing number of communal riots across the country where Hindus have been, by and large, at the receiving end, veteran Congress leader Lajpat Rai has called upon the Hindus to unite in self-defence under the umbrella organisation of Sangathan.

Bengal Pact Arouses Strong Emotions

December 1923, Coconada: While the communal conflicts have been raging in the country, Bengal has, barring a stray riot in Calcutta in May this year, remained comparatively less affected, mainly due to the predominance of the Swaraj Party in the provincial politics. On 16th of the current month CR Das, on behalf of his party, has entered into a pact with prominent Muslim leaders that aim to sort out the seeds of communal conflicts. The pact is to come into effect after real foundation of self-government in Bengal. The chief imports of their pact lies in agreeing to the Muslims presentations in the council in the proportion of their numbers in the total population together with the system of separate electorate, and giving them preference in government jobs to improve their economic conditions and bring them at par with their Hindu counterparts. While the pact agrees that the Muslims should have claim of 55% over government jobs, it provides that till this coveted percentage is achieved, still higher percentage of the new jobs ought to go to them.

To promote goodwill between communities, the pact bans playing music in processions before mosques. It also says the issue of stoppage of cow slaughter could be approached through discussion and agreement rather than by way of legislation.

The pact, being called as 'Bengal Pact', has aroused strong emotions —both for and against. The Muslims are happy and describing it as a 'path-breaking solution' to the vexed problem of communal discord. Many Hindus are bitter and unhappy at the pact which they call as 'one sided' and 'unfair'. Many leaders of the Congress Party have serious reservations too.

It is learnt that Lajpat Rai has written to CR Das pointing out that such a policy, aimed at bringing about communal unity, would be futile. Many others,whether moderates like Surendra Nath Banerjea or extremists like BC Pal are also strongly opposing this pact. But Das has remained steadfast. Subhas has been a strong supporter of this pact.

The pact was placed before the Congress, in its annual session that is under way here, for approval. But it has been rejected on the ground of being partial to Muslims and being in violation of the principle of nationalism.

1923 ELECTION, SWARAJ PARTY'S GOLDEN DEBUT

January 1, 1924, Delhi: Whereas the 1920 election was a simple 'walk away' for the other candidates as the Congress boycotted it, this year's election was a different ball game altogether. Swaraj Party's patriotic manifesto and the presence of many Congress stalwarts including CR Das, Motilal Nehru and others as its candidates, gave the party clear edge over the rest. As a result, though a recent entrant to the electoral fray, the party registered impressive victory in the Indian Legislative Assembly where it bagged as many as 45 out of 105 seats open for election and a total of 145 seats. As a result, it has emerged as not only the largest single group but also a compact, principled and disciplined formation with a clear cut political agenda. The Moderates have taken the second position with a tally of 27 seats. The Swarajists are seeing scope for floor coordination with the Moderates and like-minded Independents of whom 7 have been elected. Thus, with the right kind of coordination amongst themselves, they would be in a position to make smooth running of the government extremely difficult.

In the provinces, the Swaraj Party has earned clear majority in the Central Provinces. In Bengal provincial assembly, it has emerged as the single largest party. Its achievement here has been remarkable as, under the leadership of CR Das, the party has been able to snatch a number of seats reserved for the Muslims from the communal elements. Its performance in other provinces has not been enviable, but not too poor either. In Madras, for example, it has given some fight to the established Justice Party.

Young Swarajist Scores Sensational Victory Over Surendra Nath Banerjea

January 1924, Calcutta: Swarajists have upset many calculations in the recent election. In Bengal, a young and almost unknown politician, Bidhan Chandra Ray, contesting on a Swaraj Party ticket has defeated the veteran moderate leader Surendra Nath Banerjea. This is being seen as nothing less than a debacle and the telling evidence of the new party's popularity.

Gandhi Served 'Release Order' In Hospital Bed

February 5, 1924, Sassoon Hospital, Pune: Gandhi was awarded six years of prison term on charges of sedition only last year. However, he has not been keeping good health generally and afflicted with appendicitis problem in particular. In the meanwhile, the Swaraj Party legislators also proposed resolution in the central legislature, demanding Gandhi's release from the prison. On 11th of last month, he underwent an appendix surgery and has been convalescing here. The government has decided to release him. The release order was served today. Gandhi is not happy that the release has been ordered on health grounds. Congress workers and Indians are, however, celebrating the occasion. He would be happy, he said, if the government changed its attitude towards him and grasped the fact that non-violence formed the core of the non-cooperation movement.

According to reports received, Gandhi may not leave the hospital immediately, and take rest for few days more.

Revise The Constitution, Swarajists Demand

February 18, 1924, New Delhi: Indian political parties have found the reforms carried through Government of India Act 1919 grossly inadequate. Swaraj Party, in its election manifesto, had promised to work to improve upon the proposed constitution.

True to its promise and pledge, the party has been working enthusiastically in the central legislature to bring about improvements in the existing constitution. Working as a well-knit, disciplined political party, it has placed demands for full responsible government in India and to achieve this it has also asked for a round table conference so that a scheme of the new constitution can be drawn up for the country, while taking due care to protect the rights and interests of the minorities.

The party has also demanded that the recommendations of the round table must be adopted by th e central legislature, and sent to the British Parliament for enactment. Today Motilal Nehru put through these demands by way of an amendment to a resolution. It was passed by the Legislative Assembly by 76-48 votes, thanks to its excellent rapport with like-minded groups and effective floor strategy. The clear majority speaks about the strength of the Indian 'intent'.

Government Sets Up Committee To Review Constitution

February, 1924, New Delhi: The government is finding it difficult to ignore the Swarajists demands. They are also stepping up pressure through combination of strategies like walkouts, spurning of membership in government committees and boycotting functions organised in honour of the Governor General. Possibly, because of all of these, the government has appointed a committee under the chairmanship of Alexander Muddiman, Home Member.

The committee is expected to conduct an empirical investigation into the working of the constitution under the GOI Act 1919. For the Swarajists, the main issue, of course, is the removal of the obnoxious 'diarchy' system. In keeping with its consistent stand, Motilal has refused to be a part of the committee. It will, of course, have four leaders from the Liberal Party – TB Sapru, MA Jinnah, Sivaswamy Iyer and Paranjape.

Swaraj Party Stalls Introduction Of Finance Bill

March 17, 1924, Delhi: Though the Swaraj Party demanded a round table for revising the constitution, the government has made its unwillingness quite clear. The party, in turn, has sought to express its dissatisfaction by withholding the leave to introduce the Finance Bill in the Central Legislative Assembly. The pro-government lobby tried to push its way but the Swaraj Party and its coalition won by 60-57 votes.

May Every Drop Of My Blood Sow The Seeds Of Freedom In Every House In India – Gopinath Saha's Last Wish

March 1924, Calcutta: After a lull following the heydays of the non-cooperation movement, revolutionary activities have resurfaced in the soil of Bengal with great intensity. The law enforcing agencies are not proving adequate to meet the newly emerging challenges. Secret societies are targeting oppressive British police officers and other bureaucrats besides the latters' native collaborators.

They are sometimes issuing threats in advance, causing panic in their targets. Gopinath Saha, a young revolutionary, had made a daring plan to eliminate Charles Tegart, the police commissioner of Calcutta known for his highhanded and cruel repressions of the revolutionaries. By mistake, Gopinath had shot dead a British merchant. He was tried, convicted and hanged. He faced the trial with exemplary courage and his proud demeanour made great impression on the public. While climbing the gallows, Gopinath said: 'May every drop of my blood sow the seeds of freedom in every house in India.'[27]

Swarajists Throw Down The Gauntlet

March 1924, New Delhi: The Swaraj Party, in its election manifesto, had promised to carry the Indian nationalists' challenge to the precincts of the council and it is doing so with aplomb. It has built up a floor strategy, together with the Moderates and the Muslim group led by Jinnah. Together they number 70 out of a total of 105 elected members. Quite a few of them are veteran leaders, erudite speakers and men of sharp intellects. Already, this extended group has forced several debates upon the government, exposing the latter's vulnerabilities. In this short span, it was also able to reject the Finance Bill, which had to be carried by the Governor General on his shoulder—exercising his special powers. The government has begun to feel the heat of the new challenge.

In the provinces, where the party has majority or where it emerged as the single largest party, its leaders refused to form government under the diarchy system, as provided for in the extant constitution. However, the party has been making every effort to obstruct the functioning of the provincial ministries through legislative procedures and means so as to expose the shortcomings of the constitution. The party's aim is to expose the hollowness of the given system through continuous and consistent opposition.

Form Small Groups And Spread - Communist Strategy

March 1924: The émigré Communist Party of India, founded by MN Roy and few others in the USSR, is acting as the beacon light for the small and slowly growing tribe of Indian communists. Aware that the colonial British government is dead against allowing any Communist Party to operate in India, Roy has been in touch with the secret societies like Anushilan and Jugantar to propagate communist ideology and activities in mainland India. The strong feelings against the colonial government and the preparedness to adopt violence to achieve political goals are the glues that bind these two partners. As a strategy, the Communist Party of India has been trying to expand its activities by building up small groups across the country. Over a period of time small communist groups have been founded in

Bengal, Bombay, Punjab, United Province and Madras. Due to a ban on communist activities, these small groups, under close watch of the intelligence branches, have been working underground in a stifling environment. But they are committed to their ideology and irrepressible.

TOP COMMUNIST LEADERS ROUNDED UP

Government Alleges Plots Of Violent Revolution

March 17, 1924, Cawnpore: Over past three years, the police have been arresting communist leaders and workers from time to time. So far, they have slapped three conspiracy cases against the communists—the First Peshawar Conspiracy Case, the Second Peshawar Conspiracy Case, and the Moscow Conspiracy Case. In all these, Indian Muhajirs turned communists, trained in Russia were put to trial. Presently, the government has put a set of prominent communist leaders to trial. This has come in the wake of the government filing a charge in Cawnpore last month to the effect that it has unearthed another communist conspiracy to deprive the King Emperor of the sovereignty of India by setting up a branch of Communist International and through violent revolution. The government has been looking for leaders like MN Roy, SA Dange, Muzaffar Ahmed, Nalini Gupta, Shaukat Usmani, Singaaravelu Chettiar, Ghulam Hussain and RC Sharma in this connection. Of them MN Roy is in Germany and Sharma in French Pondicherry. Others were arrested and put on trial. The case is being called the Cawnpore Bolshevik Conspiracy case.

Indians are not quite familiar with the communist ideology. However, they have heard of the remarkable success of Lenin in throwing the oppressive Tsar of Russia off his throne and establishing the rule of the proletariats. Many Indians identify the colonial British government with the Tsar and have begun to dream of accomplishing a similar revolution in India. The newspapers cater to such imagination by spreading several stories, mostly exaggerated and unsubstantiated.

Despite being repeatedly crucified, the communists in the country are happy that the people of India are growing interested to know about their ideology and new members are enrolling. The trails in the last three cases have given the communists good mileage, thanks to the media. The latest case may surpass the past three in terms of impact, considering the stature of the leaders and their support base.

Gandhi Does Not Approve Of Swarajist Policies

March 29, 1924, Bombay: Swarajists have been able to carry on the Indian aspirations for swaraj in the hall of the Central Legislature, and that quite effectively. They have been combating the colonial government with a different strategy altogether—argument, reasoning, debating and good repertoire of parliamentary skill. In fact, the ways they have been performing their role in the legislatures, have already earned them grudging admiration and respect of the colonial rulers. Within Congress too, the Swarajists are gaining in stature and popularity.

However, Gandhi is not convinced. He is of the firm opinion that the participation in the constitutional process has been a wrong decision and pushing Congress and Indians away from the path of sacrifice. As he has been convalescing in the seaside bungalow of Narottam Morarji in Juhu, following his appendicitis operation, Motilal Nehru, Madan Mohan Malaviya and Hakim Ajmal Khan, came to meet him. There were discussions aimed at securing his endorsement for the Swarajist programmes.

Motilal tried to put before him their strategy of obstructing the government within the legislature and its rationale. However, Gandhi could not be convinced. He said one could either cooperate or not cooperate. He felt an inherent contradiction in the Swarajist plan. They held long discussion on the issue for a few days, but could not reach any agreement.

Kemal Ataturk Abolishes Caliphate

March 3, 1924, Istanbul: Kemal Ataturk, the undisputed leader of Turkey has abolished the office of the Caliph. It appears a new, rejuvenated Turkey has decided to free itself of the traditional religious sentiment. In India, the activities of the All-India Khilafat Committee have been declining in recent months. Now the abolition of the very institution of 'Khilafat' has sounded its final death knell. The question, however, is what will be the nature of next political activities of the Khilafatists leaders and workers now?

Swaraj Party Scores Handsome Victory In Election

March, 1924, Calcutta: The results of the elections to Calcutta Municipal Corporation are out and the Swaraj Party, under CR Das, has won by a convincing margin. The most striking feature of the election has been the impressive win of the Swaraj Party in the seats reserved for Muslims. CR Das has been elected as the mayor while Shaheed Suhrawardy would act as the deputy mayor. Subhas, a young man of 27 years and the political apprentice of CR Das, has been appointed as the chief executive officer. Swaraj Party is determined to leave a mark of efficiency, competence and sensitivity in its running of the Corporation while trying to Indianise its policies to the extent possible.

TEMPLE ROW IN TRAVANCORE

March 1924, Vaikom: A longstanding and simmering social conflict is waiting to explode, ironically in one of the progressive native states in the south of the country. The depressed classes and the untouchables have not been traditionally allowed to use the approach roads to the famous Shiva temple situated by the side of the picturesque Vembanad Lake in this city. But with time, raised public awareness and nationwide Congress campaign against untouchability, a team of three public-spirited persons decided to challenge the ban. Trouble began when Kunjapy (a Pulaya), Bahuleyan (an Ezhava) and Govinda Panicker (a Nair) defied the bans on the road. They were stopped by the police and allowed only one amongst the three, viz. Govinda, a caste Hindu to pass. Protests followed and all three were arrested and jailed for six months. This incident has raised a public debate. TK Madhavan, a local Congress leader, is reported to have got permission from the Congress central leaders to launch a Satyagraha here. He is organising Congress workers and other socially responsible persons to launch a movement.

RIGHT TO WALK ON 'ROADS TO TEMPLES'
Depressed Classes Stake Claim, Congress Leads

April 1924, Vaikom: The land of the Cheras, known as God's Own Country, has been ironically known for rigid caste hierarchy. Travancore, in particular, has been a citadel of orthodoxy and casteism. The depressed classes and the untouchables are not only denied entry into the temples but not permitted even to walk on the approach roads. Congress workers, enthusiastic about establishing the civil rights of these sections of the Hindu community, launched a Satyagraha on the 30th of last month by the side of the famous Shiva temple here. This splendid temple is situated on the eastern bank of the beautiful Vembanad Lake. Roads from east, west, north and south approach the temple but the depressed classes and untouchables are not permitted to use these—prohibitory boards, prominently displayed, declare the ban. Ironically, no such restrictions are imposed on people of other religions like Muslims or Christians. The crullest insult is heaved on an untouchable travelling on a bullock cart, as he is made to alight the vehicle at the entry point and use a circuitous road, whereas the cattle is permitted to pass through. Now, thanks to initiative by TK Madhavan and the Congress committee, a Satyagraha ashram has been erected some distance away in the south of the temple.

From the first day, groups of people—untouchables, depressed classes, socially responsible caste Hindus—are being sent by Congress organisers to walk through these roads, defying the ban. The police arrested them and they have been tried and punished by way of imprisonment of varying terms.

As the number of prisoners soared, the police, in a change of strategy, put up barricades at vantage points and prevented the Satyagrahis at the entry points. At this, the Satyagrahis squatted on the road in the scorching sun and held demonstrations. Public speeches were delivered denouncing the authorities. Some of those named by the protestors were held in esteem by the caste Hindus. The government deemed these as vilification of dignified people and viewed the matter seriously. Counter propaganda began against the Satyagrahis.

As the news of the Satyagraha reached other provinces and native states, people began turning up at Vaikom to participate in the programme. From the neighbouring Tamil land, EV Ramaswamy Naicker Periyar came with his wife Nagamma and a band of followers to offer Satyagraha. He was arrested but awarded a relatively light sentence of one month of imprisonment. Periyar's wife Nagamma, a public spirited woman, together with the wife of TK Madhavan mobilised a group of women from nearby villages, offered Satyagraha and courted arrest.

Although several weeks have passed since the Satyagraha began, no solution seems to be in sight as neither side is relenting. The organisers are keeping Gandhi informed of the developments here. It may be recalled that Gandhi has been carrying on crusade against untouchability and he is keeping a close watch on the movement under way here.

Untouchability A Social Curse In Travancore

Travancore and the neighbouring lands have a history of severe social discrimination. Though the harshness has reduced in recent years, the past of this place even a century ago was marked by stern discrimination against the depressed classes. Curiously, in these lands the higher castes treated themselves as polluted not only by touch but even by spatial distance—a phenomenon some describe as 'atmospheric pollution' vis-à-vis 'touch pollution' prevailing in other places. A complex and rigid caste system operated here where the Namboothiris, being Brahmins, stayed at the top followed in a serial order by the Kshatriyas, Ambala Vasis and high caste Nairs, Sudras and low caste Nairs, Untouchables and last, the Unapproachables. The system even determined the spatial distance that a person of an inferior caste was required to maintain from one of higher caste and a maze of matrix provided the data of the permitted distances between various castes inter se. For example, a Namboothiri would consider himself polluted by the touch or approach of a Nair within six feet. A low caste Nair polluted a high caste Nair by touch. The caste discrimination was maintained and enforced rigidly through various caste associations, Vaidikans and the ruler. The penance for one who got polluted by a lower caste person could be through various means, ranging from simple bathing to change of sacred thread, drinking 'panchodokam', chanting of god's name etc. The punishment could be of various degrees, ranging from mild to severe, including complete excommunication from one's caste. Significantly Vivekananda, who had toured these lands few decades ago, described the place as a lunatic asylum.

Some of these inequities dot the map of the Hindu society even now. The depressed classes are still deprived of many civil rights—the right to worship being one of the important ones. Not only they do not have the right of entry to temple of the Savarnas or the caste Hindus, they even do not have the right to use the roads surrounding the temple up to a specified distance.

Congress Conference At Sirajganj Stirs Hornet's Nest

June 1, 1924, Sirajganj: The Bengal Provincial Congress Conference held here has attracted attention of other parts of the country for more than one reason. First, the Bengal Pact, which was rejected at the Coconada Congress last December, was placed before the provincial conference here and it secured ratification. Secondly, the conference adopted a resolution appreciating Gopinath Saha's courage and spirit of sacrifice while condemning his action. Given Gandhi's strict dictum on non-violence, the resolution hurt the sensibilities of the Gandhi loyalists.

Gandhi's Ideological Difference With Swarajists

June 27-30, 1924, Ahmedabad: Since February this year, when he was released from prison, Gandhi has been involving himself lesser in Congress activities—the main responsibilities for carrying the national struggles for self-government are being carried on by the Swaraj Party on behalf of the Congress. Gandhi did not quite like that the Swaraj Party occupied the centre stage while he was in the prison. He does not agree to the Swarajist policies and programmes and therefore has reduced his involvement. No doubt, he attends the Congress session if invited, but he is focussing more on constructive activities like spinning, sanitation, untouchability, and so on. He has also been touring places, meeting people and trying to introspect as to the reasons for the failure of the non-cooperation movements that were led by him. But, there are persistent demands by Congressmen that he take over the rein again and lead the struggle for swaraj. Even though this does not look to be a possibility in the near future, to the relief and joy of the workers and delegates, he is attending the Congress session being held here.

Gandhi Administers Bitter Pill To Swarajists

June 1924, Ahmedabad: AICC session is in progress here. Gandhi is attending. He is not happy with the Swarajists who have been hogging the limelight in the national politics—thanks to his interim absence, their dramatic electoral success followed by exhibition of parliamentary skill by the Swaraj Party members in the councils, keeping the government in awe of them. He is unhappier because they are treading a path that is against his strategy of non-cooperation. Here at Ahmedabad, Gandhi has taken steps to quarantine the Swarajist influence. He has got a resolution passed that prohibits any member of legislative bodies and also practising lawyers from holding any office in Congress organisations. Swarajists, the intended victims, are looking for opportunities to salvage their prestige.

Swarajists Put Gandhi On Alert

June 1924, Ahmedabad: Swarajists gave a shock to Gandhi on the issue of a condolence resolution on Gopinath Saha, a revolutionary, who was recently hanged in Bengal for assassinating a British merchant. Earlier, the Bengal Provincial Congress led by CR Das had passed a resolution praising Saha's spirit and sacrifice while distancing itself from the violence. Here at Ahmedabad, Gandhi moved a resolution, which while taking note of Saha's love for the country, qualified it as 'misguided' and in the same breath, strongly condemned all political murders. To this new resolution, which not only diluted the obituary to a martyr but also questioned the wisdom of the BPCC, Das proposed an amendment. The amendment was defeated by 70-78 votes. Such a narrow margin suggested that the result could have gone either way. It also posed a question mark on Gandhi's hold over the delegates, while voting on such emotive issues. Last, but not the least, the result delivered a message that the Swarajists were breathing over Gandhi's shoulder, in terms of appeal to the Congress members.

AMBEDKAR FOUNDS OUTCASTE WELFARE ASSOCIATION

July 1924: BR Ambedkar, after returning from the USA with a Masters degree, had gone to the United Kingdom for higher studies. In 1923, he submitted his final thesis in LSE. Since his return to India, Ambedkar, possibly the Indian politician with the highest of qualifications, has been devoting himself to protect and advance the interests of the depressed and the untouchables in Hindu society.

Ambedkar has now founded 'Bahishkrit Hitkarini Sabha' (Outcastes' Welfare Association) with a view to uplifting the downtrodden Hindus, socially and politically, to the level of others in Indian society. As the mainstream politicians are grappling with the issue of political rights of Indians in general vis-à-vis the British government, another fight has begun within the Hindu society in earnest for equality, under his leadership.

In his tireless struggle to assert the civil and political rights of depressed classes, Ambedkar has been deposing before official commissions, organising conferences and publishing newspapers. His crusade has made him a front-ranking leader of the depressed class people.

'No Salary To Ministers'
Swaraj Party Administers Shock To Government

August 1924, Calcutta: True to its electoral manifesto, the fight against the 'diarchy' system in the provinces has been one of the main occupations of the Swaraj Party.

Significantly, 'diarchy' divided government functions under two departments, viz. 'reserved' and 'transferred'. It was only in respect to the latter that the Governor would act on the advice of the ministers, who in turn would be from the elected legislators. However, the reserved departments would continue to be administered by the Governor and his executive council, with no role of the elected representative of the people. Further, many of the key departments were categorised as 'reserved'. In a nutshell, the elected representatives would only have a limited role in the governance of the provinces under the 'diarchy' scheme.

In the Central Provinces, where it has a majority, the Swaraj Party has made the working of the diarchy nearly impossible. Even in Bengal, where it has substantial presence, though not a majority, CR Das and his followers have made 'diarchy' extremely difficult to operate. To lodge a symbolic protest, the party has managed to reject the 'salary to the ministers' for the second time in the Bengal assembly. The government is clearly embarrassed. Though the Governor will apply his special power to see it through, the party has delivered a strong message.

Swaraj Party Holds Conference

August 16-17, 1924, Calcutta: Swaraj Party has held its conference here. Large numbers of leaders and delegates converged here from all over the country. The spectacular progress in the popularity and strength of the party in less than two years of time has put the government to distinct unease and worries.

The government is smelling not only increased belligerence in the party's leadership, but also growing influence of Bolsheviks and revolutionaries in its policies and activities.

The government, in fact, suspects that many of the Swaraj leaders, especially in Bengal, have been in touch with the communists and revolutionaries. Yet, it has not been able to pin them down with the help of extant statutes. Added to this, its inability to counter the Swaraj stalwarts in parliamentary procedures in the councils and the central assembly is adding to its dissatisfaction with the Swaraj Party and its leaders. The government is reportedly mulling other options to rein in the Swarajists.

MISSION HINDU-MUSLIM UNITY

Gandhi Ends Long Fast

October 8, 1924, Delhi: Gandhi's calling off the non-cooperation movement had not gone well with large section of Indians—both politicians and civilians. By the time he was released from the prison, an alternate vision of political struggle for 'swaraj' has begun to take firm roots in the Congress. The Swarajist leaders have been gaining in stature and popularity.

Though Gandhi has been opposed to the Swarajist policies, especially those relating to 'entry into legislatures', he is not yet ready to launch any movement. For the past some time, he has been touring, meeting and interacting with people and introspecting where things went wrong last time.

Gandhi has been deeply concerned about the incidence of violence that marked his non-cooperation movement in Malabar, and later in Chauri Chaura. He has been equally concerned about the unfolding of communal violence at several places in the country, which began during the Khilafat movement and has been continuing sporadically since then. To purify his soul and expiate for the sins of his countrymen, Gandhi has decided to undertake a long fast for twenty-one days, statedly. He began his fast on 18 September and ended it today, after making a statement on Hindu-Muslim unity.

According to political observers, this fast, which has engaged the attention of national media, would again establish his relevance in Congress and the course of national struggle, despite the growing importance of the Swarajists.

Hindustan Republican Association Emerges As A Force

October 1924, Kanpur: The Hindustan Republican Association has been expanding fast. Besides in east of India, it has also been attracting many young patriots in north and north west parts of the country. Now their members from various parts of the country have met here. The Association professes to establish the Federal Republic of the United States of India through armed revolution.

Government To Use Iron Fist To Crush Revolutionaries

October 24, 1924, Calcutta: Secret societies proliferate in the country. In the absence of any mass movement against the British, the revolutionaries are trying to fill the void. Their activities are more pronounced in Bengal. In the wake of repeated revolutionary attacks on government officials, the government has passed the Bengal Criminal Law Amendment Ordinance to suppress such activities. Like Regulation III of the 1818 Act, this new Ordinance vests the government with the power of summary arrest and imprisonment without trial. It further authorises the government to try cases involving terrorists before a tribunal without jury, and denies the right of appeal to the convict. Political analysts say the Swaraj Party, adept in legislative issues and procedures, has pushed the government to the 'Ordinance' route rather than trying to get legislation enacted through the Council.

Raj's Dangerous Young Enemy
Subhas Arrested Without Specific Charge

October 25, 1924, Calcutta: Subhas has been doing a commendable job as the chief executive officer of the Calcutta Corporation, with his mentor CR Das being its Mayor. As the public spirited young CEO, Subhas has been able to add to his image and popularity in recent times.

For some time now, Subhas has emerged as a bright, promising, young, charismatic Congress leader in Bengal, with his popularity cutting across communal, social and political divides, including the revolutionaries who advocate violent political means to expel the colonial rulers from India. The British government has deep suspicion that Subhas has links with the revolutionaries, and as such, has kept him under watch of its intelligence branch. Subhas has been arrested today without any charge and sent to Alipore jail.

The government is apprehensive of Subhas' connections with the revolutionaries and had wanted to use the new ordnance against him and many others. They are treating him as a grave political risk. But the government does not have any specific proof in favour of its suspicion. As such, it has invoked the infamous Regulation III of 1818 for his arrest.

Ordinance Brings Gandhi, Das And Motilal Closer

November 1924, Calcutta: The recent measures by the government in effecting large-scale arrests of political leaders and activists through issuance of Emergency Ordinance has galvanised both Congress and the Swaraj Party leaders. On 22nd of this month they organised an all-parties unity conference in Bombay. The conference urged the government to withdraw the Emergency Ordinance and release the political prisoners arrested thereunder.

Following that, Gandhi has come down to Calcutta and held consultations with CR Das and Motilal Nehru to close ranks. It has been decided that Gandhi will be in the charge of the Khadi campaign and he will have an All-India Spinners Association, an autonomous body, to carry out his programmes and activities. The association would have its own funds and secretariat. They have agreed that the Swaraj Party would have the charge of political campaigns. It would represent the Congress in the legislatures—both in the centre and the provinces.

Political observers say this reconciliation is significant as it strengthens the nationalist voice and puts the government somewhat on the defensive. According to inside sources, Gandhi, despite his strong dislike of the 'council entry' programme, is showing his willingness to make peace with the Swarajists. He has reportedly remarked that 'My political conscience is in the keeping of the Swarajists'.[28]

League Makes Reconciliatory Gesture To Congress

1924 Delhi: The All-India Muslim League has made a critical analysis of the political situation in the country. While it gives credit to the Congress for creating powerful public opinion under the leadership of Gandhi, it reckons that the triple boycott of court, college and council has turned into a failure and that renders resuscitation of another mass movement difficult in the near future. In the given circumstances, it feels that swaraj can come easily if unity between Hindus and Muslims is achieved—and unless that happens, the Englishman will continue to be the arbiter between the two communities. The League is against Gandhi taking over the leadership of the Indian Muslims, as happened during the Khilafat. At the present moment, it feels that threat has largely disappeared and is hopeful of gaining the leadership of the community. As such, the unity and joint struggle it is now advocating have an implied assumption of the Muslim leadership being in the hands of the League.

Gandhi Sees 'Sweet Relations', States' See 'None'

December 26-27, 1924, Belgaum: The Indian States' Subjects' Conference has concluded here. NC Kelkar, a Congress stalwart, presided over it. The presence of Gandhi, who addressed the delegates, lent more weight to the proceedings. However, at the end of the conference, the delegates did not emerge with much clarity as to what to expect from the Congress in terms of its role vis-à-vis the states' people's political programmes and activities—the views of Congress leaders seemed to be divergent.

Gandhi, the president of the Indian National Congress, spoke before Kelkar, the president of the conference. He said he did not want to embitter the 'sweet relation' between the princes and their subjects, but at the same time he reminded the delegates that he had the interests of the subjects in his mind, saying, 'I need not assure you that I can never forget the people of these states and their legitimate claims.'[29] If such articulation excelled in finesses, these seemed deficient in clarity.

The delegates were again disenchanted when Gandhi said, 'My desire is to maintain sweet reasonableness in my handling the question of Indian states and I do not wish to prejudice any party.'[30]

In comparison, N C Kelkar was more forthright—he lamented the Congress' insensitivity and inadequate support to the states' people's political demands when he said in his presidential speech that, 'While the Congress is right in excluding from its jurisdiction the discussion of affairs of internal administration of Indian states, it is wrong in its general attitude of indifference towards states' questions even in their broad and impersonal aspects.'[31] Kelkar was disappointed that the Congress working committee did not care to place any general resolutions on the 'states' before the subjects' committee for the past few years.

Muddiman Committee Submits Divided Report

December 3, 1924, New Delhi: The much awaited Muddiman Committee, also known as the Reforms Enquiry Committee, has submitted two reports—one by the majority and the other by the minority, comprising of four Indian members. The two groups have widely divergent views on the issues they examined. The majority of five members have not been able to find out any serious shortcomings with the present constitution. They have, therefore, made some minor recommendations for improvement. On the contrary, the minority Indian members strongly recommended immediate abolition of the diarchy and also democratisation of the constitution. From inside sources, it is gathered that the government is planning to rest content with the majority view and just choose to ignore the demands raised by the minority members, even if these are vociferous and true reflectors of native opinion.

Gandhi Initiates Reconciliation With Swarajist Leaders Appeasement Or Deft Manoeuvre?

December 26-27, 1924, Belgaum: Gandhi was elected as Congress president last month. He has been presiding over the annual Congress session here. In the sidelines of the session, delegates are discussing a pact between Gandhi and the Swarajists, arrived at recently. On the eve of the conference, Gandhi had visited Bengal and reached an understanding with the Swarajist leaders Das and Motilal. In terms of that, he has agreed to soften his stand and treat Swarajists as integral part of the Congress organisation. He has also agreed to induct majority of members in the Congress Working Committee from the Swarajists. As quid pro quo, the Swarajists agreed to the spinning franchise.

Interestingly, this development has left many in both the camps confused and dissatisfied. Many Swarajists find the 'spinning franchise' a bothersome imposition whereas many Gandhi loyalists are surprised at Gandhi's endorsement of the council entry programme against which they fought in 1922-23. Interestingly, even the Viceroy has a point of view on this accord. He said, by this act Gandhi has sacrificed his principles.

However, some political observers feel this has been a political masterstroke by Gandhi and a part of his programme to gradually regain his supreme position in national politics.

Gandhi's Sublime Ideology Confuses States' People

January 8, 1925, Bhavnagar: Close to the Indian States' Subjects' Conference held in Belgaum, Kathiawar Political Conference is being held here. Gandhi, the president of the Indian National Congress, is presiding. He is being heard with avid interest. All that he says could be seen as signals of Congress' future policies towards states' people's movement. Gandhi said the princes should establish 'Ramraj' in their states on the basis of ideals such as austerity, reforms of revenue system etc. At the same time, he also called the subjects to prepare themselves for the 'Ramraj'. Gandhi said, people on their part must cultivate spirit of service, renunciation, truth, non-violence, self-restraints, patience etc. They must also engage in constructive activities to develop themselves. Gandhi said many reforms would be achieved automatically if the delegates put in good deal of silent work among the people.

Many delegates are not quite comfortable with such idealistic postures. The states' people's conferences are expected to deal with political goals and programmes whereas Gandhi seems to be focussing on social reforms and moral upliftment, they feel.

Dangerous Even As Prisoner, Subhas Sent To Mandalay

January 25, 1925, Calcutta: Three months ago, Subhas was arrested without any specific charge but he took the imprisonment in his stride. Undaunted by this atrocity, he continued with his work as the CEO of the Calcutta Corporation from inside his prison cell. People at large find the government measure against him irrational and high-handed. This arrest, and his novel method of handling his predicament, has only been enhancing his popularity. An irate government, gnawed by its fear of public pressure and reprisals by the revolutionaries, later sent him away from Calcutta to Berhampur prison where he was held for nearly two months. Still wary, today the government has despatched

Subhas in a ship to the prison in distant Mandalay. It considers him dangerous and a high political risk. People find this new government action as height of injustice, especially when it does not have any charge against Subhas to prove.

No Solution In Sight At Vaikom – Satyagrahis Harassed

January 31, 1925, Vaikom, Travancore: Since March last year, Congress workers have been carrying out Satyagraha to establish the rights of the untouchables and depressed classes to use the roads adjoining the Shiva temple. Confident that a success here will be replicated all over the State, they have prepared themselves for a sustained struggle. During these nine months, people have converged in this town from several parts of India to participate in the ongoing Satyagraha. This has lent the movement a national stature. Akalis of Punjab sent their people who set up camps near the site of the agitation, and provide free meals to the volunteers. EV Ramaswamy Naicker, the prominent non-brahmin leader and the originator of the 'self respect movement' from neighbouring Tamil land also visited the place during April last year and lent his voice in support of the untouchables' rights.

On 27th September last year, Narayan Guru, the venerable sage and the spiritual guru of the Ezhavas visited the venue, offered a public prayer and blessed the movement. He has also been in favour of eradication of untouchability and for equality amongst human beings.

The Satyagrahis have been keeping Gandhi informed of the developments. During November last year, on his instructions, a large delegation of caste Hindus led by Chiru Parameswaran Pillai, submitted a memorandum signed by 25,000 'savarnas' to the Maharani in favour of opening the temple roads to all sections of people, including the untouchables. But till now the regency has not passed any favourable order.

For a considerable period, the movement by the Satyagrahis was suppressed by the police and it was an issue between these two parties. But, after some time, it escalated into a wider social conflict, when a section of the caste Hindus launched a counter movement and began harassing the Satyagrahis. But the latter, having boycotted the government all these days, have not been in a position to seek redressal from the administrative machinery. The Satyagrahis are facing two-pronged attacks.

Legislators' Verdict Breaks Satyagrahis' Heart

February 2, 1925, Travancore: A section of the caste Hindus have introduced additional complications. For the last ten months, reports of violence against the agitators are disturbing the social peace in the state. On their part, the Satyagrahis, with the backing of the Congress, are in no mood to relent without clinching the issue. Last November, they had implored the regency to intervene and order the roads open to all sections of people.

Considering the complexities, the regency had left the matter to the peoples' representatives at the Travancore Legislative Council. Today, N Kumaran (secretary of Sri Narayan Guru Dharma Paripalana Yogam) introduced a resolution in the council proposing that the roads adjoining the temple should be thrown open to the public. After a hot debate, the resolution was defeated by 22-21 votes.

The outcome of the voting has come as a great shock to the Satyagrahis — quite unexpected from the representatives of enlightened people of an enlightened state. It has exposed the deep roots of casteism that still exist here. Such malady can be tackled only by changing the mindset of a large number of people. Since this appears to be a formidable challenge, possibly beyond their competence, the Satyagrahis have sent an SOS to Gandhi urging him to come to Travancore and intervene.

Swarajists Demand Repeal Of Regulation III Of 1818

February 1925, Delhi: The government has applied Regulation III of 1918 indiscriminately in several cases which included those of leaders of such high statures as Lajpat Rai. Recently, the government used it against young Subhas Bose, whom it considers a dangerous political opponent. In Bengal particularly, the government has been charging several political activists under this Regulation. The Swaraj Party has been fighting against such unreasonable measures through parliamentary process. The British regime is, however, convinced about the indispensability of the regulation to maintain law and order. In the teeth of determined government opposition, the Swarajists have been able to secure passage of a resolution demanding the repeal of this regulation and release of some political prisoners who are its victims.

The track records of the Swarajists in fighting repressive laws through parliamentary process have so far been impressive. They fought with the government tooth and nail in regard to the Criminal Law Amendment Act of 1908, Bengal and the Madras State Prisoners Act of 1850, and the Prevention of Seditious Meetings Act of 1921. They have also managed to pass resolutions for release of political prisoners victimised under such harsh legislations.

Opening Of Road Is Not The Final But First Step: Gandhi

March 10-18, 1925, Vaikom and Trivandrum: In response to the urgent request of the Satyagrahis, Gandhi paid a much awaited visit here. He was accompanied by a team that included his son Ramdas and Congress leader C Rajagopalachari. He wanted to study the position first hand. He went to meet and discuss the issue with the Queen and her Diwan in the palace. He also held long discussion with the priests and the leader of the 'savarna' (caste Hindus) but these talks turned infructuous. The priests put before Gandhi a queer argument that the untouchables deserved the 'ban' due to their 'past karma' or the deeds of the previous births. They refused to look at the issue rationally.

After discussing the issue with the various parties involved, Gandhi understood the depth of the superstitions and prejudices that plague the community psyche. He has reached the conclusion that the opening of the road is not the final but the first step in a series of reforms that must be initiated, for which the public must be educated. As an immediate solution, he instructed the Satyagrahis not to attempt passage through prohibited areas and the government, in return, agreed to remove the barricades and police outposts.

It was Gandhi's maiden visit to this beautiful land in the southern part of India and he was surprised that such grave social inequities existed here. Travancore was hitherto perceived to be one of the very enlightened native states of India. Now that the state of affairs here is known to the world due to the Satyagraha and the evil was acknowledged, Gandhi is hopeful the process of reforms will set in now. He is keen to see that the social reforms are begun and carried on.

Although Satyagrahis are not much enthused, as no immediate victory seems to have been achieved, it appears that Maharani Sethu Laxmi Bai has been impressed by her interactions with Gandhi. Her government is gearing up to begin the reform process and the roads may be opened up to the public in general—it seems to be only a matter of time.

You Reject Our Demand, We Reject Finance Bill: Swarajists

March 1925, Delhi: In February last year, the Swarajists' demands in the central legislative assembly for revising the constitution and holding a round table conference were unceremoniously rejected by the British government. The party had reacted by rejecting the finance bill, submitted for the approval of the assembly. Eventually Lord Reading, the Governor General, had to carry it through with the help of his extra-ordinary power of certification. This year there is déjà vu—the Swarajists, in coordination with like-minded parties, rejected the budget and the Governor General again had to rescue it. Though the budget has been passed, the Swarajists have registered their protest. The government is feeling uncomfortable at successive defeats in the legislature.

Bengal Emergency Ordinance Bill Thrown Out

April 1925, Calcutta: The government made a desperate attempt to pass the Bengal Emergency Ordinance as a bill, which it had issued as an Ordinance in October last year, and extensively used to torment its political opponents. Deeply antagonised by the pervasive misuse of the power of this Ordinance, the legislature under the leadership of

CR Das has thrown out the bill. There is no option left for the government, other than again the Governor using his certification power to pass it.

Gandhi Evasive On Birkenhead-Das Deal

May 1, 1925, Calcutta: Gandhi, on his way to Faridpur, addressed a large public meeting at Mirzapur Park in the city. There have been intense speculations that CR Das is at an advanced stage of political negotiations with the Secretary of State for India, Lord Birkenhead, on the issue of self Government for India. Gandhi said he was told about it by a newspaper reporter, though he claimed not having any personal knowledge about the matter. However, what he added thereafter was significant. He admitted that there was a political situation in the country today but it did not interest him sufficiently. Calling himself as an 'economist of time', he said: 'I have deliberately given my general power of attorney to the Swaraj Party', which is in charge of the political programme of the Congress Party and clarified that he has 'the fullest faith in the ability of the Swaraj Party to handle the political situation.... 'I have the fullest faith in the wisdom of Deshbandhu Das and Pandit Motilal Nehru.' Gandhi made it clear that between 'political' and 'constructive' programmes, he has chosen the latter. He said he had no intention of concerning himself with the other: 'I am more fitted for handling the constructive programme for developing our own power from within, than for engaging with diplomatic relations with the matchless diplomats from England.'[32]

Political observers say Gandhi's lecture give a clear indication that some kind of political negotiations between CR Das and the British regime are on, and possibly these are in an advanced stage.

CR Das At The Height Of His Political Acumen

May 2-4, 1925, Faridpur: The Bengal Provincial Congress Conference held here captured the eye balls of people all over the country. Bengal has been boiling due to government repression. Several events, including the imprisonment of Subhas, have generated wide-scale public anger here. Das has been channelling the rising waves of nationalist emotion in creating pressure on the government to accelerate granting of dominion status. London, however, wants to ensure that Das is able to unite all shades of opinion on the claim of dominion status and not beyond. Das was able to persuade Gandhi to attend the conference. It was a spectacle of solidarity when Das, addressing Gandhi, remarked, 'It is impossible for India to do without your guidance today and at any time'. On the other hand, Das leveraged his charisma and authority to the hilt in making large number of aggressive and impatient youth agree to the demand for 'dominion status', instead of 'complete independence'. With his statesman-like vision, he sought to convince them of what was appropriate at this juncture: Dominion Status today is in no sense servitude, it could be a true Commonwealth of Nations. The conference also condemned terrorism, to make the Congress position clear to the government. On the whole, the conference achieved important political purposes. It demonstrated the political unity between the Congress and the Swaraj party and encouraged the government to take the ongoing negotiation on dominion status to its logical conclusion.

Chittaranjan Das Dies - Country Shell-shocked

June 16, 1925, Calcutta: CR Das has been ailing for the past some time. Notwithstanding his ill health, he had presided over the Bengal Provincial Congress Conference last month in Faridpur and made it a huge success. Post conference, Das suffered serious decline in health conditions and he went to Darjeeling to attempt some recovery. Unfortunately, he sustained a brief heart attack and died. He was only fifty five. His untimely death and at this critical juncture, with negotiations for dominion status in an advanced stage, has cast a huge pall of gloom over the entire country. Nationalist India has been sent into a state of deep mourning. Affectionately and reverentially called 'Deshbandhu', CR Das will be remembered as an outstanding patriot, noble human being, statesman and at the same time an astute politician.

Gandhi was upset as he received the news and, in turn, wired to others: 'Deshbandhu is no more! God's will be done.' These words show his emotions at the bereavement of a beloved colleague and loss of an outstanding leader who just cannot be replaced and, therefore, has to be accepted as destiny's deal!

REVOLUTIONARIES DO DARING TRAIN ROBBERY

August 1925, Kakori: On 9th this month, a group of revolutionaries held up the 8 Dn train between Alampur and Kakori railway station on the Lucknow-Saharanpur route, to loot government money to fund revolutionary activities. Ram Prasad Bismil, Ashfaqullah Khan, Chandrasekhar Azad, Sachindranath Sanyal, Sachindra Bakshi, Manmathnath Gupta and others allegedly organised the hold up. Revolutionary activities have been gaining momentum in the northern part of the country and now, with this daring act of train robbery, it has become more serious. An intensive hunt for the revolutionaries has begun. Many of them have been arrested and put to trial. According to political observers, if their culpability is proved, the revolutionaries are likely to be awarded ruthless punishments.

CONGRESS OPENS ITS GATE TO THE VAST MASSES

Only 'Four Annas' To Become A Member

September 22-24, 1925, Patna: In a significant move that can potentially open up a floodgate of new membership, Gandhi has agreed to give up the insistence on the spinning franchise as a condition to becoming a Congress Party member. A resolution has been passed in the AICC meeting here, which allows a person to become a member of the Congress Party paying only four annas. Spinning has been made optional.

Motilal Pushes Swarajist Resolution, Viceroy Stonewalls

September 1925, Delhi: In the face of the determined and sustained opposition by the Swarajists to the diarchy system, the government was compelled to appoint a committee led by Muddiman last year to look into the issue. In December last year, the committee had submitted a divided report where the minority Indian members made forceful recommendations for immediate abolition of diarchy and democratisation of the constitution. But the government has taken no notice of the minority view nor has it taken any meaningful steps till now. This has been angering the Swarajists no end. That anger burst forth when the government tabled the report today in the central legislature.

Leading the opposition, Motilal Nehru has delivered a brilliant speech condemning the diarchy system. He has moved a resolution that calls for some immediate changes to make the government 'fully responsible' and also for holding a round table conference to prepare a detailed scheme for improvement of the constitution. His oratory and conviction have helped the resolution to be passed with overwhelming majority. However, Lord Reading is adamant. Unwilling to bestow importance to the resolution, he has declared that the British Parliament would not be covered by such resolutions. But, technicalities apart, the Swarajists have made their point known—they have clinched a moral victory.

RASHTRIYA SWAYAMSEVAK SANGH IS BORN

September 27, 1925, Nagpur: Today Dr Keshav Baliram Hedgewar along with five-six like-minded distinguished persons founded the Rashtriya Swayamsevak Sangh here. In his quest for freedom of India, he has had close association with revolutionaries of Anushilan Samity and Jugantar in Bengal. Later he joined the Congress under the mentorship of BG Tilak. In 1921 he actively participated in non-cooperation movement and suffered one year's rigorous imprisonment on charge of sedition. In course of time, the absurdity of revolutionary means and the limitations of the Congress programmes upset him. The persecution of Hindus in certain parts of the country during the Khilafat days and thereafter and the imbecility of indigenous political response to handle that issue compelled his perspectives about his life's mission. By making a renewed and scathing analysis of the true reasons for the country's enslavement he has concluded that Hindu Samaj must first be purged of its deep-seated evils and it has to be strengthened to be able to build a strong nation. Though there are murmurs alleging communal bias in his fledgling initiative, Hedgewar denies them. His definition of 'Hindu' transcends religion and encompasses all Indians who are inspired by the eternal cultural, moral and spiritual values and traditions of India. While the Congress and revolutionaries look at expulsion of the British as the means to secure independence, Hedgewar's thinking seems to be to make Indians strong and worthy of 'freedom'.

Swarajists Start Coming Closer To The Government!

October 8, 1925: There are clear signs that the Swaraj Party has begun to compromise on its professed ideals and respond to the overtures of the government. In July this year, hardly a month after the death of CR Das, Motilal himself accepted a 'nominated' seat in the Skeen committee appointed by the government to examine the issue of Indianisation of the army. The very next month, another veteran Swarajist, Vithalbhai Patel decided to contest for the post of president of the Legislative Assembly and got elected. Today, SB Tambe, another important Swaraj Party leader in the Central Provinces has decided to accept the appointment as a member of the Governor's executive council. It is heard that his decision has concurrence of other senior leaders, including NC Kelkar.

EVR LAUNCHES SELF-RESPECT MOVEMENT

December 1925, Madras: Formation of the Justice Party almost a decade ago had aroused much hope and enthusiasm in non-Brahmin populations, which included large number of people from depressed classes and untouchables in the Madras province. This was specially so because the Congress, the major national party, is heavily dominated by the Brahmins in Madras province. As such, the Justice Party was able to quickly mobilise the non-Brahmin people politically.

This helped the new party achieve considerable electoral success in the first election held in 1920. However, since then, the caste Hindus have managed to tighten their grip on the party. They have little interest in social reforms. The depressed classes and the untouchables gradually turned to be of lesser priority to the party. As a result, this vast, vulnerable sections of humanity has been again left in the lurch, devoid of an effective political representation.

EV Ramaswamy has now come forward to fill that political space. To uphold the dignity of numerous people living on the fringe of a caste-ordered Hindu community, he has left the Congress and started the 'self-respect' movement. Indignant at the manner the Congress has been treating non-Brahmins, he has launched a virtual crusade. His movement has a wide contour—it is not only anti-Brahmin but also anti-Sanskrit, anti-Hindi, anti-Aryan and anti-God. According to Ramaswamy, the Brahmin domination over Dravidians rests on the tripods of God, Caste and Brahminism. He would be happy to demolish these pillars, he says. Towards this end, he is directing peoples' protests against each of them. EVR, or 'Periyar' as he is popularly called, receives widespread support from the backward and depressed classes in his province.

'SELF RESPECT' MOVEMENT SPREADS IN TAMIL LAND

December 1925, Madras: The self respect movement is spreading fast in the Tamil land. Periyar is advocating burning of the 'Manusmriti', abolition of the caste system and priest craft. He is also a strong proponent of women's emancipation. Periyar has called for founding a society based on equality and justice. He is using his journal, *Kudi Arasu* to propagate his thoughts. The ripples of his movement are slowly reaching the neighbouring areas. His movement has been spreading political consciousness amongst the weaker and the depressed classes in the southern part of India.

Periyar – The Transition Of The Indefatigable Crusader

In the recently-concluded conference of the Congress in Kancheepuram, EVR has severed his nearly six-year-long association with the party. Way back in 1919, in those turbulent days of the Rowlatt Act and the Jallianwalabagh massacre, EVR had joined the Congress, responding to Gandhi's clarion call. He had given up public offices and lucrative business enterprises to spin khaddar, organise picketing at toddy shops and undertake other constructive programmes that Gandhi held before the nation.

His mission has been to usher in a system where all men and women can live with dignity and get equal opportunities to develop their physical, mental and moral faculties. However, the ambience in India in general and his province in particular, has been deterring this possibility due to the domination of the Hindu community by cast-iron caste hierarchy. His mind has consistently rebelled against the irrational, prejudiced and cruel system of oppression of the depressed and the down trodden by the privileged higher caste people. He tried to fight against such social evils from the Congress platforms but failed. Way back in 1922, he had moved a resolution in the provincial conference in Tirupur, proposing rights to every section of people to enter temples and offer worship. But the powerful high-caste lobby thwarted his attempt by quoting from the scriptures. EVR was disillusioned but kept up his crusade. Last year, he had led a powerful participation in the Temple entry Satyagraha at Vaikom in Travancore state.

However, of late, he has become convinced that he will achieve little of his mission if he stays in the Congress. He reckons that Gandhi himself is not serious about eradicating the caste system and the Brahminical domination. Impatient to put an end to this system of birth-based caste structure that only heaves injustices on, robs the dignity of and blocks the opportunities of developments of the depressed and downtrodden classes, EVR has launched the 'self respect movement', which is attracting large number of oppressed people. This messiah of the underprivileged wants to demolish the caste hierarchy. He also wants to bulldoze those scriptures, which the caste system seeks sustenance from.

COMMUNIST PARTY OF INDIA IS EMIGRÉ NO MORE

December 25, 1925, Kanpur: The émigré Communist party of India has been trying to propagate the communist ideology and enlist members through small groups. It has also tried to involve members of the revolutionary societies like the Anushilan and Jugantar, in expanding its base in the country.

Over the years, this strategy has begun to bear fruit. Now a few groups of communists have taken firm root across a number of British Indian provinces. In Bengal, Muzaffar Ahmed is leading a group. His counterparts are S Chettiar in Madras, SA Dange in Bombay, Shaukat Usmani in the United Provinces and Ghulam Hussain in Punjab.

Though these groups have been active in their respective provinces, the communists have felt the necessity to coordinate their activities across the country. With this end in view, they are holding a conference here. About five hundred people from various provinces are attending. Satyabhakta has convened it, whereas Maulana Hasrat Mohani is acting as the chairman of the reception committee. With Singaravelu Chettiar in chair, the conference has resolved to form the Communist Party of India with Bombay as its headquarters. It has vowed to establish a republican 'swaraj' of workers and peasants in the country. On this occasion, the Labour Kisan Party of Hindustan has merged itself with the new party.

Another important development is that the new party has declared its allegiance to the Comintern. Significantly, Satyabhakta, the convener was against it, and he did argue for 'national communism'. But he was outvoted on this issue.

The émigré Communist Party of India is now effectively substituted by this new organisation operating inside India. However, to the credit of MN Roy and other founders of the émigré party, it may be said that the seed that they had sown has now come up as a nice sapling. It may be mentioned that the communist activities are still banned in the country.

Notwithstanding such handicap, the indigenous version of the Communist Party, with all-India reach, is likely to add new dimension to the national struggle against colonial rule.

Swaraj Party Tries To Save Face

December 1925, Cawnpore: The Congress holds its annual session here. Sarojini Naidu presides. Though the Swaraj Party has been exposed to a series of inner dissensions, some amounting to nothing less than rebellion, it has a say in the overall policy formulation. The working committee, in consultation with Motilal, has adopted a resolution that demands that the British government should frame another constitution in the lines demanded by the Swaraj Party in the Legislative Assembly before February 1926. Failing this, the resolution warned that, all Swaraj Party members will leave the councils and remain outside till further notice and devote themselves to constructive work.

In another important move, the Swarajists have suggested that the Congress contests the election next year and pursues its policy of non-cooperation within the legislatures.

These resolutions have generated controversies. Critics of the Swaraj Party contend that at best, it is a desperate bid by Motilal to galvanise the factions who are poised to walk away and, at the worst it is a poor attempt at face saving.

Swarajists – Now Gentler Than Cooing Doves

December 1925: Notwithstanding the fact that the Swarajists gave a good account of themselves for about a couple of years, their role and performances are coming under increasing scrutiny in recent times. Cracks are visible in the integrity, unity and solidarity of the Swarajists. The death of CR Das has dealt it a body blow. After Das, the burden of steering the party has been on the shoulder of Motilal Nehru, and he is fighting to hold the spirit and the flock together. But there are not many worthy followers. With time, it now transpires that many had joined the party, not in the spirit of public service but to grind their own axes.

Although the party was against accepting any offer from the government to be a part of its committee, there has been an open advocacy in favour of accepting such offers in the name of 'responsive cooperation with the government' for past some time. Last year, the Swarajists had accepted seats in the Steel Protection Committee. Again, during August in the same year, Vithalbhai Patel was elected and he consented to be the president (Speaker) of the Central Legislative Assembly.

During the current year, even Motilal Nehru himself accepted the membership in the Skeen Committee appointed to recommend measures to rapidly Indianise the army. No less important, on the whole, the aggressive approach towards the government through the policy of uniform, continuous and consistent opposition seems to be giving way to a growing tendency to cooperate with it.

Annie Besant, a much-revered national leader, is critical that the Swarajists have lost both their goal and spirit after entering the assembly, although they had fought the election claiming that 'swaraj' was their main aim. She has lamented that before they were elected, the Swarajists roared like lion but now they have become gentler than cooing doves.[33] She said if she were a Swarajist, she would say aloud that they have been bought by the government.

Communist Call To Join Workers' And Peasants' Parties

February 6, 1926, Krishnanagar, Bengal: Although the indigenous Communist Party of India has been formed, it continues to be banned. The government has not allowed any space to the Communists to propagate their political goals and carry out activities openly. The Communists are in dire need of an overboard platform. Today, they have formed the Bengal Peasants' and Workers Party (WPP) here.

On 1 November last year, they had formed the Labour Swaraj Party in Calcutta, within the Congress. Now, it has been merged with the WPP.

More WPPs are likely to be formed in other provinces. This new outfit too, will be a part of the Indian National Congress. In fact, the WPP will form the left wing of the Congress.

As a matter of fact, the Communist Party has been exerting increasing influence over the workers and peasants. Leveraging its hold on them, the party has now urged its members to join the Workers' and Peasants' parties in large numbers.

SIX BABBAR AKALI JATHA LEADERS HANGED

Day Of Colours Turns Dark Black In Punjab

February 27, 1926, Lahore: Following the court verdict given a year ago, six leaders of Babbar Akali Jatha (BAJ) were hanged today at the Central Jail here. Ironically, this day happens to be 'Holi divas', a festival day, which people traditionally celebrate with colours. However, the hanging of these six patriotic young men has cast a pall of gloom all around. Charges were brought against them of attempting to gain independence for India and establish Sikh rule in Punjab.

It may be recalled that the Sikh struggle against the ruling dispensations has been following two courses over the past two decades —non-violent as well as violent. The Babbar Akali Jatha has been pursuing the latter path.

The non-violent struggle centres around seizing of the control of the Gurdwaras in which the Akalis have the backing of the Congress. The Akalis achieved remarkable success in this movement, acquiring control over the Golden Temple at Amritsar, Gurdwaras at Nankana, Guru Ka Bagh and many more such places of worship. Their struggle in Jaito, against the British regime demanding the reinstatement of Maharaj Ripudaman Singh in the throne of Nabha state was, however, thwarted.

The path of violent struggle was pioneered by Sardar Ajit Singh, who, nearly two decades ago traversed through Punjab urging people to take up arms to expel the British from the native soil. In the last decade, the Ghadarites' activities, their fiery patriotism, and the brutal suppression of the Ghadarites by the government made Punjab a fertile land for revolutionary activities. Founded in 1922, Babbar Khalsa Jatha may be seen as a logical successor to the revolutionary tradition.

Babbar Akali Jatha (BAJ) addressed themselves to the demobilised soldiers and Singh reformers. They also extended their hands to Hindus and Muslims who wanted to expel the British from India. They aimed at eliminating British officials and their Indian and Punjabi supporters. In 1923, BAJ had undertaken a campaign of political murders. The government was so upset by their activities that in August of the same year, it declared BAJ an unlawful association. This was followed by severe government reprisal and within a year, all its important leaders were either eliminated or arrested. Their court trials were completed in February 1925 and death penalties for six of them have been executed now.

However, the spirit of their fights has not been lost. The Central Sikh League has vowed to raise funds to help the families of these martyrs. Poets have begun composing hymns glorifying their martyrdom.

SWARAJ PARTY LEGISLATORS WALK OUT OF ASSEMBLY

March 6, 1926, New Delhi: The deadline served on the government to formulate a new constitution in the lines of Swarajist demands is over. The government has chosen to ignore it. Today, the Swaraj Party legislators have walked out of the Assembly, led by Motilal.

BHAGAT SINGH FOUNDS NAUJAWAN BHARAT SABHA

March 1926, Lahore: In Lahore, Bhagat Singh, a young and fiery patriot, has founded the Naujawan Bharat Sabha. Bhagat Singh is a nephew of the legendary revolutionary, Sardar Ajit Singh, and has dedicated himself to the service of the country at a young age. He is an atheist and a socialist and prefers anarchy to the brute colonial rule. He is influenced considerably by Marxist philosophy. The aim of the Sabha he founded is to establish an independent republic in India by organising labourers and peasants, with all its inhabitants forming a united Indian nation. Bhagat Singh aims at spreading branches of the Sabha across Punjab and even outside.

Calcutta In The Grip Of Communal Riot

May 1926, Calcutta: Calcutta came under the grip of a vicious communal riot over an Arya Samaj procession passing before a mosque, playing music. The Samajis claim that such a procession has been conducted for many years peacefully. On the other hand, Muslims insist that it disturbed their prayers.

Political observers say, rising communal tension has transformed the 'mixed population areas' to tinder boxes ready to explode at the slightest provocation. Communal amity has been under pressure countrywide right since the civil disobedience movement was withdrawn. The situation grew worse after the Khilafat movement was buried, and the large band of Khilafat sympathisers and workers were recruited by communal parties like the Muslim League. On their part, many Hindus have been organising themselves under the Hindu Mahasabha to meet these threats. The Shuddhi programmes being carried out by Hindu organisations are also adding to the communal distrust. They say the severity and the longevity of the communal riot in this important city is the manifestation of all such evils.

Motilal Left Alone To Steer The Swaraj Ship

August, 1926: The untimely death of CR Das has hit the Swaraj Party hard. He was a strong binding force in the party and a high calibre ideologue. Several leaders from Bombay and Central Provinces, who have been ardent followers of Tilak and believe in the policy of 'responsive cooperation' agreed to be part of the Swaraj Party and accepted its policy of uniform, continuous and consistent opposition, essentially due to their loyalty to CR Das who had attracted left, right and centre alike by his burning patriotism and strong emotional appeal. Now that he is no more, sections of Tilakite leaders have begun to rediscover the virtue of 'responsive cooperation'. In any case, they are witnessing a dilution of the core principles and following differences with Motilal, they have moved out of the Swaraj Party and formed a party called as 'Responsivists'. This party believes that the policy of obstructionism has not helped the party to achieve its intended mission. This group has developed a conviction that better purpose could indeed be achieved through cooperation with the government. Its members are thinking in terms of contesting the coming elections on their own.

Unfortunately, major cracks in the Swaraj party have surfaced in the Central Provinces, which once used to be its strongest fort. The desertion by such competent leaders as NC Kelkar and MR Jayakar has hit the party hard. But the worst shock was yet to come. Now, Lajpat Rai, the Swaraj Party veteran and the deputy leader in the

Central Assembly has left and formed the Nationalist Party. He is likely to work closely with Madan Mohan Malaviya, the leader of the Hindu Mahasabha.Motilal Nehru is the only stalwart, who has been left to steer the ship in the rough seas. He will have to lead this fractured, weakened party into the hustings due in few months' time.

Malaviya And Lajpat Rai Join Hands, Congress Jittery

August 1926: In a significant political development, Madan Mohan Malaviya and Lajpat Rai have come together and formed the Congress Independent Party. These two veteran leaders are disillusioned with both, the Swaraj Party and the Congress. They find Swaraj Party inconsistent and wobbling in the matter of being in and out of the council and also on the issue of cooperation with the government. As regards the Congress, they are of the opinion that it has a communal bias.

Political observers say, the desertion by these two veterans are likely to hit the Congress very hard in the coming election, which is hardly three months away. Both of them have mass followings, especially in the northern part of the country.

Subhas Elected To Provincial Legislature In Absentia

November 1926, Calcutta: Though Subhas is far away in Mandalay, his popularity has only been rising over time. There is a consensus that the government has done grave injustice to one of the most promising young leaders. In the new elections to the provincial legislature in Bengal, strong demands were raised that Subhas be elected to the Legislative Council. His name was proposed in absentia as a rival to a very popular liberal candidate, JN Basu. Support for him was so considerable that Subhas has won. He received the news in Mandalay prison as a surprise.

SHRADDHANAND MURDERED BY A FANATIC

December 23, 1926, Delhi: Shraddhanand, a much-revered social reformer and a great proponent of the 'Shuddhi movement' of the Arya Samaj was killed by Abdul Rashid, a Muslim fanatic. Since the

'Shuddhi movement' involved accepting a convert back into the fold of Hinduism, its protagonists have been incurring the wrath of the Muslim radicals. In recent times, he had been conducting 'shuddhis' for the Rajputs in the Agra-Mathura region whose forefathers had converted to Islam under compulsion by the Muslim rulers. They wanted to come back to their previous faith and the Swami helped them through his 'Shuddhi' programme. This has been generating controversies. Gandhi reportedly had reservations about doing something, which could lead to communal discord and animosity.

The Swami suffered from pneumonia and a man called Rashid had visited him, pretending that he wanted a discussion on Islam. When the man asked for water, and when the Swami sent his attendant to fetch water, Rashid launched a fatal assault on the ailing Swami with a pistol. Although the assassination of a much revered leader has caused huge public outcry, the Congress' reaction, moderated by Gandhi's view on the matter, seems to be guarded. Rashid has been arrested by police and he will be tried for the crime.

Iyenger Suggests Remedies For Communal Conflict

December 26-28, 1926: Gauhati: Congress has held its 41st annual session at Pandu here. Gandhi has attended. Srinavasa Iyenger is presiding. Iyenger has been widely known for his sharp intellect, legal acumen, patriotism and as an ardent supporter of 'independence' vis-à-vis 'dominion' status. He has resigned the office of advocate general of Madras in 1920 and taken a plunge into the struggle for 'swaraj'. He gave a head start to the Swaraj Party in Madras and has put the Congress in a good stead in the province.

The Gauhati session is affected by the gloom generated by the murder of Swami Shraddhanand by a Muslim fanatic. Even before this, the country came under the vicious grip of communal hatred and violence. What has made matters still worse is the fact that Maulana Shaukat Ali, the elder of the Ali brothers and a close aide of Gandhi, is reportedly associating himself with the defence of the murderer.

Iyenger has been taking extraordinary initiative in touring the country to restore communal amity throughout the year. In the session, he has tried to analyse the root causes of communal conflict. He has identified two sets of issues—political and religious. Iyenger contended that these two have to be dealt with differently.[34]

I Called Abdul Rashid My Brother And I Repeat It: Gandhi

December 26-28, 1926, Gauhati: There is widespread anger in people about the assassination of Swami Shraddhanand. Gandhi is in Gauhati in connection with the annual session. He moved a resolution on the issue in which the Congress expressed its horror and indignation at the cowardly and treacherous murder of the Swami and placed on record its sense of irreparable loss that the nation sustained by the tragic death of a brave and noble patriot.

Gandhi, while paying rich tributes to the martyr, held the pervasive ambience of communal distrust and hatred fuelled by irresponsible journalism responsible for the incident. He sought to remove the missgivings of the Muslims about the departed Swami, saying:

'Let every Mussalman also understand that Swami Shraddhanandji was no enemy of Islam, that his was a pure and unsullied life, and that he has left for us all the lesson of peace written in his blood.'

Continuing, he reiterated his assessment:

'Now you will, perhaps, understand why I have called Abdul Rashid a brother, and I repeat it. I do not even regard him as guilty of the Swami's murder. Guilty, indeed, are all those who excited feelings of hatred against one another.'[35]

Political observers say Gandhi has attempted to submlimate the base instincts of the communal masses to the higher human ideals, but bulk of his audience, who are ordinary mortals, may find it difficult to understand the true import of his message.

Election 1926: Swaraj Party Suffers Reverses

November 1926, Delhi: Results of general elections held recently are out. The Swarajists, who made an impressive debut in last election, have this time stumbled on their face. Except in Madras, the party has fared poorly in other places. In provinces like Bihar, United Provinces, Central

Provinces and Bombay, it was thrashed by the Congress Independent Party, the Hindu Mahasabha and the Responsivists. In Punjab, the Unionist Party has again emerged as the leader. What has hit the Swarajists further in this election is their failure to hold on to the seats reserved for the Muslims. Clearly, the Muslim communal parties have usurped that space to the detriment of the Swarajists. The absence of CR Das and with that, his secular appeal, has impacted the Muslim electorates. This loss has been most pronounced in Bengal and Punjab.

As the Swarajists struggled, Gandhi watched in silence. The election result has been a predictable outcome of their worsening condition. The eyes of the nationalists, including the members of the Swaraj Party, are again turning towards him for guidance. Gandhi also appears to be slowly warming up to move to centre stage.

Bombay Workers' And Peasants' Party Is Formed

February 1927: In continuation with the Communist strategy, to establish their overboard wing in the Congress, now the Bombay Workers' and Peasants' Party has been set up. It may be mentioned that Philip Spratt and Ben Bradley, two important Communist leaders of Britain, are in India to carry forward the Communist movement in this country and help form the WPPs, in which the Communists would exercise control. Spratt arrived in India at the end 1926 and Bradley soon after.

The Bombay WPP has declared that it would look to the Comintern for guidance, although it has not made any formal request to the international forum for affiliation.

The Arch Light Is Back On Gandhi

Preparation for the reforms of the 1919 Act had begun in 1917. It is almost time to begin preparation for the next round of reforms – a new constitution for India. The Congress, being the major political party, is expected to play a key role in engaging with the government on this issue to ensure that the new constitution is substantive in nature and extensive in scope, devolving on

Indians the maximum possible self-government — preferably granting India dominion status. It also ought to ensure that the benefit of reforms accrue equitably to all sections of Indians.

Till last year, the Swaraj Party happened to be the public face of the Congress. But in recent times, it has been showing signs of wear and tear. Worse, the party has suffered serious electoral reverses in the recent elections to legislatures, quite unlike its impressive debut in the 1923 election. The electoral setback is acting as a moral dampener.

In these circumstances, the arch light is back on Gandhi. Although he had preferred to avoid the centre stage since his release from jail in 1924, his appeal to Congress workers and leaders has remained intact. In 1924, he was also elected as the president of the organisation. Over the last two years, he has devoted himself to self-purification through a series of constructive activities. He wields great moral authority and has also irrefutable credential as a true mass leader. Congress is looking at him for leadership. Motilal Nehru is also of the same opinion.

Jinnah Offers To Forego Separate Electorates

March 20, 1927, Delhi: Government of India Act 1919 is due for revision—the next round of reforms is awaited. At this juncture, Jinnah has formulated a composite proposal wherein he has demanded: First, Sind be organised as a new province by separating it from Bombay, and, reforms, like other provinces, be introduced in NWFP and Baluchistan; Second, he has made an interesting and significant offer—that he is prepared to abandon demand for separate electorate in favour of a joint electorate with reservations of seats fixed in proportion to the populations of different communities. In Sind, NWFP and Baluchistan, he has proposed to offer concessions to Hindus in the form of reservations over and above what are their percentage to the population and expects the same benefits for Muslims in all Hindu majority provinces; Third, he has demanded that in the central legislature, the Muslims should have guaranteed reservations of one-third of the total seats; Fourth, Jinnah has sought a guarantee that no bill on communal matter can be passed, if three-fourth of the members of the community were opposed to it.

Jinnah has said that his proposals constitute a package—meaning that these could not be accepted partly. If Congress wants, it has to accept the entire bunch. Congress seems flummoxed by the proposal, coming on the eve of the next round of reforms.[36]

Jinnah's Offer – A Master Stroke?

April 1927, Delhi: Jinnah's bouquet of offers, packaged by the readiness to abandon the separate electorate system, a right close to the hearts of many Muslims, has surprised many including the Congress. At first, it seemed to have been enticed by the novelty of the offerings, and accepted it. But on a re-consideration, the Congress has rejected his proposal. Political analysts are speculating over the reasons behind the somersault.

Jinnah's demand on Sind seems to be aimed at creating one more Muslim majority province that would help him in future political negotiation. At present, Bombay of which Sind is only a part, is a clear Hindu majority province. Second, by offering Hindus more than proportional presentation in only three and, that too, comparatively less important provinces like Sind, NWFP and Baluchistan, Jinnah wants to extract the same facility for at least six important provinces, which are Hindu dominated. Third, he wants one-third Muslim presentations in the central legislature, although this ought to be about only one-fourth, based on the present demographic profile.

Jinnah has attractively packaged the bouquet by his readiness to agree to a joint electorate. If this is the bait, the catch lies in the insistence that his offers can be accepted only in toto.

Subhas' Popularity Keeps Soaring

May 16, 1927, Calcutta: Subhas has been the victim of British high-handedness. He has been kept under detention in Mandalay without any specific charge, just because the government perceives him to be a dangerous political enemy. While in prison, he has been elected to the

Bengal Legislative Council. Nationalist Indians are rejoicing. They look at it as a rebuff to the British government. Pressures have been mounting on the government to release Subhas. In the meantime, his health has deteriorated in the unhygienic condition of the jail and he is suspected to have contracted tuberculosis. Under public pressure, the government has agreed to transfer him from Mandalay to Almorah prison in north of India. He was brought in ship to Diamond Harbour near Calcutta, and was examined by a team of eminent doctors. Following this, in a surprise move, the government decided to release him today. People are celebrating.

Commission To Study Constitutional Reforms

November 8, 1927, New Delhi: Viceroy Irwin has today announced the setting up of a statutory commission to study the issue of constitutional reforms. This is towards the decennial review as provided under the Government of India Act 1919. In this connection, it may be recalled that right since 1924, the Swarajists and the Congress have been raising demands for a new constitution that addresses the aspirations of Indians.

It may be mentioned that though the Viceroy has made the announcement, the appointment has yet to get the approval of the British parliament and assent of the King. These are expected soon.

Subhas Elected President Of Provincial Congress

November 1927: The fact that Subhas was elected a member of the Bengal provincial legislature, raised the question of allowing him to be in Calcutta. His failing health emerged as another serious issue and discontents brewing in the country, particularly in Bengal, over his continued confinement in the distant Mandalay made the goverment apprehensive.

Considering him to be too dangerous if he was brought back to India, the government had offered to release him on the condition that he goes to Europe for treatment without setting foot in India. However, his health had deteriorated so much that the Government was compelled to release him on humanitarian grounds, and allow him to return to Calcutta for treatment. Subhas came back to Calcutta last May to a tumultuous welcome. His mentor, CR Das, died while he was in prison in Mandalay and the provincial Congress seemed to be in disarray in the absence of a powerful leadership. Subhas was elected as president of the Bengal provincial Congress on the 27th of October. His return to Calcutta has rejuvenated the Bengal Provincial Congress Committee. Since his return, Subhas has been amidst political activities, especially involving the youth and trade unions. There are great expectations from him.

Simon Commission To Study Constitutional Reforms

November 26, 1927, London: Indian representation in the legislative bodies had begun in 1909. Their presence was strengthened, following the reforms implemented under the GOI Act 1919. Under section 84 of the Act, it was proposed to set up a statutory commission at the end of ten years to determine the next stage in the realisation of self-rule in India. In keeping with the ten-years time interval, the British government has now begun the exercise to draft a constitution for India by 1929. On the 8th of this month, the Viceroy had announced the appointment of a statutory commission to study the issue of constitutional reforms. Subsequently, it was approved by the British Parliament and now it has received the royal assent.

The commission will be an all-white body comprising seven members of British Parliament: two Labourites, four Conservatives with Sir John Simon, a Liberal, as the chairman. Other members are Clement Attlee, Edward Cadogan, George Lane-Fox, Lord Strathcona, Stephen Walsh and Lord Burnham. Whereas such measures, including the formation of the Commission aimed at facilitating self-governance in a phased manner, are welcome to Indians, serious trouble has arisen due to the partisan manner in which the commission is constituted.

In terms of its major responsibilities, the commission is expected to study the working of the system of government at present. It is also expected to assess the extent of responsible government allowed at present and the desirability of its modification and the extent thereof.

Simon Commission 'The Butchery Of Soul': Jinnah

November 8, 1927: Simon Commission is supposed to interact with various cross sections of people in India and place its recommendations before the British Parliament that would be incorporated in the next Government of India Act. The matter of composition of the commission, with not a single Indian in it, is not only shocking, but a grave affront to Indian self-respect. The British government has sought to justify this, saying it is a parliamentary committee and it needs to be unbiased and be capable of presenting an accurate picture to the parliament. But Indians are not at all convinced.

Incidentally, way back in 1892, an Indian, viz. Dadabhai Naoroji was elected a member of the British parliament from Finsbury on a Liberal ticket. And nearly four decades after that, no Indians were found worthy of the responsibility? Further, this is an issue that concerns Indians directly—they are deprived of representation in a commission that is to draft a constitution for their country. Some are speculating this is the typical British way of evening out the score—they are out to avenge the injury inflicted by the non-cooperation non-violent movement on Britain. Not only was its political hegemony challenged before the public eye, the British economic interests were gravely threatened too. To many Indians, the all-white commission appears as an attempt to heap insult and humiliation upon them.

Political India has been reacting strongly to the composition of the committee. As soon as the news of the composition broke, Jinnah had sent a wire to the Labour Party in England protesting. He has reportedly said later: 'Jallianwala was physical butchery. The Simon Commission is the butchery of our soul'.[37]

Birkenhead Challenges India To Produce An Agreed Constitution

November 1927, London: The Conservatives or the Tories are presently on their way out as the next election is due in Britain. Birkenhead, the Secretary of State for India in the outgoing government, has been known for his hostility to Indian political aspirations. As if to deliberately wound the Indian pride and psyche, he has ensured that all members of the commission led by Simon are white people. No Indian, however eminent, found a place in it. This has surprised and angered Indians no end. Even many elite British are shocked at this move.

Birkenhead has provoked political India even more by challenging the capacity of Indian politicians to produce an agreed constitution for India. He did so while introducing the bill on the statutory commission in the parliament.

AMBEDKAR BURNS COPIES OF 'MANUSMRITI'

December 25, 1927, Mahad, Bombay: Bhim Rao Ambedkar has been able to establish himself as an undisputed leader of the depressed classes, including the untouchables. Unlike many political leaders who launched their political activities from the Congress—the major political party of the country, he has been building up a movement of the 'dalits' upon a separate platform. The reasons for this, many say, are due to his assumptions that the Congress' involvement in the 'dalit' cause, despite Gandhi's personal interest in the matter, is cosmetic rather than earnest.

Having been exposed to severe caste discrimination personally, and also having witnessed the miseries, woes and poverty of the dalit people from close quarters, Ambedkar, himself educated highly in premier institutions in the USA and UK, has been able to present the case of socio-political rights of the dalits very forcefully in course of political negotiations. Some of his actions are quite strident and appear designed to send strong messages to an otherwise indifferent Hindu society, dominated by caste Hindus.

Today, Ambedkar led a march of the Dalits to Chowdar Tank to demand the right to draw water from the public tank. In what appeared to be a symbolic act, he has also burnt copies of the *Manusmriti* (the Hindu scripture that deals with caste divisions in society). Possibly, he wanted to send a strong message of protest against the seemingly eternal oppression of the untouchables in the caste-ridden Hindu community. The event has attracted huge media and public attention. Large number of Dalit people assembled at the venue enthusiastically. They have given a name to commemorate this day—Manu Smriti Dahan Divas.

The Making Of Bhimrao Ramji Ambedkar

Born on 14 April 1891 in Mhow in the Central Province, in the Mahar Community condemned by the caste Hindus as untouchables, the boy Bhim had to consistently fight against oppression and neglect by upper castes till he went abroad, when a new world opened to him. In that vast, free, liberal world where all human beings enjoyed basic dignity, the pains, sufferings and stigmas of his fellow untouchable people back in India kept hurting him all the more.

Ambedkar had to fight his way through a series of adversities with the strength of his talent and perseverance. He earned a Masters, a D Sc and completed his legal education in USA and England in phases. In the interregnum, he pursued journalism and other socio-political activities aimed at the upliftment of the depressed classes. By now, he has been able to establish himself as the prominent face of the 'dalit leadership', despite Gandhi's abounding concern for them and keenness to abolish untouchability in Hindu society. This is because, many say, Ambedkar, while being one of the eminent intellectuals and a front-ranked social elite, has a deeper familiarity and understanding of the woes and miseries of the 'dalits', because he himself has had first hand experience of many social atrocities. As a school student, he was made to sit on the floor and his teachers did not even touch his notebooks. It made no difference that Bhim was one of the brightest students of his time.

The fact that he survived and overcame the oppressive adversities all around him, was not only because he was an exceptionally brilliant student but because he also had the courage and fortitude to take adversities in his strides. He was also lucky to have handy financial support from the Maharajas of Baroda and Kolhapur in respect of his studies overseas. But he knows too well that the vast majority of the 'dalit' did not possess exceptional talents, nor have any financial backing. Knowing the handicaps and the cruel social and economic realities most 'dalits' were subjected to, Ambedkar has been busy canvassing their cause aggressively, this as his single-point mission.

CONGRESS CALL TO BOYCOTT SIMON COMMISSION

December 26-28, 1927, Madras: Congress holds its annual session here. MA Ansari presides. The issue of Simon Commission dominates the proceedings. The session has resolved to boycott the commission 'at every stage and every form'. It has in another resolution, decided to convene an all-India, all-parties conference with a view to draft a constitution for India, acceptable to all parties. Yet another resolution has also been passed, demanding 'complete independence' for the country.

Boycott Of Simon May Be Intense, But Not Total

Simon is due to arrive in India along with his team members shortly. The commission will visit the country and hold extensive consultations with various parties, organisations and a cross-section of people, to derive inputs to draft the constitution for India. The Indian National Congress is clearly in an agitated mood. It has taken a decision not to cooperate with the commission and given a call to all Indians to boycott the commission wherever it goes. Muslim League is divided on the issue. The faction led by Jinnah, in a session held in Calcutta, is opposing the government decision and has constituted a subcommittee to hold consultations with the Congress and other organisations in favour of an indigenous initiative for drafting a constitution for India.

But fortunately for Simon and the Viceroy, the boycott is not total. The other faction of the Muslim League, led by Muhammad Shafi, a leader from Punjab, has decided to cooperate with the all-white commission. Another important leader, who has also decided to engage with the commission in defiance of the trend set by the Congress, is BR Ambedkar. He seems to be of the opinion that he can better protect the interest of the depressed people by cooperating with the commission than by avoiding it. Simon would also be visiting some of the native states, meet their princes to obtain the views of the 'Indian' India. These princes are also willing to extend their cooperation to the commission.

Committee To Cooperate With Simon Commission

December 1927: Major political parties like Congress and the Jinnah-led Muslim League have decided not to cooperate with the all-white Simon Commission. The Viceroy has ensured that an All-India Committee for Cooperation with Simon Commission is established by the Council of India. The committee is headed by Sir C Sankaran Nair and its members include Sir Arthur Froom, Rajah Nawab Ali Khan, Sardar Shivdev Singh Uberoi, Nawab Sir Zulfiqar Ali Khan, Sir HS Gaur, Sir Abdullah Al-Maman Suhrawardy, Killabhai Premchand and Rao Bahadur MC Rajah.

People Support Congress, Demand Constitution For India

December 17-18, 1927, Bombay: Congress has decided not to cooperate with Simon and urged all Indians to boycott the Commission. On the other hand, disillusioned with the government intention, Congress has begun to demand an appropriate constitution for India. It is emerging as an important political issue in the country. Though the Congress has been strident in its stand, some political formations do not subscribe to Congress views. This is making the issue somewhat controversial as well.In the above backdrop, the Congress has got strong support from a quarter, whose cause it has been reluctant to identify with all these years, despite all manners of persuasion–the states' peoples' organisations. The rulers of the native states are extending support to the Simon Commission, where as the people of these states are coming closer to the Congress stand. In the All-India States' People's Conference just concluded here, the conference, dominated by representatives from the western states, has authorised the executive committee to secure the cooperation of political organisations in British India and collaborate with them in devising a new constitution for the whole of India, including the Indian states.

People Of Princely States Expect Congress To Be Sensitive

December 26-27, 1927, Madras: Close on the heels of the All- India States' people's Conference in Bombay less than two weeks ago, another states' people's body in the same name has held a conference here on the eve of the annual session of the Indian National Congress.

If the Bombay conference indicated support for the Congress in the matter of designing the new constitution, the conference being held in Madras has reminded the Congress of its longstanding demand that the latter involves itself much more to cater to the political aspirations of the people of the native states. In a resolution, the conference has called on the Congress to widen the scope of activities, so as to include the internal affairs of the Indian states by making suitable amendments in its constitution and also to provide for adequate representations of the states in the Congress organisations.

The deliberations in both the bodies in Bombay and Madras are clear pointers to the growing political awareness of people in princely states and their urge to wipe out the borders between the princely states and British Indian provinces, in terms of Congress attention and actions. It is obvious that the Congress cannot overlook such demands for long.

Subhas Now A General Secretary Of Congress

December 1927: Subhas' popularity has been soaring. He was elected as a member of the Bengal provincial legislature in absentia. Soon after his release from Mandalay jail and arrival in Calcutta, he was elected as the president of the Bengal provincial Congress. Now, one more recognition has come on his way—he has been chosen as a general secretary of the Indian National Congress. All these three developments have occurred in the last one year.

Political observers feel, the government has mishandled his case. It has been unjust and vindictive. But they only ended up raising his popularity. Subhas has now been pushed to the all-India stage. It is quite probable that in his new role, Subhas will try to make Congress stand more militant and uncompromising at the national level.

Jawaharlal Sees Political Freedom As Basic Necessity

December 1927: Jawaharlal has returned from Europe and it seems, his political thinking has undergone important changes. In India, he has been an ardent follower of Gandhi. He participated in the non-cooperation movement enthusiastically, courted arrest and served prison terms.

Later, when the Swaraj Party moved away from Gandhi on the issue of 'council entry', Jawaharlal remained loyal to Gandhi and refrained from joining it, even though Motilal, his father, happened to be one of its key leaders. His loyalty to Gandhi has been intact, notwithstanding his inability to understand a few tenets of the latter's leadership style, dictums and approach to key issues.

During his sojourn in England, Jawaharlal had occasion to interact with social and political thinkers and leaders. Unlike his student days there, the recent visit was very different. One thing he seemed to have become convinced of, as a result of these interactions, is the imperative of social freedom and building up a socialistic structure of society. And towards this purpose, he feels political freedom of the country is a basic and enabling condition.

However, to Gandhi and other top leaders of the Congress, the thoughts of political freedom of India are yet premature. At this moment, they are setting their sight on 'Dominion Status' only and nothing else.

Jawaharlal is not able to reconcile with this Congress approach. As such, he is keeping himself free from any office in the Congress. He wants to focuss on the youth of the country and the labour movements.

Jawaharlal Has To Wait For The Crown

December 1927, Madras: According to some sources, Motilal Nehru has been trying to persuade Gandhi to make Jawaharlal the president in the Madras session. However, Gandhi, while agreeing that Jawaharlal deserved the crown, felt the time for it has not yet arrived. Gandhi's choice of president is Dr Ansari. He believes this would facilitate Hindu Muslim unity.

Jawaharlal Calls For Complete Independence Subhas Bose Supports Him

December 26-28, 1927, Madras: The Congress session is held here in a politically surcharged atmosphere. MA Ansari presides. The all-white Simon Commission has been the agent provocateur. Even though most of the veterans try to keep the tempers down, the young and the hardliners are showing distinct signs of intolerance against the colonial rulers. It has been decided to pursue a strong boycott policy against the commission.

Jawaharlal has been unhappy with the vague talks of swaraj, which is not clearly defined in the organisation. He feels the necessity of achieving political freedom as a pre-condition to building a socialist state, for which he has developed a conviction. He has pushed a resolution in the session demanding complete national independence for India, although top leaders like Gandhi, Motilal and others see no more than the 'dominion status' as the immediate goal for the country.

Subhas, another young and uncompromising leader and the newly-elected general secretary of the Congress, is also strongly advocating the demand for freedom. He has lent his support to the resolution Jawaharlal has moved. These young leaders find support from a few veterans like Annie Besant and Srinivasa Iyenger. WPP leaders of Bombay like RS Nimbkar and KN Joglekar also subscribe to such a view. However, the moderates were not ready to go beyond 'dominion status'.

Congress To Support States' Peoples' Political Aspirations

December 26-28, 1927, Madras: After maintaining a studied policy of a complete 'hands off' approach in the matter of political relations between the rulers and subjects of the native states for long years, the Congress seems to have begun a rethink. Unable to ignore the rising voices of the people of princely states, expressed repeatedly through forums like the All-India States' People's Conferences, the Congress has passed a resolution during its annual session here saying that 'this Congress is emphatically of the opinion that in the interests of both the rulers and the people of the Indian states, they should establish representative institutions and responsible Governments in their States at an early date'. The resolution is not quite strident yet, and still attempts at tight-rope walking. However, it is an indicator that Congress has begun to realise its responsibility to the people of the 'other India' or Indian India. It may be only a matter of time, before it responds to the demands of the subjects of these states in a more wholesome manner.

'Sarfaroshi Ki Tamanna' Will Now Be Sung By Millions

December 19, 1927: This month seems to be of great significance for the revolutionary movement in India. Three popular patriot-activists, viz. Ramprasad Bismil, Ashfaqullah, and Thakur Roshan Singh, arrested by the police in the Kakori train robbery case for looting government cash in 1925 and put to trial, were today sent to the gallows in three different jails in Gorakhpur, Faizabad and Allahabad.

Ashfaq earned the distinction of being the very first and foremost Muslim to climb the gallows for India's freedom. Ramprasad Bismil, a devout Arya Samaji and Ashfaq a Muslim were close friends and their friendship and executions on the same day will certainly turn into a symbol of communal unity in the country. Ramprasad was a talented poet and singer and by his song, *'Sarfaroshi ki Tamanna'*, he could instantly fill his audience with patriotic fervour. Though the oppressive colonial government has silenced this revolutionary's voice forever, now onwards his haunting song will be sung by millions of patriotic Indians, for sure.

Jinnah And Shaffi Differ On Simon Commission

January 1, 1928, Calcutta, Lahore: Two factions of the Muslim League have two different opinions about cooperating with the Simon Commission. One group, led by Jinnah, held a meet in Calcutta from 30th last month to date and decided to boycott the commission. Another faction, led by Shaffi, met in Lahore for the last two days and they have agreed to cooperate with the commission.

Independence Resolution Was Hastily Conceived And Thoughtlessly Passed : Gandhi

January 5, 1928, Sabarmati: Gandhi paid a brief visit to the Congress session held last moth in Madras. He could not attend any of the committee meetings and had to return early for health reasons. However, he was upset by the manner in which the 'resolutions involving great consequences were sprung upon the Subjects Committee' and passed without opposition. Yesterday, he wrote to Jawaharlal expressing his dissatisfaction. Gandhi mentioned that Jawaharlal was 'going too fast' while he 'should have taken time to think and become acclimatized'. Gandhi was particularly critical of Jawaharlal 'encouraging mischief-makers and hooligans', and in that context doubted if Jawaharlal still believed 'in the unadulterated non-violence'. Today, in the *Young India,* he has described the 'Independence Resolution' passed in Madras session as 'hastily conceived and thoughtlessly passed'.[38]

But Even In The Wider Sphere, Am I Not Your Child In Politics? Jawaharlal

January 26, 1928, Sabarmati: For the past some time, there has been palpable tension in the relationship between Gandhi and Jawaharlal. It apparently started when Jawaharlal had moved a resolution on independence in the Madras session and Gandhi criticised it as 'hastily conceived' and 'thoughtlessly passed'. This was like a question mark on his political wisdom and sagacity, including his newly-developed insight attained through extensive interaction with eminent thinkers and politicians in Europe. The tension was exacerbated after he wrote a letter to Gandhi questioning the wisdom of Gandhi's policies on various issues like industrial growth, centrality of khadi, prospect of India's future development on the Gandhian model, validity of dominion status claim, boycott of British goods etc. He also accused Gandhi of acting like a schoolmaster, trying to chastise students by pointing out errors but never guiding them, or giving them proper lesson. He pointed out that if the country was unable to move ahead by one political method, then surely the leaders have to think of other or additional methods.

Gandhi was shocked at this sudden outburst. On 17th of this month, he wrote a long letter to Jawaharlal mentioning that it has become evident that during the course of working with and under him, Jawaharlal has been in a state of unnatural self-suppression for long years and has overlooked those 'very things' which have now begun to appear as his 'serious blemishes...' Gandhi then wanted to redefine their future relationship. He was ready to grant Jawaharlal any freedom from the 'humble, unquestioning allegiance' that Jawahar gave to him 'all these years'. Gandhi welcomed that Jawaharlal 'carry on open warfare' against him and his views, because if he was wrong it was the duty of Jawaharlal to rise in 'revolt' after having known it. Gandhi concluded that 'the differences' between the two appeared 'so vast and radical that there seems to be no meeting ground between us'. Gandhi also suggested 'a dignified way' to Jawaharlal to unfurl his own banner: 'Write to me a letter for publication, showing your differences. I will print it in *Young India* and write a brief reply'.[39]

This response devastated Jawaharlal. Almost apologising and confirming his deep regard and affection for Gandhi, he wrote back that his letter to Gandhi was only to 'Gandhi alone' and not meant for wider audience. Jawaharlal also asked, 'But even in the wider sphere, am I not your child in politics, though perhaps a truant and errant child?'[40]

Jawaharlal's apology seems to have been accepted by Gandhi. Today, he sent Jawaharlal a wire, assuring him that he would not publish the correspondence and asked him to come to Sabarmati ashram with his father, Motilal, if at all possible.[41]

The small-duration dissension seems to have only cemented Gandhi's affection for Jawaharlal and Jawaharlal's loyalty to Gandhi.

SIMON COMMISSION ARRIVES – INDIA IS CLOSED

February 3, 1928, Bombay: The team of seven British MPs, led by Simon, has landed in Bombay. However, the major political parties have decided to boycott the commission. Today major cities and towns in the country are observing 'hartal' as a mark of protest. In Bombay, the team of John Simon has faced angry protestors carrying banners with slogan, 'Simon, Go Back'.

'Indians Have No Confidence In Simon Commission'

February 16, 1928, New Delhi: The Indian members of the Indian Legislative Assembly have become vocal too against the all-white commission. Today, Lajpat Rai has brought a resolution declaring that Indians have no confidence in Simon Commission. It was supported by MA Jinnah and adopted. The resolution will hinder any institutional support by the Assembly to the Simon Commission.

All-Parties Conference' Work On Constitution Fails

February 12-22, 1928, New Delhi: Even as the Simon Commission has just begun its work, the Indian political spectrum has organised an All-Parties Conference here to agree on a constitution. As many as twenty-nine organisations assembled here with MA Ansari in the chair. Unfortunately they could not come to any conclusion as to how to proceed.

Ramsay's Utterances Kindle Hope In India

July 2, 1928, London: Even though the appointment of Simon Commission has antagonised large sections of Indians, they were comforted by Ramsay MacDonald, the leader of the Labour Party, as he spoke in the British Labour Conference. Presiding over the conference, he said: 'I hope that within a period of months, rather than years, there will be a new Dominion added to the Commonwealth of our Nations…a Dominion that will find self respect as an equal within the Commonwealth. I refer to India'.[42] There are two reasons that give Indians hope. First, Ramsay MacDonald is believed to be a lover of India. Secondly, there is strong possibility of the Labour Party forming the next government in Britain. In such an eventuality, Ramsay taking over as the prime minister is a near certainty.

Simon Commission Faces Uphill Tasks

April 11, 1928, New Delhi: The Simon Commission has been finding it hard to carry out its mission in the face of extensive boycott and protests. Notwithstanding, it has been working over the last two months, based on whatever cooperation has been available. Today, the team has returned to England. It is likely to come back later to resume its work.

INDIANS TAKE UP BRITISH CHALLENGE

Motilal Asked To Draft Indian Constitution

May 1928, Bombay: Bulk of the Indian political spectrum has boycotted Simon Commission. As a result, Simon and his team carried out their work, based on limited interactions with those native interest groups who were willing to engage with them. The latter includes the all-India Committee for Cooperation with Simon Commission, constituted by the government, Shafi-led Muslim League, depressed classes organisations and native rulers.

In the meanwhile, various Indian political parties have been trying to work out a constitution for India. Towards this end they held an All-Parties Conference in Delhi first, during 12-22 February this year, closely followed by another attempt on 8th March. But agreements continued to elude them. There have been major differences between the League and the Hindu Mahasabha on the issue of 'separation of Sind from Bombay', and 'reservation of seats' amongst two communities. That conference achieved little, apart from appointing two subcommittees.

The Conference has met here once again but the prospect of an agreement still seems difficult. To resolve the impasse, the conference has appointed a sub-committee of nine members under Motilal Nehru, two of whom are Muslims, viz. Syed Ali Imam and Shoaib Qureshi, to draft a constitution for India.

Congress has invited the Muslim League to participate in the exercise but the latter is not willing to involve itself. As such, it has been decided that the Motilal Nehru Committee will draft the constitution and discuss the subject with the Muslim League. Critics say, as always, the League wants to sit on the fence—it likes to see the outcome. If not favourable, it reserves its right to disagree, instead of being a party to the exercise and thereby enter into a commitment.

The Motilal Nehru Report

August 10, 1928: Drafting a constitution for the country has been an enormous responsibility, particularly in view of the sharp divide between the Congress and the Muslim League on several key political issues involving the two major communities. The task was rendered even more difficult because the League did not want to participate in the drafting exercise. Motilal Nehru worked tirelessly to justify the confidence reposed in him, laboured indefatigably for the last three months at Allahabad, held twenty-five sittings and has now presented his report. Unfortunately, he did not get the full participation of the two Muslim members. Of the two Muslim members, Syed Ali Imam failed to attend more than one session for health reasons. Shoaib Qureshi did not concur with the majority view on the issue of Muslim representation in the legislatures. The report has been signed by TB Sapru, MS Aney, Mangal Singh, Shoaib Qureshi, GR Pradhan and Subhas Chandra Bose. The preamble of the report mentions a minority view in favour of 'complete national independence'.

The report has been drafted on the presumption of India as a Dominion State. This is, no doubt, a climb down from the demand for independence, echoed in the Madras session and also seemingly an inferior position than the clamour for Swaraj. However, this is seen as an attempt to carry the moderates along. The report stresses on a strong central government, saying that the country should have a federal form of government with residuary power vested in the centre. It says the government should be parliamentary in form, headed by a prime minister and six ministers, to be appointed by the Governor General. It also proposes bi-cameral legislature.

The report discards separate electorate system altogether—for any community. It also denounces the system of weightage for minorities, which it describes as bad as the separate electorate system. The report says that reservation of Muslim seats can be provided in the provinces where Muslim population is at least ten per cent. However, in such cases, the reservation has to be in strict proportion to the size of the community. They will have right to contest elections in other seats. On the issue of minimum guaranteed Muslim presence in the central legislature, the report has fixed it as one-fourth of the total as against one-third demanded in the Delhi proposal. On another demand spelt out in the Delhi proposal by Jinnah about formation of Sind as a separate province, the report said Sind should be separated from Bombay on due certification that the new province would be financially self-sufficient. However, the report has agreed to according full provincial status to NWFP. At the same time, the report has proposed a new Kanarese speaking province in south India. On the official language issue, the report suggested the use of Hindi.

Muslim League Is Unhappy With Motilal Report

August 1928: The Motilal Nehru report has found acceptance of the bulk of the Congress but the ultra nationalists in the party are clearly unhappy as it envisages only 'dominion status' for the country.

Muslim League leaders are antagonised more, but for different reasons. They are looking at the report as a virtual rejection of the Delhi proposal offered by Jinnah last year. The League perceives it as an one-sided exercise. It has branded the report as a Congress document and rejected it overwhelmingly. Jinnah is so upset that he has announced a 'parting of ways' with the Congress.

However, critics say that the League ought to have participated in the exercise from the inception. Having abdicated that responsibility, putting the blame on the door of the Congress now is clearly opportunistic.

The Congress does not seem to be much disturbed at the intransigence of the League. Confident of the strength of the report and its ability to manage the political consequences arising from it, the party has forwarded the report to the government, urging for its urgent implementation. It has also issued a threat of civil disobedience movement, if the Motilal Nehru Report is not converted into an Act by December 31, 1929. The party has hinted to the government that it has made a compromise by asking for dominion status instead of complete independence and in return expects the government to reciprocate within a year. In case the government fails to deliver within the time frame, the Congress threatened that it would revert to the demand for 'independence' instead of 'dominion status'.

Way To Ramrajya Lies Through Bardoli Gandhi Applauds 'Sardar' Vallabhbhai Patel

August 28, 1928: A successful Satyagraha carried out by the people of Bardoli has come to an end. Vallabhbhai Patel, having steered the movement as its leader, is hogging the limelight across the nation. His immaculate application of the principle of Gandhi's Satyagraha in Indian conditions, and the manner in which he led the movement extracting near total loyalty of his followers, have earned him the epitaph of 'Sardar (the leader of men)'. Bardoli, a taluk in Gujarat, has for past some years, been alternatively savaged by flood and famine. While its famished peasantry, reeling under the fury of nature, was looking for some relief measures from the administration, the Bombay Presidency government compounded their woes by raising the taxes by as much as thirty per cent in 1925. The helpless peasantry prayed, moved petitions and appealed to the authorities through civil groups. But there was no result. After having undergone the ordeals for long, the local people thought of Satyagraha as a means to get redressal and they approached Vallabhbhai. Vallabhbhai, a barrister by training from England, and a leader of high integrity, courage, will power and organising skill had earned the trust and confidence of Gandhi, during the Ahmedabad mill strike and Kheda Satyagraha.

Vallabhbhai got Gandhi's nod and checked the preparedness of the people before taking over the reins of the movement on 19th February this year. Having chalked out the strategy in fine details, he launched a non-violent civil disobedience movement in Bardoli. As an essential condition of the Satyagraha, he made it clear that the people of Bardoli would have to carry out this non-violent struggle all by themselves, without expecting any outside support and also without any rancour against their adversaries, like the revenue officials or their agents, and such others.

A master organiser, Vallabhbhai divided Bardoli in several zones and allotted a leader and his aides to each of these. Complete unity of action was ensured on the part of the peasantry, who refused to pay taxes to the government and offered themselves voluntarily for any penalty or punishment. The irate government officials tried to scare the farmers, and drive wedges amongst them but failed. As extreme punishment, they confiscated properties of some farmers but such was the fervour created by the Satyagraha that no buyer turned up to take part in the auction. Eventually, the government officials found it impracticable to coerce the farmers to pay higher taxes.

The issue began to be discussed with greater urgency and sensitivity at the legislative council meetings in Bombay. As the power of Satyagraha began to unfold, a number of Indian legislators resigned in sympathy with the cause. At last, an agreement was brokered by a Parsi member of the government. Accordingly the government agreed to restore the confiscated land and properties, forego the revenue payment for the year and also cancel the tax raise of thirty per cent until after the succeeding year.

All through the course of the Satyagraha, Vallabhbhai led the movement with great finesse. In the process, he has won the confidence of the people of Gujarat. Since the movement was watched with avid interest across the nation, he has also earned the admiration of Indians in general. People are expecting him to play a greater role in the national struggle for swaraj. Even though the Bardoli agitation was not conducted officially under the banner of the Indian National Congress, its success has given a lot of morale boost to the party against its fight with the British government.

Vallabhbhai's greatest recognition has come from none other than Gandhi. Gandhi is very happy that the Bardoli victory has come on the eve of the All- Parties Conference in Lucknow to consider the Indian-made constitution for India. He is expecting that Lucknow would pave the way for constitutional swaraj, whereas Bardoli victory has shown the way to organic swaraj or Ramrajya.[43] Today he has written to the *Indian National Herald*, referring to the two forms of swaraj.

All-Parties Conference Endorse Motilal Report

August 28-31, 1928, Lucknow: All Parties Conference has been held here to consider the Motilal Nehru Committee report. Parties from wide spectrum of political India were present. Both Jinnah and Shafi groups kept aloof. The Conference has adopted the report almost unanimously with only one dissenting vote. [44] The Sikh delegates were against reservations. Their leaders, Tara Singh and Sher Singh, insisted that if at all reservation was accepted as a principle there ought to be reservations for Sikhs and Hindus in Punjab too. They got their dissent recorded. Clearly, the Congress is trying to demonstrate consensus of political India on the issue of the new constitution to create pressure upon the British government. After adopting the proposed constitution, the All-Parties Conference has decided to place it before a representative convention to be held in Calcutta. This move is possibly to demonstrate Indian unanimity on the report, beyond doubt or reproach.

Jawaharlal Presides Over All-Bengal Students' Conference

August 1928, Calcutta: Students have been amongst important participants in the struggle for swaraj. Now, the students of Bengal are seeking better ways to increase their involvement. The first All-Bengal Students' Conference was held here. Jawaharlal presided. There are reports that students in various districts and even in neighbouring provinces are taking cue from this event.

Communists To Expose National Reformist Leaders

July 17-September 1, 1928, Moscow: Communist Party of India continues to be a banned organisation. As such, the communists are using the Congress platform to carry out their activities. Especially, the provincial Workers and Peasants Parties, the overboard wing of the Communists, are working on the Congress platform. In a number of areas, particularly in respect of trade union movement both, the Communists and other Congress leaders, have been working together. Sometimes, the dividing line between the Communists and the left nationalist leaders in the Congress is very thin. However, a new guideline from the headquarters of the Communist world may upset the ties between the two groups.

Based on the experience of the Kuomintang in China, the thesis adopted at the sixth Congress of the Communist International has called upon Indian Communists to have no truck with the bourgeoisie-led civil disobedience movement and expose the left nationalists and pseudo-revolutionaries. Gandhi, Jawaharlal and Subhas were all characterised as 'representatives of the capitalist class working against the fundamental interests of the toiling masses of the country'. This new line is a drastic departure from the one earlier advocated by Lenin, suggesting a united front with the nationalist forces. It is bound to bring the relationship between the Congress and Communists under strain with obvious implications on the leadership of the trade union movement.

Revolutionaries Declare Socialistic Intention

Chandrasekhar Azad Appointed President Of New Outfit

September 1928, Delhi: Unlike Congress, the revolutionaries are thinking in altogether different ways about the future of their country and also the methods to secure that. In a strategic move, young revolutionaries from various parts of India met at Feroze Shah Kotla ground here. The Lahore faction, led by Bhagat Singh and the Kanpur faction of HRA, led by Chandrasekhar Azad, got merged with the revolutionary faction led by Phanindra to form HSRA or Hindustan Socialist Republican Association. This new incarnation has socialism as its ultimate goal and it aims to coordinate the violent revolutionary movements against the British government throughout the country. They have elected Chandrasekhar Azad as the president of the organisation. It seems the stagnation in the programmes and activities of the mainstream political parties, their meek, compromising attitude and growing shadow of communalism over the political space have been adding to their frustration. These young, flaming souls are trying to cleanse the cobwebs from the national life by their spirit of patriotism, nationalism and commitment to socialism. To the government they are posing a different kind of challenge. Both, the 'armed revolution' and the ideology of 'socialism' are anathema to it.

Simon Commission Returns To India, Hostility Remains

October 11, 1928, New Delhi: Simon Commission team has returned to India today to resume its work. It is scheduled to visit places to enquire into issues and interact with people to collect inputs. It may be recalled that during its first visit, the team members faced intense protests. Though it has returned to India after six months, the hostility does not seem to have ebbed a bit. It is also significant that Indians have been able to prepare a constitution of their own and it has also been adopted by the All-Parties Conference. According to reports, Lahore, which is in the commission's itinerary, is preparing to give the team a hostile reception.

Lajpat Rai Hit On The Chest By Marauding Police

October 30, 1928, Lahore: Congress and many other political parties communicated their disapproval of the Simon Commission to the government much earlier. Protest meetings are erupting across cities and towns. Today, the Simon Commission arrived here. On this occasion, thousands of Indians, led by Lala Lajpat Rai, were holding a silent and peaceful protest march on the roads of the city. Under instructions from a British officer, the police hit the veteran leader in the chest hard with a baton. The action seemed not only surprising and atrocious, but it also betrayed extreme audacity and disdain of the British regime for the feelings of Indians. The Lala has been grievously hurt and he is said to be in a critical condition. This heinous action, at first stupefied the Indians, and then began to fill their heart with silent anger. A feeling of vulnerability—that they cannot protect their respected leaders from the cruel colonial rulers—has engulfed Indians. They are being reminded of the curse of being a slave nation.

LAJPAT RAI SUCCUMBS TO INJURY

November 17, 1928, Lahore: Lajpat Rai has succumbed to his injuries. This was a tragic end to the life of an illustrious leader, one of the most adored and revered leaders of the Indians. The untimely demise came not only due to the physical injury inflicted by the savage assault of an unscrupulous police official, but also the deep mental hurt he sustained by the insult and the humiliation associated with the heinous action. It was the same leader who was, in view of his exalted character and irrefutable integrity, acquitted of charges and brought back to India from Mandalay prison in 1907 by the intervention of the Viceroy and the Secretary of State. He was now assaulted like an ordinary criminal. The nation is mourning. Bhagat Singh, the young revolutionary, who was present at the procession when Lala was hurt, is seething in anger. According to some sources, he has taken a vow to avenge the hurt and the insult.

The Independence For India League Is Formed

November 1928, Delhi: Ambivalence of the Congress between 'total independence' and 'dominion status' has been bothering the left nationalists in the Congress. What is causing them more disquiet is the fact that the lack of progress in the struggle for self-government appears due to this vacillation on the part of the top leadership. The masses are ready for sacrifice and they have proved it from time to time. They also recognise the fact that in recent years, the workers' movements are gaining momentum. Under these circumstances, Indian communists and left nationalists have now come forward in an united action and formed a new organisation 'The Independence for India League' at Delhi which has the declared aim of achieving complete independence for India and reconstruction of Indian society on the basis of social and economic equality. Both Subhas and Jawaharlal have taken keen initiative in founding the organisation and they would serve as its secretaries. The League will have S Srinivasa Iynger as its president. The founders are planning to affiliate it to the League against Imperialism, which has its main office in Berlin.

This development has caused concern to the traditional Congress leadership as it threatens to snatch the national agenda and the promising young leaders away from them. It is being learnt that this development has made Gandhi think in terms of hastening his comeback, resume control and subsume the new spirit in the mother organisation.

Motilal, Srinivasa Allies In Assembly; Opponents In Party

November 1928, New Delhi: Independence for India League has opened several branches in the country since it was formed in August this year. Now it has been formally inaugurated here. Under the able guidance of veteran Srinavasa Iyer, who is its president, the League has been rising as a political force powered by its two young general secretaries, Jawaharlal and Subhas. Clearly, in a short period, it has arrived at a position to influence the policy of the Congress. The League has strong views against 'dominion status'. On this issue, its president Iyenger has growing differences with Motilal, the Congress president elect. Motilal and Srinivasa have been intimate colleagues in the central assembly and fought together against the government. Srinavasa has been the deputy leader of the Congress and acted as leader as well in Motilal's absence. But on the issue of 'independence vs dominion status', they are deeply divided.

Congress Growing In Size And Stature

December 1928: One important development in recent years seems to be that some constituencies of the Congress are organising themselves well and are pursuing programmes for enrolling new members—these include industrial workers, peasants, students, middle class youth and intelligentsia. Since AITUC was formed eight years ago, the trade union movement has been growing significantly. Peasants are astir, forming Kisan Sabhas and the young Indians are launching Youth Leagues in many places. These fronts and forums are emerging as strong support bases for young leaders like Subhas and Jawahar.

Labour Restive, Trade Union Congress Holds Conference

December 1928, Jharia: The All-India Trade Union Congress has held its ninth annual session here. The labour scene in the country, from east to west, is getting increasingly turbulent. The trade unions have been adopting more aggressive stances to realise their demands than in yesteryears. The traditional Gandhian theory of workers-owner partnership and the owner acting as the trustee is no longer popular. Even amongst Congress leaders, younger and left wing leaders like Jawaharlal and Subhas have greater acceptance. Jawaharlal has attended the conference here.

In the current year, several industrial strikes have occurred and these are at varying stages of development. On 5 March, about 14,000 workers in the railway workshop in Liluah had gone on strike. It was closely followed by a strike in the Bengal Nagpur Railway, beginning on 10 April.

In Chotanagpur belt, about 18,000 workers struck work in the Tisco plant. In the west, at least 60,000 textile workers went on strike in Bombay, causing the government and the industry deep anxiety. The large workforce in the huge British-owned jute sector, who have been working with meagre pay and difficult working conditions, may explode with their deep-seated grievances.

In several cases, left wing Congress leaders are leading the workers, Subhas being one of them. However, the Communists are gradually consolidating their hold too. Significantly, this conference has elected M Ahmed as vice president and SA Dange as the assistant secretary for the next Congress that is scheduled to be held in Nagpur next year. Both of them are Communists with credential.

IB Sees Expanding Influence Of Subhas And Jawaharlal

December 15, 1928, Delhi: According to a recent intelligence branch report, young leaders are gradually superseding the elders in the current political life. Home Secretary Haig regards this as part of the expanding influence of Subhas Chandra Bose and Jawaharlal Nehru.

As the Congress is broadening its platform to accommodate the forums of labour and youth, it is relying on young leaders like Subhas and Jawahar to play active role in harnessing the power of these new constituencies.

According to intelligence reports reaching the government, Jawaharlal has just presided over the Bombay Presidency Youth Conference in Pune, where he led a procession that displayed red flags and placards stressing on the indispensability of revolution. An IB report says, the proceedings in the conference all through were candidly Communist and revolutionary. Such reports are creating unease in the government, lest the young leaders of the Congress succumb to the communist and socialist influences.

SAUNDERS IS SHOT DEAD

December 17, 1928, Lahore: Bhagat Singh had reportedly taken a vow to avenge the death of Lala Lajpat Rai. Today, he has avanged Lajpat Rai's death by shooting Saunders, a British police officer. HSRA, the revolutionary outfit of which he is a prominent member, had chalked out the plan for this assassination. Bhagat Singh was to carry it out while other revolutionaries, Shivram Rajguru, Sukhdev Thapar and Jai Gopal would assist him. According to the plan, Bhagat Singh was to shoot JA Scot, the police superintendent who had ordered the lathi charge that eventually led to the death of Lala Lajpat Rai. However, because of mistaken identity, he shot JP Saunders, a deputy superintendent of Police to death. After carrying out his mission, Bhagat Singh has escaped. The police have launched a massive manhunt to track him.

MOTILAL REPORT

Jinnah, Sikhs Want Modifications, Convention says 'No'

December 22-28, 1928, Calcutta: Though an all-parties conference adopted the Motilal Nehru Report in its meeting in Lucknow, held in last August, and subject to only one dissenting opinion, it proposed to place it before a representative convention. In the convention now being held here, the Nehru report in its present form has met with disapproval from the Muslim League.

In an initiative apparently to resolve the dispute between the Congress and the Muslim parties, Jinnah has suggested some modifications in the report to make it acceptable to the Muslims, like increase in the elected Muslim representatives in both houses of the Central Legislatures to 'one third' instead of 'one fourth', as proposed. In the provinces of Punjab and Bengal where the Muslims already have a slender majority, Jinnah wanted reservations of seats for Muslims on the basis of population, in the event adult suffrage was not established. He wanted this to continue for ten years and a re-examination to be done after that. Jinnah agreed that Muslims would not have rights to contest additional seats after that period. On the issue of residuary powers, Jinnah wanted this to be left to the provinces instead of the centre.

The All- Parties Convention found that these demands would alter the fundamental character of the Nehru Report, and therefore, rejected them.

Sikhs on their part had strong viewpoints on two issues. First, they advocated 'independence' and argued that 'dominion status' made swaraj a two-steps process. Second, they contended that the provision of 'reservations' laid the seeds of 'separate electorate'. They are keen that no particular community holds sway over Punjab, taking advantage of the provision for 'reservation'. Since their concerns were not addressed, all thirty Sikh delegates dissociated themselves from the proceedings.

The Congress is, however, downplaying the Muslim and Sikh dissensions as inconsequential and put forth by some 'communal' elements amongst these two communities.

Workers, Peasants Hold First All-India Session

December 22-24, 1928, Calcutta: There are presently, four provincial WPPs —of Bengal, Bombay, UP and Punjab. They are holding their first all-India session here. Although the sixth Comintern Congress has been in favour of the Communists withdrawing support to the WPPs, the all- India meet has already been arranged and the WPPs are going ahead with it, backed by full-fledged support of the Communists. There is great enthusiasm around. Prominent Communist leaders like SA Dange, Sohan Singh, Muzaffar Ahmed and PC Joshi are attending it.

COMPLETE INDEPENDENCE, NOT DOMINION STATUS

Subhas Moves Amendment To Resolution

December 29, 1928 to January 1, 1929, Calcutta: The Congress holds its annual session here. Motilal Nehru presides. Large numbers of delegates have congregated. A well-disciplined band of Congress volunteers, viz. Bengal Volunteers under the leadership of Subhas has been supervising the arrangements.

In the aftermath of the Simon Commission and Motilal Report, the issue of the future constitution of the country has been hogging the lime light. One group has been in favour of 'dominion status', while the other wants the Congress to wage battle for 'complete independence'.

In the annual session held in Madras last year, Jawaharlal had moved a resolution demanding 'independence' for the country. However, Gandhi himself criticised it as 'hastily conceived' and thoughtlessly passed. In this session, Jawaharlal looks much more restrained.

Subhas, another prime young leader, is however, convinced that immediate 'independence' can alone help the country to tackle the British intrigues in creating communal divides. Gandhi introduced a resolution asking the British government to accept the demand for dominion status for India by 31 December, 1929. His resolution read: 'Subject to the exigencies of the political situation, the Congress will adopt the Nehru constitution in its entirety, if it is accepted by the British Parliament on or before 31st December, 1929; but in the event of its non-acceptance, the Congress will organise non-violent non co-operation by advising the country to refuse taxation and in such other manner as may be decided upon.'

Subhas, not happy with the climbdown from Madras session, moved an amendment to the effect that the Congress would be content with nothing short of independence. Subhas was hoping Jawaharlal would support him on this issue, but he was dismayed. It is being heard that Motilal has held Jawaharlal in check. Notwithstanding Jawaharlal's reticence, Subhas has received support from Left nationalists and Communists for his amendment proposal. However, most top-ranked leaders found Subhas' demand as premature and strident, especially when the Congress itself has asked for 'dominion status' from the government.

Gandhi has opposed the amendment proposal and it has been defeated by 1350-973 votes and the original resolution was passed by voice vote. Nevertheless, Subhas has been able to send a clear message—his amendment proposal was the declaration of the young leadership that it would not brook much delay in the matter of self-government, if not complete independence.

Interestingly, some of the senior Congress leaders are reported to have sent feelers to their friends in the British Parliament to hasten the grant of the dominion status to India, while Indians were still willing to take it. Significantly, the Sikh leaders had also made an issue of 'independence' and withdrew themselves from the All- Parties Convention.

Workers Throng Congress Venue
Demand Total Independence

December 1928, Calcutta: Annual session of the Indian National Congress is in progress here. Motilal Nehru, the man who has drafted the new constitution for India, presides. A rousing reception was accorded to him. The Congress has conveyed to the government its preparedness to scale down its demand to dominion status, provided the latter implemented the new constitution within a year.

However, a section of the leaders, more uncompromising, are clearly unhappy at the demand for 'dominion status'. They do not want anything short of complete independence. Subhas is spearheading the campaign of this section. Their demand received a boost when thousands of workers and supporters of the Peasants and Workers Party managed to reach the venue of the Congress session, held a meeting and adopted a resolution, declaring complete independence to be the immediate goal of the Indian nationalist movement. Such a strong outburst of demand in favour of independence from a well-organised body has created a great impression in the minds of the Left nationalists of the Congress.

However, the main body of leaders are not quite pleased at this, which some of them describe as 'intimidatory'. Gandhi has expressed his unhappiness at the happenings.

Civil Liberties And Full Responsible Governments
Congress Pledges Support To States' Peoples' Movement

December 1928, Calcutta: Congress has taken a step ahead to involve itself in the political movements by the people of the native states. Last year, in its Madras session, it had issued an appeal for building up representative institutions leading to responsible government in the native states. In addition to reiterating the above, the Congress has now given a call for civil liberties for the states' people and assured them of its sympathy and support to their legitimate and peaceful struggle for the attainment of full responsible governments in their states.

No doubt, such assurance from the main political party in the country, will boost the morale of a vast population of the princely states.

This new approach is being seen as a turning point in the Congress attitude towards political programmes and activities in native states.

Socialists' Hold Over Congress – Government Is Worried

December 1928, Delhi: Proceedings of the annual session of the Congress in Calcutta have created fresh set of worries for the government. There was a striking unanimity of demands in favour of 'independence', raised by hardline Congress leaders and the Communists. The government has observed a tendency of the Left nationalists and Communist revolutionaries joining hands. A section in the government foresees that the future decisions and Congress policies are likely to be influenced more and more by the younger men, notably Jawaharlal Nehru and Subhas Chandra Bose. Both of them have a pronounced socialistic leaning.

All Parties Muslim Conference Talks Tough

January 1929, Delhi: If the Motilal Nehru Report could not bring political India in alignment, it is likely to bring two adversarial factions of the Muslim League, led by Jinnah and Shafi, close ranks. There have been panic reactions on the part of many Muslim political outfits to the constitution proposed by Motilal. If there was an All-Parties Convention held in Calcutta last month to endorse the report, an All Parties Muslim Conference has been convened here by Aga Khan to deliberate on the report and recommend steps to protect Muslim interest.

This conference has listed some demands that are clearly antagonistic to the Motilal Report. Important amongst these are:(a) The only form of government suitable to Indian conditions is a federal system with complete autonomy and residuary powers vested in constituent states; (b) The separate electorate system for Muslims should continue and Muslims should also continue to have weightage in the Hindu majority provinces. The Muslims, on their part, are willing to grant the same privilege to non-Muslim minorities in Sind, NWFP and Baluchistan.

In addition, the Conference has laid down another demand that goes beyond guaranteed representation in legislatures. Now the

Conference wants a guarantee to be given in the matter of Muslim representation in the cabinets—both central and provincial.

It appears the matter is becoming more complicated because of recommendations and counter recommendations. The prospect of an agreement on the proposed constitution between the Congress and the League seems to have become even more remote after this Conference. The only party happy with the development seems to be the government.

Native States Have Relations With Crown, Not Indian Government: Butler Panel

February 14, 1929, London: At a time, when the ripples of political movements in British Indian provinces are reaching the shores of native states, their rulers can take heart from the findings of the Butler Committee which submitted its report to the parliament today. The three-member committee, chaired by Sir Harcourt Butler, was appointed in December 1927 to examine the financial and economic relationship between British India and the native states. The committee has concluded that the native states have relations with the Crown and not the Government of India. This implies that the Paramount Power has a duty to protect them.

Communist Party Calls For Anti-imperialist Front

March 20, 1929, Bombay: The Indian National Congress has already served the government with an ultimatum of one year to accept the draft constitution, and the clock is ticking. Even though the Congress has not yet launched any movement, the political temperature is rising with every passing month and the country, it seems, is going inexorably towards a climax of confrontation. At this juncture, the last thing it needs is a new political pressure. But the banned Communist Party has mounted exactly that.

The Communist Party of India held the first meeting of its underground central committee in Bombay from 17th to 19th March and adopted a political resolution calling for forging an anti-imperialist united front. The government is determined to crush the new challenge. The government has been particularly peeved over the role of Communist leaders in the series of strikes in the country, including a major one in the textile industry in Bombay. Considering these and given the increasing belligerence of the workers' movement in the country, a major offensive is feared against their leaders.

Countrywide Crackdown On Trade Union Leaders

March 21, 1929, Delhi: The Public Safety Bill has been scheduled for discussion in the Assembly today. Cautious after its defeat in the Subjects Committee earlier, the government has taken more precautions this time. It campaigned aggressively in favour of the Bill, highlighting its need and necessity while hyping up the bogey of Communism. On their part, the nationalist camp also carried out a strong counter-campaign, projecting it as a draconian Bill. They held protest meetings in all politically-aware centres across the country.

With the tempo of the adversarial campaigns pitched high, last night the government adopted an extraordinary measure that has surprised and shocked not only the political dispensation, but even the masses. It has cracked down on Communist and trade union leaders all over the country and arrested thirty-one top ranked leaders including SA Dange, PC Joshi, Muzaffar Ahmed, SV Ghate, Sohan Singh, Dharani Goswami, G Aadhikari and others.

Three prominent British trade union leaders—Ben Bradley, Lester Hutchinson and Philip Spratt—who are in India and have been working for strengthening the workers' movement here have also been taken into custody.

Political analysts feel the government action may have more than one goal. But an immediate objective may be to pre-empt a series of bigger strikes in Bombay and other places, in the wake of publishing of the Fawcett Mill Strike Inquiry Committee report. The government has supposedly the knowledge of the contents of the report and knows for a fact that it would only provoke the mill workers in Bombay to launch follow-up strikes on bigger scale. The government, by arresting all top leaders, has tried to stem any such attempts at the root.

British trade union leader, Hutchinson, who is amongst those arrested, agrees with this assessment. In addition, he feels the government, by its present action, is trying to kill many birds with one stone. First, it wants to demonstrate its determination to check the spread of Communism in the country.

Second, by such high-handed action, it wants to intimidate the working class. Third, it wants to drive a wedge between the nationalists and the Communists by giving the former a message that it is in the interest of not only the government but their own to check the Communist influence. Fourth, through this strong-arm tactics, it also wants to create a pressure upon the legislature to give in to the government thinking and pass the bill. Fifth, it wants to deter the European trade unions and Communist leaders from intervening in British India. Finally, it also wants to build a legal base though a court verdict, which it can use as a springboard to justify the ban on Communist organisations.

India Erupts Into Protests Against Repression

March 1929, New Delhi: The wide-scale, indiscriminate arrests of labour leaders, on mere suspicion, is being viewed by various sections of Indians as another instance of British high-handedness and intolerance of native aspirations. Trade union workers in the country, in particular, are raising voices of protests. The students and the youth are joining the chorus. India's bitter feelings are also echoed in the halls of the central legislature.

Trade union workers, especially in Calcutta, Bombay and other industrial areas are agitating. In Allahabad this month, a large body of students gathered to protest. They were particularly vocal about the arrest of PC Joshi. The All-Indian Youth League, presided over by Jawaharlal, has strongly condemned the arrests. In the Central Legislative Assembly, Vithalbhai Patel being the president, allowed a Congress motion for adjournment. But the government, clearly uncomfortable at the reverberation of the issue in the august legislative house, disallowed it on the pretext that the matter was sub-judice.

Jinnah Places 14-point Demand In AIML Council Meeting

March 28, 1929, Delhi: The Motilal Report has caused deep dissension between the Congress and the Muslim League. Last year, the All-Parties Convention had endorsed the report, and Jinnah's recommendations for certain changes were rejected. There was a counter to that when the All-Muslim Parties Conference was held in Delhi in January this year and made a few recommendations that went against the basic tenets of the Motilal Report. As the Congress chose not to give an appropriate political response to these, but kept up pressure on the government on the one-year time frame, the League has now formulated a distinct political proposal on the issue.

In a meeting of the council of the All-India Muslim League held here, Jinnah, the chief architect of the proposal, has laid down a list of fourteen demands that must be met in the forthcoming constitutional reforms. In essence, the League has retained the demands made earlier by the All Parties Muslim Conference and added some more items. Both, the old as well as the fresh demands, have been placed in clearer and a politically-savvy manner.The additional demands aim at safeguarding the Muslim interest in more foolproof manner. One of them is a demand that Muslims be provided adequate share in government jobs—whether state or local governing bodies, having due regard to the requirement of efficiency. Then, the League has sought for constitutional safeguards for the protection of Muslim culture. Next, the League has demanded that Muslim ministers must have a one-third share in any cabinet—whether in the centre or in provinces. Then, there is another demand that has far-reaching implication—that the central legislature should not be able to make any changes in the constitution without concurrence of the provincial legislatures. Evidently, this last demand aims to protect the interest of the community against the possibility of any future constitution amendments by a Hindu-majority central legislature.

Jinnah Calls Motilal Report A 'Hindu Document'

March 28, 1929, Delhi: In a meeting of the All-India Muslim League held here, Jinnah has dubbed the Nehru report a 'Hindu document' and registered the demands of the League before the government in the form of a fourteen-point list.

The council of the League deliberated Jinnah's fourteen points and affixed its seal of approval by adopting a resolution embracing them. Further, the resolution has also made it clear that any future constitution of India, to be acceptable to the Muslims, must conform to these fourteen points.

Clearly these additional demands have added complexities to the ongoing political equations. According to some political observers, the Congress ought to have engaged the League much earlier to clinch an agreement. It is becoming evident that the League, leveraging afterthoughts, has been adding new conditions at intervals besides hardening its position. Many of its demands are so very antagonistic to the basic tenets of the Motilal Report that the scope for a meaningful negotiation between the Congress and the League, even if it begins now, appears bleak.

Jinnah's Fourteen Demands

- The form of the future constitution should be federal with residuary powers vested in the provinces;
- All legislatures and all elected bodies shall be constructed on the definite principles of adequate and effective representations of minorities in every province, without reducing the majority in any province to a minority;
- A uniform measure of autonomy shall be gratned to all provinces;
- In the central legislature, Muslim representation shall not be less than one-third;
- Representation of communal groups shall continue to be by means of separate electorates as at present, provided it shall be open to any community at any time to abandon its separate electorate in favour of a joint electorate;
- Any territorial distribution in future, if necessary, shall not in any way, affect the majority of Muslims in Punjab, Bengal and NWFP;
- Full religious liberty shall be guaranteed to all communities;
- No bill or resolution or any part thereof shall be passed in

any legislature or any other elected body if three-fourth of the members of any community in that particular body oppose such a bill, resolution, or part thereof, on the ground that it would be injurious to the interests of that community, or in the alternative, such other method is devised as may be found feasible and practicable to deal with such cases;

- Sind should be separated from Bombay presidency;
- Reforms should be introduced in NWFP and Baluchistan in the same footing as in other provinces;
- Provisions should be made in the constitution giving Muslims an adequate share, along with other Indians, in all the services of the State and in local self-governing bodies having regard to the requirements of efficiency;
- The constitution should embody adequate safeguards for the protection of Muslim culture and for the protection and promotion of Muslim education, language, religion, personal laws and Muslim charitable institutions and for their due share in the grants-in-aid given by the State and by local self-governing bodies;
- No cabinet, either central or provincial, should be formed without there being a propotion of at least one-third Muslim members;
- No change shall be made in the constitution by central legislature except with the concurrence of the States constituting the Indian Federation.

It Needs Explosion To Make The Deaf Hear: HSRA

April 8, 1929, Delhi: There is simmering discontent in the country, particularly amongst the working classes, at the Trade Dispute Bill being shoved down their throat. The government's intimidating action in arresting top trade union leadership on the 20th night last month has added fuel to the fire. The leaders are being held in Meerut prison. The arrests are essentially on suspicion and there is little proof to justify them. The government is taking time to frame charges. Most of the politically aware Indians are aggrieved by the government's highhandedness. In the central legislative assembly, Vithalbhai Patel, the president, was to give his ruling on the result of voting on the Trade Dispute Bill today. But before the president could announce the result, there was an explosion in the assembly hall, filling it with smoke. Then arose stout slogans, 'Inquilab Zindabad', 'Down with Imperialism', and 'Workers of the World Unite'. As the panicked members began deserting the hall and the visitors the gallery, another explosion was heard. Again, the slogans rent the hall.

After the smoke subsided and visibility was restored somewhat, two young men who had hurled the bombs could be sighted—they were Bhagat Singh and Batukeswar Dutt, both leaders of the Hindustan Socialist Republican Association (HSRA). The HSRA took upon itself to protest against the draconian bill and the government's attempts at maiming the workers' voice by a series of intimidating actions. Bhagat Singh, who could not be traced by the police since he shot down Saunders in Lahore, appeared as the leader of this operation.

The two revolutionaries were seen distributing typed pamphlets, which carried the caption, 'It needs explosion to make the deaf hear'. The pamphlets carried the signature of 'Balraj', the party name of Chandrasekhar Azad. A few members of the assembly have suffered minor injuries. The revolutionaries said that their aim had been to attract national and international attention to the government's highhandedness to the workers' issues and not to kill any one.At the end of the action, the gallery was deserted. Barring a few, most members and visitors left apparently in panic. The meagre security staff inside the assembly was hesitant to approach them. But, Bhagat Singh and Batukeswar Dutt made no attempt to escape and they offered arrests. Even though he must have been fully cognisant of how he would be treated in the event of capture by the police, Bhagat Singh's steely action in offering himself for arrest, as a disciplined solider of the HSRA, has drawn acclaim.

Police Unearth Bomb Factory

April 15, 1929, Lahore: Following the bomb incident at the Central Legislative Assembly House in Delhi, the police and the intelligence began extensive operations to unearth bomb factories in the capital city and surrounding provinces. Today, the police traced the bomb factory of the HSRA in Lahore. Prominent revolutionaries like Kishen Lal, Sukhdev and Jai Gopal were arrested. The police see it as a major breakthrough in its campaign against the revolutionary networks. Several more arrests are likely to follow.

Conspiracy Case Filed Against Trade Union Leaders

June 1929, Meerut: The arrested trade union leaders have been lodged in the Meerut prison and cases registered against them in the court of the additional district judge here.

They are accused of conspiracy to deprive the King Emperor of sovereignty of India with the help of the Communist International and institute a government on the Soviet model in the country. Political observers say, in choosing the Meerut prison, the government has considered the desirability to hold the trial away from public attention and media glare.

Three leading communist and trade union leaders from Britain, viz. Ben Bradley, Lester Hutchinson and Phillip Spratt also stand in the dock.

TU Leaders, Congress Support The Accused

June 1929: The Indian National Congress has been the pioneer of the trade union movement in the country. It is visibly upset at the sudden crackdown on trade union leaders. It is a well-known fact that the Communists have been cooperating with the Congress in the struggle against the colonial regime, through forums like the Workers and Peasants Party.

In the wake of the current repression, which is undeserving and uncalled for, the Congress has a duty, as the major political party of the country, to stand up and protect the victims. The country is relieved to see that the Congress has appointed a Meerut Defence Committee, presided by Motilal Nehru, to provide legal help to the detenues.

Labour Government Announces Royal Commission On Labour In India

July 4, 1929, London: The Conservative government in Britain held office when the trade union leaders were arrested in bulk. The Labour government has assumed office in June this year and Captain Wedgwood Benn has taken over as Secretary of State for India. But so far, there has been no relief to the prisoners languishing in Meerut. However, the present government sought to demonstrate its concern for Indian labour by announcing today a Royal Commission of Labour in India. To be chaired by JH Whitley, the commission is tasked to enquire into and report on the condition of labour in industrial establishments, plantations, etc.[45]

Communists Withdraw From Workers' - Peasants' Party

July 19, 1929: The Tenth Plenum of the Executive Committee of the Comintern that began on 3rd of this month has concluded today. In a major shift in its stand, the committee has directed the Communists in India to withdraw from the Workers' and Peasants' Parties. According to political observers, the new directive may bring about important changes in the political landscape in the country, especially in regard to Congress-Communists relations. Since the Communists form the backbone of the provincial Workers' and Peasants' Parties in India, their withdrawal is likely to lead to a collapse of these parties.

'If Ever A Man Became Bold And Chivalrous... Then That Man Is Jatin Das' – The Tribune Pays Its Tribute

September 14, 1929, Lahore: Jatindranath Das, a prominent revolutionary, died yesterday while fasting in Lahore Central Jail for 63 days. He was only 24. He was arrested in the Lahore conspiracy case, together with Bhagat Singh and others. Though they were held for political reasons, they were treated like ordinary criminals in the jail. They first tried constitutional methods for redressal but that did not work. Thereafter, Das along with his colleagues went on an indefinite fast, demanding treatment as political prisoners. The government paid no heed to their protests. Following gradually-rising public interest and concern about the issue, the government, after some time, offered to look into the matter and consider some of the grievances. Upon this, and after persuasion from political leaders and people, all the prisoners except Das withdrew. He pursued his fast with missionary zeal till all their demands were actually met. The government chose to ignore the struggle of 'a single man' and took no further steps. An exceptionally long period of fasting made him die slowly; his feet and hands were paralysed one after another. At the fag end, his eye sight also deserted him. Eventually, this brave freedom fighter succumbed to death.

The accounts of his gradually deteriorating condition were brought to the countrymen by the media over last two months, creating both sympathy and admiration for this young patriot. Now, the news of his death has greatly angered people. Meetings were held across the country to pay homage to the brave soul and protest against British highhandedness and atrocities. Motilal Nehru moved an adjournment motion in the legislative assembly to draw members' attention to the martyrdom of Jatindranath Das. *The Tribune*, published from Lahore, said, 'If ever a man became bold and chivalrous for high ideals, then that man is Jatin Das, and the blood of a martyr has proved itself the best seed for all generations and the best life in the country.'[46]

As his body was being transported from Lahore to Calcutta, people in tens of thousands congregated to the railway station in Lahore to pay tribute to the departed soul.

Calcutta Comes Out To Pay Last Respect To Jatin Das

September 16, 1929: Jatin Das, an immensely spirited soul, joined the non-cooperation movement as a lad of thirteen years. His involvement with the struggle for swaraj earned him long years of prison terms, interspersed with brief spells of liberty.

In 1928, under Subhas, he played an important role in training the Bengal Volunteer Corps to handle the annual Congress session and the National Exhibition in Calcutta. His involvement with Bengal Volunteers continued as that disciplined patriotic outfit kept opening branches across the province. His courage, patriotism and dedication had endeared him to common people and Congress workers alike. Calcutta went into a state of deep mourning as the news of his death was announced. Subhas took personal interest and mobilised funds to bring his body back to Calcutta.

While the body of young Jatin Das was being transported from Lahore to Calcutta, at the stations enroute, people in tens of thousands mourned this extraordinary brave warrior of 'swaraj'. Today Calcutta came out on the streets to join the funeral procession of this revolutionary son of Bengal. It is estimated that several lakhs of people walked on the street. Subhas, along with Jatindra Mohan Sengupta, led them.

Who Should Wear The Crown Next? 'Jawahar, Of Course'

September 28-29, 1929, Lucknow: In a special meeting, the AICC has chosen the president for the Lahore session to be held in December. Over the last few months, there has been considerable pressure on Gandhi to accept the office and it continued even here. But Gandhi declined.

He has been consistently recommending Jawaharlal for this high office. In an article 'Who should wear the crown' in Young India, he wrote, "Those who know the relation that subsists between Jawaharlal and me, know that his being in chair is as good as my being in it.'[47] To the Congressmen who still persisted that he take office, Gandhi has expressed his inability, saying that his hands were too weak to hold the reins of the Congress.[48] Eventually, he prevailed and Jawaharlal's name was accepted.

To the left-wing leaders including Subhas, this has been a consummate political move by Gandhi to break their unity. Their influence was steadily rising in the Congress and, especially that of the Independence League, which had begun to challenge the aim of 'dominion status' quite hard. By co-opting their most popular leader, Jawahar, Gandhi, they feel, has tried to neutralise the Left camp.

Sahajanand Saraswati Sets Up Ashram Near Patna

1929, Patna: Swami Sahajanand Saraswati, an ascetic and a 'dandi sanyasi' who has dedicated himself to the causes of the poor farmers of the country, has set up an ashram in Bihta near Patna to work amongst them, for them. The condition of the peasantry has been miserable in many parts of India but it is particularly bad in Bihar, which happens to have a system of permanent settlement.

The zamindars are the owners of land and pay taxes directly to the government. This gives them unbridled power to exploit and torture tenant farmers. On various pretexts, the unscrupulous amongst them try to capture land from their tenants and the poor folks have practically no means to seek redress. Sahajanand has begun to give these vulnerable people a strong leadership. He has played a pioneering role in starting the Bihar Provincial Kisan Sabha, an organisation that aims at mobilising the peasants and helps them in their fight against zamindari attack on their occupancy rights. Inspired by his leadership, the peasants of Bihar across villages, are rising in protest and their voices are spreading far and wide.

Irwin Hints At 'Dominion Status' But Omits Time Frame

October 31, 1929, New Delhi: The Congress has been much exercised over the British response to its demand for the 'dominion status within a year' and time is running out. It is clearly under severe pressure to carry out its threat of national struggle, in case its demand is not met. Today, Viceroy Irwin, back from England to New Delhi, has made an important announcement. He said he has been authorised to state clearly that in the judgement of the His Majesty's government, 'it is implicit in the Declaration of 1917 that the natural issue of India's constitutional progress, as there contemplated, is the attainment of Dominion Status'.[49] Significantly, he did not mention any time limit for this but mentioned that following the publication of the Simon Commission report, yet another round table conference will be held in England.

There are mixed reactions in India. The left-wing in the Congress is clearly angry. However, Gandhi, Motilal, Malaviya and several others are looking at it as a positive development.

Dominion Status: Indian Leaders' Keep Fingers Crossed

November 2, 1929, New Delhi: The Viceroy's announcement, made a couple of days ago, has initiated intense political activity in the country. Vithalbhai, president of the Central Legislature, has leveraged his unique position to communicate with both the Viceroy and the senior Indian leaders to take the matter further through a meeting.

A cross section of top Indian leaders including Gandhi, Motilal, Jawaharlal, Ansari, Sapru, Malaviya, Moonje, Vallabhbhai, Srinavasa Sastri, Annie Besant and a few others met today and prepared a manifesto, thanking the Viceroy, signed by all of them.

They hoped that the proposed round table conference would frame a scheme of the dominion status. They also requested an amnesty before the round table. Jawaharlal, an important leader of the Independence League, was reluctant to lend his signature. However, he fell in line persuaded by Gandhi.

Jawaharlal Urges Boycott Of Whitley Commission

November 30, 1929, Nagpur: Since December last year, when he was the president elect of the AITUC, Jawaharlal has been deeply involved in trade union matters besides the youth movement. In fact, his involvement in these affairs grew so extensive that he came to regard himself as a Socialist worker. At the same time he was holding important Congress offices.

The British government has appointed the Whitley Commission to enquire into the condition of Indian labour.

However, the Indian trade union leaders suspect the intention of the government. Coming at a time when the government has locked up the top leadership in prison, the commission carrying out its terms of reference seems to be a mockery. It may be remembered that many Communist trade union leaders, who are presently lodged in Meerut jail, are against the Whitley Commission.

As he is presiding over the AITUC session, Jawaharlal has issued a press statement urging the boycott of the Whitley Commission.

Class War Is A Fact Of History: Jawaharlal

November 30, 1929, Nagpur: Jawaharlal, in his presidential speech at the AITUC session held here, said that 'class war' is a fact of history and cannot be wished away even though for those at the top, it may be easy to ignore it and preach moderation and goodwill. Critics say, such views are radically different from the Gandhian approach on the capital-labour relations. He wanted AITUC to maintain equidistance from both, the Third International and its rival anti-Communist front based in capitalist countries.

Indians In Royal Commission? No Way, Says Left

November 30, 1929, Nagpur: The trade union movement in India reached a crossroad today when the right-wing leaders and their followers parted company with the others and set up a parallel organisation with the name 'All-India Trade Union Federation'. There have been simmering dissensions between the two groups for the past some time but it came out during the AITUC session here on the question of two right wing leaders, viz. NM Joshi and Chamanlal accepting seats in the Whitley Commission, at the latter's invitation. The left-wing delegates were furious and looked at this as nothing less than a betrayal of their colleagues languishing in the Meerut jail, at the bidding of the same government which sent the Royal Commission. There was shouting, sloganeering, jeering by the left delegates and hurling of insults upon the two leaders who, otherwise, have impressive records of work for the cause of the Indian trade union movement. This ostensibly triggered the decision to part 'company'.

Dominion Status Proposal Not Acceptable: Subhas

November 1929, Calcutta: On October 31, Viceroy Irwin had announced the proposal of dominion status to solve the political problems of India and the need for a round table conference to sort out controversial issues. Whereas leaders like Gandhi and Motilal have expressed satisfaction about the proposal of dominion status in principle, Subhas has lodged his protest. In this, he is not alone.

Amongst others, Saifuddin Kitchlew has also opposed the proposal. Both of them are also opposing Congress participation in the proposed round table conference.

No Community Be Allowed Political Hegemony In Punjab

December 20, 1929, Lahore: Sikhs have been unhappy at the disproportionate political rights given to the Muslims, through the system of separate electorates and weightage. The Sikh grievances go back to the days of 1909, when the Minto-Morley reforms granted the Muslims the benefit of separate electorates as a minority community. Even the Lucknow pact made between the Congress and the Muslim League in 1916 had neglected Sikh interest. In Punjab, the Muslims happened to be the majority community and despite this, they were given the benefits of separate electorate and the benefit of weightage. As a result of the twin advantages, the Muslim population in Bihar and Orissa constituting less than 10% of the total population were entitled to 25% of the legislature seats. In contrast, Sikhs, despite constituting about 12% of the Punjab population, were accorded only 15%. Sikhs had so far refrained from making any big issue of denial of their rights. However, the Motilal Nehru report and the ever rising counter demands by the Muslim League, on behalf of the Muslim community, has been angering them. Today, while delivering a speech here, Sikh leader Baba Kharak Singh has made it clear that the Sikhs would not let any single community establish its political hegemony in Punjab.[50] His utterances have been noted by all politicians and have added a new dimension to the ongoing political controversy.

Attempt To Blow Up Viceroy's Train

December 23, 1929, Delhi: Although the government has arrested many of his colleagues, thus hitting at the root of the revolutionary activities in northern India, Chandrasekhar Azad has not lost his spirit. He has collected some followers and has made a bid to blow up the special train near Delhi, in which the Viceroy was travelling. However, his attempts failed. The Viceroy had a providential escape. The police have not been able to capture Azad.

Indians Emerge Empty Handed From Viceroy's Meet

December 23, 1929, New Delhi: The much-expected meeting of prominent Indian leaders with the Viceroy took place today but in an ambience vitiated by the recent attempt on his life. In a way, this was a right meeting held at an inopportune time. The delegation included amongst others Gandhi, Motilal, Jinnah, and TB Sapru. They tried to get an assurance from the Viceroy that the purpose of the proposed 'round table' would be to draft a scheme of 'dominion status'. But Irwin argued that the purpose of the said conference would be to elicit greatest measure of agreement and use them in framing final proposals to be submitted to the British Parliament. He made it clear that a prior assurance would limit the scope of that exercise.[51] The meeting ended without a consensus and the delegation emerged from it empty-handed, disquiet, frustrated.

Political observers are attaching considerable significance to the failure. President of the Assembly, Vithalbhai had persuaded the Viceroy to hold the meeting, arguing that unless the present top leadership could convince the Congressmen that there was a clear commitment on the part of the His Majesty's government about 'dominion status', the left-wing would hijack the Lahore session and set an agenda in favour of 'complete independence'. Now leaders like Gandhi and Motilal would have limited choice–either to concede the initiative to the left-wing or to escalate their own demand. Worse, there is little time left before the Lahore session, to explore alternative ground.

Temple Entry Satyagraha In Parvati Hills

November 1929, Poona : Untouchables and other activists began a non-violent Satyagraha at the holy hill of Parvati in Poona, on the issue of entry into the shrine. There was a confrontation and the intimation sent to the Congress. A Gandhian committee visited the site and talked to the trustees. They found that the Satyagraha has created an atmosphere of bitterness and distrust. The movement has not, therefore, received the Congress approval. But, the agitation has again brought before the nation the social treatment of the untouchables in Hindu society and the rising aspiration of the former for equality, at least in regard to basic social and civic issues.

You Can't See God By Force: Gandhi

December 24, 1929, Lahore: In the All-India Suppressed Classes Conference held here in the Congress pavilion, the delegates were eager to hear Gandhi on the entry ban on the untouchables in Hindu temples. Gandhi, while being in full sympathy with the untouchables and supporting their case, advised them not to use force to enter into temples, because, he said, that was not Satyagraha.

He clarified that they could not see God by force and that God was present in their hearts and not in temples. As regards entering the temples, Gandhi advised them to patiently undergo their sufferings and pray that the cruelty of the high caste come to an end.[52]

Critics see Gandhi's views as too idealistic for the vast multitudes of the untouchables, who have been eager to secure minimum rights to enter temples and offer worship, like others in the Hindu community. They see a danger for the Congress in keeping a vital political space vacant that can be grabbed by its political adversaries.

Congress Discards Parliamentary Programme

December 1929, Lahore: The government has not responded to the Congress ultimatum of one year to accept the Motilal Report. By giving the ultimatum, the Congress had put too much in stake. Now it has to find ways and means to make the government agree to its demand. But one thing is obvious. It cannot cooperate with this government constitutionally, when the latter has ignored its proposed draft constitution.

Predictably, the Congress has decided against participating in the parliamentary programme—it would thus not take part in the legislative bodies. This marks the end of the official policy that had allowed the Swaraj Party faction of the Congress to enter the legislature way back in 1923. Gandhi has been exerting great influence on Congress policy making.

The leaders and workers of the Congress expect Gandhi to show them the road for future struggles.

'Nothing Less Than Complete Independence'

Sikh Leaders Threaten Boycott Of Congress Session

December 1929, Lahore: Congress had asked for dominion status with a condition that the British government implement the new constitution within a year. But sections of the party, especially the young and the left-wing leaders, have become impatient for independence. The top Sikh leadership has also been unhappy with the meekness of the Congress. Last year, in the Calcutta Congress, they had differences with the Congress leadership on issues like 'dominion status' and community based 'reservations'. They went to the extent of disassociating themselves from the proceedings. Things became embarrassing, when Sikh leaders decided to boycott the Congress session to be held in this city later this month This led to a flurry of activities in the Congress Working Committee. Congress leaders Gandhi, Motilal and Ansari met Master Tara Singh and Baba Kharak Singh to inform them that the Congress has replaced the goal of dominion status by complete independence. Further, Congress also gave them explicit assurance that it would not accept a constitution that did not give full satisfaction to Sikhs and Muslims as minorities. Eventually, the Sikh leaders were convinced and they have agreed to participate.

Congress Hardens Stance, Goal Is Complete Independence

December 29,1929 to January 1, 1930, Lahore: The Congress had set a time limit of one year for the British government to implement the new constitution and in the event of non-compliance, challenged the government with a National Movement. But the government chose to downplay its ultimatum, possibly encouraged by the growing rift between the Congress and the League on this issue. At the end of the long wait came the Viceroy's vague suggestion of the 'round table conference' to sort out controversial issues. This clearly meant the government has chosen to denigrate the importance of the Motilal report that was the fruit of hard labour of a competent committee and the wisdom of the premier political organisation of the country that represented all castes and creed. It also means that the government will, from now on, make optimum use of the League as a counterweight in its negotiation with the Congress on the framing of the new constitution. But still worse, it went back on its own assurance, albeit vague, during the last meeting between the Viceroy and Indian leaders in Delhi. It has left the leadership with little option.

With the elapse of the one year period, the time for the national movement has arrived now. The workers and leaders of the party are impatiently looking at Gandhi for the 'new road map'.

Now, in the Congress session held here, Gandhi has proposed a resolution declaring 'complete independence' as the Congress' goal. This has sent waves of hope and enthusiasm amongst the delegates. Many have begun to see in this move the 'beginning of the end' of the British Raj.

In his characteristic style, Gandhi has also simultaneously held out a plan for constructive activities before Congressmen. A resolution was adopted that the All-Indian Spinners Association be organised to carry out a campaign for constructive activities involving abolition of untouchability, suppression of drinks and drug trafficking etc.

Complete Independence Okay, Roadmap Must: Subhas

December 31, 1929, Lahore: The left wing in the Congress has found vindication of its stand as Gandhi has shifted the Congress goal to 'independence'. However, it reckons that Gandhi's resolution may speak the soul of India but it is nothing more than an 'intent' without a 'roadmap'. Subhas, one of their chief proponents, wanted the resolution to lay out a 'plan' to reach that coveted destination of 'independence', like forming of a parallel government by the Congress, organising people and launching a massive civil disobedience movement to render the normal administration by the British government impossible. He sought to press these issues and create a sense of urgency in people. He moved a counter-resolution incorporating these points.

However, most delegates are more than happy with Gandhi's resolution. They feel Gandhi's shifting the Congress goal from 'dominion status' to 'independence' itself has been a momentous development. As such, Subhas's counter-resolution has been rejected.

Congress Unfurls National Flag At Bank Of River Ravi

December 31, 1929 – January 1, 1930, Lahore: In the midnight, Congress president Jawaharlal hoisted the tricolour national flag on the bank of River Ravi. Large number of people gathered to witness the momentous occasion, ignoring the chill of the winter night.

CONGRESS SOUNDS BUGLE: WANTS 'PURNA SWARAJ'

January 1, 1930, Lahore: To send a strong signal to the government that it means business, the Congress session here, presided over by Jawaharlal, has passed a resolution on complete independence, referring to it as 'Purna Swaraj' and has called the nation to celebrate the occasion on 26th January. Many feel, Gandhi has sounded the 'war bugle' by this symbolic action. However, not every one agrees. Many feel Gandhi only wants to put the government under pressure and he may not escalate the issue beyond a point. They contend the coinage of the term 'Purna Swaraj' itself is strategic, as it could be interpreted in more than one way.

Indian Spring To Substitute British Winter Festivity

January 1, 1930, Lahore: In the face of the government's refusal to consider its demand on the new constitution, the Congress has declared 'complete independence' as its goal. It has also asked all its members to resign from legislative bodies and government committees. In yet another move, it has decided to hold all future annual Congress sessions in springtime rather than during Christmas in the winter, ostensibly to save expenses on warm clothing. It may be remembered that right from 1885—the year of its birth, till now, the Congress had been holding its annual sessions during December, which happened to be a festive season for the British. For many years, the Congress used to profess its loyalty to the Empire. Even if such subservience disappeared several years ago, the Congress, somehow, did not change the time of its annual sessions, which was a kind of vestige of an emotional link that once bound the two. Now, with the new timing that tie was snapped. The underlying message cannot be missed.

Nehru's Cabinet – Subhas, Srinavasa Excluded

January 1-2, 1930, Lahore: Jawaharlal, the new Congress president, has excluded Subhas Bose and Srinivasa Iyenger from the Congress Working Committee. Over the past few years, all three leaders had worked closely on many issues, including on the platform of the Independence League. They had played key roles in passing the resolution on complete independence in the Madras session two years ago.

The exclusion of the two from the CWC has come as a surprise to many. According to reliable sources, Subhas was dropped at Gandhi's advice, whom he had antagonised by continuing with a strident position on the issue of 'independence' in Calcutta last year, and by moving a counter-resolution to that of Gandhi in the present session. Whatever be the reason, Subhas is feeling hurt at being left out from the crucial policy-making body at this important juncture of the independence struggle.

There are reports that Srinavasa Iyenger, a stalwart from Madras and a former president of Congress, has also been deeply hurt on being omitted. Significantly, both Subhas and Srinavasa are prominent leaders of the left-wing. Political observers say Gandhi has been able to deal a body blow to Left unity, by separating Jawaharlal from the rest.

Indians Celebrate Independence

January 26, 1930: The Congress has called upon people all over the country to take cue from the declaration of independence in Lahore, and asked them to hoist the tricolour in every house and establishment. It has prepared a manifesto and called upon people to read it from every platform and also pledge loyalty to the Congress. It is a long manifesto. Part of it says that it is the inalienable right of the Indian people, as of any other people, to have freedom and enjoy the fruits of their toil. It also exhorts people to express their belief that India must sever the British connection and attain Purna Swaraj or complete independence. The people have observed the day with exemplary enthusiasm, surpassing Congress' expectations and making the government take note.

From Independence To Substance Of Independence

January 30, 1930, Ahmedabad: While the announcement of 'independence' in the Lahore Congress lifted public spirit, and it was reinforced four days ago through a countrywide celebration, an article written by Gandhi in *Young India*, has begun to spread confusion amongst people and dampen their enthusiasm. In it, Gandhi has clarified that he would be content with 'substance of independence' and he espoused the concept further by stating a list of eleven points which would constitute it. These are demands such as total prohibition, desired rupee-sterling exchange rate, abolition of salt tax, reduction of land revenue etc. However, these are demands placed on the colonial government and they are far from asking for independence. Political observers say, this climb down from a high pedestal may have been occasioned by a later realisation about the country's lack of preparedness to wage a battle for complete independence. Also, Gandhi may not be ready to go for the final assault right now, and is keeping the door ajar for negotiation.

Civil Disobedience Cannot Be Stopped: Gandhi

February 27, 1930, Ahmedabad: Gandhi's climb down from 'independence' to the eleven-point 'substance of independence' has fallen on deaf ears. The government seems to be unperturbed. Gandhi has reckoned that a showdown has become inevitable. He is mobilising his wherewithal. In terms of the Lahore resolution, Congressmen have tendered their resignations from the legislatures. On the 19th of this month, the AICC adopted a civil disobedience programme. Today, he has issued a grim warning to the government in an article in *Young India*, titled 'When I am arrested', that he was ready to begin the battle with his ashramites, to start with. However, he has also addressed the concerns of the countrymen about the prospect of suddenly crying a halt to the movement, as had happened in 1922, following the Chauri Chaura incident. He has categorically written that the civil disobedience 'once begun this time cannot be stopped...so long there is a single civil resister left free or alive.'[53]

It appears, at last Gandhi has begun to mould the public mind for a long, gruelling fight and hard sacrifice.

'British Rule A Curse, It Has Impoverished Dumb Millions'

March 2, 1930, Sabarmati: Gandhi, an astute politician and leader, has mounted another attack on the British government. As a sequel to the resolution of Purna Swaraj passed six weeks ago, in which the Congress accused the British government of having ruined India economically, politically, culturally and spiritually, Gandhi is planning a full-scale civil disobedience movement on an issue that has appeal to the vast masses. Gandhi has shown great ingenuity in selecting the issue—the government law on salt, which made even the poorest Indians pay taxes on such an essential item—a compulsory food in-take everyday. A call to break the Salt Law is, therefore, expected to arouse countrywide response. Again, compared to 1921-22, Indians are more disciplined and now have better grasp of the nature of the struggle and technique of Satyagraha.

After deciding upon the issue, Gandhi has given a notice to the Viceroy of his intention to launch the Salt Satyagraha—he would break the Salt Law of the government to protest against British rule. Gandhi has prepared a list of grievances which include amongst others:

(a) The British Indian government is the most expensive in the world;

(b) The unjust expenses incurred by the administration are being met by imposing heavy taxes and even the poor are not spared. Gandhi has argued, only independence can solve these problems.

Making it plain that he considers the British rule a curse, Gandhi has written: 'It has impoverished the dumb millions by a system of progressive exploitation and by a ruinously expensive military and civil administration which the country can never afford...' [54]

He has hinted that he would undertake the symbolic 'breaking of the salt law' of the British government by marching from his ashram at Sabarmati to the Dandi coast of the Arabian Sea, and making salt out of the sea water. As per the Salt Law, making of salt by unauthorised persons or agencies is illegal and punishable. The selection of 'salt' as the focus of the movement seems to be a masterstroke as vast multitude of the common people are immediately able to connect with it. Gandhi is ready to court arrest for breaking the Salt Law. But this would be the beginning of a nationwide civil disobedience where Indians would violate any repressive government laws, court arrests and fill prisons. The Congress workers are being trained to handle the followup Satyagraha by Indians across cities, towns and villages.

Attacking The Salt Act – A Masterstroke

Salt has been a sensitive issue with a vast number of the poor in India. Right from the days of the East India Company, the British have been trying to use it as an important source of revenue, making the poor people bear the main brunt of it. The government has been holding exclusive rights on collection and manufacture of salt. During the time of Warren Hastings in 1780, the government allowed a sub monopoly of the wholesalers in its distribution. Whereas the government collected a hefty tax from the wholesalers, the latter, due to their vantage position to fix prices, played truant and escalated the price on occasions. Till the end of the nineteenth century, an average poor household, due to its low income, had to spend as much as two months of earning out of their annual income for salt alone. Easy to see that their cattle or livestock, if any, were also almost fully deprived of salt in their fodder. Thus, millions of poor Indians filled the government coffers by paying the salt tax. From time to time, there were protests galore not only from India but also sensible leaders and thinkers in England, to scrap or at least reduce this tax. As a result, the rate of salt tax was reduced for some years, ie. 1900 to 1905 but, only to be raised again. To make matters worse, in 1923, Lord Reading had doubled the salt tax and it hit millions of Indians, especially the poor, very hard. There is a greater ramification. The Salt tax can also be seen as a symbol of the oppressive overall tax regime of the British government. Generally speaking Indians, of all sections, low, middle or high income, have been made to pay taxes at high rates to maintain one of the most expensive government bureaucracies in the world. This movement against the Salt Act has the potential to kindle and spread the general discontent of the Indians against an oppressive government.Thus, Gandhi's Satyagraha, aimed at breaking the Salt Act is being seen as a masterstroke.

Your Highness, It's Not A Simple law And Order Issue!

March 1930, New Delhi: The Viceroy chose not to reply to Gandhi's long missive. Perhaps he has deemed it was not called for. However, he has sent a message to Gandhi through his secretary. The message said that the Viceroy regretted that Gandhi has chosen a course which involved breaking the law of the land, and which would pose danger to public peace. It appears, the Viceroy has underestimated the enormous power of Gandhi as a mass leader. He is committing a grave mistake of examining a politically explosive issue as a 'law and order' one.

GANDHI BEGINS HIS LONG MARCH

March 12, 1930, Ahmedabad: Gandhi has begun a long march on foot from Sabarmati today at 6.30 am. His destination is the village of Dandi in the coast of the Arabian Sea, 240 miles away. Upon reaching the sea coast, he will make salt by violating the Salt Act. That would be the first act of civil disobedience and the signal for the countrymen to take over through myriad acts of civil disobedience.

As he took his first step, there were seventy-eight male Satyagrahis following him. However, as he progressed, scores of people kept joining him. The news of his march is spreading across the country fast. The Viceroy and his government keep a watch.

'Mahatma Could Go On Boiling Sea Water Till Dominion Status Is Attained'

March 1930, Calcutta: The Anglo Indian media has been either critical or dismissive about Gandhi's movement. *The Statesman* has made a derisive comment—that the Mahatma could go on boiling the seawater indefinitely till Dominion Status is attained.[55]

The Story Of A Frail Little Man Entices Foreign Media

April 6, 1930, Dandi: Gandhi began his long march 24 days ago, amidst great enthusiasm and patriotic fervour. He arrived here yesterday. During his 240-mile long journey, people in thousands have joined him, eventually turning it into a two-mile long procession. All through the way, the government did not create any hindrance. trying to give an impression as if it was a non-event. However, the novelty of the protest has aroused the attention of people worldwide and the news of Gandhi's march is reaching them through mass media. On his part, Gandhi has ensured that his march remains absolutely non-violent. Today, Gandhi has violated the government law by picking up a lump of mud from inside the sea water, boiled it in sea water and made salt.

Civil Disobedience Engulfs The Country

April 6, 1930: On the successful completion of the Dandi march that ended with Gandhi making salt in defiance of the government law at the sea coast, the Congress has given the green signal to observe the next seven days as a 'National Week' when Indians living on the coast have been urged to make salt, breaking the provisions of the Salt Act. Tremendous enthusiasm has enveloped the country at the successful completion of the long march.

In Bengal Revolutionaries Loot Government Armoury

April 18, 1930, Chittagong: Whereas the Congress, led by Gandhi, is resorting to non-violent mass movements to obtain independence, the revolutionaries are convinced that the cunning British regime understands only one language—that of 'force'. The manner in which the government has thwarted the Motilal Report by aiding and abetting communal divide has only strengthened their conviction. Today, in the hilly tract of Chittagong in East Bengal, about hundred dedicated revolutionaries led by their leader, Surya Sen, popularly called Masterda, has carried out a daring raid on the Chittagong armoury, which is a large storehouse of government weapons. In a surprise but well-planned attack, the revolutionaries overpowered a large posse of security men and plundered huge caches of arms and ammunitions. In the confrontation, not less than eight security personnel were killed. The loot can prove valuable to the revolutionaries in their broader plan to liberate this part of the country from the British and defend that freedom. After this audacious assault, the team has moved to the Jalalabad Hills. An affront to the prestige of the mighty British empire, this act has provoked the government and it is sending strong reinforcements to capture the revolutionaries. The incident has created a sensation in the whole country.

Fakr-i-Afghan Gives New Mantra To The Fierce Pasthuns

April, 1930, Peshawar: The civil disobedience movement, started by Gandhi in Dandi in the Arabian Sea coast, is fast spreading across India—its ripples, undiminished, have now touched the distant north west frontier province. Abdul Ghaffar Khan, Fakr-I-Afghan (pride of the Pathans), has been in the vanguard of the protsts here.

Ghaffar Khan, a devout Muslim, has been for the past several years leading the Pasthuns towards the goals of eradication of poverty, illiteracy and social evils and independence of the country from colonial rulers. Drawing lessons from the life of the Holy Prophet, Ghaffar has been leading his movement along strictly non-violent lines. His near-complete identity of views on 'non-violence as both creed and political strategy', with those of Gandhi, have brought him close to the latter. Ghaffar's association with Gandhi's programme began during the Rowlatt agitation days, when he mobilised people across the province against that repressive legislation. Significantly, the Congress does not have a strong provincial chapter in this border province even to date. Thus, the prime national party has been depending on Ghaffar's mass appeal to ensure success for its programmes. This mutual association kept growing over years and Ghaffar was appointed the president of the provincial Khilafat Committee.

Only last year, Ghaffar Khan, his brother Dr Khan Sahib and their associates, launched two organisations, viz. Zalmo Jirgah and Khudai Khidmatgar—the first as a platform for the educated youth and the other for mobilising the masses, including the aged and the illiterate Pasthuns. Seen as the champions of Pasthun sub-nationalism and independence of India, these two organisations, particularly the Khudai Khidmatgar, have become extremely popular and Pasthuns have begun joining it in thousands. This year, after the Congress begun a countrywide civil disobedience programme, the provincial Congress committee here has been getting full-fledged support from the Khudai Khidmatgar and Zalmo Jirgah.

Salt Tsunami Inundates Pasthun Land

April 23, 1930, Peshawar: The political temperature has been soaring in the city. Exactly a week ago, large number of people assembled in Shahibag and they staged civil disobedience by preparing salt from the saline earth. Since then, the atmosphere in the city has been tense. The people-government relations suffered further decline when the latter prevented transit to a Congress enquiry committee, which was to arrive here to inquire into the working of the Froniter Regulations. Yesterday, there were serious public protests against the government high-handedness.

According to government sources, this morning violent public protests erupted on the issue of arrests of leading agitators including senior Congress leaders, members of Naujawan Sabha and an editor. As the arrests were being carried out, a large crowd assembled at Qissa Kahini Bazar and attempted to forcibly release the arrested leaders. The Deputy Commissioner arrived at the spot in an armoured vehicle, with a large force. A confrontation ensued and the troops were ordered to fire. This resulted in the death of twenty people and a British police officer.

According to local people, armoured vehicles were driven into the crowd, killing three and injuring several. The agitated people retaliated and set fire to the vehicles. Thereafter, the troops, upon orders of the authorities, opened fire indiscriminately. The crowds stood their ground and faced the bullets. Though reports differ, it appears hundreds of people lost their lives in the incident. They also say that the soldiers of Garwali regiment refused to open fire on the crowd, which was unarmed.

In terms of enormity of casualty and brutality, this incident is reminding a stunned nation about Dyer's brutal killing of several hundred people in Jallianwalabagh in 1919.

President Of Legislative Assembly Resigns

April 25, 1930, New Delhi: Assembly president Vithalbhai had taken keen initiative in bringing a rapprochement between the Viceroy and top Indian leaders. But the inflexible attitude of the British regime had aborted that process, following which, the Congress quit the legislature. Recently, the Malaviya-led United Party also quit the assembly. Today, Vithalbhai has resigned from his post, saying that this assembly has lost its representative character. Though he has mentioned his unhappiness with the government policy about imperial preference on cotton tariff, sources close to him say he has been unhappy about many issues, including the manner in which the government has been handling the ongoing movement. Vithalbhai J Patel has sent a letter to the Viceroy, saying:

'…thousands are prepared to lay down their lives and hundreds of thousands are ready to court imprisonment' [56]

Salt Movement Jolts Moral Right Of British To Govern

April 27, 1930: Within four days of the completion of the Dandi march, the AICC gave permission to all Congress organisations across the country to make salt and begin wide-scale civil disobedience. Thereafter, it seemed as if a spring had been released. Salt-making began to spread like wild fire. People have been making salt illegally and buying such salt illegally too, as if celebrating something sacred. Millions of Indians have been overwhelmed with patriotic feelings. But the most important thing is that they have discovered a new self-confidence vis-à-vis the blind servility that for ages dominated their mind-space and kept them dependent on the Raj.

The government had underestimated the potential of this movement. It seems it has been caught unguarded by the rapid turn of events. In a knee-jerk reaction, it has come down hard on people. Today, it has revived the repealed Press Act, 1910 to gag the domestic press. In terms of these revived provisions, it plans to demand huge security as a condition for functioning by these newspapers. It has also declared the Congress and its organisations illegal.

The government has been deploying both police and military to tackle the innumerable Satyagrahis who have been engaged in carrying out activities like picketing, distributing leaflets and other acts of civil disobedience, disregarding the lathi charges and various other forms of tortures and atrocities. More than 60,000 people in Bombay and about 50,000 in Karachi participated in civil disobedience. Jails are overflowing with Satyagrahis. In some jails, ordinary convicts have been freed to lodge civil resisters. There is abundant enthusiasm in people.

Former Comrade Lashes Out At Gandhi

April 1930, Bombay: Addressing a meeting of the All-India Muslim Conference here, Muhammad Ali Jinnah has called upon the Muslims to keep aloof from the ongoing civil disobedience movement by the Congress. He had some harsh words for Gandhi and said: 'Mr Gandhi is working under the influence of the communalist Hindu Mahasabha. He is fighting for the supremacy of Hinduism and submergence of Muslims.'[57]

Political observers say, Ali's utterances may have warmed the heart of the government. Notably, the Ali brothers had earlier acted in tandem with Gandhi and waged a common war against the British regime in the early 1920s that caused the government much anxiety. Though Gandhi and the brothers had developed some differences in 1925 over the Kohat communal riots, and have been drifting away from each other gradually ever since, they did not part company altogether. Now, this statement by Muhammad gave an indication that the differences between them have become too wide to be bridged.

Stop Us If You Can – Gandhi Dares Viceroy

May 4, 1930: Gandhi waged a peaceful, non-violent and morally sanctified battle against the British, but the government has been tackling it with brute, violent and unlawful measures. He has today written a letter to Viceroy Irwin, citing glimpses of the government atrocities on peaceful Satyagrahis in different parts of British India. He has mentioned how the bones of Satyagrahis were broken and their private parts squeezed to recover the salt they so painstakingly prepared—which was valueless to the government but precious to those volunteers. Gandhi has mentioned how the bulk of the common Satyagrahis were denied the due process of law and treated savagely; how their paddy fields were burnt and eatables snatched. At the end, he reminded the Viceroy that so much of atrocities were unleashed when the movement was only five weeks old. This reference was poignant and deliberate, to make the Viceroy be aware of the harder battle ahead, non-violent, of course!

No less important was the opening sentences of the letter which was a bold challenge: 'God willing, it is my intention…to set out for Dharasana and reach there with my companions…and demand possession of the Salt Works….'[58]

Incidentally, Congress considers Dharasana to be a government depot, though the government calls it a privately-owned salt works. Political observers say this constitutes an open challenge to the authority of the Viceroy. Irwin is likely to act expeditiously, not allowing the mater to go out of hand.

GANDHI ARRESTED AT MIDNIGHT

May 4-5 night, 1930, Karadi: A massive upsurge of people in the British Indian provinces had been challenging the moral authority of the government to rule. The government was finding it difficult to maintain law and order. Gandhi's open challenge, announcing his intention to take over the Dharasana Salt Depot has literally challenged the might of the Viceroy. The government has decided to act.

The district magistrate of Surat was assigned the difficult task. At about 12-45 am, the magistrate, accompanied by a posse of policemen, arrested Gandhi from a village near Dandi. At the time of his arrest, Gandhi was sleeping under a mango tree and his associates were also asleep nearby. It has been learnt that the government is shifting him to the Yervada prison in Pune by a bus.

He is accused of engaging in unlawful activities and placed under restraint in terms of Bombay Regulation XXV of 1827. Accordingly, he has to suffer imprisonment during the pleasure of the Government. [59]

Congress Working Committee Meets, To Intensify Stir

May 12-15, 1930, Allahabad: With Gandhi in prison, the Working Committee of the Congress met to take stock of the situation. Undaunted by the ban, it has decided to extend the scope of the movement. As a result, not only have the common acts of civil disobedience intensified, the movement has also begun to assume many different forms.

People have been boycotting foreign cloth enthusiastically. Volunteers have been picketing before foreign cloth shops, liquor shops and preventing drug traffic. Women, in particular, have been taking a leading role in these picketings. So extensive have the picketings been in scope that the government revenue from these businesses have come under stress. People are also boycotting British institutions including banks, insurance and shipping companies.

Acts of civil disobedience have already spread to other fields—like violation of forest laws in the Central Provinces, no-rent campaigns amongst both zamindars and tenant farmers in United Provinces, no-tax campaigns in Gujarat, Bengal and Bihar. In some areas, including Midnapore district in Bengal, Bardoli and Borsad talukas in Gujarat, the impact has been very high.

Sarojini Gives Demonstration Of Satyagraha

May 21, 1930, Dharasana: Mission 'Dharasana' did not end with the arrest of Gandhi. His close follower, Abbas Tayabji, a retired judge of Baroda High Court, took over and started the Dharasana campaign. But soon, he too was arrested, upon which Sarojini Naidu took charge of the campaign. She has been camping here since 15 May and has already made a few abortive attempts to enter into the Salt Works with the Satyagrahis. Today, she made a desperate bid with hundreds of Satyagrahis to break the police cordon and take over the Salt Works. But the civil resisters were brutally lathi charged. Undaunted, they kept arriving in batches. Even as the police rained steel-shod lathis upon them, the volunteers, under strict instructions from leader Sarojini made no bid to resist the attack, except for trying to save their faces and heads with their hands. Many were seriously injured. Blood flowed profusely from their bodies, many lay scattered on the streets only to be rescued by other women volunteers. Eventually, the police arrested Sarojini. But the volunteers showed no signs of retiring. It appears, this battle will continue. Today's incidents have been covered by foreign correspondents who were astounded by the novelty of the protest. Such a classic demonstration of non-violent Satyagraha is likely to be served to the world audience soon, there is little doubt.

Wadala Salt Depot Invaded By Satyagrahis

June 1, 1930, Bombay: Undaunted by the terrible police repression in Dharasana, the Congress organised a raid on the Salt Depot at Wadala in Bombay. Today, 15,000 volunteers led by Congress activists, made a determined bid to enter the depot. They kept arriving in batches and were brutally tackled by huge forces stationed there. Eventually, the volunteers were able to break the cordon and enter the depot and run over the salt pans. But they had to pay a heavy price for a transient victory. Hundreds of volunteers were injured and hundreds taken into custody. However short lived, people are considering it as a moral victory over their oppressive rulers.

Simon Commission Report A Non-event In India

June 7, 1930, London, New Delhi: Simon Commission has issued its report. In the middle of its functioning, during October last year, the Commission in an intriguing move, had sought from the British government an extension in its terms of reference to include the issue of future relations between the Indian states and the British Indian provinces. In its report, the Commission has recommended a federation of British India and the Indian states. The federal legislature will not be elected by people but by the provincial legislatures. There will be no responsible government in the centre, meaning that the powers will remain in British hand. To the provincial legislatures, near autonomy will be granted. However, these will be subject to safeguards for maintaining peace, tranquillity and protecting the legal interest of the minorities. To ensure these, the Governor will remain vested with special powers. In keeping with the Muslim demands, the commission has accepted demands for reorganisation of provinces but recommended abolition of separate electorates. Significantly, the commission has recommended that now onwards, the constitutional revision may be done in a need-based manner, instead of linking it to a pre-defined 'period'.

The Motilal Report and its opposition by the Muslim League, and then the Congress unilateral declaration of 'independence', followed by the countrywide civil disobedience movement, et al have made the discourses on the future constitution quite complex. In the noisy political ambience and amidst torrent of events, the report has failed to generate much interest. If at all, the political parties in the country have chosen to criticise its provisions, each for reasons of its own.

Ugly Face Of British Imperialism Exposed To The World

June 12, 1930, Ahmedabad: Dharasana atrocities have revealed the ugly face of British imperialism and attracted the attention of not only the entire country but the world at large, due to the presence of some foreign correspondents during police action.

Madeliene Slade, an English disciple of Gandhi, went to Bulsar in Gujarat to get a first hand account and feel of the police atrocities committed on the Satyagrahis at the Dharasana Salt Depot. Her findings have today appeared in *Young India*, it which are an account of abysmal apathy of the ruling regime.

According to her report, the police rained lathis on the volunteers, especially on their head, chest, stomach and joints; lathis were also thrust into their private parts including anus and abdomen region; men were stripped naked before being beaten; squeezing testicles till a man became unconscious; dragging wounded men by legs and arms, often beating them all the while; throwing wounded men in thorn hedges and salt water; riding of horses over men; thrusting of pins and thorns into men's bodies till they became unconscious etc.

The accounts given by Slade have caused deep revulsion amongst people towards the government.

Government At War With Indian National Congress

June 30, 1930, New Delhi: By arresting Gandhi, the government of India has achieved unintended results. The unrest in the country has aggravated even more and acts of civil disobedience are spreading thick and fast. More and more people are refusing to pay taxes, violating forest laws, boycotting foreign goods, and aggressively picketing liquor shops. On 7th of this month, the Congress went to the extent of calling on the army and police to disobey government orders. An angry government has come down hard on people. It has proscribed the Congress Working Committee. Congress president Motilal Nehru has been arrested today in Allahabad. It is reported that he may be charged for his provocative statement about what a soldier or a policeman ought to do if he was ordered to fire on civil population. Now, most of the important Congress leaders are in gaols. In a nutshell, the government has entered into an open war with the Indian National Congress.

British India Is Bleeding!

Unable to tolerate the irrepressible enthusiasm of people in taking part in the ongoing Satyagraha, the government has let loose a reign of terror across British India from the north to the south, west to east. Provinces like Bengal, Gujrat, NWFP and the United Provinces bear the main brunt of the repression. Within Bengal, Midnapore district has been chosen by the government to teach the people special lessons. They are being treated so cruelly that young people are being driven to revolutionary societies. In Gujarat, the government has been confiscating the properties of impoverished people for non-payment of rent. There is exodus of people to the state of Baroda, from the neighbouring areas in British India. In the United Provinces, repression has been on account of the no-rent campaign. In NWFP, the government has, after arresting the Khan brothers, been trying to bulldoze their supporters and sympathisers. Bombay has witnessed how ugly the face of the rulers can be. Other provinces also have their own stories to tell. The government is out to crush the movement and people are refusing to retreat. India is bleeding!

Top Prisoners Lay Down Conditions For 'Peace'

August 15, 1930, Yeravada, Poona: Viceroy Irwin has realised too well that he had underestimated the little frail man who could sway the hearts of tens of millions of Indians with such ease. His government has been rendered clueless as to how to handle the evolving situation. He has been disquiet, watching that the more he applied forces, the stronger the movement grew. At this juncture, George Slowcombe, a reporter of the *Daily Herald* has made an attempt to bring about reconciliation between the government and the Congress through dialogue and negotiations. His initiatives were transferred to liberal leaders like TB Sapru and MR Jayakar. To facilitate communication between the top Congress leaders, they arranged Motilal and Jawaharlal to be brought from Naini prison to Yeravada here, where Gandhi has been lodged. Here they held meetings for three days, starting 13th August. Other senior Congress leaders like Vallabhbhai and Sarojini also joined.

At the end of the exercise, the leaders have issued a joint statement today. They have demanded that any solution must guarantee the fulfilment of three conditions, viz. (a) India should have the right to secede; (b) India should be granted a national government responsible to her own people, including control of defence and finance; (c) India should have the right to submit the so called 'Public Debt of India' to an impartial scrutiny.

The interlocutors are to convey the outcome of the deliberations and these conditions to the Viceroy.

CITY IGP LOWMAN SHOT IN BROAD DAYLIGHT

August 29, 1930, Dhaka: People participating in the civil disobedience movement are being hauled up in large numbers. Jails are overflowing. Inside the prison, police torture is on the rise. The revolutionaries, in particular, are treated cruelly. Lowman, the Inspector General of Police of Dhaka, is infamous for committing atrocities on the arrested revolutionaries. Today, Benoy Krishna Bose, a young revolutionary, has, in broad day light, shot the IGP to death in the Dhaka medical college premise. Lowman had come there to visit an ailing colleague.

This has created a sensation in the city. After the incident, Bose was able to give the police a slip. He could not be traced despite a massive manhunt.

This is the second big attack by the revolutionaries since Surya Sen carried out a daring raid of the Chittagong Armoury four months ago. He too could not be apprehended by the government to date.

Peace Talk Fails, Back To Square One

August 30, 1930, New Delhi: Though much upset by the extant situation, the Viceroy has found the conditions put forth by the Congress leaders unacceptable. He has communicated to the interlocutors that it is impossible to hold any discussion on the basis of the 'joint statement of 15th August'.

Clearly, things are back to square one. Political observers say the government may maintain the pressure on the Congress and attempt to divert public attention.

Atrocities On Political Prisoners: Viceroy Asked To Clarify

September 23, 1930: New Delhi: Many stories have been circulating about the ongoing atrocities on political prisoners in the country's gaols. The government has been, of course, underplaying the issue all these days. But today, the matter has stirred the highest level of the government, due to the victimisation of the high-profile Meerut Conspiracy Case prisoners.

A series of excesses was committed by the prison authorities in the Meerut jail which has the capacity to hold 750 inmates, but the number of prisoners here swelled to 1100 on account of 500 Satyagrahis, also held in this jail. This year, on the 29th August night, many young boys between 9-11 years, who were arrested for violation of Sec 114 of the Cr PC in connection with a civil disobedience movement and held here, were caned on their hands. The prisoners protested shouting, 'Mahatma Gandhi Ki Jai'. These were reported to the jail superintendent who called for some of the prisoners the next day.

At that time, many other prisoners insisted they too be produced before the superintendent, resulting in a struggle. The jail wardens lathi-charged, resulting in injuries to many, including two Conspiracy Case prisoners, viz. Mirajkar and D Goswami.

The prison authorities justified their action, alleging that the prisoners attempted to break out from the jail. An enquiry was held and fourteen prisoners were identified as guilty. They were awarded punishment of thirty lashes each. The following day, when the Conspiracy Case prisoners returned from the court to the jail, they found the whipped prisoners lying in a semi-conscious state on the floor in the blazing sun, with blood oozing out, drenching their dresses.

Deeply upset at these gruesome happenings, the Conspiracy Case prisoners presented a memorandum to the Governor of UP through the Addl Session Judge of Meeurt, but it was disallowed. However, the *Hindustan Times*, having managed an access to it, reproduced the memorandum in its 4 September 1930 issue. The matter was taken up by the League against Imperialism, with both the Viceroy and the Secretary of State for India in London. Today, the Secretary of State for India has sent a telegram to the Viceroy, asking for a reply on the case.[60]

Subhas Elected Mayor Of Calcutta Corporation

September 25, 1930, Calcutta: Subhas has been elected the Mayor of the Calcutta Corporation. He received the news in jail, where he is serving a prison term. He was earlier arrested this year for his alleged involvements with the Bengal Volunteers, a revolutionary society.

It seems the British government feels uncomfortable whenever Subhas is out of prison and is in a position to pursue political activities. At the same time, the fact that he is being repeatedly anointed by the people as their representative, once as a member of the provincial legislature and now as the head of the corporation and that too, in absentia, suggests his growing popularity and mass appeal.

In, Out And Again Into The Naini Prison

October 19, 1930, Allahabad: Congress president, Jawaharlal, was arrested in April 1930 for violating the Salt Act and imprisoned for six months. At that time, he had named Gandhi and in the event Gandhi was unwilling, his father Motilal, to act as president of the Congress Party. As Gandhi was unwilling, Motilal was acting as president till he was arrested on 30 June. Jawaharlal was released from Naini prison on 11th of this month on serving his term. However, today he was rearrested here in connection with the 'no-rent campaign'. He is likely to be charged with 'sedition' and may be awarded a longer prison term. He has been again taken to the Naini prison.

Round Table: Congress Uninterested, Others Prepare

October 1930, New Delhi: Government has scheduled a round table conference in London next month. The Viceroy had announced one year ago that the government intended to hold such a conference after the Simon Commission report was published. It is expected to advance the process of constitutional reforms. However, the political situation since then has undergone drastic changes. The largest and most representative political party, viz. the Congress is no longer interested in these incremental progress and has launched a national struggle for 'complete independence'. In retaliation, the government has put nearly all top leaders in prison. So the Congress participation in the round table is out of question. The government is planning to go ahead with the rest of the parties and interest groups. It has been selecting delegates to represent the Muslim League, the Hindu Mahasabha, Sikhs, Hindu Depressed Classes, Anglo Indian community, Liberal Party and other special interest groups, besides a team to represent the government.

Significantly, all of these groups have a common interest. They would be happy with the continuation of British rule. However, each wants that the existing political equations in the country are re-organised under the safety of the British rule in ways such that the reforms confer each more political rights than the rest. Since they cannot arrive at a mutual agreement on this issue, the government is likely to have a major role in setting the agenda and steer the conference in the manner it wants. Thus, the absence of the Congress is a major advantage. On the flip side, it denudes the conference of much of the legitimacy that is necessary to arrive at a lasting political solution.

However, one thing is certain. The government is hoping the conference would distract public attention from civil disobedience, at least for some time.

AMBEDKAR ESPOUSES THE 'DALIT' CAUSE

October 1930: BR Ambedkar has been a prominent face, representing the interest of the depressed classes to the government and the political community. From 1919 through the 1920s, he has testified before official commissions, published newspapers, organised conferences, served in the Bombay legislature, taught at the Government Law College and actively supported the Temple Satyagraha. As a result he, besides becoming very popular with the depressed classes, has achieved considerable following amongst politicised untouchables and recognition from the enlightened social reformers belonging to the caste Hindu groups. He has been nominated by the government to attend the round table conference and analysts say he would go great lengths to protect the interest of the depressed classes.

'No Seat' In Round Table – States' People's Groups Upset

October 1930: The British government has invited select princes to represent the native states in the ensuing round table conference, which would meet in London to discuss the future constitutional reforms. Remarkably, the government has denied the requests of the states' people's groups for representations at the round table. The states' people are finding such denials insensitive. To them, this would mean that the viewpoints of a large chunk of people would be ignored in the new constitution. This is because the rulers of states are likely to see things from their own perspective rather than their subjects'.

Congress Absent From Round Table Conference

November 12, 1930, London: King George V has inaugurated the first round table conference in the Royal Gallery in the House of Commons here today.

There are 89 delegates – 57 from British India, 16 from the princely states and another 16 from three British political parties. Viceroy Irwin has deputed George Schuster, finance member of his council and Henry Haig, secretary of home department to provide inputs on behalf of his government and facilitate the proceedings. He has chosen other delegates from India to represent various constituencies.

Prominent delegates from the provinces include Mohammad Ali, MA Jinnah, Md Shafi, Aga Khan, Zafrullah Khan and AK Fazlul Huq from the Muslims, MR Jayakar and BS Moonje from the Hindu Mahasabha, Tej Bahadur Sapru, CY Chintamani and Srinavas Sastri from the liberals and BR Ambedkar representing the Depressed Classes.

The most notable absentee is Congress, ironically the most representative political organisation of Indian people. The British and the British Indian governments have taken care while inviting the delegates so that they do not pose serious threat to its imperial interests in India.

Round Table Mulls Federal Structure, Adopts Committee

November 1930, London: The round table conference is in progress. After the opening ceremony, the conference devoted five days in plenary session to a debate on the question whether the future constitution of India is to be federal or unitary. Significantly, the proposal of 'federation' was welcomed by the Maharaja of Bikaner, which seemed to reflect the attitude of the native states on this vital issue.

The conference has decided to approach its task through constituting several sub-committees. Important amongst these are the sub-committees on Federal Structure, Minorities, Franchise and Services, Defence, Burma, Sind and NWFP.

Jinnah Tries To Allay British Phobia Of Gandhi, Congress

November 1930, London: Though the government has been tying to pretend that the Congress absence as a non-issue, a cold doubt is gnawing its heart—would India at large accept the outcome of this conference while its largest political party is not participating in the deliberations? The British Indian government is well aware of the clout of the Congress and Gandhi over the Indian masses. They are still reeling under the impact of the unprecedented civil disobedience movement.

To allay the British fear of Gandhi and the Congress and, possibly to convince them that the conference, without Congress representative, could still be effective, Jinnah tried to reassure the government:

'Seventy millions of Mussalmans—all, barring a few individuals here and there—have kept aloof from the non-cooperation movement. Thirty-five or forty million of depressed classes have set their face against the non-cooperation movement. Sikhs and Christians have not joined it. And let me tell you that even amongst that party which you characterise as a large party—and I admit that it is an important party—it has not got the support of the bulk of Hindus.' However, these words do not seem to be sufficient to reassure the government.

Revolutionary Network In Bengal Becomes Hyper-active

November 1930, Calcutta: As the round table is in progress in London, India continues to be remarkably tense. Political observers ascribe this partly to the absence of the Congress in the negotiations that are supposed to decide on the 'constitution' of the country. The civil disobedience movement is in full swing and the jails in the country are overflowing with political prisoners. Calcutta has been a hotbed of the movement against the British government. According to leaked information from the city's jails, the police have been brutally torturing the political prisoners. It is being heard that NS Simpson, the IG Prison, is playing a key role in the persecution of the prisoners. Much of the prison tortures are occurring under his instructions. The revolutionary networks in the city are reportedly trying to assassinate him but finding it difficult, as Simpson's office is located in one of the most fortified buildings in the city—the Writers' Building.

AITUC Demands Release Of Meerut Prisoners

November 17-18, 1930: The AITUC executive committee, with Subhas Bose as the president, has adopted a resolution demanding immediate and unconditional release of the Meerut prisoners. Many trade union leaders are languishing in the Meerut prison. Although the government is accusing them of sedition, so far it has not been able to produce substantial proof against them to satisfy the court.

Bonhomie Between Muslim Delegates And Opposition

December 1930, London: The round table is in progress. So far little progress has been achieved. The Muslim delegates are reported to be hobnobbing with the opposition leaders of the British Parliament. The tacit support of the latter is reportedly encouraging these delegates to harden their attitude on issues, particularly those involving the 'minorities' and the 'federal structure'.

REVOLUTIONARIES INVADE GOVERNMENT CITADEL

December 8, 1930, Calcutta: Today, three young revolutionaries have shot down NS Simpson, IG Prison, inside the citadel of the Bengal government—the Writers' Building, its administrative head quarters. In an exceptionally daring act three revolutionaries—Benoy Krishna Bose, Badal Gupta and Dinesh Gupta managed to enter one of the most fortified buildings of the provincial capital by outwitting large posse of security personnel and have shot down Simpson in his office. Thereafter, they went on a shooting spree, attacking every British officer who came their way. The security force posted in the building retaliated and they were reinforced by a large contingent of policemen who arrived there, led by Charles Tegart, the Police Commissioner from nearby police headquarters at Lalbazar.

For a brief period, a fierce gun battle took place across the long corridors between the adversaries. After they ran out of ammunitions, the revolutionaries attempted suicides. Badal took potassium cyanide and died immediately. Both Benoy and Dinesh shot themselves with their revolvers. Both have been taken to hospital in precarious condition.

Benoy has been critically injured and is unlikely to survive. It may be remembered that this was his second major operation. It was in August that he had shot down Lowman, the IGP of Dhaka.

According to preliminary information, the premier revolutionary outfit Anushilan Samity meticulously planned this operation. The three young men had attired themselves in impeccable European dresses, to manage their entry into the fortified building without arousing any suspicion.

Iqbal Attempts To Bring Muslim Politicians Together

December 29, 1930, Allahabad: Muhammad Iqbal, the eminent scholar, philosopher and poet, is presiding over the annual session of the Muslim League here. In his presidential speech, he has dealt with a range of issues—national and international. In particular, he dwelt upon the unique socio-economic-political circumstances of the Indian Muslims, role of Islam in cementing them into a homogenous community, challenges facing them and the need for an united political action by the community to realise their aspirations and potential. Highlights from his speeches are as follows:

'Islam has been the chief formative factor in the life-history of the Muslims of India. It has furnished those basic emotions and loyalties which gradually unify scattered individuals and groups, and finally transform them into a well-defined people, possessing a moral consciousness of their own.' The Muslim society, Iqbal said, 'with its remarkable homogeneity and inner unity, has grown to be what it is, under the pressure of the laws and institutions associated with the culture of Islam.'

'The religious ideal of Islam, therefore' Iqbal argued 'is organically related to the social order which it has created. The rejection of one will eventually involve the rejection of the other. Therefore, the construction of polity on national lines, if it means a displacement of the Islamic principle of solidarity, is simply unthinkable to a Muslim.'

On the issue of unity of an Indian nation, he said it lay in mutual harmony and cooperation. In an obvious reference to non-Muslim political leaders, Iqbal said that these could not be achieved because 'perhaps we suspect each other's intentions and inwardly aim at dominating each other.' Or, may be that we 'conceal our egoism under the cloak of nationalism, outwardly stimulating a large-hearted patriotism, but inwardly as narrow-minded as a caste or tribe.'

Iqbal emphasised that each community or group is entitled to its free development on its own lines and that is certainly not inspired by any feeling of narrow communalism. He stressed that communalism in its better aspect is 'culture' without which it will be impossible to create a harmonious nation in a country like India. 'India is a continent of human groups belonging to different races, speaking different languages, and professing different religions.... The principle of European democracy cannot be applied to India without recognising the fact of communal groups.'

Iqbal endorsed the resolution of the All-Parties Muslim Conference held in Delhi for the creation of a Muslim India within India, and said that it was inspired by the 'noble ideal of a harmonious whole, which instead of stifling the respective individualities of its component wholes, affords them chances of fully working out the possibilities that may be latent in them'. Going farther on this demand, Iqbal said, 'I would like to see the Punjab, North-West Frontier Province, Sind and Baluchistan amalgamated into a single state. Self Government within the British Empire, or without the British Empire, the formation of a consolidated North-West Indian Muslim State appears to me to be the final destiny of the Muslims, at least of North-West India.'

Iqbal clarified that the Muslim demand is 'actuated by a genuine desire for free development which is practically impossible under the type of unitary government contemplated by the nationalist Hindu politicians with a view to secure permanent communal dominance in the whole of India.'

As regards the ongoing round table conference, he expressed concerns and anxieties in the proposal of a federation between the native sates and British Indian provinces. Pointing out that the rulers of the native states will constitute the single largest block in the federal legislature and the majority of them are Hindus, he warned the Muslims about a nexus between the Hindu majority and the British Imperialists operating to the detriment of the Indian Muslims. He also asserted that,

'Our demand for 33 per cent must now be taken as a demand for the same proportion in the All-India Federal Assembly, exclusive of the share allotted to the Muslim states entering the Federation'.

Iqbal appreciated the Muslim delegates in the round table conference as they have been 'pressing for a solution of the communal question before the question of responsibility in the Central Government is finally settled'. He advised that no Muslim politician should be sensitive to the taunt embodied in the propaganda word 'communalism', devised to exploit the British democratic sentiment. He put the sole test of the success of the Muslim delegates in their ability 'to get the non-Muslim delegates of the Conference to agree to our demands as embodied in the Delhi Resolution.' In the event they failed to accomplish this task, Iqbal warned, 'Then will arrive the moment for independent and concerted political action by the Muslims of India'.

Before concluding, Iqbal stressed on the need for united stand and lamented the absence of a 'herd instinct' in the matter of political action. Recognising the long present sectional bickering in the affairs of religion, he warned, 'But diversity in political action, at a moment when concerted action is needed in the best interests of the very life of our people, may prove fatal.'

Finally he sought to prepare the Muslims for the impending action, saying '...I cannot conceal from you the feeling that in the near future, our community may be called upon to adopt an independent line of action to cope with the present crisis. And an independent line of political action, in such a crisis, is possible only to a determined people, possessing a will focalised by a single purpose.'

MUHAMMAD ALLAMA IQBAL

If today there is one person who towers over scores of mundane leaders of the Muslims in India, one whom people look at with admiration and listen to with rapt attention, it is Muhammad Iqbal. He was born in Sialkot, Punjab on 9 November, 1877 in a middle-class Muslim family. His ancestors belonged to Kashmiri Brahminical order, who at some point of time in the past had converted to Islam. Iqbal's father, Nur Muhammad, was a tailor by profession. Though not formally educated, he was well versed in Islamic theology and mysticism.

Encouraged by Arnold, a British professor in Lahore, Iqbal, a brilliant student, went to England for higher studies. He arrived in Cambridge in 1905. Before he returned to India in July 1908, he could complete his BA degree from Cambridge, obtained his PhD from Munich University, Germany and was also admitted to the Bar in London. His PhD thesis was entitled 'The Development of Metaphysics in Persia'.

He fully inherited his father's passion, penchant and reverence for Islam and imparted these with the full life force of his erudition and poetic imagination. Back in India, he has steadily emerged as a prominent scholar and philosopher. He has also been expressing his thoughts and ideas through delectable poetry with great efficacy. His primary concern turned to be the revival of Islam. Based on extensive reading of scripture, history, philosophy and political science he is convinced that the fate of the Muslim world is very much in the hands of Muslims themselves.

Although as a highly educated person, Iqbal could select from a range of lucrative careers, he chose to undertake scholarly work on politics, philosophy, religion, history and economics to dominate the minds and thoughts of millions.

His abounding love for Islam and overriding anxiety to create conditions to enable Muslims to live according to strict Islamic thoughts and principles even if that led to their insularity from a secular, mainstream Indian life, vests him with a kind of communal halo.

Hindu, Muslim Problem International In Character: Iqbal

December 1930, Allahabad: As the round table is in progress in London, some tidings are reaching India in piecemeal. These are not encouraging. Muhammad Iqbal is not surprised. Right from the beginning he has not been optimistic about the outcome of such a conference. He is critical of Ramsay MacDonald, the British Prime

Minister, for failing to identify the core issue. Iqbal is convinced that Hindus and Muslims are two different nations and that the 70 million strong Muslims are a much more homogenous nation than the Hindus who are bitterly divided into castes. Iqbal regrets that the British Prime Minister in charge of the round table has been refusing to acknowledge the basic fact that the problem of India is international and not national. The only solution to it, Iqbal reckons, is the creation of a Muslim India within India.

FOUR

Capitulation And Resurrection

1931 - 1936

Capitulation And Resurrection

ROUND TABLE CONFERENCE ADJOURNED SINE DIE

January 19, 1931, London: The Round Table Conference reached a stalemate and has been adjourned sine die. Although it was attended by many delegates from India, most of them were handpicked by the government and not genuinely elected by various cross sections of people. Congress, the largest party, was not represented. However, even amongst the handpicked delegates, there was bitter acrimony on the key features of the constitution. The core disputes between the Motilal Report and the Muslim League that had generated discord in the country, again raged in the wintry clime of London with equal vehemence. The League had already structured its opposition to the Motilal recommendations through Jinnah's fourteen points and the Muslim leaders forcefully voiced those in the conference. Thus, they wanted residuary power to be rested with the provinces, continuation of separate electorates and weightage for minorities, and statutory Muslim majority in Bengal and Punjab. Even though the Congress was absent, the Liberal leaders resolutely opposed these demands. The Sikhs complicated the scenario even more by demanding that they should not be deprived of the special benefits that were accorded to the Muslims. The parties were so rigid on their respective stands that negotiations seemed impossible.

On its part, the government has been able to accomplish two important objectives for its own benefit. First, it has established the agenda of a 'federal structure' for the country comprising both British India and native states. It implies that now a new set of players, ie. large number of rulers of Indian states who happen to be loyal to the Empire will have a role in the making of the new constitution.

This, at one stroke, imparts uncertainty as to the time limit and also features of the new constitution. Second, the conference introduced the 'safeguard' clause, which gives the government extensive power to protect the political and civic rights of various minorities in the new constitution. Prime Minister Ramsay, in his concluding speech said, it was the duty of HM Government to insert such a 'safeguard' provision. Both these vest the government with scope and power to manoeuvre the contents of the new constitution when that task is undertaken again.

Let's Try To Get Congress On Board Too

January 19, 1931, London: In his concluding speech, Prime Minister Ramsay thanked the delegates for their services and suggested that it was time that the conference be suspended so that Indian opinion may be consulted upon the work that has been done. He also suggested that HM Government was willing to secure the cooperation of those engaged in the civil disobedience movement in India if they responded to the appeal of the Viceroy and join the process to carry forward the task. The reference to the Congress and the desire to get it involved in the process in future was obvious.

Round Table Conference – Victory For British Diplomacy?

January 19, 1931, London: The round table conference was called to consider the question of advancing the Indian constitution. It has come to an end, at least for the time being. At this stage, political analysts are trying to assess the implications of the proceedings held so far.

According to them, HM Government has emerged as the major

beneficiary of the conference while the gains to others, whether they be subjects of native states or people of the British Indian provinces, remain deeply suspect. They say HM Government has adopted a well-thoughtout and calibrated strategy. Their major problem has so far been the persistent demand for independence or at least 'dominion status', raised from the British Indian provinces though the people of the native states, by and large, have so far remained indifferent on the issue. In the conference, the government introduced the proposal of a 'federation' between British Indian provinces and native states as a 'game changer'.

The rulers of states have traditionally been servile to HM Government. They had nothing to lose from the proposed federation in terms of losing their independence. On the contrary, the prospect of having some kind of a role in the affairs of the whole federation was alluring. On the part of the leaders from British India, this idea of 'federation' per se could not be rejected ideologically as it held out a grander vision for the entire subcontinent.

Thus, at the beginning, when the government invited the rulers of states to join the proposed federation, the Maharaja of Bikaner accepted it. This signified a broader acceptance by his community of rulers. Interestingly, none of the Indian parties have had any idea about what would the shape and form of that federation be, which would be decided only by the delegates by due processes of deliberations under the aegis of HM Government.

Once the idea of the 'federation' was through, several committees were appointed to chalk out what would be its structure. They were to agree on the form of legislatures, methods of election or selection of members of the councils, federal finances, federal court, and so on. The government ensured that each of these committees had a fair representation of princes as its members.

There was, of course, little problem with regard to the issue of 'inner governance' posed by the proposed federation in the states. However, as anticipated by the government, serious problems arose amongst leaders from British Indian provinces on issues such as representations in the central as well as provincial councils to be allowed to various communities. There were differences, disagreements and disputes between delegates from Muslim, Sikh, Hindu, Depressed classes, Liberal leaders and others. Those proved to be irreconcilable. Around this stage, the government intervened and suspended the conference while reminding the conference that it was its bounden duty to safeguard the interests of the minorities in the constitution, whatever its form may take. It then asked the delegates to go back to consult Indian opinion.

However, the government is happy having secured two important objectives: one, introduction of federal structure as the basis of the constitution; two, a self-acclaimed role to protect the 'minorities' interest. Any future negotiations must be subject to these two ground rules. This, then pre-empts any demand for independence for all practical purposes.

Gandhi Is Released Unconditionally

January 26, 1931, Yeravada prison: The news that the first Round Table has wound up without achieving results has added to the ire of the Indian masses. While the much- hyped conference was in progress in distant London, Gandhi and his followers were languishing in British jails in India. Engaging in discussion and negotiations with its own chosen delegates while pushing the genuine people's representatives into prisons was seen as nothing but mockery on the part of the government. The anger and frustration of the masses have been reflecting in the intensification of the civil disobedience movement.

Itself no better, the government is suffering both economically and loss of credibility. It seems to have realised the impossibility of a solution to the task of constitutional reforms without participation of the Congress. Irwin is reportedly mulling reconciliation with Gandhi. After about eight-and-a-half months of incarceration in prison, Gandhi was unconditionally released from the prison today. Irwin is hoping this step would improve the political ambience.

FIRST ANNIVERSARY OF 'INDEPENDENCE DAY'
Jawaharlal Released, Subhas Enters Prison

January 27, 1931, Calcutta: In the Congress session last year, 26th January was declared as the Independence Day. Yesterday was its first anniversary. Severe repression of about nine months has not been able to cow people down. Though still banned, the Congress organised due celebration of the momentous event across the country. People confirmed their faith on the 'independence resolution' by passing an identical resolution which they called as 'resolution of remembrance'. [61] Their enthusiasm received a huge boost as Gandhi was released just a day earlier.

Significantly, the government also released most of the Working Committee members of the Congress from prison at different places yesterday. Jawaharlal was a part of the general amnesty and released from Naini. However, he was asked to rush home at Allahabad where his father Motilal was seriously ill. Such wholesale release of Congress leaders coming within a week of the conclusion of the first round table is being seen as a gesture to mend ties with Gandhi and Congress.

However, an ugly incident in Calcutta marred the spirit of reconciliation. There Subhas, presently the Mayor of the city, was leading a large procession to celebrate the independence anniversary. Without warning, the peaceful procession was attacked by mounted police who rained lathis on the procession including him. Subhas has been badly injured. In that condition he was arrested and taken to the police headquarters at Lalbazar and left practically without medical treatment. Today he was tried and awarded six months of imprisonment.

Liberal Leaders On Their Way To Allahabad

February 6, 1931, Allahabad: After his release, Gandhi arrived at Allahabad via Bombay to visit seriously ailing Motilal. Practically the entire Congress Working Committee has gathered here. The working committee adopted a resolution on 1st of the month opposing any compromise with the government. However, today the three Liberal leaders Sapru, Chintamani and Srianavas Sastri have arrived at Bombay after attending the round table. Earlier, they had sent a wire, urging the committee not to take any decision about the response to the government till they shared with Gandhi and the working committee members a first hand account of the conference. They are on their way to Allahabad. In view of the request by the Liberal leaders, the working committee has not disclosed its resolution in public.

Motilal Nehru's Last Journey

February 6, 1931, Sangam, Allahabad: Motilal Nehru had been quite upset at British indifference to the constitution, drafted by a committee under his guidance. The government ignored the ultimatum of one year issued by the Congress. On the contrary, it began a process of wider consultations with various Indian groups in the round table conference in London. His hard work seems to have gone waste. In protest against the government machinations, Gandhi began a countrywide civil disobedience movement starting with the salt Satyagraha. Motilal, though an exhausted person, actively participated in the movement and was arrested June end last year. However, as his health declined further, Motilal was released from prison after ten weeks.

During the course of the civil disobedience movement, his house in Allahabad turned into a 24-bed hospital, treating people who were beaten by the police for participating in the movement. For the last few days he was keeping very unwell and Gandhi, who came down here soon after his release from prison, has been by his side. Gandhi's spiritual presence has been giving him some measure of comfort in an otherwise distressed physical condition. On 4th of this month, his condition became acute and Gandhi accompanied him to Lucknow for a specialized medical treatment.

Today Motilal breathed his last in Lucknow. Thereafter his mortal body was brought to Allahabad. His body was wrapped in a national flag and taken to the holy confluence of the Ganges and Yamuna for last rites, where a large number of people congregated to bid him the last farewell with tearful eyes.

Gandhi To Viceroy: More Than The Viceroy, I Would Like To Meet The Man In You

February 14, 1931, Allahabad: Gandhi has been holding consultations with some of the round table delegates and also working committee members, starting yesterday. Today, the Working Committee has authorised him to negotiate settlement with the Viceroy. Accordingly, today he has written to the Viceroy seeking appointment for a meeting. In it Gandhi has requested for a 'heart to heart talk' to sort out the difficulties through discussion. Gandhi has made an appeal: 'I would like to meet not so much the Viceroy of India as the man in you'.[62]

Gandhi And Viceroy Begin Parley

February 18, 1931, Delhi: Gandhi is in Dr MA Ansari's house. His request for appointment was quickly responded to by the Viceroy, who has been looking for a way out of the present impasse. Gandhi arrived here yesterday and also began parley with the Viceroy. He has summoned select Working Committee members including Jawaharlal, Vallabhbhai, Abul Kalam Azad and a few others to Delhi to be around for consultation. The first meeting was held today.

Gandhi Asks For Postponement Of Bhagat Singh's Death Sentence, Not Commutation

February 18, 1931, New Delhi: Discussion between Gandhi and Irwin has already begun. Gandhi has brought amongst others the issue of Bhagat Singh and his two comrades who have been awarded death sentences. The country has been greatly agitated over the verdict awarded to these peerless patriots. However, Gandhi does not endorse violence in any form. Though he broached the issue, he did so rather apologetically saying: 'This has no connection with our discussion and it may even be inappropriate on my part to mention it....'[63] The Viceroy had a premonition that Gandhi would discuss Bhagat Singh and might demand commutation of the death sentence. But Gandhi's visible reservation in introducing this subject seemingly emboldened him. To his further relief, Gandhi did not ask for 'commutation' of the death sentence for Bhagat Singh, but requested for postponement as it would influence peace. The Viceroy agreed for the postponement and they proceeded to the next topic.

Azad Hee Rahein Hai, Azad Hee Rahenge

Chandrasekhar Azad Embraces Death, Defies Capture

February 27, 1931, Allahabad: Today the famous revolutionary Chandrasekhar Azad has shot himself to death at Alfred Park here. Azad came to the park to hold consultations with his comrades when he was spotted by the police in plainclothes. Soon he was surrounded by a posse of armed policemen. In a gunfight that ensued, Azad fought single handed with his enemies, and killed three policemen. When his ammunition was exhausted and there was no scope for escape, he shot himself to death.

As the news spread, a spell of gloom enveloped the city. Azad had been a man of indomitable courage and free spirit. He often said his enemies would never be able to capture him alive. Thousands of his admirers in the city are overcome with emotion, recalling his favourite couplets:

Dushmano ki goliyon ka hum samna karenge
Azad hee rahein hain, azad hee rahenge

ODE TO A EVER FREE SOUL

Chandrasekhar was born in Jhabua district in the Central Provinces, in a traditional Brahmin family in July 1906. He was barely 13-years-old when the Jalianwalabagh massacre occurred and that left a deep scar in his tender mind. In 1921, he joined the non-cooperation movement led by Gandhi while he was a teenager. When Gandhi called off the civil disobedience movement, he was left disillusioned. Thereafter, he was attracted by more aggressive and violent revolutionary ideals, which spoke of complete independence for the country and that too by force. He joined the Hindustan Republican Association and played an important role in converting it into the Hindustan

Socialist Republican Association (HSRA). He was elected as the first president of that revolutionary organisation. This new outfit aimed at building a new India on Socialistic principles. Popularly known as Panditji, Chandrasekhar had worked along with and held a special place amongst revolutionaries like Bhagat Singh, Sukhdev, Rajguru and Batukeswar Dutt for his ability to lead and inspire. Over the last few years, he had kept the government on tenterhook by a series of bold revolutionary actions. Fiercely independent in spirit, he had reportedly thrown a challenge that the British would never be able to capture him alive. This earned him the title 'Azad' or a 'freeman'. He remained true to his promise till the last day of his life. The end of this famed revolutionary came on 27 February, 1931 when he was surrounded by a posse of policemen in the Alfred Park, Allahabad. He had come to the park to meet some of his fellow revolutionaries and had no inkling of the police presence till very late. Undaunted, he launched attack on his adversaries, killing three policemen. After his ammunition was nearly exhausted, he shot himself on the head with the last bullet, seeing no way to escape.

Congress-Communist Rapport Becomes Tenuous

1931, Meerut: The plight of the detained leaders in the conspiracy case is miserable. They have been languishing in prison for several years but the court is yet to pronounce judgements. After the initial enthusiasm to rally behind the detained leaders, the Congress seems to have lost interest in them. Their preoccupations with other political issues have overshadowed the Meerut case. Also, with the sixth congress of the Comintern instructing Indian Communists to combat the national-reformists leaders created a gap between the two political formations. As a result of these developments, the Left's attitude towards the Congress in general has also begun to harden, as they feel the Congress leaders have abandoned the trade unionists and Communist leaders and the latter have now to defend themselves.

A section of Communist leaders like SA Dange and PC Joshi, however, are sticking to the old line of mutual cooperation. From

Meerut jail, they have advised other comrades to participate in the civil disobedience movement and fight for independence without any compromise. In Congress, some nationalist leaders, especially Subhas is standing firmly behind the persecuted Communists at the Meerut jail at their hour of distress. The bridge between the two sides is not completely burnt.

Gandhi, Irwin Strike An Agreement

March 5, 1931, New Delhi: Gandhi and Irwin have been holding talks over two weeks. Meanwhile, he has called select Working Committee members including Jawaharlal, Vallabhbhai, Abul Kalam Azad to Delhi. They are living in the house of veteran Congress leader, MA Ansari, in the city. Gandhi has been negotiating with Irwin and sharing the details of the progress at the end of the day with the Working Committee members. Tonight Gandhi returned from the Viceroy's bungalow at 2 am, and awoke his colleagues to inform them that a settlement had been reached.

Gandhi signed an agreement with Irwin, following which the civil disobedience movement would be suspended. In return, the government would withdraw all Ordinances issued to curb the Congress, release the political prisoners held in connection with the civil disobedience movement and even those held for offences not involving violence, from jail.

The government has agreed to return fines, confiscated properties and employment to the extent feasible. The agreement also provides that the government will invite the Congress to participate in the second round of the RTC, to discuss constitutional advancement.

As Gandhi showed the copy of the agreement to his colleagues, Jawaharlal was appalled to see clause no 2 that not only recognises the supremacy of His Majesty's Government in the constitutional question, but makes safeguarding of minority rights including reservations an essential feature of the scheme.

All these days, the Congress has been demanding complete independence and has already handed over a draft constitution for implementation. That draft provided for abolition of separate electorate system for the minorities. It was only with a view to creating pressure on the government to accept its draft constitution, followed by the demand for 'independence' that the Congress had intensified non-violent non-cooperation movement all these days, courting extreme hardship and making enormous sacrifices.

The relentless agitation had compelled the government to show white flag and begin negotiations. Under such circumstances, accepting the arbiter's role of the government and acquiescing to a mechanism that the government has cleverly contrived, appeared to be unnecessary and avoidable. Jawaharlal feels Gandhi, in his characteristic way, has hoisted a dangerous surprise upon his followers and the country by signing the agreement on these terms. He is of the opinion that Gandhi has unwittingly played into the hands of the shrewd Viceroy.

Gandhi, upon discussion with his colleagues, has appreciated the gravity of their concern. He has assured them that in his future talks and negotiations he would make it clear that the Congress would not compromise on the objective of 'independence' and it would participate in the next round table conference, only on the basis of its ultimate objective of 'independence'. It is, however, not clear as to how he can insist on that or other key issues such as 'joint electorates', after signing this agreement.

What Does Clause 2 Of Gandhi-Irwin Pact Say?

Clause 2 Reads:

As regards constitutional questions, the scope of future discussion is stated, with the assent of His Majesty's Government, to be with the object of considering further the scheme for the constitutional Government of India discussed at the Round Table Conference. Of the scheme there outlined, Federation is an essential part; so also are Indian responsibility and reservations or safeguards in the interests of India, for such matters as, for instance, defence; external affairs; the position of minorities; the financial credit of India; and the discharge of obligations.

Has India Been Short-changed By Gandhi-Irwin Pact?

As the fact of reaching the agreement is flashed across the country, there is widespread disappointment that the bargain has been a poor one. Not only the public, even many Congress leaders felt that by calling off a nationwide movement at its peak, little has been achieved and much more conceded. Besides the core issue of independence, there is visible disappointment in regard to release of political prisoners, large in number. Although the government has agreed to release the civil disobedience prisoners, there are thousands of other political prisoners, both convicted and those detained without charge, trial or conviction— many of them for years, especially in Bengal. In Lahore jail, Bhagat Singh and his associates are languishing in jail, awaiting death sentences and the whole country has been in deep sympathy with them. Then there are many Communist leaders held in the Meerut conspiracy case. Here was an opportunity to get all the political prisoners released as a goodwill gesture. But Gandhi did not put their release as a pre-condition, and thus wasted a good opportunity.

Another strategic blunder has been Gandhi's not insisting on appropriate enquiries on all cases of police and military atrocities on innocent people, and demanding corrective actions. By omitting to do this, he has allowed large number of perpetrators of savage acts to go scot free. This would, in all likelihood, encourage repetition of such acts in future.

Finally, by agreeing to reservations for minorities, he has himself negated the sanctity of the Motilal report, which the Congress seriously wanted the government to accept as India's constitution.

Subhas Released Before Full Prison Term

March 8, 1931, Calcutta: In terms of the settlement reached between Gandhi and Irwin, the government has released several prisoners. Subhas has been released before serving his full term. However, in Bengal, many political prisoners have not got the benefit. The government has brought charges of violence and is adopting a vengeful approach against them.

Gandhi To Irwin: On 'Death Sentence' If There's Slightest Error Of Judgement, Review

March 23, 1931, New Delhi: Consequent upon a settlement between Gandhi and Irwin, new hopes have been aroused in the country about commutation of the death sentence of Bhagat Singh. There are strong pressures from several quarters on Gandhi to secure this from the Viceroy. Few days ago, Subhas, in his personal meeting with Gandhi in Bombay, had made a fervent appeal to him to do something concrete. But Gandhi himself did not seem to be convinced on the merit of the case.

Thus, when he had broached the subject with the Viceroy on 18th of last month, he asked for 'postponement' instead of 'commutation'. He again raised the issue, seemingly under pressure, during his visit to the Viceroy four days ago, but perfunctorily. Now that there are strong rumours that the execution of these three revolutionaries may not even be postponed, he has today written a letter to the Viceroy. But the language of the letter refers to the 'public demand' and 'assurance of the revolutionary party' as grounds for review of the 'death sentence' rather than his own conviction, compassion and appeal. Nearly at the end of the letter he has written: 'Execution is an irretrievable act. If you think there is the slightest chance of error of judgement, I would urge you to suspend for further review an act that is beyond recall.'[64] It is doubtful if this letter can have any decisive influence on the Viceroy on clemency or even 'postponement', given his strong conviction on the issue as the head of a colonial government.

BHAGAT SINGH HANGED

March 23, 1931, Lahore: By now, Bhagat Singh has become a household name in the country. He defied the might of the British Empire. A young man well-read, with a distinct political philosophy of his own, self-less, public spirited, and fiercely patriotic, Bhagat Singh stood distinct from most others, even amongst the idealist revolutionaries.

Since his arrest in the central legislature building in Delhi, Bhagat Singh was tortured in the prison. In captivity, he resorted to a long spell of hunger strike, demanding equal rights for Indian and British political prisoners. Bhagat Singh was tried for both killing of Saunders and also hurling of bombs in the Central legislature building. He was awarded death penalty.

Today, this courageous son of mother India and darling of the masses was sent to the gallows. According to government sources, the execution was carried out this evening. Fearing public unrest, his mortal body was secretly cremated by the police near Ferozepur, on the bank of river Sutlej in the night.[65] Two of his other associates, Sukhdev and Rajguru, were also executed on the same day.

As the news spread, large number of people thronged at the funeral site and tried to collect the sacred 'remains'. A pall of gloom and anger has descended on India. His legacy is certain to prompt youth of India to keep fighting for India's independence.

Did Gandhi Do Enough To Save Bhagat Singh?

March 24, 1931, New Delhi: Indians reacted with hurt and anger to the news of execution of Bhagat Singh and his associates. Hurt because their own leaders did little to save the lives of these patriots and angry at the British regime. Demonstrations were held across the country.

In Amitsar, there was a mammoth gathering at Jallianwalabagh and police was attacked individually and collectively. In Peshawar, there was complete bandh. In the morning there were several processions in the city. In the afternoon 1,200 people assembled in Shahibag. A large meeting was held in Sadar Bazar and speeches were delivered exhorting the youth to emulate Bhagat Singh's example. In Bombay, half of the mills were closed. In Karachi 15,000 people attended a public meeting.[66]

There is a pervasive feeling in the country that the precious lives of Bhagat Singh, Rajguru and Sukhdev could have been saved, had Gandhi taken up the matter in earnest with Irwin. After all, only about a fortnight before their execution, he signed a momentous pact with the Viceroy, and he could have asked for clemency to them. Subhas had urged Gandhi to broach the matter with the Viceroy as the execution would be against the spirit, if not the letter of the Delhi pact with Irwin. But Gandhi seemed reluctant to tie up the two issues—he felt the freedom of India was more important than the savings these three young lives. Many disagreed with him on this—they felt the two were not mutually exclusive issues and certainly his words would have weighed with the Viceroy. Some analysts say that he was not convinced to take up the issue as he has been against violence as a matter of principle. At the later stage when roars of protests were raised against his indifference, he wrote to the Viceroy but ironically on 23rd March 1931, the very day on which Bhagat Singh was hanged. And even that letter was couched in such cautious wordings that it could not be presumed to constitute a simple clean appeal.

Even after the hanging, the public criticisms are continuing unabated. Gandhi has been facing protesters at several places. While travelling to Karachi by train to attend a Congress session, Gandhi had to get down at Malir, a rail station 15 miles away from Karachi, to avoid an angry demonstration.

Gandhi, Vallabhbhai Greeted With Black Flag

March 25, 1931, Karachi: The Congress session is about to begin here. The people of the city are hurt and angry over the execution of Bhagat Singh and his colleagues. As Congress leaders keep arriving in this port city, popular emotions are on display. Gandhi and Vallabhbhai Patel, the president-elect, were greeted with black flags. It is evident that the recent agreement between Gandhi and Irwin and the prospect of a progress in constitutional reforms has been overshadowed by the public wrath over Congress failure to save the precious life of Bhagat Singh.

Bhagat Singh's Spirit Is Unconquerable: Subhas

March 27, 1931, Karachi: Subhas has addressed the All-India Naujawan Bharat Sabha in the aftermath of the execution of Bhagat Singh. Whereas Gandhi has been reticent in expressing a favourable opinion of the martyr as he did not approve of violence in any form,

Subhas is always in unconditional votary of patriotic nationalistic spirit, irrespective of the means of its expression. In a moving tribute paid to the departed soul, Subhas said the spirit of revolt that Bhagat Singh symbolised has taken possession of the country from one end to another. Calling that spirit unconquerable, Subhas said the flame it has lit will not die. The government is viewing Subhas's statement warily.

'Independence' Shelved, New Aim Is 'Dominion Status'

March 29-31, 1931, Karachi: The Congress annual session is in progress here. Vallabhbhai is presiding. Nationwide grief due to Bhagat Singh's execution has cast its shadow here. A strong contingent of 'Khudai Khidmatgar' from the NWFP is attending. They gave an exemplary account of themselves in the non-violent civil disobedience programme. The most important issue before the session is the recently-concluded settlement between Gandhi and Viceroy Irwin.

Generally speaking, the pact has been viewed favourably by the masses who are unable to understand intricacies. After all, it is the first time that the mighty British Empire came down from its high pedestal and concluded an agreement with an Indian political organisation. However, those who can read the 'fine prints' have deep-seated reservations and they include many middle and senior Congress leaders. In particular, the left wing leaders spearheaded by Subhas have strong views.

There is a fundamental issue involved in the pact. By it, the Congress which earlier demanded 'complete independence', has climbed down and agreed to take part in the round table, keeping 'dominion status' as the objective. To avoid certain embarrassment, Vallabhbhai skipped the last year's 'Lahore resolution' on 'complete independence' and advanced the cause of 'dominion status'. He also maintained emphasis on social and economic issues, ostensibly to divert delegates' attention away from this sensitive issue.

The Congress official machinery has been projecting the 'pact' as a major achievement in a bid to getting it endorsed here.

Congress Puts Its Seal On Gandhi-Irwin Settlement

March 30, 1931, Karachi: The Congress session in progress here has approved the Gandhi-Irwin agreement, though not before encountering some measure of opposition. Senior leaders like Jamnadas Mehta and Swami Govindnand, in their addresses, strongly opposed the pact. Even younger leaders like Jawaharlal and Subhas had their reservations. However, they eventually decided to rely upon the political acumen and far sight of Gandhi.

The Congress Party, when deciding to take a call on the pact, seemed to adopt a similar approach. A typical reflection of this approach was seen when a veteran leader, Satyamurti while addressing the issue in the Subjects Committee meeting, pleaded that the Congress should accept the agreement, not because it was satisfactory, but because Gandhi agreed to it and the Congress has full confidence in him.

The left wing, led by Subhas, made it clear to the Subjects Committee that they did not approve the settlement. However, in view of present circumstances, they would refrain from dividing the house. With this, the deck was clear for the approval. Today the Congress passed a resolution endorsing the Gandhi-Irwin settlement and authorised Gandhi to represent it at the next round table conference.

Congress Survives Fallout Of Martyr's Execution

March 31, 1931, Karachi: The fallout of Bhagat Singh's execution on the Congress session could have been severe. But the Congress organisers have managed the issue. They brought the martyr's father to the session and made him speak in support of Congress leaders. The Congress also passed a resolution praising the courage and self-sacrifice by Bhagat Singh while condemning all acts of violence.

Gandhi Sole Representative Of Congress At Round Table

April 2, 1931: The Congress Working Committee has elected Gandhi as the sole representative of the Congress in the forthcoming round table conference and Gandhi has accepted the offer.

Political observers say this may not be a wise decision as Gandhi may have to face large number of pro-government delegates opposing him all alone in a place and arrangement determined by the government. Moreover, he has many capable nationalist leaders of all communities of proven merit to lend him able support. But the 'solo mission' seems to have become a fait accompli.

DISTRICT MAGISTRATE SHOT DEAD IN DAY LIGHT

April 7, 1931, Midnapore: Bimal Dasgupta and Jyoti Jiban Ghosh, two revolutionaries have killed Mr Paddy, the district magistrate of Midnapore in Bengal. The district magistrate was on a visit to the educational fair at Midnapore Collegiate School, when the revolutionaries shot him dead. Bimal and Jyoti are reported to be members of Bengal Volunteers. In the provincial capital Calcutta, the government is deeply vexed and contemplating serious counter measures.

Willingdon Takes Over As New Viceroy

April 1931, New Delhi: While India is in a political flux, an important change has occurred in New Delhi. Lord Irwin, the architect of the pact with Gandhi, has handed over charge to Lord Willingdon.

Censure Motion Against President Is Defeated

AITUC Breaks Yet Again – Red TUC Is The New Baby

July 4, 1931, Calcutta: The AITUC session is in progress in the University Institute Hall here and Subhas is presiding. Some Left leaders have seceded and set up the Red TUC. Even last year, a split had occurred in the AITUC in its Nagpur session, when NM Joshi group had seceded from AITUC. Jawaharlal had presided over that session.

It seems the trade union movement is increasingly coming under the influence of the Leftist leaders and ideology, thereby making the

Congress' grip to slacken. The leftist trade unions see both the colonial rulers as also domestic capitalist as their enemies, unlike the Congress, which believes that both Indian labour and Indian capitalists share common interests and ought to be partners in progress. Although Congress is trying to accommodate diverse groups on its platform, the trade union leadership is getting fractured.

The proximate reason for the current split centred round the question of who was the real representative of Girni Kamgar Union of the Bombay Textile Workers. Two groups, viz. followers of MN Roy and the official Communist Party, staked their claims.

After the Credential Committee of the Trade Union Congress gave the verdict that the Roy group was entitled to represent the union in the Trade Union Congress, the other group decided to battle it out. On their behalf, BT Ranadive brought a 'no confidence' by way of censure against the president but it was defeated by 26-24 votes. This acted as the trigger for the current split.

The followers of the official Communist Party walked out and set up a parallel body in the name of Red Trade Union Congress.

YOUNG DINESH CLIMBS GALLOWS WITH EQUANIMITY

July 7, 1931, Calcutta: Of the three revolutionaries who attacked Writers Building in Calcutta, only Dinesh had survived. He was tried by the court and awarded death sentence. A highly spirited young man of only 19 years of age Dinesh was hanged today.

Like many other young men before him, Dinesh has sacrificed his young and promising life for the cause of India's freedom, defying British punishments.

In view of the extreme anger of the British regime on these three revolutionaries, few dared to visit Dinesh in his cell to avoid the displeasure of the government. However, this young man's joy knew no bounds when the charismatic Congress leader Subhas Bose visited him in his solitary cell.

He reportedly took lot of heart from this meeting before he went to the gallows with equanimity.

Communists Call Congress 'Flag Bearer Of Capitalists'

It seems obvious that a significant section of the trade union workers are coming under the influence of the Communists. Possibly, this is due to a perception that in situations involving conflicts with Indian industrialists, the Communists-led trade unions are decisively siding with the workers. The Communists have been castigating the AITUC leaders belonging to the Congress as the flag-bearers of the Indian capitalists. They accuse these leaders of leveraging the mass movements to extract commercial concessions and advantages for the Indian capitalists and zamindars from the British government. They say Congress leaders are mobilising the economic and political discontent of the peasantry, the lower middle class and the industrial workers eventually to serve the interests of the Indian industrialists and businessmen. Another dangerous accusation is that the Congress leaders organise the mass movements at the behest of Indian capitalists and deplorably abandon these midway, when they begin to look vast and dangerous. They feel the Congress leaders, contrary to their public posture, do not want to drive the British out but need their continued presence to control and exploit the poor masses as the middle classes still do not feel themselves up to that task. All these vest the Communists with the responsibilities to organise workers, peasantry and other vulnerable sections of the Indian people to wage a real fight against the British. Congress, they argue, is a sham. Growing number of trade union members are subscribing to these hypotheses these days. The ranks of the Communist-led trade unions are swelling.

Unhappy With Official Breaches, Gandhi Meets Viceroy

July 18, 1931, Simla: Gandhi is here to hold discussions with the Viceroy about several instances of breaches of the 'pact' between him and the former Viceroy on the part of the government. While the Congress has suspended the civil disobedience, the government has not been discharging its obligations. Many farmers in Gujarat have approached the Congress to get back their confiscated properties. There is also wide scale violation, especially in Bengal, of the obligation to release the political prisoners. In the ordinary course these issues ought to have been resolved first, in a spirit of cooperation. But Willingdon, the new Viceroy, is clearly demonstrating a hardened and non-cooperative attitude. Gandhi visited Simla last month as well and held discussion with HW Emerson, Home Secretary on breaches of settlement. He is back here to pursue the same agenda. Having reached here on 13th, he held discussions with James Crerar, Home Member yesterday. Today he pursued the matter with the Viceroy. Willingdon has asked for details and promised enquiries in specific cases. Political observers say Willingdon does not want to concede anything more than what is absolutely essential. He is in no hurry to establish his government's goodwill but he would refrain from doing things that can make Gandhi reconsider attending the round table.

Communal Riot Breaks Out – Police Looks The Other Way

August 1931, Chittagong: Chittagong has been volatile in recent times. The revolutionary activities have been on the rise. The revolutionaries, swearing allegiance to both Jugantar and Anushilan Samity have been active here. Since, most of these activists are Hindus, there has been a silent antagonism towards them in some sections of the Muslims and the latter have been sympathetic to the government. After the revolutionaries in Chittagong killed a pro-government Muslim officer, the incident assumed a communal colour. With the silent acquiescence of the government, a severe communal riot has broken out here. The police are indifferent as the fire of the communal hatred has been devouring innocent lives and their properties.

Gandhi Hurries To Second Round Table Conference

August 25-27, 1931, Simla: There have been several instances of breaches of Gandhi-Irwin agreement and excesses by provincial governments. This was Gandhi's second visit to Viceroy Willingdon to bring such cases for redressal. Gandhi has been accompanied by top Congress leaders like Jawaharlal, Vallabhbhai, Abdul Ghaffar Khan and MA Ansari in the summer capital. The intermittent violation of the 'agreement' had been making Gandhi and his colleagues take stock of a situation at intervals and also a final call on whether or not to attend the round table conference at all. The Viceroy, keen that Gandhi attends the round table, has extended the needed assurance. Both, the government and the Congress, have agreed to the continuation of the Delhi pact earlier signed.

The final decision has been taken. At the last moment Gandhi, with close colleagues have boarded the train. Gandhi is scheduled to start for Europe on 29th August from Bombay. Jawaharlal is accompanying him and would see his leader off at the Arabian sea.

Second Round Table Conference

Jawaharlal, Subhas Not Optimistic About Outcome

August 1931: The British Government has scheduled the second round table conference in London in the first week of the next month. This conference would be very different from the earlier one due to one single factor — participation by the Congress. Logically speaking, this raises the probability of a meaningful outcome.

There are conflicting views in India about the desirability and likely impact of Gandhi's participation. Some Congress leaders have expressed serious reservations and they have shared their mind with Gandhi. Subhas feels the conference would be attended by those chosen by the government and obviously, have loyalty to the government. Jawaharlal is of the opinion that Gandhi would be heavily outnumbered and fiercely opposed by a motley crowd of delegates who hardly represent the Indian masses. Large sections of Indian people, however, have lots of confidence in Gandhi's leadership and his ability to deliver. They feel Gandhi can use the conference to get them 'swaraj'.

On the eve of the second round table, political experts are not optimistic about Gandhi's success. They feel, Gandhi would make his debut in the conference with some pre-existing handicaps, though, of his own makings. First, by agreeing to participate, Gandhi has abandoned the Motilal report, which was the prime reason for the unprecedented civil disobedience movement. He has, thus, committed the Congress to accept a constitution that would evolve through consensus in the conference. Second, the proposal of the conference implied an important role of the government, whether as a moderator or arbiter, of several divergent views and demands. Against this backdrop, the demand for 'independence' seems impracticable. Then, by signing the pact with Irwin, he has already conceded the demand for separate electorates, which would also limit his options. Last but not the least, acting diplomatically, the government has, through the decisions by the previous conference, pre-determined the agenda of the second conference along with the ground rules to be followed. Reopening fundamental issues or starting a de novo examination of them may be almost impossible.

British Government In Neck Deep Economic Trouble

September 1, 1931, London: As the second round table conference is set to begin, the world is in the throes of severe economic depression and Britain is severely affected. It may be noted that the British industry and business have lost a chunk of export market in India due to the Congress agitation and boycott of the Manchester cotton. The annual cloth exports from Britain to India have plummeted by about 80% to 5.5 million in 1931 from 26 million in 1929. There is considerable bitterness on this count against Congress in the economic and political circles in Britain. As such British interests, commercial and political, are least receptive to Indian nationalist demands.

Second Round Table Begins

September 7, 1931, London: The second round table conference has started today. Many delegates who had attended the first round have turned up this time and there are some new members. Gandhi would be the most prominent amongst all of them. There are representations from Congress, Muslim League, Liberal Party,

Depressed Hindus, Caste Hindus, Muslims, Sikhs, Parsees, Indian Christians, Europeans, rulers of states and officials of British Indian government.

I'm Wearing The Dress Of My Principals, The People Of India: Gandhi

September 12, 1931, London: Gandhi had started from Bombay by SS Rajputana on 29 August and reached London via Marseilles today. In the cold wintry European weather, his attires consists of a loin cloth with a shawl and a pair of chappals in his feet. This fetched him several enquiries even before he could open his mouth on important issues. To this he responded in his characteristic manner, saying: 'But I am here on a great and special mission, and my loin cloth, if you choose so to describe it, is the dress of my principals, the people of India.'[67] He seems to have sent a simple and clear message to all those who care to listen, that he would go to any extent to protect the interests of the vast masses of India in the ensuing conference.

Gandhi's Maiden Speech Makes Delegates Uneasy

September 15, 1931, London: In the first round table, Gandhi had exercised significant influence both due to his 'image' and absence. His long years of credentials as a mass leader, backed by the recent salt movement and pact with the Viceroy have created a halo around his name. Today, he delivered his maiden speech in the Federal Structure Committee, where he received almost a standing welcome, particularly from the Indian delegates.

Gandhi made it clear at the outset that he has a different mission and stand than the rest: 'I…know that there are fundamental differences of opinion between the government and the Congress and it is possible that there are vital differences between my colleagues and myself'.[68] As to what would be his role in the conference he said, 'I am but a poor humble agent acting on behalf of the Indian National Congress'.[69] Then he proudly declared the unassailable stature of the Congess, saying it is the oldest political organisation in India and 'It claims to represent all

Indian interests and all classes...above all, the Congress represents, in its essence, the dumb, semi-starved millions…in its 700,000 villages, no matter whether they come from what is called British India or what is called Indian India'.[70]

Going ahead, he revealed to the assembly the mandate that he has carried from the Congress, which happened to be its resolution in Karachi session held earlier this year and that mandate had as its underlying the 'complete independence' of India.

Giving a clear signal that he would refuse to get tied to the 'framework' that the government has carefully crafted through the first round of the round table, he made it clear that he has already studied the provisional conclusions arrived at by several committees and also the statement of the British prime minister, giving the considered policy of the government but felt that 'it falls far short of what is aimed at and claimed by the Congress'.[71] He brought in more clarity saying that the Congress expected complete independence, though it has no intention to sever connection with Britain. He said, 'Congress contemplates a partnership and connection with British people as such as can exist between two equals.'

Gandhi assured he would provide the conference with the Congress viewpoint on various issues as these are taken up for deliberations in the days ahead and expressed his desire: 'I would love to go away from the shores of the British Isle with the conviction that there was to be an honourable and equal partnership between Great Britain and India' and that the consummation would be reached during his stay.

According to political observers, Gandhi, by demanding a paradigm shift in the thinking and approach of the concerned parties, has made them uneasy. They have turned up here with the expectations of achieving some degrees of 'constitutional reforms' and of 'course' not 'independence'. The rulers of states are feeling uneasy about his suggestion that Congress represented the vast poor people of the Indian India.

Most of the delegates from British India are unhappy about his projecting the Congress as the representatives of all interests and classes, which threaten their very relevance. As regards the British, they are irritated and suppressing their anger in the cloak of civility.

Peace Talks In London, Prisoners Killed In Bengal

September 16, 1931, Kharagpur: Even though there has been a broad political settlement between Gandhi and the Viceroy, and currently the round table is in progress, there have been practically no changes in the hard attitude of the Bengal government. Thousands of political prisoners continue to languish in prisons, many of them being under trial and held in detention camps under unsatisfactory conditions. For want of space, the government has put many detainees in Buxar and Hijli jails near Kharagpur. Today, the police committed grave atrocities on unarmed prisoners. In a highhanded act, they opened several rounds of fire without provocation, killing two prisoners, Santosh Kumar Mitra and Tarakeswar Sengupta, and injuring several others. As the news flashed, condemnations followed from all over the country.

'Are We Chosen Ones Of The Nation Or The Government?'

September 17, 1931, London: The conference has resumed the sub-committees with some new members. Thus, in the Federal Structure Committee new members like Gandhi, Malaviya and the Maharaja of Baroda have joined. Leaving little scope for any new member to revisit the issue settled in the first round, the chairman of the committee in a true businesslike fashion, has urged the members to deliberate on various issues like: strength and composition of the federal legislature, election of the members, relations between two chambers of legislatures, distribution of financial resources between federation and its units, ministry and its relations with legislatures, distribution of legislative powers between federal and provincial legislatures, applicability of federal legislatures to the states, administrative relations between the federal government, the states and the provincial government, federal court etc.

Initially, some members made some laudatory comments about Gandhi's special place in India and amongst Indians. Some expressed the hope that the outcome of this conference will have high sanctity and validity because of Gandhi's participation and his representative capacity. However, as he refused to get tied to the routine stuff and began to raise fundamental issues, such positive vibes and support began to disappear. A schism has gradually been growing between Gandhi and most others. Gandhi has been demanding a special status in the negotiation on the ground that he is the spokesperson for the Congress Party, which happens to be the most representative of all Indians — irrespective of caste and creed, whereas the rest are speaking only about narrow, sectarian interests.

Also, other delegates, besides being sectarian or communal, cannot claim to be the true representatives of their constituencies, as they were nominated by the government. So even from this angle, Gandhi as the prime leader of the Indian National Congress, has greater rights to speak on behalf of all these groups. Today while speaking at the second meeting of the Federal Structure Committee, he observed, 'I have endeavoured to study, as I had not done before the list of the delegates...' and it, he said, gave him the feeling of oppression that, 'we are not the chosen ones of the nation...but...of the Government'.[72] The rest of the delegates are quite unhappy about such attitude, which nullifies their authority and relevance. Therefore, amongst the delegates, Gandhi is commanding little support and he is crusading to register his views.

Gandhi In Summit Isolation

September 1931, London: Maintaining that he is the only proper representative of all Indians — of both British India and the native states, Gandhi wants the British government to primarily consider the view of the Congress with regard to the new constitution. Gandhi is asserting that the Congress is not a communal organisation and that it is a determined enemy of communalism in any shape and form.

Gandhi laments that despite being such a comprehensive representative of the Indian people, the government is treating the Congress as one of the parties! Other delegates are not the least amused. An ego clash has already occurred and it is aggravating.

There also exists a fundamental difference in approaches between Gandhi and the rest. Gandhi is bound by the Congress' goal of 'independence' for the country and his participation is influenced accordingly. The communal and sectarian leaders, on the other hand, want to establish the rights of their community ahead of others. To most of them, 'independence' does not seem to be a priority, at least now. Rather, they may prefer the British to remain in the country, facilitate the re-distribution of political rights in their favour and protect the re-alignment for some time. Such conflicts in perspectives are operating, along with the ego-clashes to render any meaningful deliberations impossible.

Communal Issue – The Knot Refuses To Open

October 1931, London: The conference has appointed several sub-committees to inquire into and build up consensus on a number of areas like federal structure, minorities, federal finance, franchise, states inquiry. Gandhi is a member of the first two. Three committees, viz. franchise committee, federal finance committee and states inquiry committee, have drafted their reports. Two important committees, viz. on 'Federal structure' and 'minorities', both of which have Gandhi as member, are facing stiff roadblocks in arriving at a consensus. There has been unending discussion of the communal problem and several meetings of the minorities committee were held but so far there has been no effective outcome. Representatives of Muslims, Sikhs, Anglo Indians, Indian Christians, European and Depressed classes are having important differences with Gandhi.

Those Present Do Not Deserve To Be Here, Those Who Deserve Are Absent

October 8, 1931, London: The Minorities Committee is finding it exceedingly difficult to sort out the communal question. The reasons are not far to seek. It involves the rights of the communities to be present in the legislature and every community, bereft of a national perspective, wants a bigger slice for itself. Gandhi tried to bring about a reconciliation, but without success. Consensus seems impossible. While addressing the committee, Gandhi gave vent to both his disappointment and diagnosis for the impasse.

He said the cause of failure in talks lay in the very composition of the Indian delegation. Clarifying, he said those who are present are not the elected representatives of their communities while those who ought to have been here are absent.[73] Giving up any hope for a breakthrough, he has suggested that the committee proceedings be adjourned. In the meanwhile, the fundamentals of the constitution may be worked out. If no solution to the communal question is found till then, the matter may be referred to a Judicial Commission through a provision in the constitution.

According to reports, Gandhi's observations have not been taken kindly by other delegates. Their antagonism against him has grown.

National Government Wins Landslide Victory, Conservatives Sparkle

October 1931, London: The 'National Government' comprising the National Labour, Conservatives and the Liberals led by Ramsay MacDonald has earned a landslide victory in the general election held. Though Ramsay MacDonald of the National Labour continues to be the head of the government, the Conservatives have lion's share of the MPs. Out of a total of 554 seats won by the alliance, the Conservatives have more than 400 candidates. From 1929, when the Labour came to power till recently, either Labour or the National Labour had major say in formulating policies including for colonies such as India. But after this election, the Conservatives may assert much greater influence. The result of this election is likely to have impact on both the deliberations in the ongoing round table and also the policies that would be pursued by Viceroy Willingdon in India now on.

Why Bring In 'Crown' At The End Of Every Sentence?

October 23, 1931, London: While taking part in the deliberations over the issue of the proposed federal court and the terms of appointment of the judges, Gandhi criticised the fellow delegates as they kept on debating over such routine issues like retirement age etc, and inviting the wisdom of the government to provide the guideline. By attacking their attitude and the mode of deliberation, he strongly put forth his views: 'We bring in the Crown at the end of almost every sentence. I must confess that, according to the conception of the Congress, there is no question of the Crown. India desires complete independence; and if India enjoys complete independence, whoever the supreme authority there may be, that supreme authority will be responsible for the appointment of Judges and several other matters which today belong to the Crown'.[74]

Political analysts are of the view that Gandhi's uncompromising views such as these, and his attacks on the servile attitude of the delegates are making him distant from and unpopular to both the British and most of the fellow Indian delegates.

'Emergency Power Ordinances' Cooking In Viceroy's Lab?

October 1931, New Delhi: In spite of signing a peace agreement with Gandhi, the government has not initiated sufficient follow up action especially in provinces like Bengal, NWFP and UP. In Bengal, there is practically no benefit to the political prisoners, most of them continue to languish in prison under severe repression. This has been spiralling revolutionary activities in turn.

In the far NWFP, the government has been revengeful to the Khan Brothers and the large number of Red Shirt volunteers. Such policies have been creating and spreading mistrust and disquiet in that border region. In the United Provinces, many farmers have not been able to pay the 'rent' or even half of it as the prices of agricultural produces have suffered massive decline due to economic recession all around. The government's determined bid to recover the dues has only been hardening the farmers' resolve to resist.

With such political situation in India, the feelers from London about the round table reaching the Viceroy are not encouraging either. The prospect of a settlement on the 'minorities' and 'communal' questions seems to be impossible, making one thing uncertain — continuation of the British rule more or less in the present form. There are reports that Willingdon has begun to prepare for the post-round table scenario accordingly. He wants to 'hard tackle' the Congress. His office is reportedly preparing a series of Emergency Ordinances that would confer the government with enough powers to achieve such a purpose. The recent electoral success of the Conservative Party in Britain is helping matters.

Gandhi, Ambedkar At Two Ends Of The Spectrum

November 13, 1931, London: The minorities committee has failed to reach a consensus even after prolonged deliberations. The committee was supposed to submit its views by yesterday to the British Prime Minister, but failed due to the simmering dissensions within the members. On the whole, there has been a growing consolidation of interest groups against Gandhi. The Muslims, Depressed Classes, a section of Indian Christians, Anglo Indians and Europeans have combined together and prepared a joint declaration presenting their consensus views on the rights for various minority groups. This provides for inter alia separate electorate for Hindu Depressed Classes besides the Muslims. Aga Khan, who presented the declaration stressed that this was a composite offer — all parts of it would stand or fall together.

Gandhi has found the offer unacceptable. He felt the provision for 'separate electorate', claimed for the Depressed Classes, amounted to vivisection of the Hindu community. While appreciating that Ambedkar might have undergone several bitter experiences in his personal life, Gandhi urged him to adopt a broader view. Gandhi is of the opinion that the segregation and ill treatment of the Dalits or untouchables has been a grave sin on the part of the caste Hindus and they must redeem themselves by uplifting the Depressed Classes and establishing an equitable social order. The present proposal, of separate electorate, instead of addressing one of the core malaises in the Hindus, would attach a permanent tag of indignity to them, which Gandhi would not want at any cost, including even the freedom of India. His assertion has, therefore, been very forceful.

On his part Ambedkar, the leader of the Depressed Classes, has found Gandhi's approach completely unreasonable and unacceptable.

He feels Gandhi has been doing great disservice to the Depressed Classes by his objection to their demand for special political rights. He is particularly peeved that while ready to concede such rights to the Muslims, Gandhi was bent upon depriving the Depressed Classes, the most vulnerable of all Indians. He has concluded that Gandhi has become so much obsessed with fighting against the minority rights that he has even lost sight of the issue of 'independence' of the country, which is the professed goal of the Congress. He has harsh words for Gandhi, whom he finds as egotist, tactless and unsuitable for negotiation.

With the two leaders holding such completely divergent perspectives on the issue of minority rights, the reaching of a consensus has become virtually impossible. Critics say enough bad blood has been created between various groups and that no chance of any kind of reconciliation has been left, except through arbitration. In the circumstances, the Chairman has announced HM Government's resolve to go ahead and produce a constitution of India to redeem its pledge to the people of India. He asserted that the government will not allow communal differences to hinder this process.

Gandhi Crosses Sword With British PM On Communal Question

November 13, 1931, London: Prime Minister Ramsay MacDonald has endorsed the 'minorities pact', much to the chagrin of Gandhi. His argument seems to be based on the fact that a consensus on the communal question has been eluding Indian politicians for decades.

As such, when the delegates have worked out a solution that was acceptable to nearly all, it merited support from the government. On this issue, Gandhi crossed swords with him saying Congress was prepared to accept any solution that was acceptable to Hindus, Muslims and Sikhs. However, he said, Congress would not be a party to special electorate for any other minorities.

He once again reminded every one that Congress alone was the real representative of Indians of all castes, communities and creeds, saying that it represented 85% Indians including both British India provinces and Indian states. Clearly, his aggressive stand has alienated him further from other delegates.

'If A Further Ordeal Of Fire Has To Be Our Lot, So Be It!'

November 30, 1931, London: The round table is holding its plenary session. Gandhi, the lone representative of Congress, was isolated almost strategically by the government in connivance with sections of the delegation from India. Notwithstanding, Gandhi has put forth his firm, considered and statesman like views on various issues like provincial autonomy, defence, external affairs, etc. He, however, did not fail to note that despite extraordinary merits in his suggestions on various issues those were treated just like one amongst several — and this was done on purpose to demoralise him. Though disappointed with the government's handling of the proceedings, he refused to abandon hope. He declared his resolve that he would strain every nerve for an honourable settlement for his country. Because, he said, it was no joy or comfort for him to lead his countrymen to a hard fight like the one just concluded. But if that was imposed, the nonviolent warrior warned, he would not shy away: 'If a further ordeal of fire has to be our lot... I shall approach that with the greatest joy'.Political analysts are considering Gandhi's statement as significant and one that could put both the British and the British Indian government in a battle mode.

My Path May Be Opposite, Still I Offer You Thanks: Gandhi

December 1, 1931, London: Prime Minister Ramsay Macdonald in his concluding speech gave glimpses of HM Government's thinking, formulated on the basis of the deliberations held in the two conferences. He made it clear that to be entitled to responsible government, Indian political parties will have to settle the 'communal question'. Further, responsible government at the federal level, he clarified, will be possible provided both British India and the Indian states agree to join a federal structure. He added that key portfolios like defence and external affairs will rest with the Governor General.

Gandhi proposed the vote of thanks. By now he was completely disillusioned. May be he recounted repeated warnings by his deputies, like Jawaharlal and Subhas in India, against coming to the round table. However, he extended the customary thanks as a good guest would do to his host. His final words, though couched in high ethical pack, sounded like a grim, sad parting message. He said, in all probability he had come to the parting of ways: 'I do not know in what direction my path will lie, but it does not matter to me in what direction that path lies. Even then, although I may have to go in an exactly opposite direction you are still entitled to a vote of thanks from me from the bottom of my heart.'[75]

Imperialist Designs Have Aborted Round Table Meet

December 1, 1931: The second round table has come to an end without achieving its purpose — to come to a consensus on several key issues of the new constitution. Critics are not surprised. They say such an outcome was only expected, given the true motive of the British government. At this juncture they had no intention, whatsoever, of granting India self-government, let alone independence.

They achieved their hidden goal by using most of their nominated delegates as pawns and playing one against the other. The government manipulated the proceedings. Delegates were made to exhaust themselves in relatively minor matters and the core issue of independence of India, championed by the Congress, was lost sight of. Especially on the issue of separate electorates of the minorities, emotions were stoked, egos clashed and bitter acrimony swept a rational discourse.

At the end, MacDonald announced appointment of three exploratory committees, viz. States Inquiry Committee led by JCC Davidson, Federal Finance Committee led by Lord Percy, and Franchise Committee led by Lord Lothian. These committees are scheduled to visit India to examine relevant issues so that the government can draft a single Government of India Bill.

With no consensus having been achieved amongst delegates on vital issues, the prospect of achieving dominion status in near future, let alone independence, is looking bleak. Gandhi has emerged a frustrated man. The only party happy is the British government. Now it is in a driver's seat. It has already demonstrated that Congress' claim that it represents the entire India is hollow, and that political India is deeply divided and, therefore, the British Raj continues to be crucial to run the government.

Without Muslim Cooperation Any New Constitution Will Breakdown: Jinnah

December 1931: The second round table has concluded without achieving its central objectives.

Jinnah's role this time was considerably less than in the first round table. All eyes were set upon Gandhi, who had a crucial role to play in every committee. Jinnah, on his part, tried to negotiate with Gandhi to arrive at an agreement on the communal issue. On his part, he was inflexible about separate electorate for Muslims, and statutory majority of Muslims in Bengal and Punjab. He carried out several dialogues with Gandhi, alone as well as with other Muslim leaders like Shafi and Aga Khan, but they failed to reach consensus.

In the course of the present conference, Jinnah had grown suspicious about the intentions of the Congress and the British government. His cynicism was, somehow, evident and he was generally perceived as 'rigid', even by the government. According to some reports, he has become dismayed and may not even return to India from London. He is reported to have expressed his distinct feeling that there was no hope of unity and that Gandhi did not want it. Possibly he anticipates that he might be excluded from the ongoing process of 'constitutional reforms'. Anxious, lest the interest of his community is sacrificed by future negotiators, Jinnah has issued a threat to both, the Congress and the British government, saying that without the cooperation of the Muslim community, any new constitution would breakdown 'within a week'.[76] Even though he failed to hog the limelight during the pendency of the second round table, Jinnah has returned to the heart of his Muslim constituency by this loaded threat — he has ensured that he continues to be viewed as the crusader for the Muslim cause, wherever he is.

Jawaharlal Arrested For Supporting 'No-rent' Campaign

December 26, 1931, Allahabad: With the failure of the second round table conference in London, things are taking a turn for the worse in India. Jawaharlal has been in UP in connection with organising the UP provincial Conference in Etwah this week. However, it was postponed in view of Gandhi's impending arrival in Bombay. Today, Jawaharlal, along with Sherwani, president of the provincial Congress, boarded a train for Bombay. Their train was halted in Idratganj station and both were arrested. Suspecting that they could be spreading 'no rent' campaign in the province, the UP government had ordered them not to leave Allahabad.

Gandhi Addresses Sea Of People In Azad Maidan

December 28, 1931, Bombay: After the second round table conference ended, Gandhi left London on 5th December and resumed his home journey via Paris, Geneva and Italy. In Italy, he was received by the country's Prime Minister Benito Mussolini. In each of these places, numerous people were eager to see him. His long march to Dandi and the salt movement gave him publicity across the world and many people were attracted to his strategy of non-violent movements to achieve political aims. SS Pilsna, ie. the ship he travelled in reached Bombay port today.

Although Gandhi was upset by the failure of the conference, the common people, unable to appreciate the finer aspects of the negotiations, gathered in tens of thousands in Bombay to extend a warm, hearty, hero's welcome to him. Gandhi addressed the mammoth gathering in the evening at the Azad Maidan.

Besides common people, top Congress leaders from several parts of the country have converged here to welcome and get guidance from him. During his absence, Willingdon had stepped up pressure on political workers and activities, often in violation of the Gandhi-Irwin pact. The government issued draconian Ordinances in Bengal, NWFP and United Provinces.

Subhas has come over here to receive Gandhi and also discuss a few critical problems relating to Bengal. The failure of the 'round table' and the prospect of a revival of the civil disobedience movement as well as the likely government reaction to it were discussed too. These issues pose great uncertainty for India's political future. As of now, more than feeling disappointed over the barren round table, the framing of the future strategy has emerged as a priority for the Congress leadership.

How Do I Interpret These Ordinances? Gandhi Cables Willingdon

December 29, 1931, Bombay: Gandhi has been informed by the Congress leaders as to how Viceroy Willingdon had begun to prepare for Ordinances for some of the provinces, right from October this year. The massive electoral success of the Conservative Party that month in Britain and the emerging indications of the failure of the round table conference may have contributed to his activism. Both Bengal and the NWFP have been heavily repressed. United Provinces have also earned the wrath of the government for the ongoing 'no rent' campaign in the countryside.

Considering these excesses as flagrant violation of the Gandhi-Irwin pact, Gandhi has today sent a 'wire' to Willingdon, asking for a clarification in his characteristic style. Referring to the Ordinances in these three provinces, the arrests, and atrocities he has asked: 'I do not know whether I am to regard these as indication that friendly relations between us are closed or whether you expect me still to see you and receive guidance from you as to the course I am to pursue in advising the Congress.'[77]

Congress Decides To Resume Civil Disobedience

January 1, 1932, Bombay: To Gandhi's wire, the Viceroy sent a reply making it clear that he will not be prepared to discuss with him any measures adopted in relation to Bengal, NWFP and UP which, he stated, were taken with full knowledge of HM Government. Against this background the Congress Working Committee met and adopted a lengthy resolution drafted by Gandhi himself, calling the nation to resume the civil disobedience movement.

Gandhi has also sent a rejoinder to the Viceroy, stating that if he refuses to discuss Ordinances in these three provinces, the nation will resort to civil disobedience.

Interview Under Threat Is Out Of Question

January 2, 1932, New Delhi: Viceroy Willingdon has rebuffed Gandhi in his reply to Gandhi's request for an interview to discuss Ordinances. He has made it clear that an interview under the threat of civil disobedience was out of question.

Subhas Arrested, Taken To Unknown Destination

January 2, 1932, Kalyan, Bombay: Subhas has been arrested aboard a train at Kalyan railway station on the outskirt of Bombay. He was on his way back to Calcutta after meeting Gandhi. No warrant was served on him. It is learnt that there is no specific charge against him and he has been arrested under the infamous Regulation III of 1818 Act. Subhas has been taken to an unknown destination to avoid public attention.

It appears that his arrest is a pre-meditated plan of the government, which foresees an inevitable relapse of the civil disobedience movement in the aftermath of the failed round table conference.

The government is clearly uncomfortable at the prospect of a mass leader like Subhas being free amongst the public in such an eventuality. It is also being heard that the Bengal government is insisting Subhas be put in a prison outside Bengal. The provincial government clearly wants to avoid popular unrest and movement.

Struggle Will Be Non-violent: Gandhi Assures Willingdon

January 3, 1932, Bombay: Gandhi has wired the Viceroy regretting the government's decision and assured that the resurrected civil disobedience will be a non-violent struggle.

GANDHI ARRESTED

Government Shows 'Zero Tolerance' Approach

January 4, 1932, Bombay: Since his return from Europe, Gandhi did not have much time to confer with party colleagues. Today he has been arrested. The government does not want to take any risk by giving time and scope for the civil disobedience movement to resurface, at least not with the vehemence of the past years. It is on a risk mitigation exercise. Accordingly, it has begun to place top leaders of the Congress behind bars with alacrity. Subhas was an early victim. Rajendra Prasad has been arrested today at Patna. Vallabhbhai has been lodged in Yeravada jail. In Naini, Jawaharlal is serving two years of rigorous imprisonment. The government has promulgated four Ordinances—Emergency Power Ordinances, Unlawful Instigation Ordinance, Molestation and Boycotting Ordinance, Unlawful Association Ordinance and is planning to use them to facilitate brutal suppression of new protests. It has declared Congress organisations illegal.

Since Gandhi had left for the round table, an important change took place in Delhi. Lord Willingdon took over from Lord Irwin as Viceroy, and he has been in favour of pursuing a tough line in handling the Congress agitations.

Critics say, offering the bait of participation in the round table, and now crushing any attempts at resurrecting civil disobedience are all parts of a deep political intrigue. By making Gandhi participate in the round table, it has demonstrated that Indian polity is fractured. So noisy have been the differences between different interest groups that the demand for Independence, which ought to have been the Congress' core claim, has gone under the carpet. Having achieved these objectives, it wants to nip the resumption of the civil disobedience movement in the bud.

Jinnah To Settle Down In England

January 1932, London: After the second round table concluded without consensus among the Indian delegates on the key issues, Jinnah is a disillusioned man. In the first round table, he was one of the prime movers and went to the extent of assuring the government that the absence of the Congress really did not matter and ought not to come in the way of going ahead with the conference. However, instead of taking decisive actions in the conference, the government planned another round table and went the extra miles to enlist Congress participation in it. Jinnah saw this as giving exaggerated importance to Gandhi and the Congress. The second round table became frustrating, with Gandhi taking the centre stage and the long proceedings turning into prolonged mock battles of Gandhi versus the rest. Jinnah became so exasperated with the whole exercise that he decided to stay back in England. According to sources close to him, he has instructed his agents in India to sell his Indian possessions. He intends to buy an estate in England and start practising in the Privy Council. He has been admitted to the bar of Inner Temple. It is being heard that his new political ambition is to enter the British Parliament as a member.

No Government Can Hesitate To Accept Challenge: Viceroy

January 25, 1932, New Delhi: Viceroy Willingdon betrayed his attitude to the civil disobedience movement in his address to the Legislative Assembly, saying, 'There can be no compromise in resisting the civil disobedience movement…No Government worth the name could hesitate to accept the challenge.'[78] Political observers say this statement, coupled with the steps he has already initiated point to very difficult days ahead full of confrontations.

Round Table Subcommittees To Complete Their Task

January, 1932, London: Notwithstanding the on-going Congress-led agitation, the subcommittees formed as part of the round table conference have been asked by the government to complete their task. The government has also constituted a consultative committee with a view to keeping in touch with all other Indian leaders through the Viceroy.

Depression Casts Dark Shadow Over Britain

1932, London: Newspaper reports estimate more than two million Britons are out of work and living on measly weekly doles. Food riots are reported to have occurred in important cities like London, Bristol and Liverpool. The situation is depressing in other parts of Europe and United States of America as well. In Germany, few million unemployed people are expectantly looking at the Nazi Party to solve their problem. The squeeze, in which the political dispensation in Britain finds itself, has been creating severe pressure on the Government, which itself is much divided on various economic and political issues. These adverse developments seem to be playing with the temperament of the British government in tackling the Indian political demands. The last thing it can afford at this juncture is possibly to throw away the crown jewel of its worldwide empire. Even in such distressing situation, India, with its immense resources, is acting as a cushion saving Great Britain from disaster.

LT GOVERNOR ESCAPES AGNIKANYA'S BULLETS

February 6, 1932, Calcutta: The flame of revolutionary zeal is consuming Bengal — its men and even women. Ongoing repressions are fanning it. Today, at the convocation hall of the University of Calcutta, a young graduate, Bina Das, attempted to kill Sir Stanley Jackson, the Lt Governor of Bengal. Bina, a fiery patriot, is a leader of the Chhatri Sangha, and came to be known as Agnikanya or 'daughter of fire'. She had managed to procure a pistol and fired five shots at Jackson but without training in the use of firearm, she missed the target. Bina has been arrested and taken away for questioning. The incident has stirred the whole city.

Police Attack Peaceful Procession, Swarup Rani Injured

April 8, 1932, Allahabad: Undaunted by the extensive oppression across the country over its workers, the Congress had given a call to observe 'national week' during April 6 to 13, in the memory of the Jallianwalabagh massacre. Today, the police charged at a procession taken out in the city, led by Swarup Rani, widow of Motilal Nehru, injuring her seriously. It has sent shockwaves throughout the nation and generated disdain for the government across the country.

Amidst Ban Order, Congress Holds Annual Session

April 24, 1932, Delhi: Despite the ban imposed by the government, Congress managed to hold its 46th annual session here. The government, in fact, went out of its way to stop the event but failed. Two days ago, it arrested Madanmohan Malaviya, the president elect of the session in Delhi. On the same day, it arrested Sarojini Naidu in Bombay as she ventured to violate the order against her leaving Bombay. Notwithstanding, delegates kept streaming in to the city and the organisers held the session at Chandni Chowk. Ranchodlal Amritlal from Ahmedabad presided. The organisers had pre-printed resolutions that would be considered by the Subjects Committee. Those were distributed amongst the delegates. The session adopted resolutions approving 'independence', 'civil disobedience' and 'leadership of Gandhi'. The session, however, came to a hasty end as the police invaded the venue, arrested the president and many Congressmen.

According to government sources, the Muslims were indifferent to the session while Akali Sikhs posed troubles. As many as 710 people, comprising 693 men and 17 women, were arrested. They included 186 Akali Sikhs.[79]

NEW DISTRICT MAGISTRATE ASSASSINATED

April 30, 1932, Midnapore: Hardly six months ago, the revolutionaries had killed James Paddie, the district magistrate of Midnapore in Bengal. As if in a re-enactment, today, two revolutionaries. Pradyut Kr Bhattacharya and Probhanshu Pal, both members of the Bengal Volunteers, have killed the new incumbent Robert Douglas. They attacked him at the District Board House here. The success of the revolutionaries in killing important government officials, as if at will, may embolden such activities in other parts of the country. The government can ill afford such attacks. Suspecting Midnapore as a breeding ground of such activities, it is likely to come down more severely on the local people to root out the revolutionaries.

Four Months Of Civil Disobedience

May 2, 1932, New Delhi: Four months have passed and the civil disobedience movement shows no signs of abating. The government has been going all-out to crush it along with its progenitor, if possible. It has put the Congress leaders en masse into gaols and banned Congress organisations. Leveraging the freshly-issued Ordinances, it has been confiscating Congress properties and taking over Congress offices. It has banned processions, demonstrations, publications and distribution of objectionable materials. To insulate the Congress from the public, the government has made it an offence to render help to it. And to cap it all, the government has also come down hard on the nationalist press with both monetary and non-monetary threats like fine, increased security (deposit), warning etc. On its part, the Congress, despite its leadership being in jails, has been showing unprecedented enthusiasm and determination in carrying forward the movement. Congressmen are continuing with picketing, printing and distributing nationalist literature and leaflets, holding processions and demonstrations and even trying to re-possess their properties confiscated by the government. In this continuing battle between brute state power and innumerable Satyagrahis, the latter have been arrested in thousands but their spirit continues to be high.

Today veteran leader Malaviya has issued a public statement on the progress of the movement over the last four months. He cited government data of arrests of 66,646 people including 5,325 women and children. But Malaviya, quoting Congress source, claimed that over 80,000 people have so far been arrested. He also gave details of lathi charges, house searches, confiscation of properties, etc. Malaviya said at least in 163 cases, the government attempted to regulate the Press unjustifiably.

Communal Flareup Engulfs Bombay

May 1932, Bombay: Inspired by the ongoing civil disobedience movement, the aggressive campaign against foreign cloth has brought about completely unintended and calamitous consequences. Congress volunteers are picketing at piece goods shops, vending foreign cloth.

Muslims own a number of these shops. They import such stuff and earn their livelihood. Picketing at their shops created communal tension, leading to a riot. Once started, it spread rapidly and the busy commercial city has come under its vicious grip. Political observers feel this will be a setback for the Congress and will provide a handle to the government to create a deeper wedge between the two communities.

India Observes All-India Prisoners' Day

July 4, 1932: The Congress observed this day as the All-India Prisoners' Day to focus the national attention on a vital issue—uncivilised and inhuman treatment extended to large number of political prisoners. The number of arrested persons in connection with the civil disobedience movement itself is about a hundred thousand now. Then there have been large number of prisoners languishing in Bengal jails for long. The government has been adopting a revengeful attitude to prisoners in NWFP and Bengal. Such medieval practices like whipping, bar-fetters, night hand cuff are being resorted to. To impart even harsher punishments, the government has reopened the prison in the Andamans where the prisoners are reportedly being subjected to unspeakable abuses. The call of the Congress, despite all odds, has been timely and appreciated by people at large.

MacDonald Announces His 'Communal Award'

August 16, 1932, London: The second round table conference had failed to arrive at consensus on the 'communal' question, giving the British prime minister scope to arbitrate amongst the dissenting parties. Ramsay MacDonald has now done it. Today, his communal award was announced from both London and Simla.

MacDonald claims both insight into Indian problems and sympathy for Indians' aspiration for self-governance. He has formulated the communal award based on his understanding and experience of Indian dynamics. He is of the opinion that his award will offer an optimum resolution of the communal problem by catering to the political aspirations of different communities.

His award has accepted the principle of separate electorates for Muslim, Sikh, Indian Christian, Anglo Indian & European communities, besides confirming the traditional policy of weightage for the minorities. Depressed Classes amongst Hindus have also been treated as minority and allowed the right of separate electorate. Another feature of the award is the extension of the principle of weightage to the Europeans in Bengal and Assam, Sikhs in Punjab & NWFP and Hindus in Sind and NWFP. The system of weightage was tinkered with some modification in Muslim majority provinces like Punjab and Bengal.

The award provides that the reservation for these specified communities would remain operative for twenty years. It seems he has sought to produce a quick fix, 'out of the hat' solution for complex problems faced by India for ages.

Gandhi To Fast Unto Death

August 18, 1932, Yeravada Prison, Poona: The communal ward has hit Gandhi hard. He has written to the British Prime Minister and the author of the 'award' that he proposes to begin a fast unto death from 20 September, unless the award was withdrawn.

Communal Award Fails To Inspire Parties

August 1932, Delhi: Although Ramsay has been claiming he is a friend of India and that his award would help solve India's problems, most of the political parties are unhappy. They feel Ramsay, by his award, is achieving exactly the opposite of his avowed goal.

Muslim League Wants The Award To Be Improved

1932, Delhi: The Muslim League is unhappy with the Ramsay award for tinkering with the weightage in Bengal and Punjab. As per the new award, the Muslims would get lesser seats in these two legislatures than what is warranted by their proportion to the total population of the respective provinces. Although Muslims represented 56% of the Punjab population, they would be entitled to 86 out of 176 seats in the assembly. However, the retention of the separate electorate, against the teeth of the Motilal report, and the weightage of the Muslims in most of the provinces while conceding the same benefit to the Hindus only in two small provinces like Sind and NWFP, are being seen as positives. Notwithstanding, the League has been highlighting its marginal political losses in Punjab and Bengal and it is urging improvement of the award in their favour.

Willingdon Hints At A Third Conference

September 5, 1932, New Delhi: To give a final shape to the work done by the two round table conferences, Viceroy Willingdon has announced in the Legislative Assembly that a small body of representatives from both British India and the Indian states will meet in London to contribute according to a fixed agenda. This third round is scheduled to be held by mid-November this year. Significantly, most of the Congress leaders are in prisons, while the most crucial exercise for the country is proposed to be given the final shape. Political observers say, Willingdon is acting as if the Congress is quite irrelevant in this exercise, which smacks of his highhandedness.

Gandhi Is Determined To Begin His 'Fast Unto Death'

September 13, 1932, Yeravada prison: Last month, Gandhi had written to the British Prime Minister, protesting against the communal award and expressing his resolve to 'fast unto death', There was no favourable reply. Gandhi had fought like a crusader against a combined opposition, particularly against the proposal for separate electorate for the depressed classes. Now this award has confirmed that his battle was in vain. Gandhi has described this as a clear attempt by the British government to divide the Hindu community. He is convinced that separate electorate to the untouchables will result into their 'bondage in perpetuity'. He fought in the round table through debates, arguments and appeals. Now he has decided to launch his final fight — he has declared he would fast unto death in protest, but would not like to live to see this vivisection of the Hindu community. His fast would commence from 20th of this month.

Gandhi's Resolve Stirs The Country

September 20, 1932, Yeravada prison: Gandhi's momentous decision has sent the whole country astir. Leaders like Ambedkar are finding this as an undesirable pressure tactics. Many Congress leaders are also not convinced. Jawaharlal feels Gandhi is mixing religious sentimentalism in politics. He also laments that Gandhi has abandoned the goal of 'independence' while trying to help the untouchables. There are indeed few who can appreciate Gandhi's vision and the intensity of his feelings. Tagore has sent message to Gandhi endorsing his valiant defence of the unity of Hindu society. But most leaders in India, whether of Congress or otherwise including Tagore, are deeply worried about the likely impact of the fast on Gandhi's health. Letters and telegrams are pouring into Yeravada from many, trying to persuade him not to take such an extreme step. But Gandhi is firm in his resolve. Unless the separate electorate system is withdrawn, he will not step back.

Gandhi Begins His Fast, India Holds Her Breath

September 20, 1932, Yeravada prison: Gandhi has begun his fast unto death. Whether political and social leaders, or eminent individuals, or ordinary persons—tension is writ large on innumerable faces, because the underlying issue is not amenable to any easy solution. The only party who can make him withdraw is the leadership of the depressed classes, especially BR Ambedkar. But, the latter is visibly irritated and antagonised by the fast and in no mood to throw away an important political right for the depressed classes that has been achieved after prolonged struggle.

I Cannot Deliver My People Hands-And-Feet Bound To Caste Hindus: Ambedkar

September 1932: Sympathy waves are rising in favour of Gandhi, even amongst leaders of the depressed classes. They are recalling the way Gandhi has been crusading for the rights of the untouchables over the last fifteen years. In a meeting held in Calcutta, eleven organisations of the depressed classes went to the extent of passing a resolution that disapproved separate electorate for the depressed classes. But Ambedkar is unrelenting. Gandhi has been promising alternate mechanisms to address the grievances of the depressed classes, but Ambedkar does not want to leave such a crucial issue to the convention of understanding. Though he is under pressure from the nationalist press, which has been demonising him, Ambedkar is not prepared to compromise on the political rights of the depressed classes. In the face of all-round pressures, he said he would be open to only one alternative – a better guarantee from Gandhi on the political rights of the depressed classes. Ambedkar made it clear that the Mahatma must not compel him to choose between his (Mahatma's) life and the rights of the depressed classes. Under no circumstances can he deliver his 'people bound hand and foot to the caste Hindus for generations to come.'[80]

Open Hindu Temples To Untouchables: Congress

September, 1932: Gandhi's fast unto death has created great commotion in the country. People and leaders are growing concerned over his health, which is on the decline. There are intense activities – political and social across the country – all directed to save his precious life. Several Congress leaders including Rajendra Prasad, Rajagopalachari have been appealing to caste Hindus across the country to open their temples to the untouchables and to work vigorously for the removal of this stigma from the Hindu society. It is being learnt that several hundreds of temples in Allahabad, Benares, Calcutta and in the Indian states have already been opened to the untouchables.

Gandhi's Health Deteriorates, Pressure On Ambedkar

September 21, 1932, Pune: Pressure has been mounting on Ambedkar to reach a settlement with Gandhi and negotiations are going on. On this evening, Gandhi's health condition deteriorated sharply, causing great tension. Many leaders, including those from the depressed classes, have visited him in the jail. Madan Mohan

Malaviya has issued an appeal to both caste Hindu and depressed classes' leaders to bury their differences and come to a settlement. Hectic consultations are going on between the leaders of the two groups to hammer out a solution.

Rajagopalachari And Ambedkar Exchange Pens

September 24, 1932, Pune: Ambedkar has been camping in Pune for past some days and holding parleys with Gandhi's followers. At long last, an agreement has been reached in terms of which the depressed classes would forego the claim to a separate electorate as provided for in the Communal Award but in return, the Congress has agreed to give them more seats in the legislative bodies than what is promised by Ramsay MacDonald in the communal award. The agreement was signed by Malaviya, TB Sapru, Chunilal Mehta, BR Ambedkar, MC Rajah, PG Solanki, Rajagopalachari, GD Birla and others. Rajagopalachari and Ambedkar reportedly exchanged pens following the armistice.

Consensus At Poona, Modification In London

September, 1932, London: After a pact was signed with Ambedkar, the British Prime Minister accepted it with unusual speed and modified his award accordingly.

Important fallout of the episode has been Gandhi's realisation of the enormity of the problem of untouchability in Hindu society. He now seems to be convinced that he must do much more to mitigate this problem. He has begun to sensitise Congress more on this issue, and also decided to do whatever is possible in his individual capacity.

Though the majority of Indians heaved a sigh of relief when Gandhi and Ambedkar concluded their pact, significant number of caste Hindus and Ambedkar himself do not seem to be happy with the outcome. Whereas the former feel too much has been conceded to the depressed classes, particularly in provinces like Bengal, Ambedkar feels the MacDonald award would have better protected the long-term interest of the depressed classes. The communal award reserved 78 seats for the depressed classes but it gave them double voting — they could elect their own representative and also vote in general constituencies. As per the Poona Pact, the Congress agreed to give them as many as 148 seats, but the right to 'double voting' was taken away. Ambedkar feels the double vote could be a more effective weapon to ensure that a much larger number of representatives cared for Dalit interests.

Gandhi-Ambedkar Pact To Hit Bengal Provincial Congress Hard

1932, Calcutta: The caste Hindu politicians have dominated Bengal Congress for long. Under the Lucknow pact and even the subsequent Government of India Act 1919, Hindus had 60 per cent of elected seats and the Muslims 40 per cent, even though the Muslims formed the majority population. This owed essentially due to the fact that for first two decades following the formation of the Congress, its top leadership was heavily skewed in favour of the educated and affluent Bengalis, mostly caste Hindus. The educational and economic backwardness of the Muslims also contributed to the phenomenon. This hegemony was waiting to be challenged by the growing political awareness of and the spread of education amongst the Muslims.

Ramsay's award has come as a shock to the extant Congress leadership of the province, as it divided the 250 seats of the provincial legislature amongst Muslims (121 seats representing 48.4% population), Hindus (78 seats representing 39.2% population), Europeans (25 seats) and other special interests (26 seats). As the provincial Congress leadership was struggling to grope with such an earth-shaking change, the Gandhi-Ambedkar pact conceded a countrywide total of 148 seats to the depressed classes, with the largest number made available in Bengal 30, Madras 30, CP 20, UP 20, Bihar and Orissa 18, Bombay 15, Punjab 8 and Assam 7. In Bengal, a citadel of caste Hindus, it meant that out of a shrunken 78 seats, as many as 30 are to be conceded to the scheduled caste legislators. The provincial leadership of the Congress are seeing this as gross injustice. There is also a growing criticism against giving such lop-sided importance to the Europeans, who are but a miniscule percentage of the total population.

Unity Conference Attempts 'Alternative' To Communal Award

November 3–17, 1932, Allahabad: Encouraged by the indigenous solution of the separate electorate for the depressed classes issue, MM Malaviya and Shaukat Ali have taken initiatives for forging a consensus on communal issues by the Indians to replace the communal award being imposed by London. They have called for a conference and it began on 3rd of this month. As many as 121 delegates representing Hindus, Muslims, Sikhs and Indian Christians have turned up to make a serious bid towards such a lofty objective. On the first day, the conference appointed Unity Committee and it was tasked with resolving the inter-community intractable issues while the conference was adjourned.

The committee worked hard, adopted innovative approach and prepared an agreement today that specifies formula for representation in provincial legislatures. As per its formula, the minority groups derive more benefits at the expense of majority Hindus and Europeans. It also recognises the rights of Sikhs as a minority group, besides that of the Muslims. The agreement also contains 'safeguard' clause to ensure that no bill is passed, altering the religious matters of a community without its consent.

The quid pro quo for these concessions to the minority group is the formation of a central government in a short time, and acceptance by all of the 'joint electorate system', with reservations for minorities.

The conference would reconvene next month. In the meanwhile, the delegates have been advised to secure endorsements for the agreement from their respective organisations. However, as per reports, the Muslim delegates were not satisfied by the representations made available to them in Bengal. Moreover, the formula presupposed sacrifice by the European community whereas there was none from their side present in the conference to make such a commitment.

Unity Conference Is As Good As Over

December 24, 1932: The Unity Conference was reconvened. Since 17 November, there have been some developments. Both Sikh and Muslim groups submitted amended proposals seeking improved representation in provincial legislatures. A subcommittee was to resolve the differences. It could not offer a formula on the communal representations in Bengal that was acceptable to all. Further, in the first session, the conference had agreed for 32 per cent representation to the Muslim in the central assembly. Thereafter, the British Government announced 33 per cent quota for them, ostensibly to create a divide amongst communities. The usefulness of the conference is being seen as almost over.

Third 'Round Table' Ends, No Ripples In India

December 25, 1932, London: Third round table conference began in London on 17th November. To the masses of India, it did not hold any particular interest. Congress did not participate nor was it asked to. The civil disobedience movement has been in full swing and bulk of the Congress leadership has been in prison.

The fact that the Labour Party, presently the opposition in Britain's parliament, has chosen to stay away from it, has also diminished the importance of the third round table somewhat. Total delegates numbered forty-six – none from Congress. The British government already has reports of the Simon Commission as well as various subcommittees set up by the round table conferences. It is likely to act upon all of these inputs and use the present conference to give final touches to the 'constitution' it is contemplating for India.

MEERUT CONSPIRACY TRIAL
Verdicts Are Biased And Vindictive

January 16, 1933, Meerut: Top trade union leaders have been languishing in jails for over three years and a seemingly unending trial has been going on. With the passage of time, it is becoming clear that their arrests have been on suspicion, not facts. But the vindictive government will not admit its mistakes. On the contrary it has been labouring hard to fabricate false charges against these leaders.

Surprisingly, in this case, the British government, usually conscious of its international image of being just and civilised, has cast aside the growing world opinion that is speaking in support of the prisoners. The Comintern had strongly denounced the arrests almost immediately after these leaders were arrested. Since then, sympathies have been flowing from all over the world including British Trade Unions, and illustrious thinkers, scientists and politicians like Romain Rolland, Albert Einstein, Barnard Shaw, and Harold Laski. Stafford Cripps has even offered to accept the brief on behalf of the prisoners for appeal to the Privy Council.

However, the prisoners' hopes were jolted as the Additional District Magistrate, Meerut today pronounced its verdicts. In seemingly partisan and biased judgements, the court appeared keen to help the government in its intrigue against its own subjects than dispensing justice. It has imposed harsh punishments upon the accused leaders, ranging from three years rigorous imprisonment to transportation for life. It has become clear that the court even turned a deaf ear to the international voices for sanity and justice.

The anger and frustration of the government in tackling the revolutionary activities and Congress' sustained agitation seem to have found a reflection in the verdict. It has clearly made Indian people suspect the sense of 'justice and fair play' of the British government. The prisoners will certainly go for appeal in the higher court.

Viceroy's No To Temple Entry Bill In Madras Council

January 23, 1933, New Delhi: Gandhi's attempt to open Hindu temples to the Harijans had hit a roadblock at the Guruvayur temple in the south of the country. The temple authorities assigned traditional and legal difficulties in introducing the reform. Several other temples in the south toed the same line. Following this, nationalist leaders have been taking legislative initiatives to cure the ill by bringing in a 'temple entry' bill in both, the Madras council and also the Indian Legislative Assembly. The Viceroy has given sanction to the 'Untouchability Abolition' Bill in the Legislative Assembly today but refused sanction to introduce the Temple Entry Bill in the Madras Council. This is being seen as a deliberate attempt to keep Hindus a divided community.

Cambridge Student Conceives The Word PAKISTAN

January 28, 1933, London: Poet philosopher Iqbal's idea of a separate nationhood for the Muslims has found a strong advocate in the distant overseas, in the capital of Britain. Rahmat Ali, a Muslim student at Cambridge here, has prepared a small thesis in which he has called for a land for the Muslim nation that ought to be formed from the provinces of north west India in which the Muslims have a predominant presence. In this, he has included Punjab, Kashmir, Sind, Afghan (Frontier) Province and Baluchistan. He has also suggested an acronym PAKISTAN based on these constituent provinces. According to Rahmat Ali the claim that India was a single nation is a 'preposterous falsehood'.[81] Rahmat Ali is intense about his idea and trying to convince the Muslim League to take it up.

Ailing Subhas Allowed To Travel To Europe

February 1933: Subhas was intermittently arrested and released during the last three years. When the non-violent non-cooperation movement called by Gandhi was underway, Subhas was very aggressive, giving the Government a tough time. He was last arrested in January 1932. By the end of the year, his health again grew worse. It is clear that this deterioration is connected to his frequent internment and imprisonment. The government has realised that his continued detention in the prison might pose serious threat to his health. At the same time, it is not prepared to invite any political hazards if Subhas is released. The situation in the country is explosive, consequent on the failures of successive 'round table' conferences, dishonourable treatment extended to Gandhi in the second table and later, imprisonment, and resumption in the civil disobedience movement. Subhas, a charismatic leader with mass appeal, can pose significant threat, if in India. As such, it has decided to release him on the condition that he would have to go to Europe for treatment and recuperation at his own expenses.

However, it is being learnt that even in Europe, he will be kept under surveillance by secret agents. The government does not want to take any risk.

SURYA SEN ARRESTED

Host Tips Off Police For Money

February 1933, Chittagong: For nearly three years, since the raid at the Chittagong Armoury, Surya Sen, alias Masterda was able to give the slip to the police who launched several combing operations across wide areas to hunt him down. His immense popularity acted as a human shield, protecting him from the prying eyes of the police and their vast spy network. The closest the police reached was on 13 January last year, when Captain Cameroon had surrounded his hideout with a posse of policemen. On that occasion, the daring revolutionary made a desperate escape by shooting down Captain Cameroon. The government was deeply embarrassed and grew vindictive as one spirited revolutionary was challenging the might of the powerful British Empire.

Today, the police achieved a major success. Acting on a tip-off from Netro Sen, a greedy man who had provided temporary shelter to Surya Sen and his team, the police arrested him. Netro committed the treachery for the lure of cash reward and has thus incurred the wrath of the revolutionaries.

It is being learnt that the police has been brutally torturing Surya Sen in captivity. They have also registered cases against him, levelling various charges.

Vindictive Government Bares Its Ugly Fangs

1933, Delhi: The government seems to be losing all sense of civility and propriety while dealing with not only political prisoners, but even civil society. Whipping the Congress workers in jails has become commonplace. In faraway Andaman, the repression of political prisoners has become severe. This made them to go on hunger strike, resulting in death of some inmates. When Tagore, CF Andrews and other well-known people issued appeals to the government for humanitarian treatment of these prisoners, the government got so agitated that it made even the expression of such sympathy a punishable offence in Bengal. It has been resorting to many other measures for suppression of thought, speech, writing and assembly of persons.

White Paper Based On Round Tables Now On 'Table'

March 17, 1933, London: Today, the government has published the 'White Paper' containing the draft proposals for the reforms HM's government intends to carry out in the Indian constitution. The paper draws its inputs essentially from the discussions and deliberations held in the three round table conferences, and also the recommendations of the committees appointed to go into details of relevant issues like federal structure, minorities, defence etc. Broadly, it outlines a federal structure that would be operationalised by bicameral federal legislatures.

A remarkable feature of the White Paper is the importance accorded to the Indian states. In the upper chamber, viz. Council of States, the states will be entitled to have as many as 100 members out of a total of 260. In the Federal Assembly, they may have as many as 125 out of a total 375 members. What is more, the members from the states will not be representative of people but appointed by the rulers.

The White Paper stipulates that the federal structure will come into operation once states, accounting for half of the total population of all Indian states and accounting for half of the total seats allocated for the Indian states, have signed the 'instruments of accession'.

RISE OF THE NAZIS IN GERMANY

March 23, 1933, Berlin: Following the end of the first World War, after about two decades of political stability in Europe marked by Britain's hegemony, the first sign of a potential challenge to the extant power equations in the continent has arisen now. Germany under Hitler, the Nazi leader, has sent out signals of her military and imperialist ambitions.

Even if nebulous, the recent developments in Germany are of interest many nationalist leaders in India. To them, rise of any rival European nation posing threat to the supremacy of Britain is always welcome. They see the prospects of a slackening in the grip of Britain over India in such developments.

During the last World War, Indian revolutionaries had sought help from Germany to stage a country-wide armed revolt. To many nationalist leaders, the rise of Germany now may help the cause of Indian independence, some way or the other.

Since her defeat in the First World War, Germany has been lying low. In recent years, her people have been in the throes of deep economic Crises. The Communists and the Nazis were fighting street battles, adding to the chaos. Three chancellors in as many years failed to lift the country from the gloom, paving the way for Hitler of the Nazi party to take over as the new chancellor in January this year.

Though Hindenburg, president of the country, had poor opinion of Hitler, he yielded to the pressure from bankers, army officials and various right-wing politicians who were crying for order and discipline. Making the best use of his appointment, Hitler, acting with alacrity, assumed dictatorial powers in less than a couple of months.

He has established a firm grip over the country by arresting Communists and Socialist leaders. Today, the Reichstag has voted to give him the full power to rule by decree. Hitler is planning a huge boost to military power. Clearly, he has imperial ambitions. Britain is feeling uncomfortable at these developments in the continent. Nationalist Indians have a different perspective on the emerging development.

Subhas And Vithalbhai Strike Instant Rapport

March 1933, Vienna: Subhas, having left India for treatment, reached Vienna on 6th of March and met Vithalbhai Patel, the ex-president of Central Legislative Assembly and a veteran swarajist who had excellent rapport with CR Das, Subhas's mentor. Presently in Europe, Vithalbhai is furthering the cause of Indian independence by conducting active propaganda in the continent.

A rapport has quickly ensued between the two leaders—one old veteran and the other, charismatic and young. Though they have worked together on the Congress platform in India, this is the first occasion when the two have come close and got to know each other better. Vithalbhai has come to trust Subhas as a leader of great potential, who can advance the cause of India's freedom.

Government Chases Congress In Calcutta Too
Open Session Dissolves After Police Lathi Charge

April 1, 1933, Calcutta: Severe government oppression is underway across the country. Gandhi is in prison. Rumours were floated by vested interests that the Congress has given up its demand for independence of the country. Any doubts on this count have to be removed to keep up the public spirit. Since the Karachi session held in 1931, Congress has not been able to hold its full-fledged session. Last year, its bid to meet in Delhi was cut short by the government. In a bid to reinforce its image as the premier political party and to remove any misgivings, the Congress had planned to hold an open session in Calcutta.

But the government denied the party permission. The Congress continues to be a banned organisation. Sensing the Congress intention, the police have closed all parks and open spaces. Workers and leaders were trying to converge on the city from distant provinces. But many are being prevented on the way. Swarup Rani, the widow of Motilal Nehru and Madan Mohan Malaviya, the president elect, both bound for the Congress session have been arrested in Asansol on the way to Calcutta.

Despite all odds, Neli Sengupta, the India-lover English wife of the popular Bengali Congress leader JM Sengupta, presently interned, and a leader in her own right as well, led a procession of 2,500 Congressmen to the appointed destination. The session adopted a few important resolutions including condemnation of the 'White Paper', and reposed faith in the goal of independence, efficacy of civil disobedience and boycott of foreign goods.

Like Delhi, the session in Calcutta also met with an abrupt end when a large posse of policemen arrived at the scene and dispersed the gathering. Mrs Sengupta has been arrested, along with 250 Congress men and women.

'God Would Be My Invisible Medical Attendant'

May 4, 1933, Yeravada prison, Poona: The civil disobedience movement has been curbed with an iron hand by the government. Gandhi, right since the time the communal award was announced, has been actively engaged in stepping up battles against untouchability.

Though there has been considerable impact of his 'fasting' and appeal to open up the temples to the Harijans, he has not been satisfied with the progress. In the meantime, the Viceroy's refusal to sanction the Temple Entry Bill has upset him. Upon introspection, he has developed a conviction that the fault for these ills lie within himself and his associates.

In the middle of the intervening night of April 29-30, he announced that beginning from 8th May he will observe a twenty-one day fast for the purification of self and his associates. That created much commotion in the country. Concerns have been raised by several leaders, followers and people at large. But Gandhi has declared that his fasting is 'unconditional and irrevocable'. He has been trying to allay the concerns of his associates who have grown extremely concerned about his health. Today, he has written to MA Ansari, 'God would be my invisible medical attendant'.[82]

Gandhi Suspends Civil Disobedience Movement

May 8, 1933, Poona: Today has been full of political surprises, twists and turns. Determined in his mission, Gandhi commenced his fast at 12 noon sharp. Though the government earlier betrayed little concern about his programme, by 6 pm he was released from prison. Thereafter, taking every one by sheer surprise, Gandhi announced the suspension of the civil disobedience movement for a month or six weeks. He also issued appeals to the Viceroy to withdraw all Ordinances and set all civil resisters to release.[83]

The Rationale Of A Momentous Decision?

Since the Congress resumed the civil disobedience movement, huge unrest had taken over the country. The government, on its part, had been stoking the conflict too. From its actions, particularly in ignoring Gandhi and the Congress after the second round table, the government has been hinting that it would give little weight, if any, to the Congress view in the making of the new constitution. The relations between the two parties have been growing worse by the day.

The government has been responding to the mass movement harshly. Congress workers in tens of thousands have been arrested and placed in prisons. Under the doctrine of non-violent non co-operation, Congress had been boycotting legislatures. With no effective participation in governance, it has not been able to restrain the bureaucratic tyranny unleashed on helpless Indians in any manner. In jails, the civil disobedience prisoners are being dealt with cruelly and whipping has become an oft-used method of punishment.

Congress workers, and millions of patriotic Indians, on their part, were suffering these government excesses in silence and waiting for the next command from Gandhi. The two warring parties had been in an eye-ball-to-eye-ball confrontation for the last one year. The people have been making enormous sacrifices and expecting that Gandhi would take the movement to the climax to clinch victory. At this juncture, Gandhi's decision has left them shocked and perplexed.

Political analysts are also hard put to interpret today's sequence of events. Even if the first two events, ie. Gandhi's beginning the fast and the government ordering his release can be understood, the decision to suspend the movement is summoning all their skills. They say it could be due to any one or more of the following reasons. First, it may be just a case of capitulation to an oppressive government. Second, it could be that based on unsatisfactory progress in the anti-untouchability campaign. Gandhi has realised there are too many ills in Indian society which must be exorcised before the colonial government can be countered effectively. Third, it could be a shrewd political strategy. Whatever it be, it would be revealed in course of time

It's For Six Weeks: MS Aney

May 9, 1933, Poona: MS Aney has clarified that the civil disobedience movement has been suspended for six weeks.[84]

Jawaharlal Feels Suspension To Be End Of Movement

May, 1933: Jawaharlal feels the nervous energy of the nation as a whole was for the moment exhausted and it was not being recharged. Against this backdrop, Gandhi's decision to suspend the civil disobedience movement, to Jawaharlal, seems to be the end of the movement, at least for some years to come.

Gandhi's Latest Action A Confession Of Failure

May 9, 1933, Vienna: The near total discomfiture of the Congress and the news of rising government atrocities on its workers and leaders have been reaching across the seas upsetting patriotic Indians. Vithalbhai Patel and Subhas have issued a joint press statement[85] here on the political situation in India in which they said, the latest action of Mahatma Gandhi is a confession of failure as far as present method of Congress is concerned. They said there is a need for reorganising the Congress but for that, a change of leadership is imperative for it would be unfair to expect Mahatma Gandhi to evolve or work a programme inconsistent with his lifelong principles. Vithalbhai and Subhas suggested that the Congress as a whole undergo the transformation, and this would be the best course. If that was not possible, a new party composed of all radical elements should be formed within Congress. They also said the non-cooperation must not stop but it has to be made more militant and that the fight for freedom would have to be waged on all fronts.

ANDAMAN PRISONERS RESORT TO HUNGER STRIKE

May 1933, Andaman: The government has been using the notorious prison at the distant Andaman Island to confine its militant adversaries, especially the revolutionaries. In that far off place, away from the public eyes and media attention, the prison staff have reportedly been inflicting unspeakable tortures upon the helpless patriots. The cells are dingy, coated with moss. The food and water given to the prisoners are inedible and often worm-infested. There are no toilets. The prisoners are not allowed to meet each other. In such solitary existence amidst extreme hardship and indignity, the guards routinely flog the prisoners. It is also heard that the prison authorities keep inventing methods of brutal torture to chastise the prisoners who dare to show the slightest defiance.

Unfortunately, very little political protests have been raised so far in mainland India against such atrocities. According to political analysts, this could be partly due to the operation of the maxim 'out of sight, out of mind'. Another important reason, they say, could be the stress by Gandhi on 'non-violence' and his express disapproval of the political method of violence adopted by the revolutionaries.

However, unable to bear such terrible atrocities, the political prisoners in the Andaman resorted to 'fast unto death' from 12th of this month with the earnest hope that at least by this supreme suffering they would be able to attract the notice of their indifferent fellow brethren on mainland India.

After three prisoners, Mahavir Singh, Mohan Kishore Namo Das and Mohit Moitra, died in course of the fasting, people in the mainland began waking up. Demands are being raised in India to improve the living conditions of the prisoners in the Cellular jail.

Suspension Of Civil Disobedience

Calamity Of The First Magnitude: Subhas

June 10, 1933, Vienna: Gandhi's decision to suspend the civil disobedience movement without the Congress achieving any of its key objectives like independence, or even dominion status, has been baffling bulk of the Indians. Millions of them responded to his call, participated in the mass movement braving police atrocities and prisons. They were also ready to make whatever sacrifices Gandhi would ask of them to realise their goal. Now abandoning such a staggering movement midway has been breaking their hearts. There is a widespread feeling of disappointment and frustration amongst people. Unable to decipher the rationale of Gandhi's latest decision, many Congress leaders share this feeling too.

Subhas, presently recuperating in Europe, has been stunned to hear about this decision. To him, the suspension of the mass civil disobedience is a virtual surrender and a calamity of the first magnitude. This is the time when the new constitution of India is under discussion and maximum pressure ought to have been brought upon the government by strengthening the mass movement. Subhas also feels that this action has practically undone the suffering of the nation for last 13 years.

Subhas Phobia Continues

Speech In England Banned In India

June 10, 1933: Subhas, presently in Europe, was invited by Sapurji Saklatvala, a member of the British Communist Party to preside over the third Indian Political Conference organised by his party at the Friars Hall in London. Since there is a perceived ban on Subhas's entry into England, he sent his presidential speech in writing, which was read out in the conference. The British government banned the circulation of his speech in India.

Six Weeks Over, Congress Searches For The Next Move

July 12-14, 1933, Poona: Since the announcement of the suspension of the civil disobedience, Gandhi has so far not issued any further instructions. Millions are confused and waiting. Gandhi had announced the suspension for six weeks and that time limit has expired.

The Viceroy paid no heed to his requests for withdrawal of Ordinances and release of civil resisters. Against this background, few Congress stalwarts like MM Malaviya, C Rajagopalachari, MS Aney, Bhulabhai Desai, Dr Alam and Abul Kalam Azad have met here in the presence of Gandhi. The majority view was in favour of calling off the movement. However, the meeting authorised Gandhi to seek an interview with the Viceroy. On the 14th, Gandhi cabled the Viceroy, seeking an interview. Political observers see this as a major climb down.

Viceroy Refuses Interview To Gandhi

July 17, 1933, New Delhi: Viceroy Willingdon has declined to grant an interview to Gandhi. Seldom has Gandhi been ignored so bluntly and that too, after he has suspended a major movement and sending signals for peace. Political observers are of the opinion that Willingdon has sensed an impending 'total' victory, and he is stepping up pressure on his political opponent to hasten it. The condition of the Congress has become precarious. Gandhi had suspended the movement only for six weeks. He failed to resume it even after ten weeks, even though the Viceroy summarily brushed aside his pleas. It is almost impossible to regain the lost momentum.

Subhas Travels In Europe, Shadowed By British Agents

1933: Subhas has been going places in Europe and he has already visited Berlin, Rome, Prague, Warsaw, Istanbul, Belgrade, Bucharest. In Europe, Subhas has been meeting important leaders and people. He is also trying to organise Indian communities and particularly, Indian students, for the cause of Indian independence. In every place of his visit, secret agents of the British government have constantly kept him under surveillance.

No More Of Mass Civil Disobedience

July 22, 1933: MS Aney has made an important announcement on behalf of the Congress — that the programme of mass civil disobedience has been discontinued.

Plan To Handover Sabarmati Ashram
Individual Civil Disobedience

July 30, 1933, Ahmedabad: As early as on 20th July, Gandhi had spoken about the idea of individual civil disobedience to a representative of *The Times of India*. Later on, he announced his decision not to pay revenue dues, disband his now famous Sabarmati Ashram and offer it to the government. He gave due notice of his intended action to the Home Secretary of the Bombay government on 26th July. Today he has appealed to the people of Gujarat and announced his plan to march with his 33 associates to Ras on 1 August.

Gandhi Arrested – Ahmedabad Observes Hartal

August 1, 1933, Ahmedabad: Acting with alacrity, the government arrested Gandhi along with his wife Kasturba, and associate Bhulabhai Desai, in the morning today, preventing him from carrying out the march. He has been taken to the Sabarmati jail. The people of the city are hurt and angry at the series of high-handed acts. Ahmedabad observed Hartal today.

Gandhi Released Unconditionally

August 23, 1933, Sassoon Hospital: On 2nd August Gandhi was shifted to Yeravada jail. Though he was released after a couple of days, he was instructed to leave Yeravada village and confine his movement to Poona city municipal limits. He violated the order, again as a civil disobedience, was re-arrested and sentenced to one year imprisonment.

Shortly thereafter, a conflict ensued when the prison authorities refused to extend him facilities for pursuing his work for the cause of the 'Harijan'. As a mark of serious protest, Gandhi began an 'indefinite fast' on 16th August. In a span of five days, his health deteriorated rapidly and he had to be admitted to Sassoon hospital on 21st August. Today, the government has released him unconditionally.

Pressure Mounting On Jinnah To Return To India

August 1933, London: Jinnah has been receiving several requests to return to India and take over the reins of the Muslim League once again. Last month, Liaquat Ali Khan and Begum Raana had visited him and tried to persuade him. This month Nawab Mohammad

Yamin Khan met him in his west Hampstead home and tried to convince him.

Jinnah has been receiving reports about the political situation in India and the state of affairs in the League and feeling worried. What is causing him much disquiet is the lack of unity amongst the Muslim political leaders. There is another vexation — perennial ambivalence in Muslim leaders about participating in the Congress-led civil disobedience movement. Time and again, Jinnah has advised them against joining this movement. He has, every time, emphasised on building of unity amongst the Muslims.

To every one urging him to return home, he is laying down a condition — ensure unity, if you want me to come back.

Temple Entry Bill Put On Hold For One Year

August 24, 1933, New Delhi: The Indian Legislative Assembly has taken a decision that has far-reaching consequences. It would hold over the much awaited 'Temple Entry' Bill for one year. Earlier, the Viceroy had indicated that he has no intention whatsoever to give this Bill a push. He rather wanted to allow full opportunity so that the public opinion on the issue can express itself. The decision of the Assembly is in commensuration with his approach.

Political observers say, coming within a day of release from prison, this is likely to hit Gandhi hard. He may be compelled to scale down his expectations from the government even further and seize the initiatives.

MIDNAPORE'S THIRD MAGISTRATE FALLS TO BULLET

September 2, 1933, Midnapore: The cycle of repression and revenge refuses to end here. Midnapore in Bengal has been actively participating in the freedom struggle. Not only are its people responding to the Congress call with great enthusiasm, the land is also a hotbed of revolutionary activities.

No wonder its people are attracting severe ire of the government. Especially after Paddie, the first district magistrate was assassinated, a cycle of repression and revenge has been set in motion. Today, EJ

Burge, the third incumbent to the office of the district magistrate has fallen to the bullet of the revolutionaries at the police parade ground here. Such attacks, coming in quick succession, despite tightening of security measures and severe repression, are causing the government great anxiety. The mood in the air is one of retribution. People here are keeping their fingers crossed.

Harijan Work Is The New Movement For Gandhi

October 8, 1933: In a public meeting, Gandhi has announced his decision to devote himself to Harijan work till 3rd August next year.

Political observers say, Gandhi may have taken this task unto himself because he can no longer trust the government nor does he have enough confidence in the ability of Congressmen to do anything significant in the near future.

Why Sikhs Are So Upset By Ramsay's Award?

October 15, 1933, Lahore: Even a year after it was announced, Ramsay MacDonald's communal award continues to cause deep disquiet among cross sections of Indian people. A joint session of Khalsa Durbar and Central Sikh League is being held to discuss the award. Sikhs are peeved at the award's illogical approach and its discriminatory attitude towards their community. Clearly, there has been no parity in the reservation quota to Muslims and the Sikhs. For example, in UP, Bihar and Madras, Muslims were given much higher quota vis-à-vis their percentage to the total population, when compared to Sikhs in Punjab.

Province	Community	% to total population	% of reservation
United Province	Muslim	14	30
Bihar	Muslim	10	25
Madras	Muslim	6	18
Punjab	Sikh	13	<19

Again, within Punjab, the Muslims were the majority community and, therefore, they did not deserve the quota. And if the Muslims claimed special benefit on the basis of their having been rulers before the British, the Sikhs were equally deserving as they ruled over Punjab before the British. As such, they find no logic for discrimination and appeasement of one community. On the whole, the joint session resolved in favour of the abolition of communal representation in various legislatures in the country, which would constitute the way to achieve democratic 'swaraj'. The conference also declared that the Sikhs will not submit to any constitution, based on the 'communal award'.

Many prominent leaders have endorsed Sikh grievances. In the National Sikh Conference held in Amritsar in May this year, Madan Mohan Malaviya while supporting the Sikh cause had said that the British government has committed blunder after blunder and the time has come for a countrywide agitation against the award.

Beleaguered Muslim League Yearns For Unity

November 25-26, 1933, Delhi: Muslim League has become weaker and faction-ridden. Last month, the faction led by Aziz met in Howrah. Now, the other faction, led by Hafiz Hidayat Hussain, is meeting here. The Hafiz has stressed on unity in the League. He has also suggested that the party take advantage of the presence of Aga Khan and MA Jinnah in the country and hold a convention for unity. It is learnt that Jinnah is expected to visit India in a couple of month's time.

Communists Try To Regroup

December 1933: Since August this year, some of the Communist leaders have been released from jail. The party has set up a provisional committee and PC Joshi is likely to take over as the general secretary. However, the Communist Party continues to be illegal. The possibility of its members associating with the Congress in future remains to be seen.

Mission Harijan– Gandhi On Whirlwind Tour

December 30, 1933, Gandavaram: Gandhi has commenced his 'Mission Harijan' tour on 7th November. He has toured places across western, central, and southern India in addition to a visit to Delhi and surrounding places. During his visit, he has met large number of people belonging to the depressed classes, met their leaders and delegations, addressed men and women in groups, opened reading rooms, laid down foundation stones for schools, inaugurated development projects. He has also opened temples to the Harijans in various places like Selu, Lasura, Raipur, Baloda Bazar, Risama, Jabalpur, Mudunuru, Siddhantam, Kavur, Ithananagarampadu, and Vengalpadu. In addition, he laid foundation stone for a new temple for Harijans at Damoh. At Sagar he laid down foundation stone for a temple to be built by Harijans for all Hindus. Today, he is here to open a temple to the Harijans. Political observers say he has taken up this work almost as a challenge to an indifferent government and example to his anaemic colleagues.

Jinnah On A Visit To India

January 4, 1934, Bombay: Jinnah is back in India, though not permanently as yet. However, he has been received with much warmth by his supporters. A new life seems to have been infused in both factions of the League by his arrival.

MASTERDA HANGED

January 12, 1934, Chittagong: Surya Sen was arrested in February last year. The court had convicted him and awarded death sentence. There was grief and gloom all around. The heart of the people of Chittagong in particular, and Bengal, in general, pined in sympathy for him, whom they affectionately called 'Masterda'. Today he was hanged with Tarakeshwar Dastidar, another revolutionary accomplice of his. The government was so much vindictive that he was tortured even on the last day. Some jail insiders say he was dragged to the gallows unconscious.

MASTERDA, THE PRIDE OF BENGAL

Surya Sen was initiated to the revolutionary ideals as early as 1916 by one of his teachers when he joined the Anushilan Samity. In 1918, he organised the local wing of 'Juganatar' in Chittagong. A very popular leader, he became president of Chittagong district committee of the Indian National Congress in 1929. By profession he was a school teacher that earned him the sobriquet of 'Masterda'.

Amongst many of his daring actions aimed at attacking the British government and strengthening the revolutionary activities was a day-light robbery at the treasury office of Assam Bengal Railway at Chittagong on 23 December, 1923. However, his most bold act was conducting a raid on Chittagong Armoury on 18 April 1930. Subsequent to the raid, he marched to the Jalalabad hills, along with his fellow revolutionaries. Four days later, on 22 April, he was confronted by the British troops but managed to escape. Thereafter he kept hiding and changing places to avert arrest. On 13th Januray, 1932 while in a temporary refuge in the house of Savitri Devi at Patiya, he was surrounded by Captain Cameron at the head of a strong contingent of police and military. Surya Sen shot Cameroon dead while he was ascending the stairs and then gave the security team a slip. Eventually, in February 1933, Netro Sen, a traitor and in whose house Surya had taken shelter, informed the police leading to his arrest. Netro got a reward of Rs 10,000 for this tip, but later he was assassinated by other revolutionaries for this betrayal. Surya was tried and hanged with Tarakeshwar Dastidar on 12 January 1934. It is learnt that Surya was brutally tortured before executing the death sentence. He was dragged unconscious to the gallows. After death, his body has not been given any funeral, such was the cruelty of the government.

It Is Reign Of Terror In Bengal

January 22, 1934, Calcutta: The government has been ruling the country with harsh Ordinances. Bengal and NWFP, two turbulent provinces, have been chosen for special repression. The Bengal Ordinances IX and XI of 1931 had conferred the government power to conduct in camera and in absentia trial by special tribunal and special magistrates and the tribunal was authorised to take cognisance of an offence for which the accused in question was not fornally indicted.[86] Next year, provision was made to award death penalty for mere attempts to murder. [87] Today, the Bengal government has introduced a Bill in the Legislature that provides for death penalty for certain offences under the Arms Act. [88] Although the government has justified this draconian legislation in the name of fighting terrorists (revolutionaries), the provisions are being viewed as very harsh and the chances of their misuse for terrorising the whole society cannot be eliminated. People held for illegal poession of arms, explosives can be punished with death penalty.

Gandhi Focuses On Nation Building

1934: The civil disobedience movement has petered out and little, if anything, has been achieved. The government has let loose unprecedented oppression on the Indian people and the Congress is unable to mitigate their sufferings. Their absence in the Legislature further curtails their capacity in this regard. Gandhi's attempt at offering individual Satyagraha was promptly curbed by the government. The government seems much more confident in its ability to deal with the Congress.

In these circumstances, Gandhi appears to have changed his strategy. He is trying to improve the moral and ethical fibre of the Congressmen and prepare them to strive for the freedom in more effective ways. He has identified a set of key issues involved in the building of the nation and begun to undertake these himself. These involve promoting communal unity; removing untouchability; promoting khadi and village industries, basic education, adult education, equality and education of women, health and sanitation and economic equality.

His activities are also encompassing peasants and labour unions, and promotion of provincial and national languages etc. Through such multi-dimensional activities, he is putting before the Congressmen a model of leadership behaviour. Incidentally, training in these fields is expected to equip the Congressmen to discharge their leadership role effectively when India attains her freedom. Gandhi has also been touring the country to communicate his messages effectively.

However, it is not clear how far he has been able to convince the Congressmen. Most of them seem to be interested in hard political actions and movements. As such, whenever the Working Committee members have met in recent times, they were more eager to hear from Gandhi about these, clearly unable to share Gandhi's own perspectives and priorities. The lack of alignment between the supreme leader and the rest is generating some kind of confusion and listlessness in Congress.

Gandhi Suspends Civil Disobedience

February 2, 1934, Saharsha: Gandhi is here in course of his Harijan tour. He has been holding occasional consultations with political colleagues. Today he has advised Congressmen to suspend civil disobedience and taken it unto himself to offer the same.

Jawaharlal Arrested Again, Taken To Calcutta For Trial

February 12, 1934, Allahabad: Jawaharlal with Kamala, his ailing wife, was in Calcutta from 16th to 19th last month. Calcutta was reeling under Ordinance Raj. The government has been literally crushing people if it has the slightest suspicion of their involvement or support to anti-government activities. Jawaharlal, who has many colleagues and friends in the city, is deeply sympathetic to the distressed people. In the meeting he addressed, he, while criticising the terrorist acts, also expressed his mind 'against the manner in which human dignity had been outraged by indiscriminate suppression of whole populations'.[89] He thereafter returned to Allahabad via Patna. Today he has been arrested in his residence here on account of these speeches based on a 'warrant' issued from Calcutta. He is being taken to Calcutta for trial.

Calcutta Speeches Earn Jawaharlal Two Years' Jail

February 16, 1934, Calcutta: Jawaharlal has been awarded two years' imprisonment. It is clear, the Government of Bengal in particular has been acting vindictively and not prepared to brook any transgressions, even civilised dissent.

Jinnah Elected President Of The Muslim League

March 4, 1934, Delhi: Jinnah's temporary presence in India is working wonders. The two factions led by Aziz and Hafiz have re-united and Jinnah elected as the president of the united All-India Muslim League. Last month, in his absence, his nomination was filed for the Central Legislative Assembly to represent Bombay Muslims.

Swaraj Party Is Revived

April 5, 1934, Patna: Gandhi has still been touring the country as a part of his Harijan mission, which is likely to end on 3 August this year. The Congress is practically in a limbo. Today a few senior leaders including Dr BC Roy, Dr MA Ansari and Bhulabhai Desai have assembled in Patna and huddled together to chalk out the road map ahead. Gandhi is here and guiding the deliberations. They have taken stock of the stifling political situation under a harsh 'Ordinance Raj'. In the circumstances, it has been decided to revive the All-India swaraj Party and contest the forthcoming elections to the Legislative Assembly. Gandhi is reportedly in agreement.

Muslim India Cannot Lose You: Fazl-i-Hussain To Jinnah

May 15, 1934: Jinnah has been taking pains to infuse new vigour into the moribund League and he is doing it well. To lift the morale, last month he said that the League was perfectly healthy and sound.

Ironically, he himself fell sick and that held back his journey to England.

Today, he has received compliment from Fazl-I-Hussain, the Punjab premier and a leader of high stature. Fazl-I-Hussain has said, Muslim India cannot afford to lose him, being one of the very few men with such clear vision, independent judgement and strong character. He also said: 'When one sees efforts made in non-Muslim Indian quarters not to help genuinely Muslim India with a view to secure their cooperation but simply to persuade the Muslim community to entrust its future to them, the need for a strong man of independent judgement, integrity and strength of character becomes apparent and overwhelmingly great.'[90]

Jinnah values these words, coming from one of the top-ranked politicians. Possibly, this may encourage him to make his permanent return to India quicker.

Abnormal Situation Prevails Across India

1934: The government is continuing to curb civil liberties and freedom. Numerous organisations are outlawed. It is making use of weapons like emergency power, Tranquillity Act and other statutes to carry on with its agenda. Large number of books and periodicals are proscribed by the 'Sea Custom Act'. It has made possession of 'dangerous literature' punishable by long-term imprisonment. Free expressions of opinion on political or economic problems of the day are meeting strong disapproval of the censor. Such has been the intolerance that the Bengal Government warned the *Modern Review* for publishing an article by Tagore on his experiences of visit of Russia. According to the government, the article gave a distorted view of the British rule in India. On the whole it appears that the government is at war with large section of Indian people.

Now, Gandhi The Sole Representative Of Civil Resistance

May 19, 1934, Patna: Gandhi had suspended the civil disobedience mass movement in May 1933. In July last year, he had announced that civil disobedience could be conducted only at individual level. This February, he forbade Congressmen from doing that as well and reserved the right to offer individual civil disobedience to himself. In a two-day meet held here, ending today, the AICC has put its seal of approval to Gandhi's latest decision. It has also adopted a resolution allowing the Congress to contest election and enter 'councils'.

Government Lifts Ban On Congress

June, 1934, Delhi: The government has ended proscription of the Congress. However, many of its associated and subsidiary bodies like the Seva Dal, Khudai Khidmatgar, Kishan Sabhas, Youth Leagues etc. remain outlawed. The government is pursuing an 'iron fist' approach towards peasant organisations and labour unions.

Sahajanand Disillusioned By Congress Apathy

1934, Patna: Swami Sahajanand Saraswati, a Dandi Sannyasi, has been in the self-less service of the poor peasantry of India for past several years. In the political arena, he had been an ardent follower of Gandhi and involved himself in the non-cooperation movement as early as 1920. However, over the years he has found Congress and its leaders wanting in the service of the poor peasantry.

This year, when a severe earthquake struck Bihar, causing havoc to the lives and meagre properties of the farmers, Sahajanand while engaging himself in relief work found the zamindars and their agents creating more hardship to the farmers than natural calamity. He had sought Gandhi's intervention in the matter and was assured by the latter that most zamindars had Congressmen as managers and they would ensure that the zamindars help the victims in rehabilitation. Sahajanand believed as the assurance came from the Congress supremo. However, he waited in vain—neither the zamindars nor their Congressmen managers came forward to help the victims. A disillusioned man, Sahajanand severed connections with Gandhi and took up the cudgel himself to protect and help the earthquake victims. In the aftermath of this experience, Sahajanand has become a non-political man. His loyalty is now only to the peasants. His dedication to the poor peasant's cause is making him a cult figure. He is being seen as a champion of the peasants—much loved and adored.

Hinduism'll Perish If Untouchability Isn't Removed: Gandhi

August 3, 1934, Patna: Gandhi has just completed a countrywide tour with his message to the caste Hindus to eradicate untouchability. Till the end of last year he had opened several Hindu temples to the Harijans. He has called the Deprived Classes, Harijans. This year his campaigning was more focussed on overall socio-politico-economic amelioration in the condition of the Harijans. He covered larger areas this year including Madras, Bihar, Assam, Orissa, United Provinces, Central Provinces, Bombay, Gujarat, Sind and Punjab.

Having begun his tour on 7th November last year, he has criss crossed the country, having travelled about 12,500 miles by cars, train and on foot. Based on his experience, he has called upon the caste Hindus to uproot untouchability if they wanted Hinduism to survive. He delivered this central message to the Hindus:

'… I have not a shadow of doubt in my mind that if untouchability is not removed by root and branch, then Hinduism is bound to perish, for no religion can ever nurture itself on the degradations of its votaries.'[91]

Communal Award Brings About A Split In Congress

August, 1934: Congress is preparing for the forthcoming Legislative Assembly election. A serious difference arose amongst working committee members about the stand to be taken on the 'communal award'. Part of the differences was addressed by an agreement between Gandhi and Ambedkar. Another attempt was made by Malaviya and Shaukat Ali to resolve other important differences, eg. separate electorate, through the Unity Conference, but eventually it could not deliver. Malaviya and MS Aney want the Congress to reject the award but the Muslim leaders want Congress to adopt a neutral stand. Not prepared to compromise on this vital issue, Malaviya and Aney have resigned from both parliamentary board and working committee. They have formed a new party, viz. the Nationalist Party. Gandhi is reportedly quite upset with this split.

What If Congress Socialists Gain Ascendancy?

September 17, 1934: Gandhi has just completed a countrywide tour when he had a feeling of the ground realities, especially relating to the depressed classes. He has plans to take up a slew of constructive, socially relevant activities. He has, therefore, decided to stay aloof from mainstream political activities. Today, he has explained the reasons for his intended retirement from the Congress: differences in approaches with Congressmen on vital issues such as spinning and khadi, non-violence, untouchability. To him, these have been matter of conviction and creed, whereas others look at these issues as matters of policy, without adequate conviction.

He also made another important mention about the Congress Socialists. Conceding that many of them are respected and self-sacrificing co-workers and were welcomed by him to Congress, but their programmes are turning to be increasingly unacceptable to him. Interestingly, he remarked that 'if they gain ascendancy in the Congress, as they well may, I cannot remain in the Congress' [92]

To the huge number of Congressmen who were unnerved by his decision, he uttered some words of solace. He agreed to wait till the Bombay session is concluded to tender his resignation.

Gandhi And Aney Issue Joint Statement On Election Strategy

September 20, 1934, Wardha: It seems Gandhi has reconciled to the split between the Congress and the Nationalist Party, but wants that the two do not fight each other in the ensuing Legislative Assembly election.

Today Gandhi and Aney have issued a joint statement, saying that 'wheresoever it is manifest that one candidate has an overwhelming chance against another, the latter should be withdrawn'.

The two leaders also made the purpose of the statement clear: 'We may also state that we met together purely as friends and co-workers, without being deputed by respective parties. Our purpose was to find ways and means of avoiding a domestic conflict.'[93]

Socialists Launch New Party On Congress Platform

October 21, 1934, Bombay: Congress has been like a big ship, taking all Indians aboard it—individuals, parties and organisations—some holding widely differing views but all tiled by a common purpose to attain freedom. Its leftist constituents—some imbued with Socialist ideals and some more radical subscribing to Marxist philosophy and believing in class struggle—were never convinced about the efficacy of Gandhi's method of non-violent national movement.

Now that both of the major movements, led by Gandhi, stumbled on their face, the leftists felt it was time to show their dissent and put forth their views and ideology forcefully. Leaders like Narendra Dev, Jayaprakash Narayan, Achyut Patwardhan, Ashok Mehta and others have now founded a bloc of their own within the Congress and christened it as the 'Congress Socialist Party (CSP)'.

This newly born group wants the freedom struggle to be carried out in a much more radical way and it has decided to put forth its views with firmness and clarity in a bid to influence the Congress' policies. Its objectives include not only freedom from foreign power but also to end the native system of exploitation and to bring together, for this purpose, all of the anti-imperialist elements in the Congress.

As a part of the Congress, CSP wants much more active involvement of the peasants' and workers' organisation in the Congress' programmes and activities. Interestingly many traditional Congress workers who have been unhappy at the way the civil disobedience movement was suspended at first, and called off later have also been assembling under its banner. In a way it can be seen as a 'mini Congress' within the 'Congress', serving an anti-establishment role.

The emergence of the CSP is causing disquiet in the Gandhian camps and they view the concept of 'class struggle' as divisive. Following a foundational conference in Patna on 17th May this year, the Party is holding its first Conference here.

Congress Emerges Out Of Eclipse

October 24-28, 1934, Bombay: After almost three-and-a-half years, the Congress is holding its 48th session here. Rajendra Prasad is presiding. If the government thought that they have finished Congress, it is their turn to be shocked. The organisation, which was driven underground by forces of Ordinances and extensive misuse of authority, has again resurfaced reflecting all-around the glory of almost a martyr. Not only thousands of delegates, the people at large are enthusiastically celebrating its resurrection.

Gandhi had earlier declared he would retire from the Congress at the end of this session. However, he has now suggested few changes that the session has adopted through resolutions. These relate to compulsory wearing of khadi for six months to become Congress executives, drastic reduction in the number of delegates in the annual session and size of the AICC, and starting of the All-India Village Industries Association.

After this session, Gandhi would withdraw from mainstream political activities. He would be in control of the Village Industries Association and left with enough time to pursue other constructive activities, including anti-untouchability campaign, an area to which he has been according high priority, especially since the issue of communal award.

All said and done, his retirement decision has made many Congressmen and leaders nervous. They have understood the strength of their enemy quite well over last few years, and they are naturally reluctant to trudge along without their most reliable guide. Somewhat to the relief of his supporters, Gandhi said he would still take interest in it but that he would cease to shape the policies of this great organisation. Interestingly, the members of the working committee are all his known loyalists. Political observers say, though Gandhi is no longer in the policy-making bodies, the working committee members are likely to turn to him in every difficult situation and he too may not disappoint them.

Gandhi Resigns From Congress

October 30, 1934, Wardha: Gandhi has resigned from the Congress. He is expected to devote himself to constructive nation-building activities.

Joint Parliamentary Committee Report

November 22, 1934, Wardha: The report of the joint parliamentary committee on the Indian constitutional reforms has been published. When asked for his views by the *Associated Press*, Gandhi has refused to comment.

The general opinion in the Congress considers this worse than even the 'White Paper'. They feel there is an unmistakable reflection of the growing influence of the far right Conservatives in its architecture.

Poll Results Out, Congress, NP Score Impressive Victory

November 1934, New Delhi: The results of the elections to the Legislative Assembly are out. Out of a total of 105 seats offered for election, Congress has secured forty-three. After remaining underground for nearly three years, the manner in which the Congress has made such a prompt and impressive come-back suggest ground swell support for the organisation.

Jinnah On A Repeat Visit To India

December 1934, Bombay: At the end of his previous visit to India, Jinnah had left Bombay for England on 24 May. He is back in India in another temporary visit.

The League has become too much dependent on him. His absence for the intervening period of the last few months has been somewhat unsettling for them. Though he is expected to attend to organisational matters these days, Jinnah may need some time more before he can return to the country permanently.

Subhas Forced Into Exile Once Again

January 1935, Bombay: Subhas was permitted to come to Calcutta from Europe for a brief period to visit his seriously ailing father. Unfortunately, by the time he reached the city last month, his father had expired. He had reached India in November and as long as he stayed, he remained almost under house arrest. After the rituals, he has been asked to leave India. Subhas has again started for Europe.

Subhas' *The Indian Struggle* Gets Rave Reviews

January 1935: While in Europe, Subhas has been travelling across the continent canvassing support for India's freedom struggle. He has been interacting with Western thinkers, leaders as well as Indian students and communities for this purpose. He has also penned down his commentary on the freedom struggle in the country, during the period 1920-34. He was persuaded by a reputed publisher in England to undertake this project.

This book has now been published and received wide acclaim amongst intelligentsia in England and Europe. Subhas' insight and upright views have impressed readers. JT Gwynne, while reviewing the book in *The Manchester Guardian* of 17th January 1935, has written:

'Altogether, the book leaves us with a wish to see Mr Bose take a lead in Indian politics.' [94]WN Ewer wrote a review in the *Daily Herald* on 28th January, saying that this is the 'ablest work I have read on current Indian politics'. He felt that the book is the authorship of an acute, thoughtful and constructive mind and that the author, although was still under forty would be 'an asset and an ornament to the political life of any country'. [95]

The book has some harsh words for some top political leaders back home. Subhas' observations may be candid and upright, but these may not make these leaders any friendlier towards him. The British government has banned the import of the book in India on the ground that it could encourage methods of terrorism and direct action. This clearly seems to be an unwarranted step, motivated by needless phobia and denigration of a scholarly analysis of Indian politics.

Jinnah Elected To The Assembly Unopposed

February 1935, Bombay: It is being learnt that in response to sustained entreaties by a large section of Indian Muslims, especially the political leaders, Jinnah has been seriously thinking returning home. He is expected to pay a brief visit to India in the next couple of months to prepare for his permanent return. In the meantime, his enthusiastic supporters have worked for his election in the Central Legislative Assembly as the representative of the Muslims of Bombay. He has been elected unopposed.

Jinnah-Rajendra Prasad Talks Fail

March 1, 1935: Following Jinnah's return from England in December 1934, Congress leader Ansari had invited him to talk to the Congress leaders to frame a unified resolution on the constitutional reforms. Jinnah accepted the offer.

Lack of agreement on communal issue is the key hindrance to agree on the future constitution. Neither Congress nor the League is fully satisfied with the communal award. Since 28 January this year, Jinnah and Rajendra Prasad have been working on a formula for substitution of the communal award to be used for further discussion. Rajendra Prasad began the negotiations on the basis of the Congress Working Committee resolution of 1931, which envisaged joint electorate and in return offered guaranteed representations, based on percentage of population besides the right to the minorities to contest additional seats. However, eventually, the two leaders could not reach a consensus. Today, they admitted failure of the talks. [96]

Panicky Britain Plans To Step Up Spending On Arms

March 4, 1935, London: As Germany under Hitler has been indulging in massive rearmament, Britain today announced new expansion plans for its army, navy and air force. Rationalising the action, Stanley Baldwin, the British Prime Minister, said this became necessary, as his country's attempts to lead the world towards disarmament by unilateral example have failed. Britain could not just ignore the way Germany has been upgrading her military prowess. Obviously, there is great disquiet in Britain, as Germany seems to be preparing to destabilise the power equation amongst the European nations.

Punjab Tense: Shahidganj Mosque Razed To The Ground

July 9, 1935, Lahore: Shahidganj Mosque has been in the eye of the storm for past several years, particularly after the entire compound in which the mosque is situated, has been transferred to the local Sikh Gurdwara Prabandhak Committee (SGPC) in March this year. The SGPC has announced its plan to renovate the compound and demolish the dilapidated building of the mosque. Lahore has been witnessing violent protests by Muslim population including armed demonstrations targeting the Sikh clergy and the functioning Gurdwara situated within the same compound. The SGPC has added to the tension by arranging jathas from outside the city to hold counter-demonstration. The government has so far managed the situation by persuasion, police action and protection, troop deployment, curfew and such other measures. The SGPC has reportedly obtained the necessary municipal permission for the renovation and last night went ahead with the demolition. The work started before midnight and the dilapidated shrine was razed to the ground before sunrise. As words spread, there has been huge commotion in the city. The troops and police have cordoned off the whole areas. Curfew has also been clamped to avert any serious communal conflict.

Shahidganj Gurdwara-Mosque Conflict

The Shahidganj complex, situated outside Lahore city has a Mosque and a Gurdwara. Of the two, the mosque has ceased to be used as a place of worship before 1852, when right to private use was permitted legally. The Muslims argue that the mosque was constructed during Moghul Emperor Shah Jahan's reign, well before the Gurdwara. According to available reports, during the Sikh rule of Punjab, the complex was taken over by the Sikhs and it was used as residence by the Sikh clergy. From the 1850s, after Punjab came under British rule, Muslims kept approaching the Court from time to time reclaiming the place. Sikhs resisted claiming that Muslims used it not as place of worship but to conduct trials for the Sikh prisoners, and the place has been sanctified by rivers of blood of those Sikh martyrs. The Court did not entertain the Muslim claims essentially considering its conversion to private use. Under the SGPC Act, the Gurdwara here has been placed under the management of the SGPC in March this year. The SGPC has decided to renovate the entire complex that involves the demolition of the dilapidated Mosque. The legal verdict could not settle the strong religious fervours of the two communities that are at odds with each other. Political activities are likely to gain further momentum after the present incident.

Government Of India Act 1935 Passed

Constitutional Reforms Introduced

August 2, 1935, London: In 1933, the government had released a white paper that incorporated the proposals formulated by the third round table. These proposals were put before the Joint Select Committee on Indian constitution. This committee was constituted by taking sixteen members each from the House of Commons and House of Lords, twenty representatives from British India and seven from the princely states. Lord Linlithgow presided over its working. Today, it has been passed as the Government of India Act.

New Constitutional Reforms – Too Little Too Late

After decades of struggle, Indians have finally come to see the new constitution for their country coming from the British Parliament. They are deeply disappointed. Let alone independence, there is no talk of dominion status. The Government of India Act 1935 is essentially in the nature of constitutional reforms and that too grossly inadequate considering the peoples' expectations. Even the reforms, incorporated in the Act look as mere intentions at the present time.

On the whole, the new Act has provided for little effective power of self-government to the Indians and retained the ultimate power to the Governor General in the centre and the Governors in the provinces—though the position is somewhat better in the latter case. In terms of presence in the Central Legislature, the Act gives undue advantage to the princely states and nominated legislators.

The Act envisages a federal structure for India, comprising the British Indian provinces and the princely states and it has also introduced the retrograde 'diarchy' system. The Federal Legislature would be composed of two houses, viz. Council of States or the Upper House and Federal Assembly or the Lower House. Whereas these houses may have the satisfaction of discussing issues related to the country and her people, the real power would continue to vest in the Governor General. Foreign and Defence subjects remain in his hand.

The legislative powers of the Central Council are truncated. There is a negative list in respect of which it cannot legislate. Further the Viceroy can veto a legislation that it has passed and certify one into law that it has rejected. The Viceroy has discretionary powers to dismiss ministers, suspend the legislature and even the constitution.

The scope for representations in the councils through general election is also limited. There are complex quotas allocating seats to various segments of the population based on religion, gender, community, profession etc. Only seventy-five seats out of a total of 260 seats in the upper House and 86 out of a total of 375 in the lower House are open to general election. In terms of number of representatives to the two Houses, the Act is disproportionately weighted in favour of the princely states and the nominated representatives.

The federal part of the constitution will become operational only after specified minimum rulers of native states sign the 'instrument of accession'. Till the time the federal part of the constitution becomes operational, the Central government would function under the Government of India Act, 1919 under which the Governor General would continue to wield very wide powers in relation to administrative, legislative and financial matters. In the provinces, the Act has granted near autonomy. However, the Governor has been given the power to declare state of emergency when he can suspend the constitution and assume all powers. The Act provides for elections to the provincial legislatures, subject to the system of separate electorates. On the contentious issue of communal representations, the Motilal Report had provided for joint electorate system and in return a guaranteed Muslim representation in the legislature to the extent of one fourth of the total strength. The Act has provided for separate electorate system for population segments. It has guaranteed Muslim representation to the extent of one-third of the total. Clearly, the Act has overwhelmingly endorsed the demand of the Muslim League. On the whole there are 1,585 seats in the eleven provincial legislatures. After taking care of special allocations, only 657 seats remain as general seats. The new Act has failed to meet domestic expectations. It has hardly given Indians their share in the governance, which they have been waiting for over last fifteen years, ie. since the 1919 Act. The government made fullest use of the acrimony between the Congress and the League in retaining the substantive power in the Governor General.

Jawaharlal Calls 1935 Act 'New Charter Of Slavery'

1935, Delhi: The new constitution is a testimony of the victory of British diplomacy. The government played the communal card with such consummate skill that the major parties lost sight of the 'independence', 'dominion status' or even the demand for a fair measure of self-government and kept fighting over other issues including separate electorates.

The radical reforms that were anticipated in 1929 did not arrive at all. The truncated form in which it arrived six years later now is nothing more than sprinkling of measly charity through provincial autonomy in selected areas. Various parties who fought each other bitterly during the round table conferences are realising their follies and short-sightedness. It has become manifest that the British government has walked away with the trophy by conceding to the Indians the bare minimum.

Indians will have lots of responsibilities but little resources. Gandhi, presently retired from the hustles bustles of politics and busy in constructive activities in his ashram, feels that the new constitution is unworkable. Jawaharlal has called the Act a 'new charter of slavery'. [97] Jinnah feels that the new constitution has been forced 'upon us'. He feels it is 'now the duty of various leaders to put their heads together and chalk out a definite and common policy with regard to the constitution.' [98]

LURE OF OFFICE DANGEROUS: GANDHI

1935: The Government of India Act has provided for elections in the eleven British Indian provinces along with the scope to form government. Apparently, the lure of forming governments at various provinces is attracting the ordinary members and leadership of both Congress and Muslim League. However, Gandhi is cautious.

He clearly sees the potential of slippages through corruption. As he discusses the new Act with his colleagues, it becomes evident that the British offer for native parties to form provincial governments is a trap indeed. The autonomy available to the provincial governments is available only for specified lists.

Thus, even if the Congress is able to form government, it will not have sufficient power to implement its agenda whereas it will be responsible to rise up to the peoples' expectations.

To make matters worse, many of the Congress leaders may be corrupted by power. Gandhi's own experience, while conducting the non-cooperation movement has already convinced him that most of the Congressmen are yet far from ready to assume serious responsibilities. Considering the pros and cons, Congress is in a state of ambivalence in regard to chalking out its course of action. Internal debate is raging.

IMPACT OF 1935 ACT

Princely States Major Concern For Congress

1935: The future of the princes and their subjects has emerged as a significant issue for the Congress Party, after the prospect of federation has been spelt out in the 1935 Government of India Act. To nationalist India, it leaves much to be desired. Amongst its several shortcomings are included the position of princes of Indian states in the federation.

Now it has become important for the Congress to see that in the proposed federation, the rulers of the princely states do not form a solid bloc at the centre, totally unrepresentative of their subjects. Yet another worry is the possibility that the dissidents amongst Congressmen may build up power bases in these states through agitations.

The morale is, from now, Congress has to devote more attention to the peoples' issues in the princely states. Hitherto, they had a hands-off approach. Now genuine grievances of people of the states can no longer be ignored. Congress may have to start taking more initiatives.

Princes Hesitant To Join The Federation

1935: On their part, the princes of native states have their own reservation about joining the federal government. They are apprehensive of losing some of their autonomy because in the proposed federation, the central government would retain the responsibility of defence and external affairs.

Further, Section 93 gives special power to the Governor General to take over power if constitutional machinery breaks down. The princes are reluctant to accept British paramountcy, especially the special responsibility of the Governor General under the Act.

They have another fear—in the event they join the federation, their people are likely to demand administrative and economic reforms. In view of several such reservations on the federal provisions in the Act, they are unlikely to join the federation in a hurry.

Congress Unhappy With 1935 Act, May Fight Election

1935: As regards the provincial elections, the initial response in the Congress was cautious and guarded. However, a rethink is taking place. Jawaharlal has been a vehement critic of the new constitution, especially the federal part of it. But he is sensing that the process of electioneering would help the Congress reach its policies and programmes across the land, down up to the small town and village level. Further, Congress can develop its internal strength by working in the legislature. At the same time, the party can also fight against the objectionable provisions of the GoI Act 1935 and also for its improvement from within the legislatures. There is yet another factor. For past some time, Vallabhbhai Patel has been building up the election machinery within the party by his hard and dedicated efforts, which can benefit the party significantly.

However, there are serious reservations amongst many leaders about forming government, if elected. But the party feels that issue can be taken up once the occasion arose—the AICC can take appropriate decision at the appropriate time in consultations with the provincial Congress Committees.

Subhas Makes Important Political Contacts In Europe

1935: Subhas has been in Europe for over two years. One of his first contacts was senior Congress leader Vithalbhai Patel. Convinced that Subhas would be able to carry forward his unfinished work, he has made Subhas the trustee of not only his ideas but of his huge funds. Vithalbhai, engaged in carrying the propaganda of the awareness of India abroad, had died in October 1932. On the issue of making Subhas a trustee, a misunderstanding has unfortunately developed between him and the late Vithalbhai's relatives, including Vallabhbhai Patel. Subhas has been hurt due to this controversy.

Despite his ill health, Subhas has been taking pains in building and developing contacts with important people. He has met Bernes, de Valera and Romain Rolland, amongst others. He also met members of the Nazi hierarchy to explore the possibility of securing their support for India's independence.

Man-made Law Versus Divine Law

September 1, 1935, Rawalpindi: Following the demolition of the Shahidganj Mosque, the Muslims are angry. But they have been kept under leash by the Unionist Party government. The Courts have repeatedly rejected their claims on the mosque. But their contention is based on the dictum of the Sharia—that once a mosque is dedicated as 'waqf' to the God, it remains a mosque forever. In the emerging situation of conflict between the man-made law and the divine law, they are preparing to make any sacrifice to see the latter prevails.

Today, the Muslim protesters have concluded a two-day conference in the Imam Bazaar mosque here, with a view to formulating measures for restoration of the Shahidganj mosque. A separate organisation, viz. Majlis-I-Ittihad-I-Millat has been created to wage the struggle and Pir Jamaat Ali Shah of 'sajjada nashin' (clan of Sufi saints), has been appointed as its Amir (chief).

The choice is strategic to a large extent. The protest movement since July this year has been mostly led by urban organisations without much success. Pir Jamaat has huge followings in the countryside. His leadership may encourage villagers in thousands to enrol as volunteers for the cause and thus bring in a synergy between urban and rural populations in support of an Islamic cause.

Another factor that weighed in his favour is his extensive following, including many in the armed forces, whose support too could be anticipated. Last but not the least, with a revered Pir as the Amir, the bulk of the Pir community is expected to come forward and strengthen the movement.

The conference has decided large-scale civil disobedience as an effective weapon to achieve the aim of the movement. The conference has asked Muslims to observe September 20th as the Shahidganj day to force their cause.

Jawaharlal Released , To Attend Ailing Wife

September 4, 1935, Almora: Jawaharlal's wife Kamala has been seriously ill and undergoing treatment in Europe, while he is serving his prison term for two years. Both Gandhi and Tagore had cabled the Viceroy urging for Jawaharlal unconditional release. Today he has been released by the government. Jawaharlal is expected to proceed to Europe expeditiously.

Though I Was Born Hindu I'll Not Die A Hindu: Ambedkar

October 13, 1935, Yeola: BR Ambedkar has been crusading for long years in various manners using different forums to secure basic human rights for the depressed classes. Gandhi has also been trying since long to remove untouchability from the Hindu community. He increased his endeavour many fold following the publication of Communal Award in August 1932. However, a recent event in Kavitha village in Ahmedabad district in Gujarat, has exposed the limitations of all such reform activities.

In Kavitha, the untouchables sent their children to the common school in the village. This antagonised the caste Hindus so much that they demanded that these children must be sent back home forthwith. When the untouchables persisted, the caste Hindus deprived them from farm labour, stopped their animals from the common pasture and even dropped kerosene oil in their well. The atrocities were so enormous that a hundred families of untouchables were compelled to think about shifting from their ancestral habitation.

The incident has greatly disappointed and angered Ambedkar. Today, in a conference of depressed classes being held here, he has called upon the untouchables to renounce Hinduism and embrace any other religion which guaranteed them equal status. Reflecting on his own life, he reckoned that he was unfortunately born to a Hindu untouchable family which was not in his power, he solemnly declared that though he was born a Hindu, he will not die a Hindu. [99]

Both, the incident at Kavitha and its reactions from the top leader of the untouchables, reveal that individual efforts and sacrifices, howsoever earnest those may be, are inadequate to rectify the deep seated malaise in the Hindu community. Possibly, this calls for nothing less than a revolution in social psyche.

Jinnah Takes Over League Leadership

October 24, 1935, Bombay: Jinnah had sailed for England in April 1935. Now he has returned permanently to India.

In the wake of the passage of the GoI Act 1935, legislative elections are likely to be held in British India. The Congress is already seized of the matter and has begun to prepare. At this juncture, the Muslim League is rather listless. Putting an end to its anxiety, Jinnah has returned to India. He has been received with open arms. Soon after, he has begun the task of consolidating the Muslim League in earnest.

He has already been elected to represent Bombay Muslims in the federal legislature in New Delhi. For all practical purposes, Jinnah is back in the centre stage of Indian politics in an amazingly short time. Significantly, Gandhi is still keeping himself away from the Congress and active politics—he is focussing on constructive social programme and activities. Critics say Gandhi's absence from practical politics is helping Jinnah in more than one way.

Pir Jamaat Talks Of A Million Volunteers For Shahidganj

November 9, 1935: The Shahidganj controversy has brought the communal relations between the Sikhs and the Muslims to a nadir. In fact, a serious communal riot broke out between the two communities on 23 October.

The movement, spearheaded by Majlis-I-Ittihad-I-Millat, has not been able to achieve much so far, notwithstanding the support received from a number of religious divines and rural folks. Part of the reason seems to be the tough postures by the Unionist Party government led by Fazl-I-Husain. He looks at Shahidganj matter as a political issue and not a religious one. He is not ready to antagonise the British government on an issue that the Courts have repeatedly decided against. Provincial Governor Herbert is also clearly against the ongoing movement, which keeps posing threat to the law and order situation of the province. It is true that some Unionist leaders, individually, are lending support to the Pir Jamaat-led movement, but they are not prepared to go beyond a point.

Pir Jamaat on his part, even tried to enforce boycott of Hindus and Sikhs, but found it difficult to implement the scheme. In these circumstances, he has convened a joint conference of Muslim leaders and ulemas to chalk out the path to carry the struggle forward. Emotions are running high and it was decided to enlist one million volunteers and raise a large corpus to vindicate the Muslim rights over Shahidganj.

Political analysts, however, say that these programmes are too grandiose and may fall flat in the face of tough government actions. They also doubt Pir Jamaat's ability to take such tough agenda ahead, especially because he has several connections with the wealthy and powerful Muslims in the provincial government. One of his prime *murids* (followers) is the brother-in-law of Sikandar Hyat Khan, influential Unionist Party leader.

Pir Jamaat May Go For Haj Pilgrimage

January 1936, Amritsar: The movement by the Majlis-I-Ittihad-I-Millat on the Shahidganj Mosque issue is ebbing out. The call for enlisting a million volunteers has proved illusory. There is mounting criticism against Pir Jamaat. Many say rich Muslims are undermining the movement and using the Pir as their tool. Some condemn him for having nexus with the government. Like the last flicker of a lamp, Pir Jamaat has convened a conference here. Unfortunately, rather than coming to his help, the conference is proving to be a platform for criticisms by his detractors because its arrangements and control are mostly in the hands of wealthy Unionist Party followers.

Pir Jamaat finds his position simply untenable, and is known to be mulling to embark upon 'Haj' pilgrimage shortly, to salvage his credibility.

Socialists And Communists Come Closer

January 20, 1936, Meerut: The second Congress of the Congress Socialist Party is being held here. In the session, a thesis has been adopted in which it is declared that there is a need to build a 'united Indian Socialist Party based on Marxism and Leninism'. This is being called the Meerut thesis and it has marked a new height in understanding and cooperation between the Socialists and the radical left in Congress.

RAJANI PALME DUTT IMPRESSES JAWAHARLAL

February 1936, Laussanne: Jawaharlal was released from prison on 4 September last year to be by the side of his seriously-ailing wife, Kamala, undergoing treatment in Germany. A number of prominent people like Tagore, Andrews, Attlee and a few others had urged the government to set him free. Jawaharlal flew to Europe at once. Early this year he moved Kamala from Badenweiler in Germany to Lausanne in Switzerland. He has been staying in a Swiss pension.

Since his arrival, he has been in contact with Rajani Palme Dutt and Ben Bradley, both Britain-based leaders but long involved in Communist and trade union movements in India. Bradley even had undergone a prison term in connection with the Meerut conspiracy case. Jawaharlal is staying in the Swiss pension where Rajni Palme Dutt is living. Both of them are having long talks, which is reinforcing Jawaharlal's Socialist orientation. Dutt has been holding such beliefs from 1927, which have grown stronger during his association with the League against Imperialism. Both Dutt and Bradley have formulated a thesis. One of the main points in it refers to the need of securing collective affiliation of the trade unions and peasant organisations.

The Dutt-Bradley Thesis

Rajani Palme Dutt represents the lineage of Romesh Chandra Dutt, whose scholarly work helped nationalist leaders get an objective insight into economic issues of India under the British empire. A worthy carrier of that lofty tradition, Rajani has established himself as a Socialist thinker of great repute in Britain and Europe in his own right. His father, Dr Upen Chandra Dutt, had migrated from Calcutta to England and established a medical practice in Cambridge. Known for charitable disposition and patriotic spirit, Upen's house became a favourite rendezvous of Indian nationalist leaders visiting England. Rajani, whose middle name was borrowed from his Swedish mother, developed love for India and Indian people under the influence of his father. As he grew up, Rajani emerged as an intellectual genius and eminent Marxist ideologue. He has been dedicating his life to selfless work for the Communists and working class movement in Britain. Right from 1927 he has been associated with the League against Imperialism.

Rajani has worked together with Ben Bradley in formulating a thesis, which seems to be very relevant to countries like India. The Communist Party of India owes a lot of debt to Bradley, a prominent Labour leader in Britain, who had shown exceptional involvement in the trade union movements in India. In fact, he was arrested in the Meerut conspiracy case and faced rigorous incarceration for more than five years in the prison, along side Indian Communist leaders including SA Dange.

Based on their observations and understanding of the Indian situation, particularly in regard to the condition of the peasantry and working classes and their role in the national struggle for freedom, Dutt and Bradley formulated a thesis recently. This thesis helped the Communist Party of India to emerge as a national political force.

One of the cardinal features of the thesis underscores the need for widening the base of the Indian National Congress, the main political party spearheading the national struggle against Imperial rulers, by securing collective affiliation of trade unions and peasants' organisations[100].

Jawaharlal Returns Home

March 10, 1936: Despite best medical treatment and attention, Kamala Nehru died in Europe on 28th last month. Jawaharlal has today returned to India.

Jawaharlal Elected Congress President For Second Time

March 1936, Allahabad: Nehru was in Europe attending his ailing wife, Kamala, when he got the news of his election as the president of the Indian National Congress, this would be his second stint as president after a gap of nearly six years. He will preside over the Lucknow session.

On return to India, he observed that the Congress had developed factionalism and the two major groups, viz. Gandhi loyalists and Congress Socialist Party, were in cold war with each other, with both sides progressively hardening attitudes. He is uncomfortable at the 'atmosphere of suspicion, bitterness and conflict in the party organisation'.

During his sojourn in Europe, Jawaharlal spent days in intellectually stimulating ambience, discussing ideologies and their relevance to world problems. Now real politik at the ground is repulsing him. He feels that his Socialistic thoughts and activities are now being viewed by a section of his colleagues in the Congress executives with apprehension. He will preside over the Congress session in Lucknow next month.

Prevent Office Acceptance By Congress: Subhas

March 4, 1936: Subhas is in Europe in forced exile. However, his heart is in India. Jawaharlal is the current Congress president and is in a key position to formulate Congress policies.

There are rumours that the Congress might accept the new constitution, contest elections and form governments. Subhas, currently in Europe, is afraid that this could be a dangerous trap laid by the government and Congress would commit a blunder if it fell for it.

Subhas has sent a missive to Jawaharlal, the current Congress president, that he must prevent 'office acceptance by the Congress' by any means. Subhas has also expressed the hope that 'Mahatma Gandhi will be more accommodating towards you than towards anybody else.'[101] Subhas is eager to come back to India but the government has warned him not to make any such attempt.

Subhas Determined To Return To India, Come What May

March 27, 1936: For more than one-and-a-half decades, the British government was not comfortable with Subhas's participation in Indian politics. For most of this period, they had tried to keep him in prison and that too without valid charges. During the last two years, they forced him into exile in Europe. Subhas, though upset, has utilised this period in cultivating relationships which have resulted in important and influential people in the continent favouring India's freedom. But now he is eager to be back in his motherland and resume the fight from here. Last year the Government of India Act was passed and it set the stage for launching the next round of the national struggle. For the present, Subhas is keen to take part in the Lucknow session. In Europe, he was warned by the British consul in Vienna of arrest, should he dare to set his foot in India. But Subhas has decided to ignore the government threat and come back, irrespective of the consequences.

Subhas Arrested As He Sets Foot On Indian Soil

April 8, 1936, Bombay: Subhas had started for India on 27 March on board SS Cante Verda vessel, ignoring the government threat. The government carried out its threat to arrest him as soon as he stepped on to Indian soil today. Large numbers of Indians are feeling strongly against such unjust treatment accorded to one of their prominent leaders. This arrest has added to his popularity across the country.

All-India Kisan Sabha Chooses Sahajanand President

April 11, 1936, Lucknow: All India Kisan Sabha has chosen Swami Sahajanand Saraswati as its first president. The process involved participation of prominent leaders like NG Ranga, EMS Namoboodiripad, Pandit Karyanand Sharma, Rahul Sankrityayan, P Sundarayya, Rammanohar Lohia, Jayaprakash Narayan, Narendra Dev and others. There are expectations. It is hoped, under the leadership of Swami Sahajanand, a self-less and dedicated soul, the All-India Kisan Sabha will play an important role in guiding and directing the peasants' struggle across the country.

Jawaharlal Encourages 'Socialism' As Congress Goal

April 12-14, 1936, Lucknow: The Indian National Congress has been holding its 49th annual session here. Jawaharlal presided. Impressed by thinkers like Dutt and Bradley, Jawaharlal, as the Congress president, has been entering into debate with Gandhi, Patel and others over the adoption of socialism as the official goal of Congress. His efforts in this line have been endearing him to younger Socialists like Jayaprakash Narayan, Narendra Dev and Ashok Mehta who now view him as the leader of the Congress Socialists. Under their pressure, Congress has passed the Avadi resolution, proclaiming socialism as the model for India's future government. However, Jawaharlal's active support for passage of this resolution has come under serious criticism from other top leaders, including Gandhi and Vallabhbhai Patel.

Whereas Jawaharlal is emerging as a popular leader and the spokesperson of the Congress Socialists, the Gandhian faction is becoming disquiet. Gandhi himself has a clear political philosophy, which is grounded on Indian soil. If he has been listening and even appreciating Jawaharlal's elucidation of Socialistic views, it is due to his personal liking for the latter. Most certainly, he is not a wee bit enthusiastic about a shift of Congress policy to the socialism of the West. In comparison, Gandhian leaders are much more impatient with Jawaharlal's new ideological moorings. Their opposition to Jawaharlal would be much more strident but for Gandhi's soft corner for him. Given the dynamics of the party, it is clear a conflict is likely between the two camps—sooner or later.

Congress Rejects New Constitution

April 13, 1936, Lucknow: The annual session of Congress is in progress here. The Congress has rejected the new constitution for India.

Conflicts Between Right Wing Leaders And Socialists

April 12-14, 1936: Jawaharlal presided over the Lucknow session of the Congress. His speeches here clearly reflect his commitment to socialism. He has suggested amendment in the Congress constitution to make provision for the organic affiliation of separate, functional peasants and workers organisations to Congress. Critics say, the Dutt-Bradley thesis has exercised considerable influence upon him. If accepted, this can potentially alter the balance of power between the right wing and the Socialists, due to the sheer numerical strength the latter would derive due to from the new membership. The issue has, therefore, created tension and conflict between the two groups.

Committee To Consider Need For Mass Contact

April 14, 1936, Lucknow: Before the end of March of the current year, Congress Socialists like Achyut Patwardhan, Kamaladevi Chattopadhyaya and AP Sinha submitted identical draft resolutions that the Congress recognises the need for a closer participation of the toiling masses in the struggle for independence. For this purpose, the Congress asked the working committee to work out, in consultations with trade unions and peasant organisations, the scope for amendments to the Congress Party's constitution, providing for representation of organised workers and peasants.

The right wing of the Congress sensed the danger inherent in the proposal and resisted the move. They could crystal gaze the consequence—the broadening of the base of the organisation by including constituencies, which were rather the preserve of the Congress Socialists. In this raging conflict, Jawaharlal in his presidential address on 12 April 1936 came close to supporting the Socialists' stand. He said, one way the Congress could increase its contacts with the masses was to organize them as producers and then affiliate such organisations to Congress. This implied that the Congress could have individual as well as corporate membership. Political observers say Jawaharlal's approach on the issue has been influenced considerably by Rajani Palme Dutt and Bent Bradley's thesis.

Despite the views of the Congress president, the right wing Congress leaders were not impressed. They held their ground. Two days after Jawaharlal spoke, they sought to diffuse the issue by passing a rather routine resolution in favour of a three-member committee to consider the need for mass contact. This committee, to be headed by Jairamdas Daulatram, will have Rajendra Prasad and Jayaprakash Narayan as the remaining members.

Linlithgow Takes Over As The New Viceroy

April 1936, New Delhi: Lord Linlithgow has taken over as the new Viceroy of India.

Hindi As Lingua Franca Agitates Urdu Press

April 24, 1936, Nagpur: In the course of a speech delivered at the inaugural conference of the Akhil Bharatiya Sahitya Parishad here on the 24th, Gandhi referred to the 'Hindi' language as 'Hindustani' without making any reference to Urdu, and described it as the future lingua franca of India.[102] He is being severely criticized by the Urdu press. So scathing are these criticisms that even Gandhi's ardent Muslim supporters are hesitant to say anything in his defense. Critics say, even some of these supporters themselves are deeply concerned at Gandhi's preference for Hindi.

Gandhi has been trying to resolve the complex issue of language in the country by coining a term 'Hindustani', by which he means both Hindi and Urdu. As regards script, he has been suggesting that both Devnagri and Nastalic Persian be accepted, and it should be left to the free will of each writer to decide which script to use. In these circumstances, such sharp attack on him on the basis of a single speech has been shocking.

Gandhi lamented that the whole atmosphere is charged with suspicion and no person's declarations and actions are above suspicion. If the current explosions are any indication, this Hindi versus Urdu issue portends ominous signals for much communal discord and can poison the political atmosphere.

Subhas Interned In His Brother's House

April 1936, Kurseong: Subhas was arrested in Bombay on 8 April this year on return from Europe. Large numbers of Indians were shocked and sad at the sustained injustice meted out by the government to him.

There were protests even in England. Sensible people there described his arrest without any valid charges as 'unfair'. However, the government is adamant. Government sources allege that Subhas has been plotting to introduce the Irish method of warfare in India. The government has interned him in his brother Sarat Bose's house in Darjeeling, far from the hustle and bustle of Calcutta and the country's politics. The last thing the government wants is to allow Subhas to participate in politics, especially when the provincial elections are due. They also know that Subhas can alone unsettle much of their political calculations in Bengal, given his popularity cutting across communal divides.

Jinnah, Rejuvenated League Deliberate On Elections

April 26, 1936, Bombay: The League has held its twenty-fourth annual session here. It has taken stock of the evolving political situation in the country and set in motion its preparation for the provincial elections. Conscious that it is lagging behind the Congress in terms of organisational strength and reach, and also the fact that the Muslims in the country are divided in their political loyalty to multiple parties, the League under Jinnah has laboured hard in the session to draft an appropriate electoral strategy across the eleven provinces.

At the beginning, it faced a setback — it seemed impossible to mobilise all Muslim leaders under the League. In more than one province, the regional Muslim leaders have already floated parties and formulated their programmes to fight elections. Thus, regional Muslim leaders like Fazlul Huq of Krishak Praja Party in Bengal, Syed Abdul Aziz in Bihar, Sheikh Abdul Majid Sindhi in Sind and some others have already taken the plunge and begun preliminary campaigns.

Under the circumstances, the League has empowered Jinnah to constitute a central parliamentary board. Jinnah can also authorise the central board to affiliate boards in various provinces for contesting elections on the tickets of the League. It is being seen as a deft move. Because the League does not have the organisation and the reach across the eleven provinces and choose candidates, it is adopting such a loose decentralised model. It would be happy to secure the allegiances of the Muslim candidates and in return give them the tickets. In another imaginative move, the League has extended invitations to the regional Muslim leaders, heading their own political parties, to serve as members of the parliamentary board of the League. Fears of personal and provincial rivalries have made some of these leaders accept the invitation from the League.

Iqbal Praises Jinnah's Election Strategy

June 3, 1936: Jinnah's election strategy, built up in a short time frame, has earned appreciation from many in the League and League sympathisers. In a meeting of the All- India Muslim League held under the presidency of Iqbal, the president has hailed Jinnah's initiative in forming a Central Muslim League Parliamentary Board for election of the members for provincial assemblies.[103]

MUSLIM LEAGUE DRAFTS ITS ELECTION MANIFESTO

June 9, 1936: The Muslim League has adopted its election manifesto today. While affirming that the position of Muslims should be protected and safeguarded in any future constitutional architecture, it has asserted that such a demand does not smack of communalism. It has stressed that for the sake of a stable national government, the minorities must be made to feel they can rely upon the majority with complete sense of confidence and security. It has stressed for a new social order with specific attention to the poor and backward Muslims, and to protect the religious life of the Muslims. Other demands are mostly secular and economic like:

- To make every effort to secure the repeal of all repressive laws;
- To resist all measures which are detrimental to the interests of India and which encroach upon the fundamental liberties of the people and lead to economic exploitation of the country;
- To reduce heavy cost of administrative machineries, central and provincial, and allocate substantial funds for nation building departments;
- To rationalise Indian army and reduce military expenditure;
- To encourage development of industries;

- To regulate currency, exchange and price in the interests of economic development of the country;
- To stand for the social, educational and economic upliftment of rural population;
- To sponsor measures for relief of agricultural indebtedness;
- To make elementary education free and compulsory;
- To take steps to reduce the heavy burden of taxation;

Congress Socialists Strident Against Indian Princes

1936: Since the formation of the Congress Socialist Party, the leaders of all India states' people's conferences have been coming closer to the prominent Congress Socialist leaders, to influence the Congress' policy of intervention in the internal affairs of the princely states. They have been quite critical and vocal about Gandhi's 'hands-off' policy.

Young and firebrand Socialist leader Jayaprakash Narayan is taking an extreme view on the issue. In his book, *Why Socialism*, published by the All-India Congress Socialist Party, he has called for extinction of the system of princely rule. He feels even the presence of constitutional princes would be meaningless in free India, an unnecessary burden and a perpetual obstacle for the growth of democracy. Jayaprakash seems to be somewhat ahead of his time. The Congress' official policy does not, as yet, endorse such views, however strident and forcefully espoused. Both the Gandhian camp in the Congress and the AISPC are still reconciled to the idea of constitutional monarchy heading responsible governments.

Congress Intervention In Native State Mysore A Testing Laboratory?

1936: The Congress policy in terms of scope for intervention in the states' peoples' causes has been evolving, generally growing with passage of time, induced by the rising political aspirations of the people of the native states Its growing ambit has come under test in the native state of Mysore, where a simple issue of enrolment of new members by the local Congress, has snowballed into a Satyagraha

—thanks to the personal involvement by the Congress president, Jawaharlal.

NS Hardikar, the Bombay secretary of the Karntaka PCC, had started a membership campaign to improve the stature of the KPCC within the Congress. He had the backing of Jawaharlal for this drive. During the campaign, Hardikar faced opposition in the state and he invoked support from Jawaharlal. The latter came forward to strongly endorse Hardikar's campaign and asserted that every activity of the Congress should be carried out in the states, especially enrolling new members and forming Congress committees, as long as the activities were not in direct conflict with the state government. The conflict situation, if any, he said, ought to be referred to the Congress leadership for necessary direction. Notwithstanding the statement by Jawaharlal, the opposition continued. Ultimately, the Congress leaders in Mysore undertook a civil disobedience campaign with Nehru's approval. There have been arrests, which have, in fact, strengthened the unity between Mysore and the National Congress.

Political experts say the event at Mysore will go a long way to influence the relevant Congress policy in the times ahead.

Ideological Differences Mar Debut AISF Conference

August 12, 1936, Lucknow: The debut conference of the All-India Students' Federation has been held here. Student representatives have congregated here from all over the country. Besides promoting the students-specific causes, the conference is expected to open up vistas for students' participation in the Indian freedom struggle. Issues like failures of two rounds of non-cooperation and civil disobedience movements, unsuccessful round table conferences, the hanging of Bhagat Singh and his associates, the Meerut conspiracy case and emergence of the Congress Socialist Party professing Marxism and class struggles, have been sending ripples across the student community and the conference is expected to construct a regular channel for continuing interaction between them and the political leadership. Jawaharlal has inaugurated the conference, while Jinnah Chairs it as its president.

The presence of the two prominent leaders holding adversarial positions on a number of issues has been reinforcing the importance of the event. However, there were simmering cold tensions between the two groups of supporters and those showed up in some unpleasant incidents even as the two leaders were speaking to the large student body.

Jawaharlal, in his inaugural address, reportedly described 'communal problem' as a nuisance and creation by the rulers in the subject countries. Jinnah, known to believe in much deeper connotation of the communal issues, was probably not amused. As Jawaharlal spoke, Muslim students demanded a break for the Meghrib prayers and this incensed their Hindu counterparts, who burst into protests.

Jinnah's dissatisfaction with Jawaharlal's reference to the 'communal issue' entered into his presidential speech. Possibly voicing his lament over perennial disagreements amongst major political parties in the country on such issues, he deplored the lack of a common platform in the country where the best minds of all communities could meet and discuss ways and means to solve the various and potentially insoluble problems.[104]

He also came down direct and hard at the Congress Party by calling it a predominantly Hindu body, while Muslims, who have a separate entity, are represented by the Muslim League. At this, he was reportedly booed and hooted.These incidents have marred the spirit of a momentous occasion. Another politically significant event happened after the conference ended. A few Muslim student leaders met Jinnah after the conference. It is reported that they discussed forming a parallel student body for the Muslims—the All-India Muslim Students Federation.

Political analysts consider the impending break-up of the all-India student body as reflection of the communally-surcharged political atmospherics. They feel, the parting of ways at the student level may lead to further hardening of positions between the Congress and the League.

Ambedkar Founds Independent Labour Party

August 15, 1936, Bombay: In view of the impending elections, Bhimrao feels the interest of the depressed classes cannot be left at the sole custody of the Indian National Congress (INC). So, here in Bombay, his stronghold, Bhimrao has founded the Independent Labour Party. It would take part in the ensuing elections. According to reliable sources, this new party can give INC a run for its money in many constituencies—it has strong command over the depressed classes.

Right Wing Congressmen, Socialists Don't See Eye To Eye

December 1936, Faizpur: A cold war has been going on between the Congress Socialist Party and the right wing Congressmen, over the issue of granting corporate membership of the party to the organisations of peasants and workers. This would require amendment in the Congress constitution. If the amendment is carried out, the Socialist faction, with greater control over the peasants and workers, would emerge a clear gainer, establishing tighter grip over the levers of power. The Gandhian group is thus fighting tooth and nail against the move.

In the Lucknow session in April this year, the Congress deliberated on the need to involve the workers and farmers in its organisation and give them scope to contribute in shaping of its policies. To explore the issue further and to consider the need for mass contact, a three- member Daulatram Committee was appointed. Now it has been decided to merge it into a constitutional committee. Obviously, corporate membership would involve constitutional amendment.

However, considering the fact that Rajendra Prasad, a Congress stalwart and Jayaprakash Narayan, a bright young passionate Socialist holding two extreme opposite ideological views on the issue, are on the panel, it is doubtful if the committee would be able to recommend some actionable measures to the Working Committee.

Congress Socialists Are Gaining In Stature

September 1936: There is simmering tension between the Gandhian block and the Congress Socialist Party. The former is ideologically rooted in the Indian soil. It is also a disciplined and organised force under leaders such as Vallabhbhai Patel. In comparison, the Congress Socialist Party led by young, talented leaders like Jayaprakash Narayan and such others deeply imbued by socialism, is a new entity but showing lots of promise. Thanks to the success of that ideology in uplifting the lots of the masses in the USSR, the CSP is able to place its views with confidence and force. Jayaprakash Narayan in his book, *Why Socialism*, has not hesitated to call Gandhi a reformist, in the unenviable sense it is understood in Socialist history. Elaborating, Jayaprakash has written, 'Reformism is interested not in securing social justice, but in covering up the ugly fissures of society.' Clearly, Jayaprakash believes the solution lies in revolutionary socialism.

For its bold, daring stance, the CSP is attracting public attention. There is yet another reason why CSP is gaining importance — its supposed ability to help the Congress in the ensuing provincial elections.

Within the Congress, there is a clear recognition of the fact that the CSP leaders are closer to the collective bodies of people like the trade unions, peasant organisations, youth leagues etc. and in a position to influence the opinions of the individual members of these bodies. Ideally, the Congress should mix the organising abilities of the Gandhian group with the mass appeal of the CSP, to get best results in the ensuing elections.

Congress Decides To Contest Provincial Elections

December 1936, Faizpur: Though most political parties of the country resented the meagre doses of self-government offered by the new constitution of 1935, they have been gradually turning around to collect the trickles of British charity.

The Congress Party, examining the long-term implications of participating in the provincial elections, was taking time to intimate its decision. The delay was driving many smaller parties to the limit of their patie nce, so keen have they grown to share the spoils of power.

Now, at the session here, the Congress has decided to contest the provincial election but has postponed its decision on 'office acceptance'. It has come as a big relief to all others, including the British Indian government. Elections without the Congress would not have lent it any measure of credibility. The Congress Party has made the decision after much debate and deliberations. The major challenge before the party now is to reach the vast massses of the country and convince them of the Congress goals and policies. Important leaders are preparing to go for mass contacts—Jawaharlal has decided to give a lead.

Critics, however, say with this decision, the Congress has accorded legitimacy to the new constitution and betrayed defeatist attitude. A long course of struggle, which it began by organising protests against the Simon Commission, followed by the Motilal Report, the Dandi march, the civil disobedience movement, Gandhi's participation at the round table and resumption of civil disobedience movement have all come to a naught now.

The Government of India Act 1935 negated many of the cardinal assumptions about India's problems, and the mode of their solution, which were practically the fruit of the Congress' experiences of over three decades.

But instead of leading a determined protest against the ill-spirited constitution thrust upon the country, the party has been meekly acquiescing to it. Its decision is an ominous compromise, with crafty machination of the government that aims at driving a permanent wedge between communities by dangling before them the lure of office and power.

Though some Congress leaders have sought to rationalise the decision, saying that it would help them fight the new constitution through the legislatures, such possibilities are farfetched. For example, even the Swaraj Party had earlier entered the legislature to fight the government from within, but it lost its way in less than four years.

They say, the actual fact is that the Congress has lost vital energy to fight a powerful and shrewd enemy. Worse, at a later stage when the lure of office begins to lurk, it would become more challenging to restrain the bulk of the Congressmen, and retain the integrity of the party in its fight against the British Empire.

Jawaharlal Talks To Millions

1936: Jawaharlal Nehru has literally criss-crossed the country over 130 days. He has addressed over a thousand meetings and communicated the messages of the Congress to a few million people. He has received enthusiastic response in most of these places. This augurs well for the Congress. Vast bodies of peasants and workers in cities and towns are veering round to the Congress viewpoint. These are likely to result into electoral benefits, for sure. Most other important leaders are also actively canvassing to ensure electoral success. This, of course, does not include Gandhi who sees himself above party politics and identifies himself with the whole country. Subhas, another important leader with appeal to all communities, is unable to participate—he is under house arrest.

Communist Party Of India Makes Another U-turn

December 1936, Faizpur: In accordance with a changed directive of the Comintern towards popular front policies, Indian Communists are effecting a revision in their relations with the Indian National Congress. They are now strengthening the Congress Socialist Party—the left wing of the Congress. It is ironical that the Communists had a different assessment of this very same Congress left wing, when the latter had launched this party. They had branded it as 'Social Fascist'.

The Communist Party of India has now decided to adopt a policy for forging a broad 'anti-imperialist peoples' front' with Congress Socialists, trade unionists and left-wing Congressmen. This new stand is expected to improve the relations with the Congress and particularly, with those in Congress who have leftist or Socialist view. CPI is now expected to penetrate far deeper into the Congress Party.

EPILOGUE

This volume stops here after chronicling the story of India's struggle against the British Raj till the end of 1936. Clearly, political India is at an important cross-road, somewhat confused, groping for 'a response' to the latest British offer to contest elections and form government in eleven British Indian provinces under the new constitution.

Over last two decades (1915-1930), Indian political parties have been demanding *swaraj*, complete independence or at least dominion status from the Raj. The new constitution, as incorporated in the Govt of India Act of 1935, gives them none of these.They are merely being asked to run provincial governments while the Raj would continue to retain the key levers of powers to itself.

At the federal level, the situation is worse. In the crippled legislature, that would have large numbers of nominated members from the native states loyal to the British and possess no authority over the 'cabinet', the Viceroy would enjoy unfettered power to rule.

The parties realise, and bitterly so, that the Raj has exploited their internal differences to the hilt. What is more, they also realise that through the much-hyped 'round table conferences', their powerful adversary has also succeeded in exposing their irreconcilable rifts to the world at large. They are now left with no space to hide their own adequacies.

And having succeeded in fixing the blame squarely upon Indian politics for the constitutional logjam, the Raj is now trying to shove an ignoble political offer down their throat. For predictable reasons, there were dissensions and unrest within the Congress Party against it. Several young, radical and socialist leaders rejected the federal part of the constitution outright and even want the party to stay away from forming the provincial governments. The offer of the Raj was debated, deliberated, and the extant political landscape was carefully scanned. The opportunity cost of not taking up the offer was examined meticulously, too. At the end of it all, the Congress has decided to bite the bullet. Its major rival, the Muslim League, has also begun to prepare in earnest. Jinnah has returned to India to lead the League's campaign.

Political analysts point to the dangers ahead. The very nature of the new constitution that gives inadequate access to resources and power, but imposes enormous responsibilities on the provincial governments, would make it difficult for the native political parties to deliver and meet public expectations. At the same time, access to the executive power, however meagre, portends the threat of enticing them into corruption. On the whole, chances are more that through their lack of performance, they would end up further legitimising the continuation of British rule. In the testing times that lie ahead, a single factor that can help them is the prospect of the major political parties working in a cooperative framework for the general good of Indians. However, the recent developments in the political space almost pre-empt such possibilities. Not only are the Congress and the League growing intolerant of each other, their top leaders too are fast moving apart.

Post-election, the political situation in the country may become very different from what it is in 1935. It remains to be seen how the political parties decide about entering office, the manner in which they handle the task of governance, and above all, how they once again bring to centre stage the goal of 'independence' or at least the 'dominion status' in their continuing political engagement with the

Raj. With the British ever ready to employ the weapon of 'divide and rule', resurrecting these goals and pursuing them aggressively in a fractured polity is bound to pose serious challenges. However, 1937 is knocking at India's door and the reader may not have to wait for long. They are cordially invited to Part II of this book.

Reference

1. http://archivesmanipur.nic.in/whoswho.htm#THE%.20ANGLO
2. *Inside Congress,* Swami Shraddhanand, p 25
3. *The Story of My Experiments with Truth: An autobiography,* M K Gandhi, p 175
4. Sri Aurobindo on Nationalism :Selected writings and speeches, p 79-80
5. Sri Aurobindo on Nationalism :Selected writings and speeches, p 188
6. http://www.indiankanoon.org/doc/1430706/]
7. www.sriaurobindosociety.org/sriauro/theysaw.htm
8. Organiser, Volume 44, p 17
9. http://punjabrevenue.nic.in/gaz_sang3.htm, Also, *Nationalism and British Raj,* S R Bakshi, p 1-2
10. Jinnah: Man of Destiny: Prakash Almeida: p 59
11. An Indian Diary by Montagu quoted in: *Political and Social Conflict in South India:* The *Non-Brahmin Movement and Tamil Separatism,* Eugene F Irschick, p 77
12. *Collected Works of Mahatma Gandhi* [hereafter CWMG], vol 17,. p 4 [e-version]
13. www.sscnet.ucla.edu/southasia/History/British?Crawling.html

14. English Writings of Rabindranath Tagore: A Miscellany: 16Rabindranath Tagore: pp751-752
15. CWMG: vol 19 – e-version pp137-142
16. www.workingmuslim.org/pers/khilafat.htm quoting 'The Islamic review April, 1920 issue p 140-141
17. CWMG vol XVII p 504
18. *Raj to Swaraj: A Text Book on Colonialism and Nationalism in India,* Ram Chandra Pradhan: p265
19. CWMG vol XXII: p 59
20. CWMG vol XXII: p 302-305
21. CWMG vol XXII: p 377
22. CWMG vol XXII: p 377-381
23. CWMG vol XXII: November 1966
24. Report of the CD Enquiry Committee Report (hereafter CDECR): page 2
25. CDECR : page 50
26. Home Political File 53/1927-KW; NAI], http://www.indianetzone.com/21/hindustan_socialist_republican_association_indian_extremist_organisation.htm
27. *Netaji Subhas Chandra Bose: The great war for political emancipation,* Harihara Dasa, p 197
28. *Communism and Nationalism in India,* Shashi Bairathi, p 84
29. CWMG Vol XXV: p 522-523
30. *Congress and the People's Movement in Princely India: Ambivalence in Strategy and Organisation* by Barbara N Ramusack
31. *Congress and Indian Nationalism in the Pre-Independence Phase* by Richard Sisson and Stanley Wolpert, p 383
32. CWMG vol XXVII: p 4-9
33. *Ambedkar And His Writings:* A Look For The New Generation: Dr Raj Kumar, p 83
34. *Autobiography,* Rajendra Prasad, p254-255
35. CWMG: Vol XXXII: p 458-462
36. [http://www.humsafar.info/1927.php
37. http://www.humsafar.info/1927.php
38. CWMG vol XXXV: p 432-433

39. CWMG vol 41 pp 120-122 [e-ver]
40. *Mahatma Gandhi and Jawaharlal Nehru: A Historic Partnership,* Madhu Limaye, p 379
41. CWMG vol XXXV: p 546
42. *Labour's Way with the Commonwealth,* George Lansbury
43. *The Path to Indian Independence: Gandhi and Nationalism,* Simone Panter-Brick: p 129
44. www.nichr.edu.pk/Downloads/AIML.pdf
45. www.indianlabourarchive.org/col/ncl.htm <22.11.12.>
46. Bhagat Singh, An Immortal Revolutionary of India, Dr Bhawan Singh Rana, p 77
47. *Early Aryans to Swaraj,* Volume 10, Editors S R Bakshi, S Gajrani, Hari Singh (hereafter Bakshi EATS): p373
48. Bakshi EATS: p 378
49. *The Indian Struggle* 1920-42, Subhas Chandra Bose (hereafter Subhas TIS), p 189
50. http://www.sikh-history.com/sikhhist/events/partition.html <22.12.12>
51. *The Transfer of Power in India,* V P Menon, p 41-42: 1952
52. CWMG vol XLII: p 313-314
53. TIS: p 199
54. CWMG Vol XLIII: p 1-8 (esp p 3)
55. http://www.mkgandhi.org/articles/the%20story%20of%20Salt.htm <15.12.12>
56. *Studies of Indian History: Bihar Through Ages,* Volume 4, S R Bakshi & R Chaturvedi: p 43
57. Jinnah, Pakistan and Islamic reality: The Search for Saladin: Akbar Ahmed: p 122
58. CWMG vol XLIII: p 389-393 (esp p 389)
59. www.mkgandhi.org/apinchofsalt/Chap01.htm <24.11.12>
60. Home, Political File no 120/1931, NAI
61. Jawaharlal Nehru Autobiography, p 257
62. CWMG-Vol XLV, p 175-176,(esp p 176)
63. www.mkgandhi.org/article/bhagat_singh.htm <24.11.12> & CWMG-Vol 51, p 151
64. www.mkgandhi.org/faq/q26.htm <26.11.12>

65. File no 18/3/31-Poll 1931; Govt of India, Home Dept: Fortnightly report ending 31st March 1931: NAI
66. File no 18/3/31-Poll 1931; Govt of India, Home Dept: Fortnightly report ending 31st March 1931, NAI
67. Subhas TIS: p241
68. ttp://archive.org/stream/indianroundtable029565mbp/indianroundtable029565mbp_djvu.txt <8.12.12>
69. ttp://archive.org/stream/indianroundtable029565mbp/indianroundtable029565mbp_djvu.txt <8.12.12>
70. ttp://archive.org/stream/indianroundtable029565mbp/indianroundtable029565mbp_djvu.txt <8.12.12>
71. ttp://archive.org/stream/indianroundtable029565mbp/indianroundtable029565mbp_djvu.txt <8.12.12>
72. TIS: p 242
73. CWMG vol XLVIII: November 1971: p 116
74. CWMG Vol XLVIII: November 1971: pp 216- 217
75. CWMG-Vol XLVIII: November 1971: p 373
76. Jinnah's Early Politics: Iyan B Wells, p 233
77. CWMG-Vol XLVIII: November 1971: p 459
78. www.gandhiserve.org/information/chronology_1932/chronology_1932.html
79. File no18/7/Political 1932 Govt of India Home Dept: Fortnightly Report on Internal Political situation for the month of April 1932, NAI
80. *History of the Indigenous Indians:* T H P Cheutharassery: P 144
81. http://www.columbia.edu/itc/mealac/00islamlinks/txt_rahmatali_1933.html <7.12.12>.
82. CWMG Vol LV: p 106
83. http://www.gandhiserve.org/information/chronology_1933/chronology_1933.html
84. http://www.gandhiserve.org/information/chronology_1933/chronology_1933.html
85. *Selected Works of Vithalbhai J Patel,* Volume 8 p 1518
86. 'Penal Strategies and Political Resistance in Colonial and Independent India' by Ujjwal Kumar Singh' in *Challenging The Rule(s) of Law: Colonialism, Criminology and Human Rights in*

India: Ed. Kalpana Kannabiran and Ranbir Singh: p236

87. Subhas TIS: p 306
88. trove.nla.gov.au/ndp/del/article/32792325 <7.12.12>
89. *Jawaharlal Nehru Autobiography, p 500*
90 http://thejinnah.webs.com/calenderofevents.htm
91. *Economic Philosophy of Mahatma Gandhi, Shanti Swarup,* p 26
92. CWMG: Volume LIX, p 3-12
93. The Hindu, 21-9-1934
94. *Netaji Rediscovered,* Kanailal Basu, p 294
95. *His Majesty's Opponent,* Sugata Bose, p 101
96. http://www.humsafar.info/1935.php <18.12.12>
97. http://www.cambridgetrusts.org/assets/documents/Lecture_1.pdf <1.12.12>
98. *The Path to Indian Independence: Gandhi and Nationalism,* Simone Panter Brick: p 147
99. *Religion and the Legitimation of Power in South Asia, K Ishwaran,* Ed. Bardwell L Smith: E J Brill, Laiden, p 95: quoting 'The Conversion Speech of 1935'
100. http://www.marxists.org/archive/dutt/great_son.htm quoting Labour Monthly, Vol.57, No 3, March 1975 Unity Publishers <9.12.12>]
101. *A Bunch of Old Letters,* Jawaharlal Nehru: p 166
102. CWMG vol LXII: p 344-347 (esp p 346)
103. http://www.humsafar.info/1936.php <14.12.12>
104. http://thejinnah.webs.com/calenderofevents.htm

BIBLIOGRAPHY

The Story of my Experiments with Truth: An autobiography, M K Gandhi, Master Mind Books, Bangalore: Reprint 2011

Sri Aurobindo on Nationalism, Selected writings and speeches, Sri Aurobindo Ashram Pondicherry, 2nd edition 1996

History of Indian National Congress 1832-1947, Girija Kanta Mukherjee, Meenakshi Prakashan 1974

Education and Politics from Sir Syed to The Present Day (The Aligarh School), Shan Mohammad, APH Publishing Corporation, 2002

The life and work of Syed Ahmed Khan, George Farquhar, Irving Graham, Oxford University Press, 1974

History of Modern India, S N Sen, Revised 3rd edition 2006, New Age International (P) Limited Publishers, (about Anglo Mahomedan Defence)

An Indian for All Seasons: The Many Lives of R C Dutt, Meenakshi Mukherjee, Penguin Books India, 2009

An Advanced History of Modern India, S N Sen, Macmillan Publishers India Ltd, 2010

The Tibetan Independence Movement: Political, Religious and Gandhian Perspectives, Jane Ardley, Routledge, 2002

Organiser, Volume 44, Bharat Prakashan 1992

Nationalism and British Raj, S R Bakshi, Atlantic Publishers and Distributors,1995

English Writings of Rabindranath Tagore, A Miscellany, Volume Two, Rabindranath Tagore, Sahitya Academy, Reprint 2006

Report of the CD Enquiry Committee Report or CDECR 1922, Tagore & Co Madras, 1922

Labour's Way With The Commonwealth, George Lansbury, Methuen & Co Ltd, 1935

The Transfer of Power in India, V P Menon, 1952, Orient Longman Ltd

History of the Indigenous Indians, T H P Cheutharassery, APH Publishing Corporation, 1998

Selected Works of Vithalbhai J Patel, edited/compiled by Ravindra Kumar, Mittal Publications, 1995

Dadabhai Naoroji: The Grand Old Man, Issue 13 of Indian Freedom Fighters Series, S R Bakshi, South Asia Books 1991

Dadabhai Naoroji: A Biography of Vision and Ideas, Verinder Grover, Deep & Deep Publications, 1998

Political Thinkers of Modern India, Adi H Doctor, Mittal Publications 1997

Mahadeo Govind Ranade, Prabhakar Janardan Jagirdar, Publications Division, Ministry of Information and Broadcasting, Government of India 1971

Swami Vivekananda in India: A Corrective Biography, Rajagopal Chattapadhyaya, Motilal Banarasidass, 1999

Gokhale, A Political Biography: A study of his services and political ideas, D B Mathur, Manaktalas, 1966

The Indian Enclyopedia, Biographical, Historical, Religious, Administrative, Ethnological, Comercial and Scientific, Volume 1, Ed Subodh Kapoor, Cosmo Publications, 2002

The Emergence of Indian Nationalism: Competition and Collaboration in the Later Nineteenth Century, Anil Seal, Cambridge University Press, 1971

Congress and Indian Nationalism: The Pre-Independence Phase, Edited by Richard Sisson & Stanley Wolpert, Oxford University Press, 1988

Political Thought and Leadership of Lokmanya Tilak, N R Inamdar, Concept Publishing Company 1983

Books on the Lives of Sri Aurobindo, Peter Heehs, Columbia University Press, 2008

On Nationalism, Selected writings and speeches, Sri Aurobindo, Sri Aurobindo Ashram Pondicherry, 2nd edition 1996

Tilak and Gokhale: A comparative study, Mohammad Shabbir Khan, Ashish Publishing House 1992

Tilak and Gokhale: Revolution and Reform in the Making of Modern

India, Stanley A Wolpert, University of California Press 1977, Berkeley, Los Angeles, London

Indian Political Thought, Urmila Sharma, S K Sharma, Atlantic Publishers and Distributors 2001, New Delhi

Lions of the Punjab Culture in the Making, Richard G Fox, University of California Press, 1985,

Dalit Inheritance in Hindu Religion, Mahendra Singh, Kalpaz Publications 2006, New Delhi

Inside Congress, Swami Shraddhanand, Phoenix Publications 1946, Bombay

History of the Freedom Movement in India (1857-1947), S N Sen, New Age International (P) Ltd Publishers, New Delhi, 2009

Freedom Struggle and Anushilan Samity (Vol 1), Niahrranjan Ray, Anushilan Samity, 1979

The Sikhs of the Punjab (The New Cambridge History of India), J S Grewal, Cambridge University Press 1998,

Freedom Movement in Punjab 1905-29, Satish Chandra Mittal, Concept Publishing Company 1977 Delhi

A Comprehensive History of India Volume 3, P N Chopra, B N Puri, M N Das, A C Pradhan, Sterling Publishers (Private) Ltd New Delhi, Reprint 2005

Communal Crimes and National Integration A Socio-legal Study, Praveen Kumar, Readworthy Publications, 2011, New Delhi

Studies in Indian History: Punjab Through the Ages , Volume 3 & 4, Editors S R Bakshi Rashmi Pathak, Sarup & Sons, New Delhi, 2007

Glimpses of Indian National Movement, M Abel, ICFAI University Press, Hyderabad, 2005

Down Memory Lane: Reminiscences of a Bengali Revolutionary, P K Ray, Gian Publishing House New Delhi, 1990

M N Roy, A Political Biography, Samaren Roy, *Orient Blackswan, 1997*

India and The First World War, Budheswar Pati, Atlantic Publishers and Distributors Pvt Ltd, New Delhi, 1996

The Black Hole of Empire, History of a Global Practice of Power, Partha Chatterjee, Princeton University Press, 2012, New York Oxfordshire

The Voyage of the Komagata Maru, The Sikh Challenge to Canada's Colour Bar, Hugh J M Johnston, University of British Columbia Press, 1989

An Account of the Ghadr Conspiracy, 1913-1915: F C Isemonger, J Slattery, Archana Publications 1998

In the Cause of Freedom, Radical Black Internationalism from Harlem to London 1917-1939, Minkah Makalani, University of North Carolina Press, 2011

Partners of British Rule: Liberators or Collaborators? Mohinder Singh Pannu, Allied Publishers Private Ltd, 2005

Jinnah, Man of Destiny, Prakash Almeida, Kalpaz Publications, 2001

Indian Revolutionaries, A Comprehensive Study 1757-1961, Volume 5, Shrikrishan 'Saral', Ocean Books (P) Ltd, 1999

Hindu Consciousness, the Congress and Partition by K L Tuteja in 'The Partition in Retrospect', Editor Amrik Singh, Anamika Publishers and Distributors (P) Ltd, 2000

'Presenting' the Past, Anxious History and Ancient Future in Hindutva India: S P Udayakumar, Praeger, 2005

Social Equity in Indian Society, The Elusive Goal, P A Augustine, Concept Publishing Company, 1991

Advanced Study in the History of Modern India, Volume II (1813-1920), G S Chhabra, Lotus Press, 2005

Raj to Swaraj, A Text Book on Colonialism and Nationalism in India, p265, Ramchandra Pradhan, Macmillan India Ltd 2008

The Non-Brahmin Movement and Tamil Separatism, 1916-1929, Eugene F Irschick, University of California Press, 1969

Mahatma Gandhi, Sankar Ghose, Allied Publishers Ltd, 1991

Struggle for Economic Freedom and Social Justice of Scheduled Caste in South India, Y Ashok Kumar, Kalpaz Publications, 2005

Jawaharlal Nehru: A Biography, Frank Moraes, Jaico Publishing House, 2008

The Collected Works of Mahatma Gandhi Volume 17, (Electronic Book), Publications Division, Government of India '98-1999

The Collected Works of Mahatma Gandhi Volume 19, (Electronic Book), Publications Division, Government of India, '98-1999

The Collected Works of Mahatma Gandhi Volume 20, (Electronic Book), Publications Division, Government of India, '98-1999

The Collected Works of Mahatma Gandhi Volume 26, (Electronic Book), Publications Division, Government of India, '98-1999

The Collected Works of Mahatma Gandhi Volume 31, (Electronic Book),

Publications Division, Government of India, '98-1999
The Collected Works of Mahatma Gandhi Volume 41, (Electronic Book) Publications Division, Government of India, '98-1999
The Collected Works of Mahatma Gandhi Volume 51, (Electronic Book), Publications Division, Government of India, '98-1999
The Collected Works of Mahatma Gandhi Volume 53, (Electronic Book), Publications Division, Government of India, '98-1999
The Collected Works of Mahatma Gandhi Volume 54, (Electronic Book), Publications Division, Government of India, '98-1999
The Collected Works of Mahatma Gandhi Volume 61, (Electronic Book), Publications Division, Government of India, '98-1999
The Collected Works of Mahatma Gandhi Volume 63, (Electronic Book), Publications Division, Government of India, '98-1999
The Collected Works of Mahatma Gandhi Volume 65, (Electronic Book), Publications Division, Government of India, '98-1999
The Collected Works of Mahatma Gandhi Volume 68, (Electronic Book), Publications Division, Government of India, '98-1999
Collected Works of Mahatma Gandhi Volume 27, Publications Division, Government of India, September 1965
Collected Works of Mahatma Gandhi Volume 22, Publications Division, Government of India, November 1966
Collected Works of Mahatma Gandhi Volume 25, Publications Division, Government of India, May 1967
Collected Works of Mahatma Gandhi Volume 27, Publications Division, Government of India: March 1968
Collected Works of Mahatma Gandhi Volume 32, Publications Division, Government of India: April 1969
Collected Works of Mahatma Gandhi Volume 35, Publications Division, Government of India: August 1969
Collected Works of Mahatma Gandhi Volume 42, Publications Division, Government of India, December 1970
Collected Works of Mahatma Gandhi Volume 43, Publications Division, Government of India: January 1971
Collected Works of Mahatma Gandhi Volume 45, Publications Division, Government of India, July 1971
Collected Works of Mahatma Gandhi Volume 48, Publications Division,

Government of India, November 1971
Collected Works of Mahatma Gandhi Volume 59, Publications Division, Government of India, November 1974
Collected Works of Mahatma Gandhi Volume 62, Publications Division, Government of India, October 1975
Advanced Study in the History of Modern India, 1920-1947, G S Chhabra, Sterling Publishers, 1971
The Shaping of Modern Gujarat, Plurality, Hindutva and Beyond, Achyut Yagnik, Suchitra Sheth, Penguin Books India, 2005
Party Politics in Indian National Congress, R K Parashar; Anamika Publishers and Distributors Pvt Ltd
Dr Ambedkar Life and Mission, Dhananjay Keer, Popular Prakashan Ltd 1995
Ambedkar And His Writings: A Look For The New Generation, Dr Raj Kumar, Kalpaz Publications, 2008
What Congress and Gandhi have done to the Untouchables, B R Ambedkar, Gautam Book Centre, Reprinted 2009
Mahatma Gandhi, Political Saint and Unarmed Prophet, Dhananjay Keer, Popular Prakashan, 1973
Challenging The Rule(s) of Law, Colonialism, Criminology and Human Rights in India, Ed Kalpana Kannabiran and Ranbir Singh, Sage Publications India Pvt Ltd, 2008
Haryana, A historical perspective, Satish Chandra Mittal, Atlantic Publishers & Distributors, 1986
Faith and Philosophy of Sikhism, Sardar Harjeet Singh, Gyan Publishing House, 2009
Perspectives on Sikh Gurdwaras Legislation, Surjit Singh Gandhi, Atlantic Publishers and Distributors, 1993
Madras: Chennai, a 400 year Record of the First City of Modern India, Edited by S Muthiah, Palaniappa Brothers, 2008
Gandhi and Anarchy, C Sankaran Nair, Ulan Press, 2012
The future of Indian politics: a contribution to the understanding of present day problems, Annie Wood Besant, Ulan Press, 2011
Freedom Movement in Punjab 1905-29, Satish Chandra Mittal, Concept Publishing Company, 1977
Hindu Muslim Relations in British India: A Study of Controversy, Conflict

and Communal Movements in Northern India, 1923-1928, Gene R Thursby, E J Brill 1975, Leiden Netherlands

Swaraj Party and Gandhi, S R Bakshi, Atlantic Publishers & Distributors,1996

The Satyamurti Letters: v2, The Indian Freedom Struggle Through the Eyes of a Parliamentarian, Editor K V Ramanathan, Prentice Hall India, 2008

Life and Times of Deshbandhu Chittaranjan Das, Rathindra Nath Sen Northern Book Centre,1989

Netaji Subhas Chandra Bose: The Great War for Political Emancipation, Harihara Dasa, National Publishing House, 2000

Autobiography - Rajendra Prasad, Penguin Books India, 2010

Communism in India, Gene D Overstreet, & Windmiller, Marshall, Overstreet, University of California Press, 1960

Communist and Socialist Movement in India, Chandrika Singh, Mittal Publications, 1987

Three Giants of South Asia, Gandhi, Ambedkar and Jinnah on Self-determination, Editor Prof Richard Bonney, Media House Delhi , 2004

The Path to Indian Independence: Gandhi and Nationalism, Simone Panter-Brick, I B Tauris & Co Ltd, 2012

Communism and Nationalism in India: A study in interrelationship,1919-1947, Shashi Bairathi; Anamika Prakashan, 1987

Early Aryans to Swaraj: Volume 10, Editors S R Bakshi, S Gajrani, Hari Singh: Sarup & Sons, 2005

Studies of Indian History: Bihar Through the Ages: Volume 4, S R Bakshi & R Chaturvedi, Sarup & Sons, 2007

Jinnah, Pakistan and Islamic Identity, The Search for Saladin, Akbar Ahmed, Routledge 1997,

An Autobiography Jawaharlal Nehru, Penguin Books, 2004

India's Struggle for Independence 1857-1947, Bipan Chandra, Mridula Mukherjee, Aditya Mukherjee, Sucheta Mahajan and K N Panikkar, Penguin Books, 1989

The Indian Struggle 1920-42 Subhas Chandra Bose (edited by Sisir K Bose & Sugata Bose, Netaji Research Bureau, Oxford University Press, 2011

Why I am an atheist, An Auto-biographical Discourse, Bhagat Singh, Hope India Publications, 2005

Ambassador of Hindu-Muslim Unity, Jinnah's Early Politics, Ian Bryant Wells, Permanent Black, 2005

The Selected Works of Subhas Chandra Bose, 1936-1946 Volume 2, Ed Ravindra Kumar ,Atlantic Publishers & Distributors, 1992

Imperial Power and Popular Politics, Class, Resistance and the State in India c1850-1950, Rajnarayan Chandavarkar, Cambridge University Press 1998

Social Background of Indian Nationalism, A R Desai, Popular Prakashan Pvt Ltd, 1948

Revolution Highway, Dileep Simeon, Penguin Books, 2010

History of the Indigenous Indians, T H P Chetharassery, APH Publishing Corporation, 1998

Social and Political Thought of Mahatma Gandhi, Bidyut Chakrabarty, Routledge, 2006

Mahatma Gandhi and Jawaharlal Nehru, A Historic Partnership 1916-1948, Madhu Limaye, B R Publishing. Corporation 1989

His Majesty's Opponent, Subhas Chandra Bose and India's Struggle Against Empire, Sugata Bose, Penguin Books, 2013

Awakening Indians to India, Debanita Satpathy, Central Chinmaya Mission Trust, 2003

The Princes of India in the Endgame of Empire, 1917-1947, Cambridge Studies in Indian History & Society, Ian Copland, Cambridge University Press, 2002

Andaman and Nicobar Islands, A Saga of Freedom Struggle, R V R Murthy, Kalpaz Publications: 2011

Economic Philosophy of Mahatma Gandhi, Shanti Swarup Gupta, Concept Publishing Company, 1994

Rural Development and Social Change, Thoughts of Swami Sahajanand, Dalip Kumar, Deep & Deep Publications Pvt Ltd, 2007

International Studies in Sociology and Social Anthropology, Volume 25 Religion and the Legitimation of Power in South Asia, General Editor, K Ishwaran, Leiden, E J Brill, 1978

From Movement to Government, The Congress in the United Provinces, 1937-42, Visalakshi Menon,, Sage Publications India Pvt Ltd, 2003

Political Philosophy of Rammanohar Lohia, Alternative Development Perceptions, K Gopinath Pilllai, Deep & Deep Publications, 1994

Netaji, Rediscovered, Kanailal Basu, Author House, 2010

Dr Ambedkar and Untouchability, Analysing and Fighting Caste, Christophe Jaffrelot, Permanent Black, 2005

Ambedkar and Buddhism, Bikshu Sangharakshita, Motilal Banarasidass, 2006

A Bunch of Old Letters, Written Mostly to Jawaharlal Nehru and Some Written by Him ,Asia Publishing House, 1958

From Plassey to Partition, A History of Modern India, Sekhar Bandyopadhyay, Orient Longman Pvt Ltd, 2006

Gandhi's Passion, The Life and Legacy of Mahatma Gandhi, Stanley Wolpert, Oxford University Press, Oxford 2001

Congress, Muslim League Tussle 1937-40 A Critical Analysis, Abida Shakoor Compiled by Q Z Hasan, Hajira Kumar, Aakar Books, 2003

Why Socialism, Jayaprakash Narayan, All India Congress Socialist Party, 1936

Nehru Selected Works, General Editor, S Gopal: Sangam Books, Volume 3, 1975

Nehru Selected Works, General Editor, S Gopal, Sangam Books, Volume 4, 1976

Nehru Selected Works, General Editor, S Gopal, Sangam Books, Volume 6, 1979

Nehru Selected Works, General Editor, S Gopal, Sangam Books, Volume 7, 1979,

Land, Labour and Power, Agrarian Crisis and the State of Bihar (1937-52), Usha Jha, Aakar Books, 2003

The Garrison State, Military Government and Society in Colonial Punjab 1849-1947, Tan Tai Yong, Sage Publications India Private Ltd, 2005

History of the Freedom Movement in India, Volume I, 2, 3, Firma K L Mukhopadhyay, Calcutta, 1971, 1975 & 1977

Copies of Fortnightly reports (various issues), Home Department, British Indian Government

INTERNET BILBLIOGRPAHY FOR PART I

http://www.hindu.com/thehindu/mp/2003/05/26/stories/2003052601080200.htm
http://www.storyofpakistan.com/articletext.asp?artid=A119
http://www.mgutheses.in/page/?q=T%200064&search=&page=&rad=
http://sites.google.com/site/cabinetmissionplan/gandhi-offer-of-jinnah-pm-ship-to-jinnah-1947
http://www.san.beck.org/20-6-LiberatingIndia1934-50.html
http://www.ggdc.net/maddison/articles/moghul_3.pdf
http://books.google.co.in/books?id=Q9sI_Y2CKAcC&pg=PA13&dq=history+of+muslim+league&hl=en#v=onepage&q=history%20of%20muslim%20league&f=false[A History of Pakistan and its origin: Christophe Jaffrelot]
http://books.google.co.in/books?id=OC3FjTWOS28C&pg=PA109&dq=Krishak+Praja+Party+Muslim+League+in+Bengal&hl=en#v=onepage&q=Krishak%20Praja%20Party%20Muslim%20League%20in%20Bengal&f=false[Bengal [Bengal Tiger and British Lion; An Account of the Bengal Famine of 1943: Richard Stevenson, Lionheart LLC, USA: 2005]
http://www.ambedkar.org/ambcd/41G.What%20Congress%20and%20Gandhi%20CHAPTER%20VI.htm
http://www.san.beck.org/20-6-LiberatingIndia1934-50.html
http://sites.google.com/site/cabinetmissionplan/ss4-m-j-akbar
http://www.nihcr.edu.pk/Latest_English_Journal/3.%20Nationalist%20Politics,%20Samina%20Awan.pdf[
http://www.wengewang.org/simple/index.php?t22618_2.html
http://www.gandhiserve.org
http://www.mkgandhi.org/swmgandhi/chap08.htm
http://www.subhaschandrabose.org
http://sites.google.com/site/cabinetmissionplan/speeches-and-statements-by-jinnah-1938---1940
http://www.siasat.pk/forum/showthread.php?63614-Sindhi-leader-who-sacrificed-himself-in-the-laboratory-of-provincial-autonomy
http://www.baachakhantrust.org/AbdulGhaffarKhan.pdf [
http://www.freerepublic.com/focus/f-news/1945851/posts

http://www.columbia.edu/itc/mealac/pritchett/00islamlinks/txt_iqbal_1930.html
http://www.columbia.edu/itc/mealac/pritchett/00islamlinks/islam_articles.html
http://sites.google.com/site/cabinetmissionplan/durga-das-3
http://www.columbia.edu/itc/mealac/pritchett/00islamlinks/txt_jinnah_lahore_1940.html
http://www.humsafar.info/(VARIOUS YEARS 1876-1948)
http://www.spartacus.schoolnet.co.uk/PRmacdonald.htm
http://sites.google.com/site/cabinetmissionplan/durga-das-2
http://pu.edu.pk/images/journal/studies/PDF-FILES/Artical-5-Vol-12-1-2011.pdf[
http://www.indiankanoon.org/doc/1416180
http://www.marxists.org/history/international/comintern/2nd-congress/ch04.htm#v1-p115
http://aicc.org.in
http://www.marxists.org/archive/roy/1923/02/03.htm
http://www.marxists.org/history/international/comintern/sections/britain/periodicals/labour_monthly/1929/03/x01.htm
http://pu.edu.pk/images/journal/history/Previous%20Issues/qalb-i-abid%20and%20massarrat%20abid.pdf
http://www.democracy-asia.org/qa/india/Manjari%20Katju.pdf[Design
http://www.archive.org/stream/nehrusmotilaland006223mbp/nehrusmotilaland006223mbp_djvu.txt
http://www.marxists.org/history/usa/eam/ci/comintern.html
http://www.marxists.org
http://www.archive.org/stream/balgangadhartila00tilauoft/balgangadhartila00tilauoft_djvu.txt
http://dictionary.sensagent.com/bengal+presidency/en-en/
http://www.aurobindo.ru/workings/sa/01/0317_e.htm
http://www.nihcr.edu.pk/Downloads/Chronology.pdf
http://pu.edu.pk/images/journal/studies/PDF-FILES/Artical-1-Vol-12-1-2011.pdf
http://www.archive.org/stream/storyofina035471mbp/storyofina035471mbp_djvu.txt

http://www.global.ucsb.edu/punjab/journal_14_2/kamran.pdf [
http://pu.edu.pk/images/journal/history/Current%20Issues/Q.%20Abid%20%20M.%20Abid.pdf
http://sites.google.com/site/cabinetmissionplan wavellstrongarminggandhinehruaugust
http://punjabrevenue.nic.in/gazfzpr3.htm
http://www.periyar.org/html/dk_movement_eng.asp
http://www.periyar.org
http://www.houseofdavid.ca/round_tab.htm
http://www.marxists.org/history/international/comintern/index.htm
http://www.sriaurobindoashram.org/research/show.php?set=doclife&id=14
http://dspace.vidyanidhi.org.in:8080/dspace/bitstream/2009/4168/3/SHU-1995-047-2.pdf
http://www.marxists.org/archive/dutt-clemens/1926/12/x01.htm
http://archive.org/stream/congresscaravan035201mbp/congresscaravan035201mbp_djvu.txt
http://orissa.gov.in/e-magazine/Orissareview/jan-2007/engpdf/39-43.pdf
http://www.bhavans.info/heritage/rashbose.asp
http://www.indianetzone.com/21/hindustan_socialist_republican_association_indian_extremist_organisation.htm
http://www.marxists.org/archive/campbell-jr/1960/40_fighting_years.htm
http://www.indianetzone.com/7/communist_party_india.htm
www.mahatmaphule.com/lifesketch.html

Note: The above websites were accessed during years 2012, 2013 and 2014. All of them were visited last on 4 June 2014

INDEX

D

O

P